D1171287

ADULT DEPARTMENT

1. Fine Schedule
   - 1- 5 days overdue . . . . grace period, no fine
   - 6-10 days overdue . . . . 25¢ per item
   - 11-19 days overdue . . . . 75¢ per item
   - 20th day overdue . . . . $2.00 per item
2. Injury to books beyond reasonable wear and all losses shall be paid for.
3. Each borrower is held responsible for all books drawn on his card and for all fines accruing on the same.

FOND DU LAC PUBLIC LIBRARY
FOND DU LAC, WISCONSIN

COLONIAL VIRGINIA

A HISTORY

A HISTORY OF THE AMERICAN COLONIES
IN THIRTEEN VOLUMES

GENERAL EDITORS:
MILTON M. KLEIN & JACOB E. COOKE

WARREN M. BILLINGS
JOHN E. SELBY
THAD W. TATE

COLONIAL VIRGINIA

A HISTORY

kto press

A DIVISION OF KRAUS-THOMSON ORGANIZATION LIMITED
WHITE PLAINS, NEW YORK

First printing

Printed in the United States of America

The paper used in this publication meets the minimum
requirements of American National Standard for
Information Science — Permanence of Papers for
Printed Library Materials, ANSI Z39.48-1984.

Library of Congress Cataloging-in-Publication Data

Billings, Warren M., 1940–
  Colonial Virginia.

  (A History of the American colonies)
  Bibliography: p.
  Includes index.
    1. Virginia—History—Colonial period, ca. 1600–1775.
2. Virginia—History—Revolution, 1775–1783. I. Selby,
John E. II. Tate, Thad W. III. Title. IV. Series.
F229.B613   1986   975.5'02   86-139
ISBN 0-527-18722-4 (alk. paper)

TO
THE MEMORY OF
RICHARD LEE MORTON
(1889–1974)

CONTENTS

ILLUSTRATIONS

EDITORS' INTRODUCTION

The American colonies have not lacked their Boswells. Almost from the time of their founding, the English settlements in the New World became the subjects of historical narratives by promoters, politicians, and clergymen. Some, like John Smith's *General History of Virginia*, sought to stir interest in New World colonization. Others, such as Cotton Mather's *Magnalia Christi Americana*, used New England's past as an object lesson to guide its next generation. And others still, like William Smith's *History of the Province of New-York*, aimed at enhancing the colony's reputation in England by explaining its failures and emphasizing its accomplishments. All of these early chroniclers had their shortcomings but no more so than every generation of historians which essayed the same task thereafter. For it is both the strength and the challenge of the historical guild that in each age its practitioners should readdress themselves to the same subjects of inquiry as their predecessors. If the past is prologue, it must be constantly reenacted. The human drama is unchanging, but the audience is always new: its expectations of the past are different, its mood uniquely its own.

The third century of the appearance of John's Smith's history and the bicentennial era of American independence present an appropriate occasion for a fresh retelling of the story of English-American colonization. Underlying the earliest histories were conscious or unconscious needs for national exaltation, self-justification, or moral purgation. The present series, by contrast, seeks simply to reexamine the past through the lenses of the present and to illuminate that present in the light of our colonial past.

Bicentennials aside, there is ample justification for a modern history of each of the original colonies. For many of them, there exists no single-volume narrative published in the present century and, for some, none written since those undertaken by contemporaries in the eighteenth century. The standard multi-volume histories of the colonial period—those of Herbert L. Osgood, Charles M. Andrews, and Lawrence H. Gipson—are too comprehensive to provide adequate treatment of individual colonies, too political and institutional in emphasis to deal adequately with social, economic, and cultural developments, and too intercolonial and Anglo-American in focus to permit intensive examination of a single colony's distinctive evolution. The most recent of these comprehensive accounts, that of Gipson, was begun as far back as 1936; since then a considerable body of new scholarship has been produced.

The present series, *A History of the American Colonies*, of which *Colonial Virginia* is part, seeks to synthesize the new research, to treat social, economic, and cultural as well as political developments, and to delineate the broad outlines of each colony's history during the years before independence. No uniformity of organization has been imposed on the authors, although each volume attempts to give some attention to every aspect of the colony's historical development. Each author is a specialist in his own field and has shaped his material to the configuration of the colony about which he writes. While the Revolutionary Era is the terminal point of each volume, the authors have not read the history of the colony backward, as mere preludes to the inevitable movement toward independence and statehood.

Despite their local orientation, the individual volumes, taken together, will provide a collective account that should help us understand the broad foundation on which the future history of the colonies in the new nation was to rest and, at the same time, help clarify that still not completely explained melodrama of 1776 which saw, in John Adams's words, thirteen clocks somewhat amazingly strike as one. In larger perspective, *A History of the American Colonies* seeks to remind today's generation of Americans of its earliest heritage as a contribution to an understanding of its contemporary purpose. The link between past and present is as certain as it is at times indiscernible, for as Michael Kammen has so aptly observed: "The historian is the memory of civilization. A civilization without history ceases to be civilized. A civilization without history ceases to have identity.

Without identity there is no purpose; without purpose civilization will wither."*

It is perhaps ironic but not entirely accidental that the first of the English settlements on the North American mainland should constitute the subject of the last published volume in this series of histories of the American colonies. By the eve of the Revolution, Virginia was not only the largest, most populous, and most valuable portion of Britain's mainland empire but also the province with the longest history, the oldest legislative assembly, the earliest system of African slavery, and perhaps the most arresting array of political leaders to have graced the stage of American colonial history—from John Smith and Walter Ralegh at one end to Thomas Jefferson and George Washington at the other.

Compressing the lengthy, richly textured history of the Old Dominion into a single volume is a challenge that Professors Billings, Selby, and Tate have met by drawing on their close familiarity with the sources, their own writings, and the work of the "new generation" of Virginia historians, with their interest in demography, family history, social class structure, and historical archeology. The history of colonial Virginia that emerges from their collective pen reaffirms some old truths, modifies others, and opens up several entirely new prospects. The proud boasts of the province's contemporary historians, its affluence arising from the tremendous European demand for its tobacco, and the stately life style of its planter aristocrats could never totally conceal the tensions and insecurity that characterized the life of the colony from its beginnings.

Claiming to be a rib hewn from Britain's side, Virginia never truly mirrored the mother country. A large, unfree labor force, mostly white in the seventeenth century and black in the eighteenth; planter aristocrats who possessed neither the wealth nor the leisure of the English country squires; an Anglican church establishment never firmly based and in the eighteenth century shaken by the onslaught of evangelical Baptists; a self-governing provincial elite always circumscribed in its power and under increasing British restraints after 1763;

---

*Michael Kammen, *People of Paradox* (New York, 1972), 13.

and growing inequalities producing greater social and economic stratification all belie the traditional portrait of a self-confident, English-style aristocracy.

Nevertheless, this homegrown elite managed to dominate Virginia's political, economic, and cultural life and in the years leading to the Revolution provided extraordinary leadership for the coalition of rebellious colonies. Conservative by instinct and interest, these planter aristocrats asserted vigorous claims to colonial autonomy that were eagerly accepted by their neighbors. Their radicalism was less ideological than circumstantial: they were propelled forward by the tide of events. Like colonists elsewhere, Virginia's leaders were torn betwen cultural loyalty to the mother country and insistence on retaining the right to "internal" self-government to which they had long been accustomed. The Revolution moved Virginia's leaders on to the national scene, but they never shed their parochial outlook. The colonial legacy of the Old Dominion was both mixed and ambiguous, perhaps more like that of the other British colonies than has heretofore been suspected. Virginia's colonial history, then, viewed in conjunction with the histories of the other twelve colonies, helps clarify the meaning of a revolution whose inception, however fortuitous, produced consequences so momentous that they live with us still.

MILTON M. KLEIN
JACOB E. COOKE

PREFACE

Writing the history of colonial Virginia within the compass of a single volume is a difficult task. The Old Dominion was, in the first place, the oldest, largest, and most populous of the British colonies in America. This circumstance requires scholars who intend to study its history to deal with an extensive array of persons and events and to examine an equally extensive body of past writing and—despite the loss of many of the colonial records—original sources.

For a long time historians tended to solve the problem in two ways. They wrote most often about some briefer period of the total colonial past in Virginia. Few undertook major studies that extended from colonization to independence, confining themselves instead to perhaps the seventeenth century, to the high point of colonial development in the early and mid-eighteenth century, or to the coming of the American Revolution. Second, much of the writing exhibited a preoccupation with the illustrious planter elite who have come to represent colonial Virginia in the popular mind.

No one can take away a certain central importance of the planter elite in the history of the colony, small though they were in number. Yet a wave of major scholarship in the last two decades has produced a more complicated explanation for the development of that remarkable group and has confined the large planters' dominance of life in Virginia to a period not much longer than the second quarter of the eighteenth century. The new generation of Virginia historians has called attention to the tenuous, unstable character of life in the first years of the colony; to the implications of a labor system always dominated by unfree workers—at first primarily indentured white servants and then black slaves; and, in the late colonial era, to the effects of rapid development of interior regions of the colony, an increasingly diverse population, and serious dislocation in the tobacco trade, which formed the major economic base of the colony. One cannot now write a brief synthesis of the history of colonial Virginia without drawing into it these newer themes, while at the same time retaining what is of enduring significance in the older ones.

Our solution to these problems—perhaps somewhat more practical than ideal—has been to divide the task among three authors. We would not, however, have undertaken the volume in such a manner had we not from the first established our essential agreement on the major contours of the history of colonial Virginia and had we not shared a conviction that the best periodization of that history is tripartite. Such a division recognizes (1) a perilous but ultimately successful period of development extending to about 1689; (2) a major transformation of the social and political order that began at least by the 1680s and culminated during the third and fourth decades of the eighteenth century; and (3) a time of crisis that began to appear by the middle of the eighteenth century and reached its climax in the imperial conflict that led to the American Revolution.

Each author has therefore assumed responsibility for one of these periods, Warren M. Billings for 1607–1689 (Chapters 1–5), John E. Selby for 1689–1750 (Chapters 6–10), and Thad W. Tate for 1750–1776 (Chapters 11–14 and a brief Epilogue). We had no expectation that we could eliminate every difference in style and emphasis among us, but we have sought to make our transitions as smooth and logical as possible and to avoid repetition or contradiction. We hope that we have achieved a satisfactory degree of unity and coherence.

For a subject on which the scholarly work is moving so rapidly, lack of annotation, however much it conforms to the design of the series and produces a more readable book, also presents difficulties of its own. We hope the bibliographical essay, which is organized in a manner that seeks to emphasize the work on which we have drawn, will both guide the reader of this volume in further exploration of the subject and make our debt to a great number of Virginia historians apparent.

The three of us wish to dedicate the volume to the memory of one of those historians, Richard Lee Morton. His two-volume study, *Colonial Virginia* (Chapel Hill, 1960), which was one of the last efforts to provide a general overview of the history of the colony, capped a lifetime of dedication to the study and teaching of Virginia history. We began our association with the College of William and Mary, where Dick Morton taught for forty years, after his retirement, but the three of us—Warren Billings as an undergraduate student and John Selby and Thad Tate as members of the history faculty, are grateful for the opportunity they had to know him and to see him still vigorously at work.

We also wish to acknowledge our debt to the editors of this series, Milton M. Klein and Jacob E. Cooke, for their patience and helpful suggestions. We join with them in relief that the entire series of thirteen volumes is now complete. Warren Billings wishes also to acknowledge the receipt of a summer research grant from the University of New Orleans that aided his work on the volume. Thad W. Tate incorporated into his chapters work that he initially completed under a fellowship from the American Council of Learned Societies. He is also indebted to John M. Hemphill II and Jack P. Greene for their careful reading of his chapters and to Jennifer Hall for enabling him once again to delay his confrontation with the word processor by her skillful preparation of his section of the manuscript.

A short note on dates is warranted. Continental Europeans abandoned the Julian calendar in 1582, when they replaced it with one devised by Pope Gregory XIII. That change required advancing dates by ten days; thus October 5, 1582 became October 15. The English continued to use the old style for another one hundred seventy years. Until they adopted the Gregorian calendar in 1752, they also began their year on March 25. It was therefore customary for seventeenth-century Virginians to write both years, e.g., January 1, 1600/01, in the interval between January 1 and March 24 through the years 1607 to 1752. That usage is retained in Chapters 1 through 10 of this book.

Williamsburg, Virginia   WARREN M. BILLINGS
December, 1985   JOHN E. SELBY
                                            THAD W. TATE

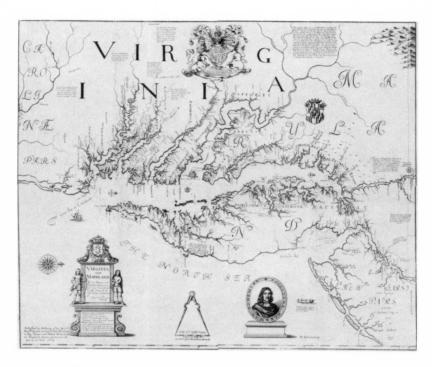

Augustin Herrman's map of Virginia and Maryland, 1670. The map is visually interesting for its presentation of the Tidewater Chesapeake as a single geographic region despite its separation into two colonies and also for its orientation, which places the east at the bottom of the map. That arrangement suggests the perspective of Europeans who approached Virginia from seaward. Courtesy of the Library of Congress.

COLONIAL VIRGINIA

A HISTORY

1

WESTWARD HO!
ENGLAND'S ROUTE TO VIRGINIA

First light broke across the eastern horizon. Three small vessels beat cautiously westward. A week had passed since the storm. Forced to run before the towering seas, they had been driven far from their intended course. But their admiral believed that he had now recovered his bearings. Some of the other mariners lacked his confidence, until the nippy morning breeze mingled the pungent odor of the sea with scents of land at springtime. Heartened by the smell, lookouts strained anxiously in the dawn to find an end to the trackless ocean that had been their little fleet's companion since the start of the voyage. Day brightened. Then they spied their landfall, the headlands that marked the entrance to Chesapeake Bay.

Carefully, the skippers sailed their ships into the bay. Leadmen, who clung precariously to each ship's fore channel rigging, took repeated soundings which they bellowed out for the masters' and the helmsmen's benefit.* Decks bustled with activity. Passengers came

---

*Leadmen were of especial importance to seventeenth-century mariners trying to negotiate previously uncharted waters, for they gave the captain and the helmsman an indication of the water's depth. The technique of sounding was relatively uncomplicated. The only equipment required was a piece of small-diameter rope, usually 100 fathoms (600 feet) in length, to which was attached a heavy lead weight. Every fathom was marked by a different colored piece of string or leather. To take a sounding, the leadman got up in the fore channel rigging and heaved the lead well forward of the ship's bow. He then paid out line until the weight reached bottom. If done properly, the weight found bottom just as the line came perpendicular to the leadman,

topside for a first glimpse of this strange new land. Seamen scrambled
to man the braces and halyards or scurried aloft eagerly awaiting orders
to douse sail. Other hands stood beside the anchors, ready to heave those
great weights overboard. Slowly, the convoy bore past the southern
cape and slipped further up the bay in search of a suitable anchorage.
Some eight miles to the west of the bay's mouth the orders echoed
across the water, and the stillness of the morning was broken by the
squeak of rigging and the splash of anchors that brought sails and hulls
to rest. At last, on this April morning in 1607, the vanguard of
England's immigrants to the New World had reached their destination—Virginia.

*   *   *

England's route to Virginia had been a long one, albeit neither so long
nor so old as that of the hated Spaniard. From the beginning of the
great Age of Discovery until the middle of the sixteenth century,
Englishmen stood apart from European explorations of the newfound
lands in Africa, the Americas, and Asia. They were racked by troubles
that kept them home. First was the Hundred Years' War with France,
which ended in 1453. It was soon supplanted by the Wars of the Roses,
debilitating contests for the Crown between the Yorkists and Lancas-
trians which only ended when Henry Tudor vanquished Richard III at
Bosworth Field in 1485. Fighting with the Scots and the French
dragged on into the next century. Then came Henry VIII's breach with
the Church of Rome. Thereafter, disputes over the character of the
nation's religious practices threw monarchs and commoners alike into
a turmoil that did not quiet until the accession of Elizabeth I.

The new reign ushered the realm into an era of relative calm. Even
so, the face of England was altered considerably by changes in the
economy and the social order as well as in politics and religion.
Advances were made in agriculture, industry, trade, and commerce.
Agricultural methods improved and new products were raised, while

---

whereupon he called off the mark closest to the water's surface. The procedure was
repeated at regularly spaced intervals, but the closer to shore, the more soundings he
would take. Thus he might have called out "By the mark, twain," meaning that his
ship had two fathoms of water beneath her bottom.

landowners became more aggressive in their efforts to exploit their holdings commercially. The wealth of the Spanish Indies and its subsequent influx into the European economy inflated prices and wages at staggering rates. Nonetheless, more money in circulation meant more to invest. Industry grew, though never at a rate that could threaten the preeminent place of agriculture in the English economy. Trade expanded, first into its traditional markets on the Continent and then into places opened up by the discoveries of new worlds. Merchants devised methods such as royally chartered trading companies that enabled them to marshall the influence, capital, and manpower necessary to the success of long-term ventures in faraway places. From these undertakings would come experience that had ready application to later colonizers. For all of these changes, though, the reign was not one of untrammeled expansion and limitless opportunity. In truth, to listen to the Elizabethans tell it, they lived in bleak times in which depression and war threatened their national existence.

Their perceptions of the alterations in England's social fabric were no less acute. The number of Englishmen, for reasons that demographers cannot explain, started rising at the beginning of the century, and it continued to multiply rapidly for a hundred and fifty years thereafter. Although the economy expanded, it did not grow fast enough to accommodate the needs of the new millions. Wages failed to keep pace with prices and rents. Perhaps as many as half the population left their homes and took to the road, where they joined others driven from the land by the commercialization of agriculture. And so it appeared to many, by Elizabeth's day, that England was dangerously overcrowded. Rigid enforcement of old and new vagrancy laws bespoke that concern, as did the belief that overcrowding threatened order throughout the kingdom.

Elizabethans regarded order and rank, laced with authority and obedience, which were reinforced by every social institution, as the ingredients of the proper society. They did not, as we do, think of society's being divided into classes. Instead, there were three distinctions among men: the monarch; those who governed—nobles, gentlemen, merchants, lawyers, clergy, even yeomen; and, in Sir Thomas Smith's words, "the sort of men which do not rule." Where an individual stood depended wholly on how he fit into a complicated scheme of ranks that only luck or the monarch might change, and in an age as fluid as Elizabeth's changes in rank occurred often. That very mobility betokened a turbulent society on the move.

A hunger for adventure and achievement became the hallmarks of the times, and the queen herself was their embodiment. Her entire life was an adventure in keeping her head and her crown. Endowed with a ready wit, she also possessed a broad learning that was remarkable even for the highborn women of her day. Ever the realist in religion and politics, Elizabeth abated religious tensions by striking a compromise between reform and tradition. She sought peace with her nation's foes while she encouraged her merchants to further England's commerce and trade. Her use of her power was firm but benign: by yielding gracefully in small matters, she had her way when things counted most. To be sure, not all of her countrymen found her rule congenial. Some plotted against her life, zealous reformers wished to purify the church of its popish practices, while adherents to the old faith longed to restore the church to communion with Rome. Despite these discordant notes, Elizabeth spared her people religious strife, civil war, and foreign involvements.

Her achievement was to give Englishmen an opportunity to turn their restless and creative energies elsewhere, and, until 1603, when the "great land-lady of England [was summoned] to appear in the star-Chamber of heaven," scores of the queen's subjects did just that. Playwrights and poets, essayists and historians, statesmen and soldiers, merchants and craftsmen, explorers and seamen helped to cut England loose from the past and to point it in new directions. They prided themselves on being a breed apart, blessed by an especial genius. No one captured those feelings better than William Shakespeare, who in *Richard II*, had his character, John of Gaunt, speak so tellingly:

> This royal throne of kings, this scepter'd isle,
> This earth of majesty, this seat of Mars,
> This other Eden, demi-paradise,
> This fortress built by Nature for herself
> Against infection and the hand of war,
> This happy breed of men, this little world,
> This precious stone set in the silver sea,
> Which serves in the office of a wall
> Or as a moat defensive to a house,

Against the envy of less happier lands,
This blessed plot, this earth, this realm,
this England. . . .

*   *   *

In these circumstances, it is hardly surprising that the Elizabethans should have cast their eyes westward and begun to think of carving out their own place in the New World. Their tastes for discovery and empire were honed many times over by news of wondrous findings that filtered into England throughout much of the sixteenth century. They thrilled to stories of great wealth from the Indies, of unusual plants and animals, of exotic remedies for common ailments, and even of extraordinarily strange people, who scarcely seemed human because they neither dressed, nor talked, nor worshipped as the English did, and, oddest of all, because their skins were not white. Told and retold, these tales were the stuff of colonial promoters—Richard Eden, John Frampton, Thomas Nicholas and the two Richard Hakluyts among them—who looked beyond their mere curiosity about unimaginable places and creatures. In their mind's eye, they saw that proud, Protestant England had as much right to share in the rewards of discovery as did the Spanish or the Portuguese. Honor, glory, and profit, their arguments ran, would come to those who took up the cause of overseas expansion, and their stress on these seemingly limitless possibilities helped to determine English thinking about America.

Of all the publicists, none were more influential than the Hakluyt cousins, though neither man ever sailed the oceans. The elder Richard was a Herefordshire man and a lawyer of indifferent abilities. What lawyerly skills he lacked he more than offset with his grasp of England's economic and social problems, as well as with his connections to merchants and others who ventured beyond the seas. His understanding led the first colonizers to seek his advice, and in that way he played a key role in fashioning the earliest plans for an English presence in America. The younger Richard was also a man whose chosen profession, the clergy, did not match his true calling. As a geographer and an editor, he gave a lifetime to preparing essays and compilations of sailors' narratives that popularized the value of colonization. His *Discourse on the Western Planting* (1584), *Divers Voyages touching the Discovery of America* (1582), *The Principall Navigations, Voiages and Discoveries of the English Nation* (1589) were the work of a masterful propagandist who provided compelling justifications for England's need to take its share of the New World. Beyond that, his persistent devotion to an idea helped keep it alive in times when his contemporaries' visions of empire dimmed.

Other Elizabethans also began to garner practical experience that would aid in future colonizing ventures. Those who attempted to conquer Ireland learned firsthand the techniques and the difficulties of planting settlements in hostile environments. Fishermen, who knew the way across the Atlantic to the Grand Banks and certain characteristics of the North American coast, provided direct knowledge of likely places to settle. Then too, the activities of John Hawkins and Sir Francis Drake showed that peaceful competition with Spain for colonies was an impossibility. If the English wished to erect their own profitable New World colonies they would have to wrest part of the Americas away from the Spanish.

Elizabeth herself, at last, took an interest in fostering colonial development, but only to the point of encouraging it. In 1576, she sent Martin Frobisher to find the fabled Northwest Passage by traversing the Arctic Ocean. He failed, of course, to sail over the top of the globe, as he did in his attempt to colonize Baffin Island, but his cargo of fool's gold and several Eskimos excited other courtiers to build on his failure. Now, it was the turn of Sir Humphrey Gilbert. The queen granted him letters patent to found a colony in June 1578. Gilbert intended to settle Newfoundland, which he believed to possess a more salutary climate that Baffin Island because it lay in the approximate latitude of the British Isles. His attempt was no more successful than Frobisher's. He lacked the capital to sustain it adequately. The site was inhospitable. Beyond fish, the land and its natives held little that could be exploited for profit. With his loss at sea, Gilbert's adventure came to naught.

Enter Sir Walter Ralegh.*

---

*Although the form Raleigh is the more familiar spelling, it was never used by Ralegh himself. He used the spelling Ralegh throughout all of his adult life, and that

Ralegh is a difficult man to assess. Adventurer, warrior, courtier, poet, historian, colonizer, his accomplishments ought to have ranked him among the greatest of the Elizabethans, but they have not. His very versatility made him a dilettante. The tragic events that led him to the block to die the traitor's death in 1616 have cloaked him in martyr's garb. Yet Ralegh commands attention because of his part in England's first steps toward empire and because of his connection with the fabled "Lost Colony."

He sprang from gentle but impoverished West Country stock whose other sons Carew Ralegh, Adrian, John, and Humphrey Gilbert all had long, intimate ties to colonizing ventures in Ireland and America. Ralegh's own appetite for an American adventure was first aroused when he sailed on Gilbert's initial expedition. Upon returning, his attentions were diverted elsewhere while he steadily improved his position at court, but when Sir Humphrey perished, it was Ralegh who pressed for a renewal of Gilbert's patent in 1584.

Ralegh profited from his half-brother's failure. For one thing, he resolved to try to plant considerably south of where Gilbert had expected to settle. The area he had in mind lay closer to the Spanish colonies, which was a possible disadvantage, but its climate was more agreeable than the cold wilds of Newfoundland. For another, Ralegh decided to dispatch a small survey party to scout the site, and in April 1584 he sent Philip Amadas and Arthur Barlowe with two ships to America.

Amadas and Barlowe reached the coast of what is now North Carolina early in July. They spent several weeks reconnoitering the vicinity of Roanoke Island for a good harbor and for a place to erect a plantation and initiate trade with the natives. The ships returned to England by September, bringing a bag of pearls, several venturesome Indians, and many tales about the wonders of this part of America. Barlowe wrote the account of the expedition in glowing, if fanciful, terms that made the land seem worthy of the name that his master gave it—Virginia. In return for the honor, the Virgin Queen knighted Ralegh.

Encouraged by the queen's gesture, Ralegh enlisted the younger Hakluyt to memorialize her, in the expectation that she would give

---

is why it is employed here. On the point, see Robert Lacey, *Sir Walter Ralegh* (New York, 1974), p. 11.

financial aid to another expedition. Hakluyt's memorial, *Discourse on the Western Planting*, set forth every argument for planting colonies—from augmenting trade, to ridding England of surplus population, to furthering religion—that promoters advanced over the next two centuries. But to no avail: Elizabeth offered no more than her encouragement and the loan of a navy vessel.

Undaunted, Ralegh proceeded on his own. He sought further advice from the elder Hakluyt, who counseled him to send a company of specialists in botany, map making, drawing, and similar skills who might prepare the way for a more permanent settlement. Acting on the suggestion, Ralegh sent just such a group, commanded by Richard Grenville and Ralph Lane, back to Roanoke Island in 1585. Among its number were the artist John White and a young Oxford scholar, Thomas Hariot, both of whom were to produce accurate, naturalistic depictions of the natives, their ways, and the Carolina flora and fauna. The expedition made a slow crossing, arriving too late in the season to plant crops. Damage to their supplies, coupled with Indian difficulties, led to a hard winter, which was compounded by Lane's ineptness. When spring came and Sir Francis Drake appeared, Lane and his men inclined toward returning home. As they considered their situation, a storm destroyed what few supplies Drake had brought. That disaster stiffened Lane's resolve to leave, and he persuaded Sir Francis to take the company back to England. Grenville arrived some weeks later with a major supply; finding no one, he put the stores on shore in the care of some of his men and sailed off in search of Spanish shipping. Ralegh's American plantation lay in ruins.

Despite the outbreak of war with Spain, Ralegh mounted another try in 1587. He placed the men, women, and children he recruited under the leadership of John White, whom he named his deputy governor. The inclusion of families, coupled with his generous promises of land and orders to erect a borough form of government, suggest that Ralegh intended this attempt to become permanent. On Lane's advice, Ralegh also instructed White to select a more congenial site on or near Chesapeake Bay, though the colonists were to call at Roanoke Island to fetch Grenville's men. When the colonists reached Roanoke Island, the pilot refused to go farther, so White and his people unloaded and began to establish themselves. For reasons that have remained unclear, White chose to go back with the ships. His arrival in England coincided with the threat of the Armada. Four years passed before the English could undertake to resupply the colony. White returned to a deserted settlement. Save for the cryptic word "Croatoan" that was carved into a tree, the colonists had vanished without trace.

The long-accepted explanation of their fate was put best by the Virginia historian Robert Beverley II, who wrote in 1704, "It is supposed that the Indians seeing them forsaken by their country and unfurnished of their expected supplies, cut them off. For to this day they were never more heard of." Modern scholars take a different view. Based on evidence that is far from certain, they conclude that the main body of settlers abandoned Roanoke Island and went to live on the Elizabeth River near the Chesapeake Indians. They intermarried with the Chesapeakes and acculturated to native ways, but they were wiped out by Powhatan, who destroyed the entire Chesapeake tribe on the eve of the Jamestown settlement.*

Whatever its fate, the "Lost Colony" finished Ralegh as a colonizer. Indeed, his signing away of certain of his patent rights indicated a loss of interest in the colony even before anyone in England knew of its disappearance. His dream of colonizing America never was the focus of his undivided attention. Rather, it was one facet of a nimble intellect in an era whose participants were intrigued by astounding discoveries and great possibilities. It was of a piece with his other business enterprises and a way for him to strike out against Spain. And, it was, at least for a time, a way to further his ambition for power.

*   *   *

The Armada and the Anglo-Spanish War that followed in its wake drove further colonizing activities to a temporary halt. Both also contributed, indirectly, to an eventual redefinition of English conceptions about what colonies ought to be. Even though the promoters had always stressed the commercial worth of colonies, the merchants had not been among the first to reach for opportunity. Instead, the earliest adventurers were courtiers. Frobisher, Gilbert, and Ralegh used their connections to secure the government's blessings, and they employed

---

*The argument is largely that of David Beers Quinn in his *England and the Discovery of America, 1481–1620* (New York, 1974), pp. 432–482.

their personal wealth to found settlements. Their hope was that in erecting domains, which would be sustained by the tribute of subject natives, they would augment their existing fortunes. Colonies built on such schemes attracted little interest from merchants, who saw no profit to themselves in such enterprises. To them, the loss of the Roanoke colony demonstrated the ultimate folly of the courtiers' ideas. Nevertheless, their thinking changed as the war dragged on. For one thing, the younger Hakluyt convinced them that England stood to gain by settling in America, even though gold mines and northwest passages might not exist. For another, as the seventeenth century opened, a need for colonies was being linked to a general effort to increase trade. Modest efforts at settling both the New England and Virginia coasts began soon after the century turned, but the queen's death stopped further expeditions until James I's attitudes were known and the war ended.

Peace returned in 1604. A short while later, Richard Hakluyt, Sir John Popham, the Lord Chief Justice of England, Sir Thomas Smythe, an official in the East India Company, Sir Thomas Gates and Edward Maria Wingfield, both old soldiers who were Hakluyt's associates, among other well-connected public men or merchants from London, Bristol, and Plymouth, laid plans for a new colony. Their first move was to draft a charter. Chief Justice Popham, it seems, did most of the drafting, although he may have received advice from Sir Edward Coke, the attorney general, and John Doddridge, the solicitor general and possibly even the assistance of Robert Cecil, the earl of Salisbury, the king's principal secretary. As soon as Popham finished, the group petitioned the king for a patent that would validate Popham's work and permit them to attempt the settlement. James granted the appropriate letters patent on April 10, 1606.

The charter divided the North American continent in two, assigning the northern half to the West Country patentees, with the southern part going to the Londoners. Next, it authorized the establishment of two privately funded and managed joint-stock companies, one centered in London, the other in Plymouth, and held both accountable to a royally appointed council in London. James guaranteed that the colonists and their descendants "shall have and enjoy all liberties Franchises and Immunities within anie of our dominions. . . . as if they had been abiding and borne within this our Realme of England." The charter also contained an exhortation to proselytize the natives. Finally, it provided lengthy instructions on how settlement should proceed, as it put the burden of government in the hands of resident councils.

Supplemental instructions amplifying the charter provisions were subsequently drafted. Most had to do with the responsibilities of the resident councils or advice that the patentees thought pertinent. One, however, enjoined that "for the good Government of the people to be planted in those parts and for the good ordering and disposing of all causes happening within the same, the same to be done for the substance thereof, as neer to the Common Lawes [of] England, and the equity thereof, as may be."

Although that statement, together with the charter's promise of individual rights, can be construed as evidence of an intention to transfer English society in its entirety to Virginia, it was not. These adventurers were less bent on social engineering than on devising an efficient business organization that would make the undertaking pay. Both provisions were for the convenience of the resident officials; indeed, they were viewed as means of stretching the odds in favor of success. In time, the colonists would put these guarantees to uses that no one in 1606 could have anticipated.

Helping Dame Fortune is why, among other considerations, the patentees also turned to the joint-stock trading company for their model of organization and management. The device was a familiar method for pooling capital, talent, and knowledge. It had proven itself in the development of trade with eastern Europe and the Orient. Apart from the advantages it offered the merchant with capital to risk, it offered another attractive possibility. Someone who lacked money could gamble his labor as a company servant against a share of the expected profits. That feature was the one which the patentees hoped to turn into a tool to recruit emigrants from the ranks of the poorer sorts of Englishmen.

* * *

Seven men comprised the London Company. Sir Thomas Smythe, Sir William Romney, and John Eldred were merchants. Both Sir Henry Montagu and Sir William Waad were lawyers and influential Londoners. Montagu was the city's recorder, while Waad held the post of lieutenant of the Tower. The remaining two, Sir Walter Cope and Sir George More, were also public men. Smythe and his colleagues envisioned their initial attempt as pathfinding and pathbreaking. Once it had established a toehold, then a more permanent colony would follow.

Eight months passed before the company fully organized an expedition and sent it off toward Chesapeake Bay. Its first order of business was to name the resident council, recruit settlers, purchase supplies, and hire vessels. Company officials picked an odd lot for leaders. Four were mariners. Of these, Christopher Newport and Bartholomew Gosnold had close ties to the company, as well as direct knowledge of the Chesapeake. The other two, John Ratcliffe and John Martin, were of no great reputation or connection. A fifth councillor, Edward Maria Wingfield, was recently one of the suitors for the charter. The sixth was the wildly tempestuous George Kendall, who, it seems, was a spy for Lord Salisbury. Last was John Smith, a farm boy from Lincolnshire with a nose for hair-raising adventures and wits to match, who learned much about command and survival during the years he soldiered on the Continent. Newport was in command until the expedition reached Virginia. About 104 men and boys agreed to sign on as colonists. Half their number were gentlemen; the remainder were either laborers or assorted craftsmen and artisans. Supplies, which took a while to secure, were stockpiled. Summer passed into fall before longshoremen began to stow them aboard two ships and a pinnace, the *Susan Constant*, the *Godspeed* and the *Discovery*.*

The loading proceeded while the company drew up the last of the instructions and attended to remaining details. All seemed in readiness by the third week in November, but as the *Susan Constant* was being moved to a different mooring she collided with another ship. She sustained no major damage, though the accident delayed the departure until late December, when all repairs were finished. The colonists climbed aboard on the 19th, and on the next day the little convoy stood

---

*A pinnace was a sailing craft that ranged in dimension from a ship's boat to a vessel capable of carrying men and supplies across the oceans. The *Discovery*'s smaller size made her useful in exploring little known coastlines. Because she drew less water than either the *Susan Constant* or the *Godspeed*, she could be used to scout closer to shore.

down the Thames for the Chesapeake. Ahead lay a four-month journey
and wonders and hazards that few could have foretold.

*   *   *

Captain Newport and his companions came to the Chesapeake little
prepared for what they found. No Englishman had yet explored the
great bay and its tributaries; no one had mapped the terrain; and no one
had described its natural features in any detail. What these settlers
thought they knew of the region in April 1607 was grounded largely
in ignorance. Their misunderstanding flowed from the pens of promoters and explorers, who had invariably depicted Virginia in fabulous
language as a new Eden peopled by natives who were alternately simple
and friendly or cunning and dangerous, but always savage. Newport's
men expected to find a garden where they might be fruitful and
multiply, and there to have dominion over every living thing.

Virginia was no Eden, but it was a place of beauty and bounty
nonetheless. Its landscape varied from the Atlantic coastal plain to the
unknown hinterland, as did the soil and climate, and the native
Virginians were neither simple nor savage. From the first sighting,
these and other physical characteristics excited the settlers' curiosity
about the place. Inquisitive colonists speculated endlessly on what they
saw, and they left accounts of their observations. Whether the observer
was John Smith, John Hammond, Robert Beverley, Hugh Jones,
Thomas Jefferson, or any one of dozens of others, the word pictures that
emerged from their combined writings provide the modern reader with
a wealth of detailed information about Virginia's pristine condition.

Geographically, the area that encompassed colonial Virginia was
vastly greater than the modern Old Dominion. James I's charter of
1606 originally defined it as the territory between 34° and 45° north
latitude; that is, all the land from the Passamaquoddy Bay in Maine to
the Cape Fear River in North Carolina, extending westward to the
Pacific Ocean. The founding of New England, Maryland, and the
Carolinas reduced the northern and southern boundaries almost to their
present-day lines, though the western limit remained uncharted.
Within these borders, then, what was colonial Virginia comprised four
distinct topographical regions that ranged from the seacoast into the
interior of the continent.

The first of these regions was the Tidewater. Tidewater contained all of Virginia between the fall line and the Atlantic Ocean. Located approximately a hundred miles inland from the seacoast, the fall line was the point at which the eastern waterways ceased being tidal; hence the name Tidewater. Its distinctive feature was the Chesapeake Bay, formed by the mainland and a large peninsula that the English aptly named the "Eastern Shore." The bay was fed by numerous creeks and small rivers, in addition to four major tributaries—the James, the York, the Rappahannock, and the Potomac—into which flowed streams of lesser proportions. Lying beyond the Tidewater was the Piedmont, a land that rose gently upward as it rolled toward the Blue Ridge Mountains, the eastern chain of the Appalachians. The Piedmont was a region of considerable size that ran from forty to one hundred and forty miles in breadth. It was watered by the upper reaches of the Chesapeake Bay river system, as well as by several other streams. Back of the Blue Ridge was the Great Valley of Virginia, whose western edge extended to the far range of the Appalachians. Pierced with numerous passes all along its length, the Valley was actually part of a much larger one that stretched from New York to Georgia. It served as a highway in the eighteenth century, as settlers moved along its floor in search of new land. Last came the main ridge of the Appalachian Mountains and the trans-Appalachian West.

Colonial acquaintance with these regions and their particular natural characteristics developed in stages over the seventeenth and eighteenth centuries. The fall line, the Indians, and the colonists' dependence on the sea link to the mother country combined to confine the settlers to the Tidewater. Consequently, the Piedmont and the Valley were known only to a handful of Indian traders or other venturesome souls before the early 1700s. Some of these explorers probably traveled beyond the far mountains, but the tramontane west remained one region whose character was virtually unknown to English Virginians until well into the eighteenth century.

Virginia had a mild climate. Spring would begin in the Tidewater by mid-March, and within four to six weeks the danger of frost would pass. From then on, bright, sunny days would warm into July and August, the hottest months of the year. Thunderstorms would interrupt the oppressive heat, providing respite for both man and crop. John Hammond, who wrote *Leah and Rachell, or the two fruitfull Sisters of Virginia and Mary-land* (1656), noted that the heat was abated at other times by a "continual breaze of Winde which never failes to cool and refresh the labourer and traveller." Another, more violent, feature of summer's weather was the occasional hurricane. The first sustained break in the sultriness of summer would come in late September. October's frosts would bring that loveliest of all Virginia seasons, fall, followed in turn by the cold, leaden-sky months of winter. Through the year, temperatures would fluctuate from below 0° to 100°, though the mean range was less extreme. Precipitation averaged around 40 inches a year, with the greatest amounts of rainfall coming between April and September. December, January, and February would bring snow. More often than not, however, what moisture fell in those months would take the form of a biting drizzle that magnified the winter's dreariness.

These seasonal conditions changed as the distance from the coast and the elevation of the land increased. Although it was a matter of days or weeks, rather than months, spring arrived later beyond the fall line. To the west, summer was neither so long nor so hot, but the winters were sharper and longer. Rain in winter was less abundant; snow, more so.

"The colour of the earth," noted John Smith, "resembleth . . . Fullers earth, marle, and divers other such appearances. But," he continued, it was "a black sandy mould, in some places a fat slimy clay, in other places a very barren gravell." Smith's depiction of soil conditions came closer to actuality than he realized. The coastal lowlands were covered with loam, an alluvial soil rich in organic matter, but farther upriver the loam was mixed with sand and clay. Although Tidewater soils were "lusty and very rich," in Smith's words, their texture was light, meaning that, when cultivated, they soon lost their nutrients and eroded easily. Some combination of sand, clay, and limestone, or just limestone, constituted the soils in the Piedmont and beyond.

No matter what its composition, the land supported plant and animal life whose immense variety is now difficult to imagine. The kinds of plants were so great that even as late as 1785, when Jefferson first published his *Notes on the State of Virginia*, he could write "there is an infinitude of . . . plants and flowers." Out of this "infinitude," what easily drew the early colonists' attention were the trees: they were everywhere. They ranged from the coastal forests of pines, whose scent the offshore winds carried miles out to sea, to interior stands of walnut, hickory, oak, chestnut, elm, beech, poplar or numerous other species. These woods were so thick as to be free of undergrowth, but they did not completely cover the land, especially in those regions where the Indians had burned back the brush to facilitate hunting. Indian clearings and old fields, meadows and dunes, marshes and tidal flats, bogs and swamps, river bottoms and mountain valleys also dotted the landscape with open areas that provided living spaces where flowers, berries, medicinals, tobacco, and small grains could flourish.

The rivers and bays teemed with edible fishes and crustaceans, while aquatic vegetation supported countless waterfowl. Land animals of all sorts and sizes, and in great populations, seemed to thrive everywhere. According to the anonymous author of *A Perfect Description of Virginia*, published in 1649, the colonists had already named "above 20 severall kinds" of mammals and more than "25 severall kindes" of birds by the middle of the seventeenth century, but he indicated that there were many other species "that have no English Names." One of these, which he styled a "Passonne," caught his countrymen's particular fancy because it "hath a bagge under her belly into which she takes her young ones, if at any time affrighted, and carries them away." Another writer, who commented on the staggering numbers of migratory fowl he had witnessed, recalled seeing flocks of more than 500 turkeys and seven-mile-long strings of flying ducks.

* * *

It is a conceit of Virginians of Old World extraction to think of their forebears as *the first* Americans. Some whose ancestry derives from the earliest English colonists refer to themselves as the "First Families of Virginia." Of course, the distinction of being first goes to none of these. Instead, it belongs to a group of people who John Smith wrote were "of a colour browne," the true native Virginians—the Indians.

Arriving at a fair, accurate portrayal of them as they existed before contact with Europeans is no small task. Because the natives had no written languages, no records represent the Indians' viewpoint. All that is known of them, therefore, comes either from European accounts or from archaeological remains. Both forms of evidence have limited worth, however. Rare was the Englishman who overcame his cultural chauvinism to the point that he could recount what he saw without varnishing the truth, especially after the settlers perceived the Indians as a menace to their well-being. Artifactual remnants have much to tell about the natives' material possessions, but they are of little value for an understanding of their intangible cultural belongings. How to fit the Indians into their appropriate niche in the history of the Old Dominion has also been a problem. It is one that Virginia historians have been content to leave to anthropologists, at least until recently. Once a concern for the specific contributions of ethnic Americans began to inform historical thinking, as it has for the past decade or so, it became possible to reconsider the evidence with an eye toward discerning significant cultural relationships between the Indians and the English.

The origins of the Indians are cloaked in mystery, and only one point seems beyond dispute: they did not arise in Virginia. Instead, they descended from the archaic tribes of nomadic *homo sapiens* who, beginning perhaps as early as 50,000 B.C., emigrated in stages from Asia by way of a land bridge between Alaska and Siberia. Through succeeding millennia, these ancient people developed distinctive languages and cultural traditions as they spread across the Western Hemisphere and eventually into Virginia. Artifacts taken from excavations at the Conover site in present-day Dinwiddie County have disclosed that the earliest Indian presence dates from only about 9500 B.C. We know little else about these ancient Virginians, except that they and their descendants continued to grow through different levels of social complexity. By 1607 they were as elaborate and varied in their ways as the English were in theirs.

Just as Gaelic, Welsh, and English, together with its several dialects, were the languages of the British Isles, Virginia's original inhabitants spoke in tongues that derived from one of three linguistic stocks, Algonquian, Iroquoian, and Siouian. The Algonquian speakers occupied the territory east of the fall line. West of the falls lay the domain of the Siouian tribes; those who spoke Iroquoian ranged along southeastern portion of Virginia and the area north of the Potomac.

No one knows how many Indians were alive in 1607 or in 1776: neither natives nor colonists kept head tallies. Accordingly, any calculations are conjectural, and, because there is no longer a way to arrive at precise tabulations, they differ greatly. The difficulty can be seen in the estimates of the number of natives who lived near the colonists' original settlement. John Smith put it at 5,000, but modern guesses range from double that figure to upwards of 170,000. One thing is clear, nevertheless. Prolonged proximity with the Europeans led to rapid depopulation. The effects of Old World diseases, alcohol, loss of tribal lands, and warfare were so devastating that after less than a century of contact, Robert Beverley could write of the original inhabitants of Tidewater, "the *Indians* of Virginia are almost wasted." What was true for them was no less true for those who lived beyond the falls.

Although divided by language, all of the natives shared cultural characteristics. Their largest unit of social organization was the tribe. Individual tribes had defined territories over which they might range, but the idea of private tenure did not exist, although a concept nearer to the civil law doctrine of usufruct* did. Tribal members lived in family groups inside palisaded villages of houses fabricated of wood and its byproducts. The line of descent was through the mother, rather than the father, as was the English custom. Marriage was held to be sacred, though divorce was permitted, but infidelity was thought of as the most unforgivable of offenses.

Ceremonies, dancing, and games were important rituals for social occasions of great moment such as warfare or religious festivals. Religions aimed at balancing nature's elements and placating evil spirits. Beyond performing the spiritual role, priests were valued for their knowledge of ailments and their remedies. In truth, what the colonists came to call the "Indian physick" was generally superior to European medical practices.

There were no accumulated bodies of law such as the common law or prescriptions of individual liberties, which the English revered as the bedrock of their polity. Nevertheless, the Indians' sense of justice and morality was finely drawn, albeit in a manner different from that of the English. Offenders were not haled into courts to answer for their misdeeds or to have their fates weighed by juries. Tribal leaders had the power of life and death, and they punished those who murdered, stole, or transgressed tribal mores in other ways.

---

*I.e., the right to temporary possession or use of a property belonging to another without causing damage to it.

A palisaded Indian village resembling those that the Virginia colonists would have found in 1607. An engraving by Theodore de Bry (1590) from a watercolor painting by John White, who was a member of the first and unsuccessful Roanoke expedition in 1587. The Virginia and eastern Carolina Indians had such similar cultures that the White drawings are assumed to provide a good picture of both groups. Virginia State Library photograph.

The Indians were experts in extracting a living from the land while retaining a balance with their natural environment. Surrounded by abundant wildlife and fish, Indian mean were accomplished hunters and fishermen who developed the community hunt, the net, and the weir as harvesting tools. Other tools were fashioned from bone, wood, or stone; their design differed little from similar European implements. Whenever possible, the natives built their villages on lowlands, where the land usually required little clearing and the soil was most fertile. Women maintained small family plots in the villages. They also assisted in farming the principle fields which the men cleared and prepared. Skilled in agriculture, the Indians cultivated tobacco, melons, beans, and corn, which were the staples of life. They often produced as many as three crops of corn in a single season. Such productivity was a direct result of their farming techniques. Long before the seventeenth century, they had learned to sow their crops in hills which they laid out in rows. Hilling not only established stronger stalks and root systems but also helped to retain moisture, as it cut down on weeds. Their practice of planting different crops between rows also served to replenish the soil's nutrients, thereby reducing the necessity of continually clearing new land. Such methods were unknown to Europeans in 1607, and more than a hundred years passed before the eighteenth-century agricultural revolution brought them into general practice.

The intrusion of the English into this native world presented the first Virginians with bewildering problems. What sort of relationship should they have with the whites? What, if anything, should they borrow from white culture? Could they maintain the integrity of their culture in the face of the onslaught, or must they inexorably give in to an amalgamation with white society? As events proved, the choice of answers was not always theirs to make.

The Algonquian-speaking Indians of the Tidewater became the first to confront these profoundly vexing questions. Their tribes, numbering three dozen or more, were bound together in a loose association dominated by a leader the English called Powhatan. Although its cohesiveness resulted from the strength of Powhatan's personality, the association was a well-defined polity. A chief, often a woman, ruled every tribe. Collectively, several tribes were governed by other chiefs, known as lesser *werowances*, who were in their turn subordinate to a council of priests, relatives, and werowances that shared dominion over the whole with Powhatan, the great werowance.

Europeans, some of whom first showed up on the Chesapeake coast in the 1520s, were no strangers to the Powhatans. From that date, contact was intermittent, as the occasional vessel put into bay in search of provisions, fresh water, or a temporary safe harbor. At times such as these, the intruders kidnapped or lured unsuspecting natives aboard ship and took them beyond the horizon, never to return. Spanish Jesuits attempted to establish a mission in 1570, but the effort was soon abandoned. (It is just possible that these missionaries were assisted by Powhatan's chief subordinate, Opechancanough. Opechancanough was taken to Spain in 1560, some scholars believe. From there he was sent to St. Augustine, before returning to the Chesapeake with the Jesuits.* Then, too, Powhatan's men had wind of the Ralegh expeditions, and some had seen Captain Newport when he scouted the bay in the 1590s. Such experiences bred caution, and so, in 1607, the Powhatans greeted the latest of these strangers warily.

The English did not threaten the natives at first. Their numbers were small, and they died off almost as rapidly as they came. Powhatan therefore seemed inclined to leave them be, in the apparent belief that they would probably tire of trying to settle an alien country. In the meantime, the strangers had their uses. Their aid might be enlisted against Powhatan's enemies to the north and west. Perhaps they would also trade cloth, iron pots, steel tools, even firearms, for furs or foodstuffs and for the secrets of growing corn and tobacco. Beyond these possibilities, neither Powhatan nor his minions discovered any benefits from prolonged relationships with the English. Watchful waiting was the proper course to pursue. The determination of the colonists and the London Company to persevere in the face of all obstacles soon proved the folly of that policy. Once the Indians discerned that intention, their hostility toward the whites stiffened, and from that day forward they resolved to rout the English from their homeland. Their decision led to a seventy-five-year war of attrition, the

---

*This is the view of Carl Bridenbaugh, who developed it in his book, *Jamestown, 1544–1699* (New York, 1980). He argued that Opechancanough and the Indian taken by the Spanish explorer, Pedro Menendez de Aviles, and called Don Luis were one and the same person. The argument rests largely upon circumstantial evidence.

result of which was cultural devastation. That choice also helped to sire the tragic pattern of Indian-white relations that, differing only in particulars, repeated itself until the last of the natives were subjugated at the end of the nineteenth century.

*   *   *

How did those who came to colonize respond to what they found in Virginia?

Among the first reactions was relief—relief at having survived the Atlantic crossing. To inexperienced landlubbers, the passage was an exquisite test of their endurance. Seemingly trackless, unending water surrounded them as soon as England dropped behind the eastern horizon. The wind was unpredictable. Just spending weeks or months aboard ship had its own frights. Captains rarely encouraged their passengers—assuredly not in the instances where skippers trafficked in slaves—to come topside. Conditions below deck were dreadful. Deepwater sailing vessels of the colonial period were never designed with comfort in mind. They were small and seldom surpassed a waterline length of one hundred feet. Cargo space was at a premium, which meant that settlers and their belongings, together with pigs and chickens, cows and horses, were all jammed tightly into cramped holds. Hot meals were a seldom-seen luxury; cooking invited the danger of fire. Garbage and excrement, which wound up in the bilges, fouled air already made noisome by inadequate ventilation. Seasickness was ever-present. Disease carried off the weak, the sick, and the very young, though not always quickly or easily. Indeed, captains sometimes allowed suckling infants free passage because they knew that such children rarely survived the crossing. Even with these trials, many passengers agreed with Governor Francis, Lord Howard of Effingham that the trip was merely "tedious"; but an early colonist, Richard Frethorne, spoke for them all when, upon landing in 1623, he described his safe arrival as "no smale joy."

That feeling of joy was short-lived because new arrivals next had to adjust to the Virginia wilderness and the separation from the familiar surroundings of home. Experienced settlers graphically styled these collective adjustments as "the seasoning." Seasoning was never easy. Sometimes it happened swiftly; sometimes it was so slow as to be imperceptible. Failure to adjust had painful or deadly results. On the one hand, as small a thing as refusing to accommodate one's dress to new conditions caused misery to those who, in Robert Beverley's acerbic words, "make no distinction between a cold and a hot country: but wisely go sweltering about in their thick Cloaths all the Summer, because they used to do so in their *Northern* Climate; and then unfairly complain of the heat of the Country." On the other hand, those who failed to come to terms with the climate, illness, or plain loneliness perished. But the ones who became seasoned saw themselves as blessed with special favor, and from this sense of blessing came the eventual belief that they and their progeny were a chosen people.

From the beginning, colonists were fascinated by what they first saw of Virginia. George Percy, who went ashore in 1607, later marveled at having discovered "faire meddowes and goodly tall Trees, with such Fresh-waters . . . , as I was almost ravished at the first sight thereof." As they grew more accustomed to their surroundings, the mystery and much of the inaccurate knowledge faded, but they never quite lost their fascination for the natural qualities of the country. In the 1780s, for example, Jefferson described the Natural Bridge as "the most sublime of Nature's works.*

The sheer quantity of land was a powerful attraction. So far as anyone knew in 1607 the amount was boundless, and for the English, whose homeland was a small island, that thought was mind-boggling. Owning ground was what made gentlemen back home. In Virginia a man could take of it as he desired and do with it as he pleased. Very quickly, that realization bred a belief that Virginia was a place without limits; and, over the long run, that conviction had profound consequences for the colony's future.

---

*Jefferson went on to say of the bridge, which lies west of Lexington, "You involuntarily fall on your hands and feet, creep to the parapet and peep over it. Looking down from this height about a minute, gave me a violent head ache. This painful sensation is relieved by a short, but pleasing view of the Blue Ridge. . . . It is impossible for the emotions, arising from the sublime to be felt what they are here: so beautiful an arch, so light and springing, as it were up to heaven, the rapture of the Spectator is really indescribable . . . " The quotation is from his *Notes on the State of Virginia*, ed. by William Peden (Chapel Hill, 1954), 24–25.

2

SETTLING DOWN: JAMESTOWN

The London Company's ships arrived at their destination none too soon. After four months at sea, the colonists were eager to be rid of tight quarters, sickness, and moldering rations, even if the landing meant trading the hazards of the ocean for the uncertainties of the Virginia wilds. But there was another reason why they longed to be ashore: the expectation that the business of establishing the colony would put an end to the bickering among their leaders.

Quarrels had broken out even before England fell behind the horizon, their apparent origin being friction between John Smith and Edward Maria Wingfield, who took exception to what he perceivd as Smith's lack of deference to his social superiors. By the time the fleet had reached its first stopover, the Canary Islands, the disagreement had warmed to the point where Wingfield accused Smith of fomenting mutiny and had him arrested and confined for the duration of the voyage. The feud brought credit to neither man. Nevertheless, its significance lay not in how it damaged Smith's or Wingfield's reputations but in what it augured for the future of the soon-to-be-established settlement. It signified fundamental discord within the leadership—a dissonance that would curse Virginia with divided counsel during all the years the company managed Virginia, just as it would cause the Crown to vacate the charter in 1624.

*   *   *

Whatever their hopes, coming to anchor on April 26 quickly shook the English from their reveries. All the landsmen wished to go ashore and renew their acquaintance with *terra firma*, and they clamored to be in the initial landing party, but Admiral Newport paid them no heed. Instead, he picked some thirty men, a few gentlemen but mostly seamen and soldiers, to go with him.

Once the party was in the longboat, it made for the nearest shore. Lookouts in the bow were alert for any sound or sight of Indians. Nothing broke the morning stillness but the muted sounds of the Englishmen's own voices and the rhythmic cadence of their oars biting water, or an occasional bird call. Ashore, a quick check of the beach seemed to indicate that no natives lurked nearby, and the party walked slowly inland.

The explorers spent most of the day scouting the meadows and refreshing themselves at the frequent brooks they found. Aside from enjoying the first taste of fresh water since leaving the West Indies and marveling at the scenery, they discovered nothing, in George Percy's words, "worth the speaking of." Night fell before Newport decided to return to the fleet, though a nearly full moon afforded light enough to guide him back to where he had left the longboat. No sooner had he given the order to retire than the English discovered they were not alone. Suddenly a small band of Indians, who had evidently stalked the party from the moment it landed, charged them. A brief skirmish followed, in which, according to Percy, the attackers "hurt Captaine Gabrill Archer in both his hands and a sayler in two places of the body very dangerous." The soldiers fired their weapons, but to no great effect; and once the natives spent their arrows, they retired "into the Woods with a great noise." Apart from the injuries to Archer and the seaman, everyone returned to the fleet intact, though a bit unnerved by the experience.

That night the leaders, all save Smith, assembled in Newport's cabin on the *Susan Constant*. They gathered there to witness the opening of the sealed boxes that company officials had entrusted to the admiral and Captain Gosnold, together with instructions to open them only when the fleet was safely in Virginia. Someone, quite likely Newport, broke the seals and took out what proved to be identical lists of the seven names of those whom officials back home had designated to sit on the resident council. In addition to Newport and Gosnold, the list included Wingfield, John Martin, John Ratcliffe, George Kendall, and Smith. Now the business of locating a place to settle could begin.

Next day, the ship's carpenters fitted up and rigged the dismantled shallop that the colonists had brought along. The shallop was sloop-rigged, and it could be rowed when there was no wind. Smaller and more maneuverable than the *Discovery* but larger and more accommodating than a longboat, she would be handy for exploring.

When the shallop was ready, the colonists began to scout the bay. They searched the south shore first, and within a matter of days they had landed at both capes. The southern one they named Henry, after the prince of Wales; the northern one they called Charles, after the prince's younger brother. Their exploration also revealed that their first anchorage had actually been in the mouth of a large river, which they styled the James to honor the king, perhaps in the hope that he would reward these adventurers as Elizabeth had done Ralegh. That discovery led them to probe the James's north shore around what is now Old Point Comfort. They found the native village of Kecoughtan, whose inhabitants welcomed them, and they relaxed there some days before working their way farther up the James. About forty miles above Old Point Comfort, Newport anchored the fleet off another village, Paspahegh, where he and his charges were again entertained by the natives. While at Paspahegh, the admiral sent George Percy with the shallop to investigate higher up the James. Percy returned to Paspahegh on May 12 to report finding a site, soon to be known as "Archer's Hope," that seemed ideal for the settlement. Game and trees abounded, and the site had fresh water and a good anchorage. Wingfield and others decided not to settle there, however, opting instead for another location which seemed more nearly consistent with the company's written instructions and with sound military precautions. On the morning of the 13th, the fleet anchored off the place the colonists called Jamestown.

What made this site more desirable than Archer's Hope was its configuration. It was a pear-shaped peninsula about two miles long and approximately a mile wide. In 1607, a narrow isthmus— since washed away—joined the "island's" western end to the north bank of the James. Surrounded almost completely by water, the place could be defended against attack with seeming ease. Moreover, it lay about sixty miles inland from the coast, a great enough distance to give the settlers ample opportunity to prepare to repel any incursions the Spanish might wish to mount. Game and trees appeared to be abundant. A final advantage was the proximity of deep water to the shoreline. Soundings revealed a six-fathom channel almost against the bankside, which meant that Newport could tie up to trees and the ships' cargoes could be off-loaded without lighters.

The site had liabilities, though. Much of the island was an uninhabitable marsh that bred great quantities of mosquitoes. High ground, such as it was, mainly rimmed the shoreline or ran out into the marsh in ridges—what locals now refer to as "fingers"—and it, too, was infested with insects that preyed on humans. There were no springs that could provide potable water. The marsh water was brackish—that is, partly salt—as was the James. Apart from these liabilities, the Paspaheghs considered Jamestown as tribal hunting ground, and they did not take kindly to the strangers' disturbing an area that was vital to their well-being. Never sensitive to Indian ways, the English failed to consider how their intrusion might affect their relations with the Paspaheghs. Unfortunately, none of these drawbacks was apparent to men unskilled in pioneering but impatient to choose a spot where they could begin settling.

In keeping with the company's instructions, the councillors met on the 13th to elect a president. They chose Wingfield. The election was followed by a debate about what to do with Smith; at Wingfield's insistence, he was denied his council seat. That done, Newport relinquished his overall command of the expedition to Wingfield.

The next few weeks were spent in getting settled. Seamen put the supplies ashore, at least those they did not pilfer and sell to the colonists or eat. One crew of colonists worked at clearing trees so that others might sow crops and build shelters. Another gang cut a cargo of clapboards and sassafras root which they loaded into the *Susan Constant* and the *Godspeed*, along with some ore samples. At first Wingfield expressed reluctance to fortify the encampment, for fear he might violate the company's injunction not to "offend the naturals," but the "naturals'" mounting hostility quickly led to the construction of a stout triangular fort. Toward the end of June, things appeared well enough in hand for Newport to sail for England to fetch more supplies and colonists. On the 22nd he weighed anchor, leaving behind the *Discovery* and what he thought was a thriving colony of about a hundred men. So far, the only disappointment was the lack of cargo more profitable than lumber and tree roots.

A conjectural drawing by Frances Dayton of the first fort erected at Jamestown. Although some authorities now believe that the original fort may not have enclosed any buildings, the juxtaposition of an Indian fortification such as that depicted on page 21 and this English one effectively symbolizes the uneasy relationship between the two peoples. Colonial Williamsburg photograph.

Appearances were deceiving. Between the time of Newport's departure and his return six months later, the condition of the colony passed
from tenuous to bad to worse to desperate, as the leaders quarreled and
the men starved. Although no one doubted his courage or his
commitment, Wingfield could not lead. His animus towards Smith
divided a council already riven by disagreements over the colony's
future. The other councillors suspected him of hoarding supplies, and
that suspicion finally led to his replacement as president by John
Ratcliffe. Ratcliffe's election eased tensions a bit, though the bickering
and talk of conspiracies continued. One such rumor even led to George
Kendall's expulsion from the council and his execution as a Spanish
spy. Slow death by disease and starvation magnified the leaders'
divisions. Everyone arrived in Virginia weakened by the effects of a long
shipboard confinement, but no one took time to recuperate. Instead,
the colonists plunged immediately into the arduous labors of settlement. They were no less profligate in the consumption of their stores.
No one saw a need to husband them so that they would last until
Newport could bring more, and that recklessness brought on a critical
shortage of food and drink. Beef, cheese, and hard tack were gone
before midsummer. Only some wormy barley and wheat remained, and
what there was of that was doled out in meager portions. The supply
of ale dwindled. Thirst drove the men to drink from the marsh or the
river, and the briny water turned their stomachs. And there was the
heat of an oppressively humid Tidewater summer.

The outcome of their situation was predictable. Less than two weeks
after Newport left the colony, the men started to sicken and die so
quickly, as John Smith later remembered, "that the living were scarce
able to bury the dead." Half of them were gone by September. Succor
for the rest came from the Indians, who shared their crops as soon as
they ripened. (They would have cause to regret that kindness.)
Nevertheless, the dying continued, and when Newport returned in
January 1608 with more supplies and settlers, only thirty-eight men
were still alive.

One may wonder that the English starved in the midst of abundance.
Their debility is one explanation, but there were other reasons they did
not save themselves by hunting or fishing. Clearing the land reduced
the animals' habitat on the island, so the game went elsewhere. Then,
too, just because the colonists had guns and nets, that did not mean

they could take wildlife with impunity. The brutal reality was that few knew how to hunt or fish. Smith acknowledged as much when he wrote the company in 1608, "though there be fish in the Sea, foules in the ayre, and Beasts in the woods, their bounds are so large, they so wild, and we so weake and ignorant, we cannot much trouble them."

Newport stayed until April. He took Wingfield and Gabriel Archer with him when he left for home. His presence and their removal helped to stabilize the council, but a basic problem remained unresolved. None of the councillors seemed capable of leading—certainly not Ratcliffe, who turned out to be as disagreeable as Wingfield and was also indolent. When Ratcliffe's term expired in September, Smith reluctantly agreed to assume the presidency.

*   *   *

Among the most remarkable of the early colonists, Smith remains as controversial today as he was during his lifetime. His betters looked on him as an upstart, which in a sense he was, because he had elbowed his way into the Virginia venture by dint of ability rather than by virtue of his pedigree. Something of a braggart, he seldom refrained from holding his tongue in those matters in which he believed his experience was superior to that of others. His accounts of the colony's beginning, vividly written, still make good reading, but they are not unimpeachable. Smith, like others of his contemporaries, had a penchant for embroidering the truth. Many of his escapades cannot be confirmed by accounts independent of his own, which has led historians to discount some of his more colorful tales. Whatever the flaws of his writing, Smith's vigorous leadership indisputably kept Virginia from coming closer to failure than it did.

Smith's emergence began with his restoration to the council in the summer of 1607. That September Ratcliffe named him supply master; and in that capacity he traded with the Indians for food, stockpiling enough to ease the shortages. He soon became the colonists' most experienced negotiator. While exploring the Chickahominy River in December, some of Powhatan's braves took him prisoner. They held him captive for several weeks, during which, by his telling, Powhatan's favorite daughter, Pocahontas, saved his life. He became so respected for his bravery that the Indians set him free. Whatever the truth,

Smith's captivity had a beneficial result for the English. The natives were not hostile as long as the feisty captain remained in the colony. He had a closer brush with death after he returned to Jamestown in January 1608, when he was condemned to hang for letting two of his men be killed by the Indians. Newport's timely arrival spared him the noose. After he and the others stabilized the situation at Jamestown, Smith spent much of the spring and summer exploring and mapping the upper reaches of Chesapeake Bay. He found neither gold nor the passage to the Orient, but when he came back, he was elected president.

Newport dropped anchor off Jamestown with the so-called Second Supply soon after Smith assumed his duties. What the supply did not include was suitable colonists. Of the seventy who shipped over, half were gentlemen and two were women, the colony's first. A dozen laborers and an assortment of artisans skilled in refining gold and making glass or tar came, but not husbandmen who might adapt their knowledge of agriculture to growing sufficient food. Newport also carried new orders from the company. He was to seek out Powhatan and crown him, thereby making him subject to the English and validating their ownership of the land. Company officials also wanted him to query the natives not subject to Powhatan on the whereabouts of the Roanoke Island colonists. Then Newport was to look for the South Sea and gold. Smith was not overjoyed at the admiral's coming. But orders were orders, and they would be obeyed.

Of course, Newport did not find any gold, and he did not discover the South Sea. Powhatan would not be crowned, though he exchanged a mantle and an old pair of shoes for Newport's coronet. Questioning the western Indians about Roanoke only reconfirmed what the Powhatans had already told the English: there were no survivors. In the end, all that Newport carried back to England was another cargo of lumber and a tart letter from Smith in which he castigated the company for its unrealistic expectations and the lack of competent laborers. "When you send againe," he wrote, "I intreate you rather send but thirty Carpenters, husbandmen, gardiners, fisher men, blacksmiths, masons, and diggers up of trees, roots, well provided; then a thousand of such as we have; for except wee be able both to lodge them, and feed them, the most will consume with want of necessaries before they can be made good for any thing." The unskilled, he concluded, could not satisfy the company's "desire of present profit."

Despite Newport, silly orders from London, and incompetent settlers, the colony fared well under Smith's presidency. He took steps to improve conditions at Jamestown even before the second supply arrived, and work on those improvements continued after Newport's departure in December. As winter approached, he oversaw the construction of additional housing, as well, and the accumulation of enough corn to make it through the cold weather. When the supply proved to be rotten, Smith dispersed the settlers, some of whom he sent to Old Point Comfort and others to the falls of the James. By that precaution, he prevented another famine and lessened the outbreak of diseases related to malnutrition. The winter was hard, and it caused suffering, but most of the colonists lived to see the spring.

Smith also concluded that a healthy dose of military discipline would put the colony on a more orderly footing. He therefore organized everyone into work gangs whose size varied with the task to be done, just as he drilled them in the use of firearms, and only the sick were excused from the regular routines of work and drill. He achieved a measure of order, as well as a reduction of dissidence and idleness. Moreover, the sight of healthy, disciplined Englishmen performing the manual of arms served as a caution to the natives.

Winter passed into the spring of 1609, and Smith set the men to gathering cargoes for the expected ships from England. In mid-July a lone vessel limped up the James bearing Samuel Argall, who had news of a reorganization of the colony's government and the impending arrival of a third supply. Argall's intelligence set off the dissenters anew, and when former councillors Archer, Martin, and Ratcliffe reappeared with Argall, they attempted to overthrow Smith. They did not succeed at first. What finally did in the doughty captain was an injury that resulted from an accidental gunpowder explosion. His debilitating wound made him an easy mark for his enemies, who overthrew him and put George Percy in his place. Desperately in need of medical attention, Smith left for England in October, never to return.

Smith deserved credit for keeping Virginia a going venture. His resort to military discipline as a model of organization foreshadowed company policy, just as his tactic of intimidation remained basic to the settlers' policy toward the natives. Yet none of Smith's accomplish-

A contemporary engraving of Captain John Smith, the most important leader of the Jamestown colony in its first years, from his 1616 *Description of New England* after an engraving by Simon van de Passe. Colonial Williamsburg photograph.

ments reconciled the differences among company officials and colonists over how best to exploit Virginia profitably or who among Englishmen were best suited to do the exploiting. After 1609 Smith would have little direct say in the resolution of those problems, but he continued to be an enthusiastic promoter of Virginia until his death in 1631.

*   *   *

The backers of the London Company expected a return on their investment within two years. When Newport came home for the first supply, his account of what he had seen, along with his cargo—especially the putative gold ore—appeared to validate that expectation. Prospects for quick rewards were dimmed, though, by the colonists' difficulties in establishing a thriving settlement. And so, by the winter of 1608–1609, members of the company undertook a review of their operation with an eye toward making it pay. Their reexamination led to a fundamental overhaul of the company, the provisions for which were embodied in a new charter which James I granted early in 1609.

The charter streamlined the company's corporate structure and reorganized the colony's government. To raise additional, much-needed capital, the new company was granted the privilege of selling its stock publicly. Gone was the old royal council. Henceforth, a treasurer and a Council, elected by the stockholders, would now direct operations from London. Executive authority for Virginia was put into the hands of a governor, who served at the company's pleasure, and who was empowered to choose his own councillors as well as the colony's other subordinate officers.

Buoyed by the enthusiastic response of investors, Sir Thomas Smythe, the new treasurer, and the others set about the revitalization of Virginia. They chose Thomas West, Lord Delaware as Virginia's new governor. Delaware, a sometime privy councillor who had soldiered in the Low Countries, was expected to use his political acumen and military experience to stabilize the colony. The services of two more experienced military officers, Sir Thomas Gates and Sir Thomas Dale, were secured as well. Smythe, as of May 1609, had succeeded in raising supplies and recruiting some five hundred new colonists, including women and children, all of whom were loaded aboard a convoy of nine vessels and dispatched to America.

Unable to leave with them, Delaware relinquished command to Gates. A disagreement over the precedence between Gates, Sir George Somers, admiral of the fleet, and Christoper Newport, now vice admiral, led the three leaders to sail on the flagship *Sea Venture* instead of on separate vessels. Events proved that to be a costly error of judgment.

Contrary winds kept the fleet in sight of England for weeks, but when they shifted, the ships were storm tossed for much of the crossing. Plague set in and killed several dozen passengers. Off the West Indies a hurricane struck, sinking a ketch with all hands. The *Sea Venture* was wrecked on Bermuda,* though the crew and passengers survived. Leaderless, the remnant of the convoy straggled up the coast and arrived at Jamestown in August.

The arrival of four hundred new settlers was more untimely than welcome. It was too late in the season to plant extra crops to accommodate them. Besides, none of them was well enough to do anything useful. Their weakness made them all the more susceptible to life-threatening disease. Sick or well, all ate from the limited stores. The food dwindled to nothing as bitingly cold weather broke across the colony. When there was no more to eat, death relieved the hungry, as well as those who suffered from typhoid or dysentery. A survivor remembered the tribulations of the winter of 1609–1610 as "that time . . . we called the starving time; it were to vile to say, and scarce to be beleeved, what we endured." Of five hundred colonists who were alive in the fall, a mere sixty lasted into spring.

Meanwhile in Bermuda, Gates and his companions salvaged what they could of the *Sea Venture*'s tackle and used it in the construction of two pinnaces which they fashioned from timber they cut on the island. They then sailed to Jamestown, landing there in May 1610. Sizing up the situation as too desperate for repair, Gates resolved to abandon the colony. He was on his way down the James when word came that Lord Delaware was in the bay with men and fresh supplies. Jamestown was spared, at least for the moment.

Delaware set about putting things to right. Like John Smith, he assigned each colonist specific tasks, and he forced them all to adhere

---

Sea Venture's wreck and Gate's ensuing adventurers are supposed to have provided William Shakespeare with the idea for his play, *The Tempest*.

to a strict work schedule. And, like Smith, he produced results. Reports from his Council and from Gates, who had gone home to consult with company leaders, indicated a flourishing colony, but the hopes they sired in those officials were dashed when Delaware unexpectedly reappeared in London. Virginia made his lordship sick "upon the point to leave the world," and in March 1611, he fled home in search of a cure. His account of more death and Indian trouble dispirited Smythe and the others, but they did not give in to despair.

Back to Virginia went Gates and Dale, Gates to replace Delaware and Dale to fill the newly created post of marshall. The pattern for that office came from the military. In English armies of the day, the marshall was the officer who maintained discipline in accordance with the rules of martial law. In place of martial law, the company prepared a series of stringent regulations for Dale that represented a mixture of military and civilian legal practices, which became known as the *Lawes Divine, Morall and Martiall* following their codification and publication by William Strachey in 1612. Thus Dale's appointment and the *Lawes* bespoke the company's decision formally to impose a military model of organization on its struggling colony.

This combination of Gates and Dale worked. A stickler for detail, Dale enforced the stringent provisions of the *Lawes* to the letter; and, by degrees, he produced tractable colonists. Together, the governor and the marshall encouraged experiments with potentially useful crops as they introduced a measure of private landownership and enlarged the number of settlements along the James River basin. They also managed to pacify the natives, especially after 1613, when Samuel Argall took Powhatan's favorite daughter, Pocahontas, as a hostage. Despite these achievements, Gates and Dale came no nearer to finding the path to profitability than had their predecessors.

*   *   *

John Rolfe found the way.

Englishmen, he knew, had a fondness for tobacco. The attraction of the weed had grown steadily ever since smoking had taken the fancies of the fashionable back in the 1580s. Some of Ralegh's colonists introduced the custom. Ralegh was a smoker himself, and his example quickly made the habit acceptable. When tobacco was available, it sold quickly at handsome prices. Suppliers had difficulty meeting the demand because their main source was the sweet-scented tobacco raised in the Spanish Indies. Strangely enough, the English were aware that tobacco would grow in England. Agriculturalists were writing pamphlets on its cultivation there in the early 1600s, but few tobacco fields dotted the English landscape.* Colonists also observed the natives using tobacco in their ceremonies, though they disdained what the Indians smoked. A stubby plant, the Virginia variety, *Nicotiana rustica*, produced smallish, thick leaves, which were, according to one Englishman, "poore and weake, and of a byting taste."

Rolfe's genius lay in his seeing in these disparate bits of information a possible way to wealth. Rolfe reasoned, if the Indians could raise tobacco, why could not he? Only he would go them one better: he would grow the desirable West Indian species, *Nicotiana tabacum*. Urged on by Gates and Dale, he used the time and the land that they allowed all colonists for private enterprises to discover which of those strains he could adapt to Virginia cultivation and how it might be cured for transport to English markets. Success did not come at once. His experiments took two years to produce the first four barrels of cured leaf, which Gates took to England in 1614. Here, at last, was something, in the words of a fellow colonist, Ralph Hamor, "which everyman may plant, and with the least part of his labour, tend and cure will returne him both cloaths and other necessaries."

What happened next is a familiar story. Tobacco planting quickly became the colonists' chief preoccupation. Every available acre, including the streets of Jamestown, was sown with tobacco as hopeful planters sought to copy Rolfe's success. Within three years of his first cargo, they shipped nearly 50,000 pounds of the leaf home, the best of which fetched 3s. a pound. The great tobacco boom was on. Virginia's future was assured. That was John Rolfe's achievement.

Officials in the London Company did not greet tobacco with the same enthusiasm as their colonists did. Their first inclination was to discourage its culture, both because they knew how James I despised smoking and because they remained convinced that their only hope of a return on their investment lay in other, more exotic, staples.† But

---

*E.g., C. T., *An Advice how to Plant Tobacco in England* (London, 1615).

†In *A Counter-blast to Tobacco*, printed in 1604, James denounced smoking as "a

they unwittingly contributed to a tobacco-based economy, when in
1616 they declared a promised dividend in land, instead of cash. That
was followed the next year by the institution of the headright system,
a scheme which promised 50 acres of land to anyone who bought his
passage, as well as an additional 50 acres for every other person he
brought at his own expense. These prospects heightened, rather than
diminished, the attractiveness of tobacco.

Sadly, the lure of riches blinded the greedy would-be planters to the
consequences of following Rolfe's example. Within a matter of years,
Virginia became a place where some men could escape the restraints of
English society and exploit the labors of others for their own
aggrandizement. As they elbowed their way to the head of an emerging
colonial society, such men doomed the colony to a single-crop economy
whose bound laborers were its mainstay. These transformations were
part of Rolfe's legacy too.

*   *   *

Ten years after the birth of Jamestown, the London Company was in
trouble. Nothing had gone as any of its members had expected. No one
found gold mines, a new passage to the Orient, or rare commodities on
which to erect a flourishing trade. The "naturals" were a disappointment. They hindered more than they helped. Colonists perished faster
than they could be shipped out of England, and Virginia's widespread
reputation as a charnel house made the task of recruiting willing
settlers more difficult. Those who lived almost always seemed to turn
into indolent troublemakers who ran up expenses and produced
nothing of value. The amount of money required to keep the colony
afloat surpassed even the most sanguine of imaginations. Efforts to
maintain solvency through the reorganizations of 1609 and 1612 were
failures. Not even the proceeds from the sale of lottery tickets that the
charter of 1612 authorized as a means of financing Virginia brought in
sufficient operating revenues. Demoralized stockholders were beset by
doubts that they would ever recover their investments, let alone any

---

custome lothsome to the eye, hateful to the nose, harmfull to the braines, dangerous
to the lungs, and in the blacke stinking fume thereof, neerest resembling the horrible
Stigian smoke of the pit that is bottomlesse."

returns on them. Those uncertainties rent the leadership further into factions as Smythe's stewardship was openly challenged. Thus, the company stood at the edge of bankruptcy as it marked the tenth anniversary of the foundation of its struggling colony.

Despite everything, none of the Londoners was ready to write off Virginia, and in 1618 they mounted a massive salvage effort. Smythe was shunted aside, replaced by stockholders who favored Sir Edwin Sandys. Sandys came to the treasurer's post committed to a broad plan of reform. He gambled on the ability of the company to profit from the colony's production of staple commodities, though tobacco was not to be one of them. To encourage such production, he believed in the necessity of inspiring the transfer of as much of England's traditional social order as the wilderness and the colonists' own inclinations would permit. He embodied his ideas in various commissions and instructions that were soon known as the "Great Charter." Among these were plans for new forms of landholding, the replacement of the *Lawes Divine, Morall and Martiall* with rules that more nearly resembled local law at home, and an improved local administration, including a more representative governing authority. He also sought to lure seasoned colonists into becoming subsidiary developers, promising liberal grants of land and political authority as inducements. The so-called particular plantations arose out of that scheme, whose promoters gave them exotic names like Berkeley, Bermuda, or Flowerdew Hundred.* Finally, Sandys raised new supplies and settlers, including a contingent of women, and sent them off in the charge of a new governor, Sir George Yeardley. An old Virginia hand, Yeardley was knighted to give his new dignity added weight.

Landing in the colony, the new governor issued writs calling for the election of leading colonists to meet with him in an assembly at Jamestown. They assembly convened on July 30, 1619 in the church, the only building large enough to accommodate Yeardley, his six councillors, and the twenty elected representatives who would be known until 1775 as burgesses. Their session was cut short by "the intemperance of the weather and the falling sick of divers of the Burgesses," but it set a precedent for the slow development of

---

*Developed by Sir George Yeardley, Flowerdew Hundred has attracted considerable attention in the last decade because of its richness as an archaeological site.

self-government and representative political institutions in Virginia and elsewhere in English America.

Such precedents were not the main concern of the burgesses or of Sir Edwin Sandys. Making money was; and at first, Sandy's gamble held the prospect of paying off. Recruitment and the promise of cheap land swelled the colony's population to its highest level to date. The presence of women, children, and a few families were hopeful signs. Equally encouraging were the spread of agriculture and the adaptation of customary legal usages. But none of these things happened swiftly enough to ease the company's fundamental fiscal distress. Moreover, Sandys himself became the object of contention, as investors loyal to Sir Thomas Smythe constantly pointed to his successor's failure to fulfill his pledge to remedy the company's ills. Then the Crown withdrew the lottery, and with the loss of that privilege went the only steady source of capital. Worse was still to come. In the spring of 1622 London buzzed with the shattering news of the Indians' sudden attack on the unsuspecting and unprepared colonists.

*   *   *

Prolonged peace had lulled the colonists into believing that their dream of white intruder and red native living in harmony was a reality. Things had been tranquil ever since Powhatan had come to terms. His daughter's marriage to John Rolfe in 1614 stood as a symbol of better relations. The Indians viewed the years after 1614 differently. They smarted at the contempt the English showed for their customs. It was a marvel that people who thought them *savage* should so depend on them for survival. They resented the attempts to convert them to English ways. Apart from the firearms and trade goods, little in what they understood of English culture appealed to them. Ultimately, they saw the expanding English settlements for what they were: a threat to the survival of their culture and to their continued existence as a race of free people.

How to respond to these threats? The choice of options, having been narrowed when the Indians first mistook the settlers' intentions, was small. They could remain at peace, give up more of the land, and accept assimilation on the whites' terms; they could move west; or they could try once and for all to wipe the English out. We do not know the extent to which these alternatives were debated before 1622. We do know that for as long as Pocahontas and Powhatan lived, the natives remained friendly and acceded to increasing demands on their territory. Some followed the example of Pocahontas and converted to Christianity.

Pocahontas died in 1617, her father was gathered to his ancestors the next year, and Opechancanough became the great *werowance*. By all accounts, Opechancanough had one ruling desire, to be rid of the English, but he was too clever to let his passion overcome his judgment. He could not attain his objective if he were overhasty. Realistically, his one hope of success lay in a massive assault along the entire line of settlements and in the suddenness of his stroke. Mounting such a strike required time, secrecy, coordination, and the proper moment. And so he quietly laid his plans and marshaled his fighting men while he feigned friendship, even to the point of telling the new governor, Sir Francis Wyatt, in 1621 that the sky "should sooner fall than [peace] dissolve." A year later, he struck.

The attack came on Friday, March 22, 1622, a day on which Opechancanough thought correctly, the English would be the most unsuspecting. Three hundred and forty-seven settlers—a third of the colony's population—died that day. The "Massacre," as the English would call it, more raids, disease, and famine almost destroyed the colony, but Opechancanough failed to keep up the pressure and lost his advantage. Once the colonists recovered from their shock and disarray, they retaliated; and both sides settled down to a brutal war of attrition that dragged on sporadically until the late 1620s.

It was a war that took its toll in more than lives and property. Opechancanough served notice that he and his people had opted for war rather than assimilation or immigration. The colonists made their choice as well. After 1622, they dropped all pretense of friendship for the original Virginians. Henceforth the natives were seen as nothing more than a barbaric impediment to settlement that was to be avoided or destroyed as the situation warranted. Opechancanough's war also helped to bring down the London Company.

*   *   *

The war and its demands sapped the stockholders' will. Their resilience gone, they grew ever more peevish and combative. Sandys was the focus of much of the contentiousness. His extravagant promotions added to the strains of a colony at war, as did his rapid dispatch of new settlers, more of whom perished from disease than from Indian arrows. The Crown intervened in an attempt to calm the dissension, but the intervention failed. King James, whose patience had worn to its limit, finally decided that more drastic measures were in order. In November 1623, he instructed his attorney general, Thomas Coventry, to sue the company on a writ of *quo warranto* to show cause why it should not lose its charter. Six months after Coventry brought the suit in the Court of King's Bench, the court ruled for the king and voided the charter.

James appeared to favor reconstituting the company, but putting it under more direct royal control. He appointed a commission headed by Privy Council President Henry, Lord Mandeville to advise him on a proper course. The commission's work was cut short by James's unexpected death on March 27, 1625. Six weeks later, having no better idea of what he should do, the new monarch, Charles I, proclaimed Virginia a royal colony.

Explanations for the bankruptcy of the London Company as an agency of colonization abound. Fabulous expectations, inadequate capitalization, inept colonists, divided government, incompetent leadership, loss of will—all of these reasons, and more, contributed to the failure of the company. Yet even in loss there was benefit. The early settlers taught future colonizers practical lessons about the New World. The English gained a toehold in North America, and that start ultimately led to the creation of an empire. The door was opened to the future economic and social development of Virginia. And the transplantation of English social values, government, and law to an American setting was encouraged. That contribution alone gave the years of the London Company their significance.

3

A HALF-CENTURY OF GROWTH

The Virginia of 1675 only faintly resembled the place that Charles I had proclaimed a Crown colony half a century earlier. From the Eastern Shore to the fall line, scattered communities of settlers and tobacco fields replaced Indian villages and virgin land. Gone were the early adventurers who viewed their sojourn in the wilderness as temporary. In their stead came immigrants who intended to stay and take from the land whatever they could. Their commitment to prospering in the New World, in addition to their sheer numbers, gave shape and substance to Virginia society. Gone, too, was the nearly formless resident government of the London Company. That had given way to distinct provincial and local governing institutions, a body of indigenous law, and a discernible political structure. In a word, Virginia changed during these five decades from a tenuous outpost in a colony hewn roughly to the shape of its English antecedents.

* * *

One distinctive feature about Virginia after 1625 was the remarkably free environment in which it grew. Until 1676, inexperience and inattention kept the home government from devising a consistent policy for managing its first American dominion. Events, as well as distances, combined to slacken the bonds between colonists and mother country. Innocent of direction from England, the colonists were largely left to do as they chose.

The collapse of the London Company forced the task of governing

Virginia on Charles I. Neither the king nor his advisors quite knew
what should be done with the colony. Their only certainty was the
conviction that the powers of Virginia's government now inhered in the
Crown and should not be turned over "to any Company or Corporation,
to whom it may be proper to trust matters of Trade and Commerce, but
cannot bee fit or safe to Communicate the ordering of State Affairs be
they of never so Mean Consequence." Nonetheless, both Charles I and
the colonists themselves first appeared to favor returning the colony's
management to a reconstituted company, an option that remained a
lively possibility for almost two decades. What killed it eventually was
a neglectful king, together with the planters' own recognition of the
advantages to be gained from the inattention of the Crown.

Charles's mounting difficulties with his Parliaments and his Puritan
adversaries pushed his concern for Virginia aside. Beyond appointing
governors and councillors and conducting infrequent correspondence,
the Crown mostly left Virginia to the Virginians throughout the years
leading up to the Puritan ascendancy. The effect was a further
weakening of the political links between mother country and infant
colony at a crucial time in Virginia's development.

As for the early royal governors, they made little effort to become
closely associated with the colonists. In truth, they were often at odds
with the leading Virginians who served on the Council of State. By the
mid-1630s such frictions gave rise to disputes that culminated in the
expulsion of Governor Sir John Harvey because he would not share
power with his councillors. His replacement, Sir Francis Wyatt,
calmed the situation somewhat, but Wyatt also viewed his tenure as
temporary. The appointment of Sir William Berkeley in 1641,
however, signaled a new direction in the executive leadership of the
colony.

Of all the governors who served in the Old Dominion before 1776,
Berkeley was one of the few who became thoroughly identified with
leading Virginians and their interests, even when those interests were
opposite to the Crown's. His staunch loyalty to the house of Stuart, his
haughtiness, his stubbornness, and his vindictiveness have all contributed to the unflattering portrayals that typify his treatment at the
hands of Virginia scholars. In truth, much about him is not endearing,
but to dismiss him as a petty tyrant is to overlook his part in insuring
Virginia's development without direction from London.

Born in 1606, Berkeley was a younger son of Sir Maurice Berkeley of Bruton in Somerset, and the brother of John, Lord Berkeley, who sometimes figured prominently in the politics of Restoration England. For William Berkeley, an accomplished playwright with some influence at court, the posting to Virginia offered an opening to advancement that usually remained closed to younger sons in England. Save for the eight years of the Commonwealth period, he retained the loyalties of leading colonists during most of the thirty-five years he governed and lived in Virginia. He requited their ambitions even as he hoped to make Virginia a land of close-knit communities with a diversified economy and a deferential social order. Toward those ends, he abetted the rise of the General Assembly into a miniature Parliament and sanctioned a decentralization of power between the provincial and local governments that assured the great men an untrammeled control of local affairs. In exchange, he enlisted their support for his handling of Virginia's external affairs and their help in ways to diversify its economy. By these measures he attracted men who saw in his schemes the means to fulfill their own desires.

Berkeley's proclivity for sharing his authority with greedy constituents greatly lessened the strength of his office. His approach to governing did not lead him to use subordinate offices as devices for insuring loyalty to himself or to his sovereign, and he showed no disposition to stay the growth of the General Assembly. As a result, local government and the Assembly grew independent of his control, and independent of the Crown as well. It was just such independence that the later Stuarts would attempt to curtail after 1676.

Berkeley faced a major Indian uprising shortly after he arrived in Virginia. Alarmed by the spread of the English settlements, Opechancanough, now enfeebled and blind, planned another campaign to drive the aliens from his homeland. He attacked in April 1644. Although his men killed more of the English than they had in 1622, a quick response by Berkeley, as well as the colony's increased size, prevented the Indians from attaining their objective. The fighting dragged on for two years, during which Opechancanough was captured and murdered in his jail cell. Peace came when Necotowance, Opechancanough's successor, surrendered the remnants of the once-powerful Powhatan organization and agreed to go to a reservation. Thereafter, Berkeley formulated an Indian policy which aimed at preserving the subjugated natives and preventing future difficulties. That policy served him well, in the main, until it began to break down in the 1670s.

Events in England loosened the ties to Virginia even as they dictated an uneasy future for the colony. Armed conflict broke out across the kingdom in the summer of 1642, and the start of civil war cramped the Virginians. No strangers to the controversies that divided their kinsmen at home, some colonists were themselves devoutly loyal to the Church of England and the Stuart monarchy, while others adhered to the Puritan cause. Whatever their feelings, they were intensified by an understanding that no matter what the outcome, it would affect everyone. A triumph for Parliament could mean a resurrection of the London Company, since many of its surviving investors supported Charles's opponents. Re-creation of the company would undermine the freedom allowed by a negligent Crown. Berkeley's appointment temporarily put such concerns aside, but another persisted. The tobacco trade in all its permutations was vital to the well-being of the colony, and the civil war interrupted normal commercial relations. Faced with such realities, the colonists tried to be neutral: they were outwardly loyal to the king, though they were at pains not to offend Parliament.

Their neutrality succeeded, but only for as long as the struggle between roundhead and royalist remained in doubt. The situation changed as soon as the Puritans beheaded Charles and overthrew the monarchy. News of the king's execution evoked an angry reaction to Oliver Cromwell and the new Commonwealth regime from both Berkeley and the General Assembly. Parliament retaliated by passing an act in October 1650 that forbade foreign ships from trading in Virginia without a special license. Again the Virginians responded with hostility. They averred their loyalty to the Stuarts anew, but they also encouraged the Dutch to increase their trade with them.

Such independence could not go unchallenged. Virginia was too important to continue beyond the control of Parliament. Accordingly, the Commonwealth government now resolved to take matters in hand. It appointed four men of moderate Puritan leanings as a commission in charge of a military force and dispatched it to Virginia. Instructed to reduce the colony by peaceful means, if that were possible, the commissioners left in the fall of 1651, arriving in the mouth of the

James early the next year. The two who survived the passage tried to negotiate with Governor Berkeley, but he refused their entreaties, whereupon they sailed their vessels upriver abreast of Jamestown and threatened to bombard the capital. Hastily Berkeley tried to organize his defenses, and for a brief moment it seemed if England's civil war had come to Virginia. But no blood was let. Berkeley surrendered on March 12, 1651/52, content, it seems, with having displayed the colonists' loyalty to their late sovereign, as well as serving notice on the new masters of the possible consequences of too much tampering with Virginia's government.

The commissioners were generous in their terms. They spared Berkeley the indignity of having to swear fealty to the Commonwealth, and he was permitted to retire to live a quiet life at his plantation, Green Spring. The colonists were to "have and enjoy such freedoms and priviledges as belong to the free borne people of England." Churchmen were permitted the use of *The Book of Common Prayer* for at least a year, providing that was the wish of a majority in local parishes. Those colonists whose consciences did not allow their submission to parliamentary authority were given twelve months to take their property and leave Virginia. Aping Parliament, the House of Burgesses took over the governing of the colony.

Changing from royal to parliamentary rule did not lead to conflicts between Anglican and Puritan Virginians. In truth, the transition was easy. Save for the staunch royalists, men who had held office under the king continued to do so under Cromwell. Moreover, the Cromwellians were more concerned with securing the Virginians' allegiance than they were with any extensive refashioning of Virginia's government. As things stood at home and abroad, Cromwell and his associates could ill afford to compound their difficulties by adding Virginia to their list of preoccupations. Once they won its surrender, they left the colony alone. On their part, the colonists kept their distance, too. Their sympathies for the Stuart cause ran high throughout the Commonwealth years, as most prayed or hoped for restoration of the monarchy. Few mourned the collapse of the Puritan experiment when it at last came to an end in 1660. Except for a further attenuation in the governor's power to influence local affairs, the interregnum left little of a lasting impression on the colony.

As much as Virginians welcomed the return of Charles II, his restoration was not the blessing they expected it to be. Leading colonists assumed that the return to royal authority would mean a resumption of the Crown's indifference to Virginia, but that hope proved illusory. The restored king and his closest associates brought with them visions of empire that translated into a policy of political and commercial imperialism. Berkeley and his friends opposed the new imperialism at first, and then they ignored it. Ignoring the Crown would work only so long as its attentions were engaged elsewhere and Berkeley kept Virginia peaceful. By 1676 both of these conditions changed, and in the aftermath of Bacon's Rebellion, the Virginians were forced to accept limitations on their freedom.

*   *   *

A second distinctive feature of Virginia's growth after 1625 was the character of the colonists who populated the Old Dominion. Apart from a few thousand Africans and an even smaller contingent of continental Europeans, Virginia was settled by Englishmen. So obvious is that observation that its importance is easily missed. It meant that the Old Dominion's customs, language, and law would be English in origin, and all non-English immigrants would forever be compelled to cast off their own ways and take on those of transplanted Englishmen. Furthermore, the English whom Virginia attracted were of a special type, and that very peculiarity left an indelible stamp on the social order they created.

They came intending to replicate what they knew of the homeland's social customs. Like others of their countrymen, they presumed a society that fit everyone into a hierarchy of vocations ranging from the monarch to the lowliest subject. Callings in England determined social standing, as individuals were ranked according to means of livelihood. High status was given to those who lived off unearned incomes or engaged in gentle pursuits, whereas those who labored with their hands were deemed less worthy. Although rigid, these graduations were not inflexible, and upward mobility was possible for those blessed with talent or born with luck. Commerce, the church, the law, the military, service to the monarch—all of these provided ways by which men, irrespective of origin, might rise up the social staircase. Grounded in the ownership of real property, this structure was inseparable from the political order because it and the state coincided with a broader, more general social authority. The "better sort," as England's natural leaders, carried the great burden of governing others. Accordingly, in the words of the devotional writer Richard Allestree, they "on whom God hath stamped so much of his own power and authority" expected "all honour and esteem" from their social inferiors, and they got it. Social inequities were accepted as the normal course of things. Few questioned the eternal verity that some men were born to exploit while others were ordained to be exploited. Virginia appeared as a haven for both kinds of Englishmen.

All were drawn by a commitment to their own advancement and a belief that land, labor, and tobacco opened the way to wealth and improved social standing. Each of these venturesome immigrants left England in search of the promise of a richer life in Virginia. Their sense of that promise was singular. As John Smyth of Nibley summarized it, "temporall possessions are the life of a man, and by riches is worshipp and honour preserved in familyes, whereas by poverty they grow contemptible." The guiding precept was a quest for personal aggrandizement. To immigrants so imbued, the colony offered the nearly perfect freedom to hunt for private gain. Like some great magnet, Virginia attracted a disproportionate share of ruthless, avaricious men who were callous in their exploitation of others.

* * *

Any consideration of the peopling of Virginia by the English is grounded in large measure on conjecture. Records such as censuses, tithing lists, or parochial registers, on which demographic analyses might be based, are now almost entirely lost, if they were ever kept in the first place. Only two contemporary censuses survive for the period before 1675, as do several listings of tithables, a register, and an estimate or two. Nevertheless, recent devotees of what is known as "the new social history"* have been remarkably adroit at extracting new insights from

---

*The "new social history," which draws on quantitative analytical techniques, aims at elucidating the demographic and economic attributes of a population over time. Developed by French and English historical demographers, the genre first attracted historians of colonial New England, and for the last two decades, it has dominated the

such fragments, and, because of their collective skill, it is now possible to describe many features of Virginia's colonial population in precise, albeit broad, strokes.

These settlers were not all dispossessed cavaliers, as later generations of Virginians once believed. Royalists there were among the immigrants, but the gentry, the landed aristocrats, lawyers, doctors, clergy, or other professionals showed little inclination to trade the comforts of their privileged positions at home for the colonial wilds. Neither were the immigrants England's dregs, as Virginia historians have sometimes maintained. Assuredly, convicts and other social undesirables found places between the decks of Virginia-bound vessels, but the colony was never a dumping ground for felons. Rather, the bulk of immigrants came from that varied class which Stuart Englishmen called "the middling sort," whose standing ranged from near poverty to near greatness. They were yeomen, husbandmen, craftsmen, or the younger progeny of substantial families with ties to England's mercantile communities. Most of them were males. They were young. And most became indentured servants.

No matter what their origin, sex, or age, the immigrants hailed from all over England. The majority lived in the southeastern part of the realm around London and the Home Counties. Looking for work, they flocked to the City, to Bristol, to Liverpool, and to other ports. Finding none, they eagerly sought passage to America. Those with connections hoped to turn them to advantage, just as those who had nothing more than their own labors to gamble expected a profitable return on them.

The number of new settlers swelled after 1625. A census made in the wake of the dissolution of the London Company fixed the number of colonists at 1,200. Half a century later, when queried by the Privy Council about how many people inhabited the colony, Governor Berkeley responded, "We suppose, and I am very sure we do not so much miscount, that there is in Virginia above forty thousand persons, men women and children." On its face, the increase seems substantial, if not dramatic, until one considers another of the governor's responses to the same set of queries. In answer to a question about how many people arrived annually, Berkeley calculated that around 1,500 immi-

---

writing of Virginia's colonial history.

grants landed in an average year. If that figure were multiplied by 50, then it might be assumed that upwards of 75,000 English settlers went to the colony between 1625 and 1675.*

That being so, what accounts for the divergence between the two calculations? In a word, emigration was injurious to Englishmen's health. Death's hand exacted a frightful toll as the price of entry into a new world. Thousands came and thousands died, carried off by overwork, starvation, epidemics, and natural causes faster than they could be replenished by new births. The birthrate was kept low by the small number of fecund women in proportion to the total population. Because many women were servants, they put off childbearing until they served out their indentures. Only the steady flow of new arrivals sustained the colony to 1675 and for some time beyond.

As the number of inhabitants increased, so did Virginia's colonized areas as the new settlers fanned out over Tidewater. The pattern of settlement first radiated out from Jamestown along the James River basin, the lower end of the York-James peninsula, and the southern tip of the Eastern Shore. Thereafter, pioneers pushed north and west of the York into the land watered by its tributaries, together with those of the Rappahannock and Potomac river systems. By 1676 all of Virginia east of the fall line was to some degree dotted with English settlements.

*   *   *

The post-1625 settlers contributed to the evolution of a social order based partly on traditional values and partly on Virginia realities. They held to their view that society was composed of unequals, just as they continued to believe that a man's calling determined his social position. But a blurring of customary distinctions occurred. For one thing, landownership was not restricted to the few. Land existed in abundance, and anyone could become a landowner; at least that was the promise if not always the practice. Primogeniture, the legal device Englishmen employed to keep real estate in the hands of the few by requiring that it descend to the eldest son, never worked either. Even though possession of land helped to fix an immigrant's status, its mere

---

*Modern estimates of the colony's population growth are somewhat smaller than that which may be achieved by using Berkeley's figures.

acquisition did not assure a high place in Virginia society. For another, settlers unaccustomed to work stood little chance of survival. That truth had been evident since the days when John Smith bemoaned the presence of too many gentlemen among the first immigrants. In contrast to English society, in Virginia the fundamental social division was between bondsmen and planters.

Indentured servants and slaves constituted the lowest of Virginia's social groups. They accounted for more than half the colony's total population at any time before 1675. Young, predominantly male, and resentful of authority, they were difficult to control in a colony whose rulers often lacked the ability to make any of its residents answer for their behavior. Nevertheless, these colonists were a class to which the planters were tightly bound. Bondsmen represented a major financial investment for the planters, and their labor was prized as fundamental to the goal of personal aggrandizement. Consequently, the recruitment and maintenance of a labor force became a primary concern. To fill the need for workers, the planters hit on two solutions, indentured servitude and chattel slavery.

Indentured servitude first appeared as a device for recruiting laborers in the company period, and laws giving it definition were among the first acts of the General Assembly in 1619. Thereafter, servitude became a matter of the colony's statute law, as virtually every subsequent Assembly turned its attention to defining legal relationships between master and servant. These laws were harshly punitive and weighed heavily in the master's favor, though they did allow servants some access to the courts. The shape that servitude took represented a variation of a traditional form of bondage, apprenticeship. Like an apprentice, servants contracted with masters to work for specified periods of time, usually four to seven years. Masters generally agreed to pay the costs of transporting servants to Virginia, to maintain them for the duration of their terms, and to give them freedom dues—corn, tools, and clothing—when their contracts expired. They sometimes promised to provide a piece of land or other goods as well. Whatever the agreed terms, they were written out in a document that lawyers styled "a covenant merely personal," but which was commonly called simply an "indenture." Indentures could be sold or willed like any other personal belonging, and so long as servants were under contract, law and social convention deemed them the property of their master. Despite its resemblance to apprenticeship, servitude diverged markedly from its model. Its purpose was not to teach skilled craftsmanship; instead, its intent was to bring restless young Englishmen to the colony and then force them to become tractable agricultural workers. That done, once they had served out their indentures they were free to shift as they might, assuming that they outlasted the dangers of their bondage—and many did not.

Before 1675 chattel slavery was not important as an alternate labor system. A few Africans came to Virginia several years before that notorious but unnamed Dutch ship captain sold his infamous cargo of "twenty Negars" at Jamestown in 1619. Their arrival did not herald the start of a large influx of blacks into Virginia. The African population remained small for most of the century, though it did begin to swell in the decades after 1660. Slavery was at least as old as indentured servitude, but not every African who migrated to Virginia wound up a slave. In the beginning, whether or not black colonists were cast into slavery depended on conditions that are not now always easy to fathom, though it is clear that their religion and former status, as well as English feelings, influenced their lot. The idea of slavery was no more foreign to the English than was apprenticeship. Their grasp of its meaning was forcibly put by a sixteenth-century judge of the Prerogative Court of York, Henry Swinburne, whose *Treatise on Testaments and Last Wills* the colonists esteemed as an authoritative source of legal information. "Of all men which be destitute of liberty or freedom," wrote Judge Swinburne, "the Slave is in greatest subjection: for a slave is that person which is in servitude or bondage to another, even against nature." Moreover, Englishmen mistrusted all foreigners, but they were particularly wary of blacks, whose strange ways and color kindled intense hostilities and suspicions. Holding Africans as servants in perpetuity therefore came rather easily to people who considered the exploitation of their less fortunate fellows as the natural order of things. Nonetheless, until the numbers of blacks increased, white colonists were slow to define precise legal relationships between themselves and these aliens. And so slavery was practiced for years before 1662, when the General Assembly began the process of giving it statutory definition. Until then, slaves sometimes managed a legal escape from bondage, and, like servants who survived to complete their terms, passed into the ranks of the colony's freemen.

Virginia's freemen divided into four groups based on social standing, vocational status, and wealth. At the very bottom was the underclass. Any conclusion about these colonists is mainly speculative; they had little, and they left even less behind as a testament to their existence. Former servants and slaves wound up in this group, as did the failed immigrants, the runaways, the dispossessed, and assorted other unfortunates. All were without land or other means of support, and that rootlessness was what made them dangerous. To survive, they roved the countryside, finding what work they could or preying on their more substantial neighbors. Even so, they, like any other free men, were permitted the vote, at least until 1670. The franchise was restricted in that year to freeholders, that is, men who owned or rented at least fifty acres of land, because the underclass had swelled to such a size that the better sort of colonist perceived it as a threat. For these Virginians, the colony's promise of betterment was a mockery indeed.

Standing just above the underclass were the small planters. Some of these had immigrated with just enough substance to get to Virginia, acquire a tract of land, and try to make a go of tobacco planting. Others were former servants who were lucky enough to survive their terms and scratch their way higher up the social ladder, while still others were artisans or tradesmen who had left England in search of more promising employment. Those for whom it is possible to determine landholdings generally owned fewer than two hundred acres, which suggests the group's lack of success in the competition for choice tracts. Although they may have wished it, few small planters ever held public office, apart from occasional appointments to petty local posts. This too is an indication that the small planters came up short in the hunt for improvement. How much the passage to the colony bettered their lives, like those of the underclass, is open to debate.

By contrast, the colonists who comprised the middle rank of planters were quite successful. They left England with enough capital and connections to assure a modest start. Acquiring servants and land, they eagerly threw themselves into tobacco farming, but they also used their ties to England's mercantile centers to engage in a variety of commercial pursuits as well. The more adept of these colonists employed the time-honored technique of strategic family alliances to further their ambitions. They also developed interests in colonial politics as yet another means to fulfill their desires, and they sought to become officeholders. Middling planters filled an assortment of offices, both local and provincial, and a few of them even made their way into the House of Burgesses. Ultimately, the middling planters bridged the gap between the bottom and the top of Virginia social ranks. It was to this level that the lower orders could aspire in the likelihood that some might actually rise to it, just as middling planters formed a link with colonial society's top rung, the great planters.

The scions of the Lees, the Carters, the Byrds, the Diggeses, the Ludwells, the Beverleys, the Carys, the Fitzhughs, the Harrisons, the Masons, the Blands, the Wormeleys, the Pages, the Washingtons, and those of the several hundred other families who made up Virginia's planter aristocracy in the Revolutionary generation had all begun to progress toward gentility by 1675. They landed expecting to re-create the traditional connection between social position and political author- ity, and in so doing to claim the right to lead their fellow colonists. As younger sons of the well-to-do, the accident of birth gave them an edge the others did not enjoy. Using their advantage, they elbowed themselves to the head of colonial society, amassing as they did fortunes in land, servants, and offices as well as complex ties to each others' families. But their pretension to rule lacked the imprimatur of immemorial custom, for it rested on nothing more than their consid- erable ability to outdistance their competitors. That fact, in addition to the time it took Virginians to sort themselves into their distinctive hierarchy, contributed to the social tensions that characterized the Old Dominion for much of the seventeenth century.

*   *   *

A distinctive social hierarchy bespoke other changes which the English accepted as they gradually adjusted their traditional ways to life in Virginia. Somewhere to live was a first concern to colonists, but they did not build log cabins. (The log cabin was not known in the English colonies until the early eighteenth century, when Scotch-Irish immi- grants borrowed it from Scandinavian settlers living near Philadelphia and adapted it for use along the trans-Allegheny frontier.) Instead, the English relied on their own vernacular housing styles and construction methods, which were readily tailored to Virginia's climate and building materials. A colonist's first dwelling was likely to be a cottage. Ordinarily a one-room affair, the cottage was built of plaster and laths, called "wattle and daub." It frequently lacked doors, windows, or finished floors, and it was roofed with thatch. Sometimes a catted fireplace and chimney, constructed of logs chinked with clay, provided heat and illumination, but just as often a fire pit set in the middle of the room and a hole through the roof fulfilled the same purpose. Cottages normally served only for as long as it took a colonist to build something better.

That something better was the frame house. Such a dwelling was usually a single-bay, rectangular structure, one and a half stories high. It was framed in hand-hewn timbers held together with pegs called treenails. The outer walls were covered with clapboards that the builder either split with an axe or sawed with a pit saw. Brickmakers began manufacturing bricks at an early date, but few brick houses were built before 1700. What brick construction there was consisted mainly of churches and public buildings. Surviving examples of brick houses indicate that their builders did little more than elaborate on the basic design of the common frame dwelling, for none of them is distinguished by its architectural character or its scale. Governor Berkeley's house, Green Spring, was the notable exception. Berkeley started the house in the 1640s, and within two decades he had transformed it into the grandest manor house in Virginia. As such, Green Spring became one of the seeds for the architectural ideal of the stately plantation mansion that flourished in the eighteenth century.[*]

Few of Berkeley's fellow colonists could afford to emulate him, but the quality of housing improved as the century passed. Durand of Dauphine, a French Huguenot who visited Virginia during Governor Efffingham's administration, remarked that the colonists he observed were "comfortably housed." He also noted that "whatever their rank, and I know not why, they build only two rooms with some closets on the ground floor and two rooms in the attic above; but they build . . . according to their means," which revealed that Virginians of the 1680s still retained an affinity for the basic one-and-a-half-story home.

---

[*]Green Spring survived until 1806, when it was demolished and soon forgotten. The site was subjected to intensive archaeological investigation in the 1950s, which revealed much valuable data about the house and Governor Berkeley's activities as a builder and planter.

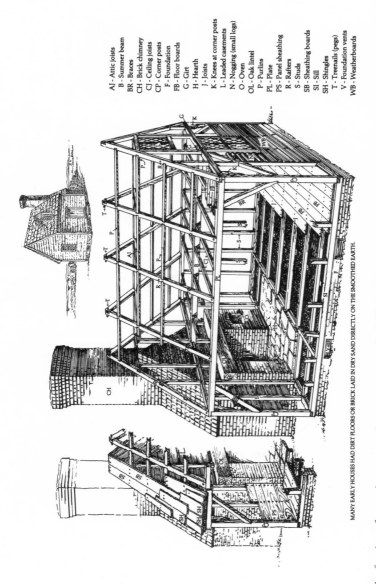

AJ - Attic joists
B - Summer beam
BR - Braces
CH - Brick chimney
CJ - Ceiling joists
CP - Corner posts
F - Foundation
FB - Floor boards
G - Girt
H - Hearth
J - Joists
K - Knees at corner posts
L - Leaded casements
N - Nogging (small logs)
O - Oven
OL - Oak lintel
P - Purlins
PL - Plate
PS - Panel sheathing
R - Rafters
S - Studs
SB - Sheathing boards
SI - Sill
SH - Shingles
T - Treenails (pegs)
V - Foundation vents
WB - Weatherboards

MANY EARLY HOUSES HAD DIRT FLOORS OR BRICK LAID IN DRY SAND DIRECTLY ON THE SMOOTHED EARTH.

The framing of an early seventeenth-century story-and-a-half single bay house and a similar finished dwelling (inset). Conjectural drawing by H. Warren Billings.

Bacon's Castle, built about 1655, by Arthur Allen, is an unusually early example of a large brick Virginia house. It suggests that a few of the more affluent colonists began to build substantial dwellings before the end of the seventeenth century. The high-Jacobean style of the west elevation with its steep gabled roof and its stepped and curved parapet is unique in Virginia. Virginia State Library photograph.

Virginians filled their houses with an array of furniture and personal belongings that varied according to the householder's wealth. Some got by with little more than modest furnishings, a few utensils, and the essential tools. More affluent householders stuffed their living quarters with beds, tables, chairs, chests, quantities of pots, pans, dishes, linens, and even silverware. Items like weapons, flocked mattresses, edge tools, or cast-iron pots—things the colonists could not manufacture or obtain readily in Virginia—were highly valued and often willed to a favorite relative.

Clothing varied as much as household furnishings; it was a badge of one's social distinction as much as protection against the elements. Well-off settlers stocked their wardrobes with numerous articles of diverse quality, and when the occasion called for it they could dress in fine, expensive attire that befitted individuals of their station. Both the quality and quantity of wearing apparel declined on the lower rungs of the social ladder. Even though a colonist might own several outfits, one did not usually expect a daily change of clothes. For one thing, woolen or leather garments were not easily cleaned; for another, manufacturing any clothing was laborious and time consuming. It was made to last, and the usable shoes, doublet, bodice, and skirt, like the pewter porringer or musket, were passed from generation to generation until they wore out.

As for the householders themselves, all were not heads of families in the traditional understanding of the word *family*. The reason they were not was the direct consequence of English migratory patterns before 1675. Young, unmarried men comprised the majority of Virginia's settlers, which meant that the number of families composed of husbands, wives, and children was small in comparison to the total population of the colony. Accordingly, its society was largely bereft of the family's assumed steadying influences. Such a society contrasted sharply with England, where the traditional family was seen as society's fundamental element, as well as its microcosm.

An immigrant family of parents and children was subjected to strains of adjustment unknown in England. The passage to Virginia not only threatened the survival of members but also marked a physical separation from familiar surroundings and customs that nurtured or reinforced ageless roles and values. Little in Virginia spanned the void. Supporting institutions—the church, the government, and the social hierarchy—were themselves in the process of being and becoming; consequently, they were less capable of nurturing and reinforcing than their English counterparts were. Life expectancies were shorter in Virginia than in New England, so it was commonplace for perhaps as many as a third of the colony's children to suffer the loss of at least one parent. Frequent orphanhood blurred traditional nuclear family arrangements. Uncles, aunts, brothers, sisters, or some other legal guardians became parental figures in households of orphans, stepbrothers, stepsisters, and half-siblings ranging in age from newborn to young adults.

Wives and widows undertook responsibilities outside the household. Some held real property in their own right or managed it for their minor children. Others conducted their family's business affairs; still others appeared in the courts as attorneys in fact to represent their own or someone else's legal interests.

Despite the temptation to see in these and similar activities indications of an improved status for colonial women, they were not. Prevailing thought held them to be the "weaker vessel." They were not cherished for their intellect; instead, they were esteemed for the ability to produce children or to bring economic advantage to a marriage. Widows were desirable, especially to the ambitious immigrant who saw marrying one as the surest, speediest way to an alliance with established Virginia families. Typical were the three marriages of Elizabeth Willoughby, a granddaughter of Thomas, who emigrated in 1617 to what became Lower Norfolk County. Elizabeth's first husband was Simon Overzee, a disagreeable and unscrupulous Dutch merchant, who had business ties to her father and various other planters in both Virginia and Maryland. Overzee died in 1660; a year later Elizabeth married George Coleclough. A younger brother of a London grocer, Coleclough rose to prominence as a justice of the peace and burgess before his death in 1662. Scarcely had he grown cold in his grave than Elizabeth married another man of mercantile origins, Isaac Allerton. The connection was timely for Allerton, for he soon took his seat on the Northumberland bench, which launched his career in the House of Burgesses and the Council of State. Colonial property and family law also kept married women in an inferior position that differed not at all from what it had been in England. As in England, too, a wife owed her husband, in the devotional writer Richard Allestree's words, "Obedience . . . , Fidelity . . . , and Love, and together with that all Friendliness and Kindness of Conversation."

Like their relatives at home, Virginia Englishmen expected the neighborhood, the church, and the government to help sustain the family, though each never quite matched the expectation. "Neighborhood" assumed a somewhat different connotation than that which attached to it in Old or New England. Apart from Jamestown, there were neither towns nor villages nor hamlets which could serve as corporate focal points of neighborly activities. Each plantation was a small community, linked to others that lay within walking distance. This network provided opportunities for social and commercial contacts that led in turn to amusement or help in time of need and, when neighbors did not get along, to less fruitful associations.

The Church of England came to Virginia in 1607. Its teachings gave spiritual solace in an uncertain world, but from its beginnings until the end of the colonial era it always had difficulty satisfying its intended purpose. Before 1675, it was a hierarchical church without its own bishop or structural supports. There were never enough clergymen to fill all of the vacant parishes. Laymen assumed many of the responsibilities for maintaining individual parishes. The parish vestry, which in England was a lay body concerned with relieving the poor of their distress, came to occupy a key place in parish government as well as being a means of introducing some men to public office. Vestrymen recruited ministers, maintained parish property, cared for the infirm or the indigent, and prosecuted moral offenses in the county courts. The weight of these duties meant that the office was filled by local political magnates or else men whom the mighty considered potential recruits to their company. Churchgoing brought these individuals into regular contact with the larger parish community. It also gave every parishioner the chance to trade gossip or other information with people outside the immediate neighborhood. Clergy or readers always provided time during services to publish proclamations and to announce the next militia drill or elections for the House of Burgesses. These social purposes for attending church explain the origin of the custom of tarrying in the churchyard after worship that continues to this day in those rural parishes whose beginnings trace to the seventeenth century.

Courthouses were gathering spots for colonists who sought respite from their chores or whose problems required legal remedies. Actually,

only a few courthouses as such existed before 1676. Instead, a room in
the house of the presiding justice of the peace doubled as a courtroom,
and his table served as the bench. On court days, justices, sheriffs,
clerks, jurors, plaintiffs, defendants, witnesses, attorneys, and spectators, all of whom usually knew one another personally, crowded into
the room or milled about the yard during sittings. There was ample
time to talk about the weather or the latest happenings, and someone
almost always had a bottle or tall tales to share with any bystander who
would partake. All of these qualities gave the sessions a feeling of
intimacy, an air of informality, and a sense of immediacy, as well as a
leavening of indecorum, that have long since disappeared from modern
judicial proceedings. They also bespeak an emergent social order in
which scale and complexity were more modest than in our own.

*   *   *

John Rolfe's experiments had spared Virginia from collapse, and in the
half century after 1625 the cultivation and marketing of tobacco
became the colonists' economic lifeblood. It was the prospect of taking
up planting that drew settlers to the Chesapeake. Trade in the weed
provided colonists with things they were incapable of manufacturing
for themselves, just as it afforded opportunities for enterprise, and in an
economy in which hard currency was always scarce, tobacco became the
medium for exchanging goods and services.

The enticement of tobacco was its promise of riches and the seeming
ease with which a crop might be grown. It was a desirable commodity
that commanded high prices in Europe. The yield per acre was high.
If cured properly it could be stored for long periods. It weighed less
than other agricultural commodities, which meant that it could be
profitably shipped in the cramped holds of the tiny merchantmen
which plied the vast seas between Virginia and Old World markets. To
raise a crop, a prospective planter needed only a piece of ground, a
handful of tobacco seed, some labor, a buyer, a bit of luck, and he
could prosper—at least that was the theory.

Here, as elsewhere in the affairs of men, there was more than a little
distance between idea and reality. Although the supply of land in
Virginia appeared limitless, not all of it was immediately suitable for
cultivation or of the same degree of fertility. Indian fields or other open

areas were the easiest to plant, but there were never enough of these to accommodate everyone, so time and energies had to be expended in cutting back the forests. Planters adapted the Indian method of slashing and burning wooded parcels, starting their first crops among the stumps or blackened tree hulks.

However the colonist came by his cleared fields, the soil had to be worked for planting, and that was no easy task. Few planters owned plows. Owning one was of no particular advantage. The implements bore little resemblance to their efficient modern descendents, for they could do no more than scratch the surface of the topsoil. Instead of plowing, planters depended on servants, who used broad hoes to break up the sod; but like the seventeenth-century plow, a broad hoe could not penetrate much below a depth of six inches. Consequently, repeated turnings of the light, alluvial Tidewater soils contributed to their eventual erosion.

Erosion was slowly worsened by primitive farming methods. The English knew little of fertilizers, and they showed even less inclination to learn from the Indians, who had perfected ways to restore or maintain the nutritive properties of the land. Whereas the natives were given to rotating crops or to planting those that replenished nutrients alongside those that withdrew them, the English had little regard for care of the land. Their one concession to soil conservation was the periodic idling of fields in the belief that they would regenerate naturally. No land, not even the fertile land the colonists reckoned Virginia to be, could withstand indefinite exploitation. When the planters' fields reached the point at which they could no longer sustain productive growth, they were abandoned in favor of others, starting a pattern of reckless land usage that continued far into the future.

Raising a crop of tobacco was more troublesome than it seemed to those who had never grown one. Throughout the growing season, tobacco demanded constant attention, from starting the seedlings; to setting young plants in the field; to worming, suckering, and topping them as they developed; to cutting, stripping, and curing the matured leaves. All of this work had to be accomplished within a rather tight timetable from spring, when it began, to fall, when the tobacco ships arrived. Growing tobacco, like any type of agricultural endeavor, had its risks. Disease, too much rain, too little rain, rain at the wrong time, wind, hail, hurricanes, competition from one's fellow planters, high

labor costs, runaway servants, shipping losses, bad prices—all figured
into the return on the effort. In spite of all of these challenges and
more, the allure of tobacco culture was so seductive that no amount of
effort to channel the Virginia economy in other directions—not even
the diversification schemes of the ever-persuasive Sir William
Berkeley—succeeded.

Tobacco continued to fetch high prices at least until the 1650s, and
that was reason enough for immigrants to bank their hopes on a weed.
After mid-century, though, translating expectations into pounds,
shillings, and pence proved more chancy. Marylanders also grew
tobacco, as did settlers in North Carolina. Their production increased,
as did the Virginians', and what they all raised was often of inferior
quality, which meant that it was not readily sold. Overproduction,
which was chronic by the 1660s, drove down prices, as did the vagaries
of a market sensitized by civil strife in England, the adjustments
brought on by trade restrictions imposed by the navigation system, the
Anglo-Dutch wars, and a one-crop economy.

Once it was grown, the tobacco had to be sold, and from Rolfe's day
forward Englishmen developed an extensive trade in the leaf. Every
planter was therefore engaged in trade to some extent, since they all
produced for an overseas market on which they were also dependent for
laborers and for commodities they did not make for themselves. Who
they traded with was largely a matter of personal ties, for like so much
else of the world of seventeenth-century Englishmen, business was
carried out within the context of family or friendly relationships. The
basis of the trade was the consignment system, by which a planter
arrranged to have his crop shipped abroad to a merchant who acted as
his sales agent. The merchant sold the crop for what he could get; then
he subtracted shipping costs, duties, and his commission. He depos-
ited the net proceeds, if any, to an account on which the planter could
draw. Anyone who knew someone in Virginia could take tobacco on
consignment. That being so, Englishmen from virtually every mercantile calling participated in the tobacco trade, which accounted for the
variations in the commercial links between Virginia and the mother
country. Planters and merchants found additional financial opportunities in the servant trade, land speculation, and brokering credit. The
variety and the value of the tobacco trade eventually made homebound
Englishmen increasingly more aware of the worth of Virginia to the

nation's own well-being. That awareness abetted the Restoration imperialists' desire to curb what was seen as a too-independent colony.

* * *

The London Company conceived the General Assembly as a resident body that could dispatch routine administrative, legislative, and judicial matters. It grew into a miniature Parliament, however, and that development was something neither its creators nor the Crown intended. In truth, the very right of the General Assembly to exist appeared to be in jeopardy when the company fell. Charles I failed to include a provision for its continuation when he commissioned Sir Francis Wyatt as the colony's first royal governor. The oversight may have had less to do with Stuart antipathy to representative government than with the Crown's sheer ignorance of the best way to manage its new responsibility. Whatever the cause, the Assembly remained in legal limbo for some time. Even so, Virginians regarded the Assembly as a useful instrument of government and something of a hedge against a revived company. Wyatt and his successors regularly called it into session, while leading colonists campaigned to gain the Crown's sanction; and in 1639 Charles finally legitimized it.

Despite the uncertainties of those early years, the Assembly's transformation was already afoot. Originally, the intent of the company was for the governor and the Council to handle the routine management of the colony, but that design soon required modification because it was predicated on an assumption that the colonists would develop compact settlements. So long as settlers stayed close to Jamestown and their number remained small, the company's scheme could work, but neither of those conditions continued much beyond the Crown's assumption of control. Thereafter, the Council's part in local affairs narrowed while its judicial, advisory, and legislative responsibilities enlarged.

The Council sat as a court four times a year, and for that reason it was first known in its judicial capacity as the "Quarter Court." The Quarter Court heard both civil and criminal cases, but with the adoption of the county form of government in 1634, its jurisdiction was modified. Civil matters below a value set by the Assembly were turned over to county courts, whose decisions might be appealed.

Felonies, that is crimes for which the penalty was loss of life or limb, remained the Quarter Court's exclusive province, but the trial of lesser offenses was also gradually assigned to the local benches. In such cases there was no appeal. A reorganization act of 1662 reduced the court's number of terms to three and changed its name. From that date until the conclusion of the colonial period, it was called the "General Court"—a title "more sutable," in the statute's wording, to a tribunal "where all persons and causes generally have audience and receive determination."

The councillors advised the governor and gave their consent in the formulation of provincial policies. Their president, always the senior member, acted as governor whenever the incumbent was absent or there was a lapse between terms. As a body, the councillors also had a say in who was appointed to what offices, the more lucrative of which they kept for themselves. Their right to have such a voice came only after they ran Governor Sir John Harvey off in 1635 because he was unwilling to share political control over Virginia's affairs with them. Their point made, it was not lost on Governor Berkeley, who won them over by his willingness to share his authority and by his careful cultivation of their sensibilities.

Collectively, the Council comprised one of the three elements of the General Assembly. (The other two were the governor and the House of Burgesses.) Individual councillors participated in drawing up bills and managing the burgesses. Their approval was required for any act to pass into law.

Popular myths to the contrary, the General Assembly did not spring to life as a two-house legislature vested with all those attributes that are now associated with popularly elected legislative institutions. Disagreement still exists over just when the councillors and the burgesses started to sit separately. Where once it was customary for scholars to maintain that the division occurred in the 1680s, more recent inquiry suggests that it happened forty years earlier. Whenever it took place, it was only the first of many steps towards bicameralism, an infant idea that would not fully mature until after 1787.

On their part, the men who served in what eventually became the House of Burgesses moved gradually toward establishing their legislative prerogatives. At its very first meeting in 1619, the Assembly laid down a precedent for judging the qualifications of members when the burgesses ejected two of their number whose credentials they deemed invalid. Apart from controlling its membership, the House of Burgesses assumed wider authority to direct its internal procedures. There are hints that by the 1640s it regularly disciplined refractory members. Around mid-century it established a standing committee on elections, which by the 1660s was recommending the expulsion of burgesses for religious nonconformity. The House set its own rules of order, just as it controlled the appointment of its speaker and clerk, at least until the time of Governor Francis, Lord Howard of Effingham. One such set of rules, which dates from the 1650s, enjoined strict "attendance on the House," required "the party that speaketh [to] rise from his seate and be uncovered," and cautioned members to avoid appearing on the floor "disguised with overmuch drinke." The speaker and the clerk were the chief officers of the House, so its right to name them gave the burgesses considerable freedom from the governor's meddling, as well as a liberty that Parliament did not yet enjoy.

Other privileges were added. A statute of March 1623/24 freed members from arrest during sessions. Another claimed a share of the power to tax. By the end of the decade some degree of fiscal control had been established, and in 1666 Governor Berkeley expressly recognized the right to raise public revenues as an exclusive prerogative of the House of Burgesses. When the Assembly erected county governments, it set a precedent for its regulation of local affairs. This prerogative was much augmented before 1675, and it was one that exceeded Parliament's control of English localities. Parliament did not have the authority to create counties or their courts, and English local magistrates drew a considerable degree of their powers from customary rather than statutory law.

* * *

When the General Assembly began to perfect the county-court form of local government, it laid the groundwork for changes that profoundly affected the character of Virginia's political and legal order. In doing so, the legislators divided the authority of government between themselves and the newly erected courts. Then that division was greatly enlarged by statutory additions to the responsibilities, customs, and local conditions of the county courts. The competence of the county courts expanded as the Assembly assumed a more purely legislative responsibility, while the governor's broad authority to direct the political life of the colony was eroded by tradition and by Berkeley's willing acquiescence. As the courts became important centers of power, their members began to see in seats on the bench the means to satisfy their ambitions. The court system therefore became the institutional mechanism for setting the foundations of a ruling elite that possessed the attributes of traditional ruling classes. This process was played out in a political arena full of petty disputes, constant bickering, nasty infighting, and occasional violence. These political qualities combined with other changes in Virginia society to produce the disorder that marked the Old Dominion before 1676.

The Assembly's division of Virginia into counties in 1634 represented the culmination of years of searching for an effective means of local government. Both the officials of the London Company and their royal successors expected that the governor, the Council, and the Assembly itself would share the burden of the colony's routine administration with four boroughs and with the proprietors of several private plantations that had been seated before 1618. That hope proved illusory. For one thing, a growing population meant more misdeeds to punish and civil matters to settle than such a small group of individuals could dispatch. For another, the founders of particular plantations assumed greater responsibility for administering and, after 1622, defending their settlements. Then, too, the Assembly complicated things in 1624 when it ordained "that there shall be courts kept once a month" in two of the corporations. Within less than a decade the number of these courts rose to eight. The Assembly intended the monthly courts to provide the means of judicial administration and defense in freshly inhabited regions as speedily as conditions warranted. Nonetheless, their establishment only clouded already confused and overlapping jurisdictions, which made the tasks of governing unnecessarily slow and cumbersome. The county courts seemed to be a way out of that difficulty, and their beginning marked the start of a statutory differentiation between local and provincial governments in the colony.

At first there were eight counties. A ninth was added in 1636, but its size was such that the Assembly divided it the next year. The number stayed at ten for more than a decade before the influx of settlers necessitated the addition of more. Another six were carved out of the frontier by 1656, and the number rose to twenty by 1668. From that date until 1691 the Assembly created no new ones, which had the effect of closing off easy access to county offices.

Justices of the peace, a sheriff, and a clerk, who were nominal appointees of the governor, their deputies, and several subordinate officers such as constables and tithe-takers constituted the county courts. Their responsibilities were akin to those of their English counterparts. Individual justices, for instance, resolved minor controversies, took depositions, or issued warrants, while the entire complement sat in monthly sessions to hear the criminal and civil matters that fell within the full court's competence. Sheriffs served warrants, arrested defendants, conducted elections to the Assembly, executed the sentences of the courts, and collected taxes. Clerks kept the records of court proceedings and enrolled wills, deeds, business papers, and, on occasion, even private letters.

Although the General Assembly first assigned the courts jurisdiction only in petty matters, it soon expanded their authority to include a wide arc of colonial life. The fundamental lines of their power were plotted in less than two decades. Within another ten years, that power was rendered nearly absolute when the courts' preeminent position was imbedded in the revised statutes of March 1661/62.

As in England, the county courts enforced the law and saw to the needs of their respective communities. But their authority was broader than that of their English models, for they were an amalgamation of assorted administrative, admiralty, civil, criminal, and ecclesiastical jurisdictions. Furthermore, their powers derived from statutory law, just as they were themselves the creatures of the Assembly instead of customary usage. The justices turned their offices into the link between Virginia's political and social ranks as they made themselves its *de facto* rulers. They came close to replicating the familiar bridge between the great power and high social standing, just as they made themselves more independent of direct royal rule.

* * *

The development of the General Assembly and the county courts was of a piece with the arrogation of a more general lawmaking authority.

Enlarging the scope of legal activity not only gave form to Virginia society, it also compelled the colonial men of law to grapple with the question of bending their knowledge of English law to a Virginia setting. The English who colonized Virginia transported more than their kinsmen, bondsmen, or material belongings. They also took the very things that marked them as Englishmen—their culture and their law. The transformation of the lawmakers' understanding of both therefore constitutes an important element in early Virginia history.

Colonial Englishmen were part of a culture which regarded law as the glue that held men together in civilized society. Its "end, and aime," according to the legal commentator Edward Bulstrode, "is no other than this, that the people may live happily, the Instruments, and sinews of all outward blessings, being good Laws." English law, like that of the Continent, embraced the subject's precious possessions—his life, his family, his reputation, his possessions, his beliefs—but its form was set apart from other Western legal traditions. They were called civilian systems; that is, they were codified and derived from Roman precepts, whereas English *common law* was pluralistic, uncodified, and lacking in a single focus. Common law accumulated through the centuries as case law, statutes, custom, and precedent, and it represented the collective wisdom of generations of Englishmen about the proper constitution of society. It set the standards of taste and morals, it maintained the peace, and its ceremonies were reminders of its place as the arbiter of social conduct. Above all, however, common law ultimately defined English culture because it gave Englishmen the collective identity that distinguished them from other Europeans.

One did not need to be a lawyer to understand the cultural significance of common law. All he need do was look around, and no matter where he turned, he saw that law was part of his life. The desire to escape the complex webbing was what drove men to Virginia's apparently freer environment. Once in the colony, though, the routines of existence required regulation; without order, chaos would reign and identity would be lost. That was terrifying to men who felt keenly their separation from England. Leading colonists therefore began to turn to what they knew, or thought they knew, about law in order to give purpose, direction, and definition to their lives. They were thus the instruments by which English conceptions of law were transplanted to the Old Dominion.

Throughout the nearly two decades that the London Company managed Virginia, it recruited the colony's leaders from England's ruling classes. Those men were well schooled in English law and custom. They had been educated at the universities or the Inns of Court; some knew martial law, and they all enjoyed ties to the court and Parliament. Despite such qualifications these men were to leave only a slight impression on colonial law. Few survived or stayed in Virginia long enough to make much of a mark. Furthermore, there was little agreement before 1625 as to which of England's legal traditions were most suitable to a struggling colony. The question of what law should prevail was only vaguely addressed before the formulation of *The Lawes Divine, Morall and Martiall*. The Charter of 1618 supplanted *The Lawes*, but that change merely introduced the possibility of adapting a more familiar form of law. Thus it was the members of the post-1625 general assemblies, together with their counterparts in local government, who assumed the greater role in grafting English common law to colonial needs.

Few of these individuals were trained lawyers. What they had learned about law came largely from experience or from a variety of law books that circulated on both sides of the Atlantic. Their exposure to this literature reminded them how English local officials discharged their public obligations, and it tended to magnify the eminence of these officeholders. It likewise accented the primacy of local law and custom. That emphasis served chiefly to reinforce colonial lawmakers' previous experience with English local law by calling to mind their past contacts, as well as to sanction the belief that local tradition best suited their own needs in the New World.

Their backgrounds turned the lawmakers into reformers of sorts. Inimical to the constraints they believed English society imposed on them, they sought to build a legal order in the unfettered environment they thought Virginia offered men of their kind; that is, a place where they might stalk their fortunes in virtual freedom. Hostile to the complexities of England's courts and procedures, they greatly simplified their own. Lacking the lawyer's innate conservatism, as well as his deep attachments to old customs and precedents, they had less affection for the usages of the past. Their desire to dominate inclined them to experiment and to judge those experiments by the standard of efficacy. What answered the problems of the moment was of immensely greater value than adhering strictly to the conventions of the ancients. They were willing to appropriate anything in their books and their experience, as well as to create from whole cloth remedies for what they saw as the concerns—economic, political, or social—of their time. What they saw as the great imperatives frequently resulted from their own ambitions for aggrandizement. The laws they wrote, the supporting legal institutions they constructed, the very society they helped create—each of these reflects their efforts to gain wealth and to maintain dominion over those whom they governed.

* * *

The 1670s marked a turning point in Virginia. Sir William Berkeley was an aging governor who felt the weight of his years. His method of governing had not contented all of his constituents. Those outside the circle of privilege turned restive, as taxes increased and their economic position worsened. Signs pointed to trouble with the Indians. Far away in London, Charles II, his brother, James, duke of York, and their underlings considered ways to curb the colony's independence, and they looked for an excuse to toss Berkeley aside. A man named Nathaniel Bacon would give them that.

4

BACON'S REBELLION

One day in April 1676, Henry Isham, James Crews, William Byrd I, and Nathaniel Bacon got together for a drink. These four friends were no ordinary upcountry colonists. A well-to-do Charles City County planter, Isham had ties to the faction that opposed Edward Hill, one of the county's leading political figures. Although Crews and Byrd were militia officers who held seats on the bench of Henrico County, neither man belonged to the inner ring of justices who ran the county. Bacon was a relative of Governor Berkeley. He sat on the Council of State, but he too was a comparative newcomer to Virginia politics.

Their conversation that day was not the usual stuff of such convivial visits. Instead, the four spoke of "the Sadness of the times" and "the Fear they all lived in, because of the Susquahannocks who had . . . committed many murders upon them." For Byrd and Bacon, those "murders" had struck close to home; both had recently lost servants. Worse still, Governor Berkeley seemed incapable of defending the frontier from further attacks, but he refused to give in to pleas to let the settlers meet the threat in their own way. Because he controlled the Indian trade, his insistence on protecting the tributary Indians smacked of pecuniary motives, while his plan to stop the raids with a string of forts surely doomed more colonists to barbaric deaths.

In the course of their musings, someone mentioned that some planters who lived on the south side of the James River were no longer willing to wait for the governor to act. A number had already armed themselves, and they were camped across the James at Jordan's Point. Isham, Crews, and Byrd suggested to Bacon that the four of them should visit the encampment to see what was going on. When they came to the campground, cries of "A Bacon! A Bacon! A Bacon!" went up from the volunteers as they pressed the councillor to lead them. He obliged.

*   *   *

"The Sadness of the times" was nothing new. Virginia had been cursed by bad times for the past fifteen years. There was a difference in 1676, however. Terrified by Indians and disaffected with Berkeley, former servants, small planters, disgruntled office seekers, and men who were just plain angry followed Bacon into civil war.

Bad times started with the Stuarts' restoration, which altered the relationship between England and Virginia. Charles II, James, duke of York, and their minions returned to power animated by a vision of empire predicated on social order, military security, political obedience, and the exclusion of the Dutch from the colonial trade. Achieving these ends augured limitations on Virginia's independence. The earliest of these came in 1660, when the Restoration Parliament enacted the first in a series of statutes that settled the navigation system on the colonies over the remainder of the seventeenth century. These laws were intended to provide imperial control and regulation of foreign trade and the subordination of colonial interests to those of England. Virginians, especially those who ruled, resented the trade legislation because it curtailed their access to lucrative markets and threatened their freedom.

Governor Berkeley went to London in 1661 to oppose the navigation acts. His lobbying failed. Undaunted, he saw in his failure the opportunity to make real his image of Virginia. He had long envisioned the colony as a prosperous place of compact settlements, a varied economy, and a deferentially hierarchical society where men were free to pursue their ambitions without much direction from London. Such a Virginia, he believed, would be of greater benefit to his sovereign than the tightly controlled imperium Charles II now appeared to favor.

The ideal he sought depended on diversifying the economy of the colony and obtaining financial backing from the Crown. At first, English officials saw some advantage in encouraging Berkeley to work toward his goal, but they ventured nothing out of the royal coffers; and when they realized that smaller tobacco crops meant reduced revenues from tobacco duties, encouragement turned to opposition. Moreover, while Berkeley got the enabling legislation through the General Assembly, he failed to persuade the planters in great numbers to take up the cause of diversification, and by 1669 he abandoned the effort. Failure cost the planters dearly in taxes and the governor in debased political coinage.

As the ordinary planters saw it, Stuart imperialism and Berkeley's diversification were ill timed. By the 1660s overproduction of tobacco was a fact of life that kept prices down and planters' debts up. The requirement that all Virginia-grown tobacco be sold only in England saturated the market there and created surpluses that brought colonists "soe very little for their labores as it will not cloath them and their Families." Diversification only added to their increasing tax burden, already made great by the costs of county government. Mounting taxes in turn focused their animosities on the men who controlled the county courts.

By the 1660s men of well-established families had monopolized local offices for themselves and their progeny. They turned the counties into the basis for representation in the House of Burgesses, as they in practice had made membership on the bench a prerequisite for a seat in the Assembly and an opening to the Council of State. While charting these lines of political authority, the justices laid down the substructure for a native ruling class. Possession of the office of justice of the peace symbolized the holder's superior standing as one who had outdistanced everyone else in the quest for riches and preferment. Having won the place, he sought to pass it on to succeeding generations of his family through family and political alliances with other justices.

That change had promoted neither tranquillity nor order. If anything, it made matters worse. Monopoly came just as the rapid multiplication of county offices waned. No new counties were created after 1668, and the closing of this avenue to preferment intensified the competition for existing offices. Then too, county magnates, being men of new wealth and status, had neither the mystique of a ruling class nor the acceptance of those they intended to rule. Their place at head of Virginia society derived from their success in a high-stakes game for aggrandizement rather than the sanction of tradition and immemorial usage. Public office was less a place of public trust than an opportunity for their individual profit. They misused their enormous and often ill-defined authority, and they showed little sensitivity to those whom they governed. Insecure, they fought one another continually, which gave to county politics a nasty, irresponsible quality that was typical of the 1660s and 1670s.

Political contentiousness exaggerated the fears that free Virginians had of the colony's bound laborers and former servants. Young, mostly male, and decidedly unruly, the servants accounted for more than half of Virginia's population. Overworked and ill treated, disgruntled servants and slaves were prone to running away, crime, and rebelliousness. One such servant revolt was averted in 1663 only because an informer betrayed the plot before it hatched. Laborers who served out their time joined a burgeoning rootless underclass that preyed on other colonists. Members of this underclass had no loyalties except to themselves, and that made them all the more dangerous because, as Secretary Thomas Ludwell observed, "of us being in a flat open country full of great rivers pressed at our backs with the Indians [and] in our bowells with our servants."

Ludwell's comment voiced the concern that leading colonists might someday face the danger of having to fight the Indians and a foreign invader while simultaneously having to contend with rebellious servants. Although there had been no general war with the Indians since the peace of 1646, relations between the two antagonists remained tense. Twice before the summer of 1675 the tension might have given way to all-out warfare had not Berkeley acted swiftly to prevent it. The Stuart imperialists' attempt to cut the Dutch off from trading with England's colonies raised the prospect of war with Holland and the specter of a Dutch invasion of Virginia. Not unmindful of the weak state of the colony's defenses, Berkeley and the Council of State pestered Charles II with requests for military stores, but, except for a few siege guns, some powder, and a decrepit frigate that could not "keep the sea for want of masts and reparations in her hull," none was forthcoming. Instead, the Crown forced Berkeley to forsake his own costly plan to protect Virginia for a worthless and expensive fort at the mouth of the James River. Events proved the correctness of the Virginians' arguments against such a fort: when

Dutch raiders attacked in 1667, during the Second Anglo-Dutch War, they merely sailed into the James out of range of the fort's guns and burned tobacco ships at will, a feat they were to repeat six years later in the midst of their third war with the English.

The burning of tobacco ships again pointed up Berkeley's failure to protect the Old Dominion. None of the taxes for forts and arms brought results, and the governor's defensive schemes became the targets of loud complaints. The disaffection boiled over in the fall of 1673, after the Assembly ordered the rearming of local militias, the cost of which was to come from additional county taxes. Rate payers in New Kent and Surry counties balked at the new assessments. In Surry, the protestors tried to prevent the sheriff and neighborhood justices from collecting the levy in Lawne's Creek Parish, but they were quickly arrested. Shortly thereafter, the entire "Company of Giddy Headed and Turbulent persons" was tried and sentenced as rioters.

That such a riot should have happened in Surry County is understandable. Surry was something of a backwater community. Its southern and western borders were vulnerable to attack by the Indians, and its people were not among Virginia's most prosperous. Surry planters resented taxes for whatever purpose, the more so because they regarded the magistrates who exacted them as abusive, "short arsed" rascals.

The Surry and the New Kent incidents should have alerted Berkeley to the probability of more serious trouble, but he perceived them as nothing more than the rantings of a few malcontents. Eventually he pardoned the Surry dissidents, while the real troublemakers, the Surry justices, went unpunished, as did other venal politicians across Virginia. His lack of perception was a sign that advancing age had blunted his judgment at the very time that his capacity to lead was coming into greater doubt.

Never a gentle man, Berkeley's waspish temperament made him more cantankerous the older he got. As close friends died, he replaced them with the colony's younger politicians or its more recent immigrants, but few of these men were as intimate with him as his departed colleagues had been, and he was quick to quarrel with the more forward of them. More and more he turned to the opinions of his remaining friends like the Ludwell brothers and Robert Beverley. He also relied on his second wife, Frances Culpeper Stephens, Lady Berkeley, whom he married in 1670.* These "interested persons," noted the impudent royal customs official, Giles Bland, filled the governor's ears "continually with strange stories which being antient [he] is apt to believe." Thus, there was plenty of leeway for bickering and infighting, even within the inner circle, as everyone jockeyed for the most favorable position against the day when the old man either died or stumbled into the king's disfavor. As for Berkeley, he showed no inclination or ability to check the discord.

Until the mid-1670s the governor was lucky. He had been spared worse than he received only because no one was willing to make the frustrations and anxieties of the discontented his own and so challenge Berkeley's leadership. His fortune soured in 1675.

*   *   *

On a July morning in 1675 a band of Doeg Indians raided Thomas Mathew's plantation in Stafford County. They stole some hogs and killed an overseer before slipping back into Maryland, satisfied that they had balanced their accounts with Squire Mathew, who had refused to pay them for some trade goods. When the Stafford militia commanders heard the news, they mustered the militia and marched into Maryland, where they killed a few Doegs. Unhappily, they also dispatched some innocent Susquehannocks, whose countrymen retaliated with a series of murderous attacks along the Virginia-Maryland frontier.

Word of all this made the long, slow circuit from Stafford to Jamestown, and by the time Governor Berkeley finally learned of these latest troubles, it was difficult for him to winnow truth from fancy. He was alarmed, but he hesitated to act until he had better information, so he hastily convened the Council of State on August 31. Following the meeting, he ordered two Westmoreland County justices of the peace, John Washington and Isaac Allerton, to investigate the situation, and, if need be, to call up enough of the local militia to punish the offending natives.

Allerton and Washington gave no heed to the letter of their

---

*Berkeley married his first wife sometime around the year 1650, but little is known of the woman or her background, not even her name or when she died.

instructions. Instead, they speedily gathered "a fitt number of men" and contacted the Maryland government, whose help they sought in tracking the marauding natives. The Marylanders sent troops to join the Virginians, and the combined force sallied forth in search of the Susquehannocks. Late in September, they found their enemy holed up in an abandoned fort on the Maryland side of the Potomac. The Susquehannocks appeared willing to negotiate, but they stood their ground after the English treacherously murdered five of their chiefs during a parley. Lacking cannon to dislodge them, the English besieged the stronghold. Their siege was abruptly lifted some seven weeks later, when, under the cover of darkness, the Susquehannocks slipped off into the forest. Surprised by what had happened, the enraged colonists could do no more than rail at their own stupidity and burn the fort before going to their homes. The expedition had been an expensive failure.

Over the next few months frontier settlers paid the cost as the Susquehannocks exacted a full measure of revenge for their slain leaders. They struck fringe settlements all along the fall line, although the brunt of their assaults fell on the settlements that were scattered across the upper reaches of the Rappahannock. The worst of these occurred in January 1676, when thirty-six colonists died in a single attack. After that, the Susquehannocks were satisfied that they were avenged, and they sent messengers saying they were ready to conclude a peace. Berkeley refused to deal, and, slowly, they withdrew into the interior.

Their retreat did little to calm the situation. Seeing the English caught off their guard, other natives grabbed the opportunity to settle scores of their own. Who the "others" were was a point of heated dispute between Berkeley and the frontiersmen, and it remains a matter of controversy among historians even now, but the effect of what they did is unquestionable. Where the Susquehannocks were content just to kill Englishmen and to carry off supplies, these Indians burned and pillaged at will. Horrified by the suddenness and the extent of the devastation, the frontiersmen panicked. They convinced themselves that the long-feared combination of "the Indians" had come to pass. Urgent appeals for help went out to Jamestown.

Berkeley wasted little time in replying. Instructing the lieutenant governor, Sir Henry Chicheley, to assemble 300 men, he commanded him to succor the settlers and engage whatever marauders he found. But before Chicheley marched, Berkeley did something that was wholly out of character with his reputation. He countermanded his orders and demobilized the troops, saying that he intended to lay the whole Indian business before the next session of the Assembly.

To say the least, his decision not to show the flag dumbfounded everyone. He gave no reason for it, nor could any of his friends. What was stranger still was his failure to grasp its impact. Not only did Chicheley's recall leave defenseless Englishmen unprotected, it made the governor look indecisive. When boldness was needed, he appeared unmanly, even cowardly. Perhaps those who whispered that advancing years had dulled the old man's wits were right.

Amid wild rumors and reports of new raids, the Assembly convened on March 28. Uncertainty hung in the air. None of the legislators knew quite what to expect from their governor. These were pliable men whose dependence on him was as great as their fear of the Indians. Even his detractors among the burgesses and councillors were reluctant to voice their concerns openly. He had, after all, carried the colony through bad times before, and he might again. Expediency dictated that they follow his lead.

Acting on Sir William's recommendations, the Assembly committed the colony to fighting a defensive war and left the major decisions for its prosecution to Berkeley. The plan was similar to that created after the 1644 Indian war. It authorized a garrison of 500 men, some of whom were to construct and man nine forts situated at the heads of the rivers and other strategic locations. The remainder were to range between the forts in search of the natives. However, the law prohibited the commanders from attacking enemy raiders "untill order shall come from the governour." To pay for the scheme, the Assembly voted new taxes.

There was little in these measures to soothe panic-stricken colonists or to dispel doubts about Berkeley. They were greeted with universal condemnation all across Virginia as the raids continued and as critics pointed out that static forts were no defense against a mobile enemy who struck without warning. People on the frontier repeatedly petitioned Berkeley, begging him to commission someone to lead them against the Indians. Unmoved by their pleas, he turned a deaf ear to them, even to the point of forbidding further complaints.

In April a story circulated in Charles City County that several large bands of natives lay within fifty or sixty miles of the county's borders south of the James. This intelligence (later proven false) aroused the inhabitants, who "beat up the drum for volunteers to go against the Indians" and sent a delegation to Jamestown seeking someone to lead them. Again Berkeley refused to countenance the request. This time, however, the angry petitioners were not to be denied. No sooner had they returned to Charles City than they began arming and looking for a leader. They found him the day Nathaniel Bacon came to visit their encampment.

*   *   *

By leading the revolt against Berkeley, Bacon made himself a pivotal figure in Virginia history. His followers cherished him as their savior; his enemies abominated him as a traitor. Echoes of that angry, partisan division of opinion still reverberate in the judgments of scholars who have never agreed on the man's character or motives, let alone his proper niche in Virginia's history.

Who was this Nathaniel Bacon?

Anyone attempting to answer the question must confront a daunting truth: no one *really* knows. There are no Bacon pictures, no Bacon archive, no Bacon diaries; only fragments remain. A scrap here, a snippet there—that is the stuff from which to delineate the man. The remnants are pliant enough to shape him into the patriot who struck the first blow for American independence, into the Indian-hating opportunist who ruined the reputation of a popular governor, or into someone else. So he continues as the haunting figure who vexes Virginia historians almost as much as he taxed his antagonists.

Born the son of Sir Thomas Bacon of Friston Hall, Suffolk, in 1647, Nathaniel Bacon grew to manhood in the comfortable world of the English country gentry. Like other gentle youths of his day, he dabbled at a university and legal education and took the grand tour of the Continent, all before he attained his majority. He courted and wed Elizabeth Duke, over the stout opposition of her father. The marriage in 1670 caused Sir Edward Duke to disown his willful daughter. An improvident young man with responsibility for a family, Bacon was soon strapped for ready cash. After unsuccessful attempts at gaining his fortune by fraud or by lawful means, he was packed off to Virginia. There he might prosper under the watchful tutelage of his relatives. One of these was a cousin who also bore the name Nathaniel Bacon. Cousin Bacon, who lived in York County, was the colony's auditor general, as well as a councillor. Another, Governor Sir William Berkeley, was a cousin by marriage. Thus did Sir Thomas's rapscallion son emulate other Virginia immigrants: he went to the Old Dominion looking for a fresh start; and, as many before him had, he expected to turn his connections to his advantage.

Nathaniel and Elizabeth Bacon arrived in the colony in 1674. That August he bought a working plantation from Councillor Thomas Ballard. The main tract lay forty miles above Jamestown in Henrico County on a neck of land at the bends of the James that the colonists called "the Curles";[*] the remainder was located at the falls. Within six months of his landing, Bacon was appointed to a vacancy on the Council of State. Few Virginians had risen so high so fast.

There is no record to indicate his regular attendance at the Council before 1676, though he may have sat in the Henrico County sessions, which was his prerogative as a councillor. Despite an evident lack of interest in his new duties, his sudden exaltation marked Bacon as someone of influence. As such, other colonists found him attractive, and by the time of the Indian troubles a circle of notable men had gathered round him.

Isham, Crews, and Byrd were neighbors with whom he shared an abiding animus toward Indians and a wish to profit in the Indian trade. Beside these three, there was Richard Lawrence, the shadowy Oxford scholar turned Jamestown ordinary keeper and sometime burgess for Lower Norfolk County. Among the others was Giles Bland, a royal customs collector, who cheekily nosed about in the province's business, alleging that Berkeley cheated the king of his customs and besmirching the name of Sir William's favorite, Secretary Thomas Ludwell. The circle also included William Drummond. A sturdy Scot, Drummond was no friend to Berkeley. They had first fallen out in disagreements over land grants in North Carolina, where Drummond was once governor and Berkeley was a proprietor. Then they quarreled about the costs of building the fort at Jamestown for which Drummond was a

---

[*]The site is now occupied by Curles Neck Dairy farm.

contractor. Also in the group was William Carver, a ship captain who made his home in Lower Norfolk County, where he was a justice and member of the General Assembly until he lost the seat in 1671.

The less prominent members included men such as Thomas Hansford, Thomas Cheesman, Joseph Ingram, and Gregory Walklett. Hansford and Cheesman were York County militia officers. Of old York families, neither they nor their kin had prospered as well as had other families in the county. Their connection to Bacon was through his cousin, the auditor general. Ingram, a merchant whose real name was Johnson, and Walklett, "an Indian gowne man" had "come to Virginia a little before Bacon's business broke out." Partners, the two men settled on the New Kent frontier.

To have such friends was heady wine for anyone who had come as far as quickly as Bacon. Some of them expected him to do what the governor would not. And in those frightful days of early 1676, Bacon may well have judged his place and his ties as such that Cousin Berkeley would allow *him* to lead the volunteers against "the Indians."

*   *   *

The last thing the governor wanted was a mutiny to add to his other troubles. On learning that Bacon had accepted command of the Southside volunteers, he sent word, cautioning his kinsman against turning mutineer and demanding that he come to Jamestown. Bacon ignored the warning, choosing instead to continue preparations for his campaign. He went over into New Kent for more volunteers, and he wrote the governor for a commission to lead his army lawfully. Angered by what he took to be Bacon's contempt, Berkeley impetuously mobilized his own force of men, with whom he hurriedly set out to head Bacon off before he marched beyond the frontier. Too late: by the time he got to Henrico, Bacon was gone, and he looked foolish for his exertion.

Now the two men's disagreement assumed a different hue. A tired, angry, and bewildered Sir William returned to the capital, where on May 10 he petulantly proclaimed his antagonist a rebel and removed him from the Council of State. He then issued a proclamation dissolving the General Assembly and calling for the first general elections in fourteen years. The new assembly would deal with the Indian threat and remedy any other grievances that the voters presented to their burgesses. Furthermore, Berkeley challenged the electorate, which he now expanded to include freemen as well as freeholders,* to find any fault in his leadership. "Supposeing I who am the head of the Assembly may bee their greatest Greviance," he concluded, "I will most gladly joine with them in a Petition to his Sacred Majestie to appoint a new Governor." Attempting to undercut Bacon's popularity still further, he drafted a "Declaration and Remonstrance," which he ordered read out in every county court in advance of the new Assembly. In it, he justified his outlawing of Bacon, as he reminded the colonists of their duty to Charles II, and he vowed anew to redress their grievances.

Meanwhile, Bacon was off hunting Indians. He and the volunteers marched southwest of their campground. Near the site of modern Clarksville, they encountered some friendly natives, the Occaneechees, in their stronghold. The Occaneechees told of a party of Susquehannocks camped close by. From that point, the story of what happened next becomes muddled. Seemingly, Bacon talked the Occaneechees into attacking the Susquehannocks, which they did, taking some prisoners and a quantity of booty in the course of their assault. After that Bacon and his newfound allies evidently squabbled over an equitable division of the captured food and plunder, and the quarrel led to a fight with the Occaneechees. As Bacon later explained it, "we fell upon a town of Indians, consisting of 3 forts strongly mann'd beginning our fight after midnight close at their port holes." He had done what Berkeley would not, or could no longer bring himself to do—kill Indians. To the frontier settlers, he was the most popular man in Virginia. That popularity won him a seat in the new House of Burgesses when the saucy voters of Henrico chose him to represent them.

Bacon sent his friend Crews, himself newly elected a burgess, to the capital to learn Berkeley's intentions. Berkeley said nothing. Nonetheless, Crews relayed the advice of several councillors who urged

---

*Traditionally, those Englishmen who met certain real property qualifications known as a freehold were entitled to vote in parliamentary elections. The Virginians took these requirements for their own, although they did not exclude free adult males from voting until 1670. Because of "tumults at elections" freemen were denied the vote by statute in 1670.

Bacon to come to town and beg forgiveness. Fearing harm, Bacon chose not to come to Jamestown unattended. Instead, he boarded his sloop and sailed down from Curles Neck on June 6 with fifty men at arms. Anchoring a short distance off the town, he sent Berkeley a messenger to see if he could take his seat in the House. Berkeley ordered the town gunners to fire at the sloop, which retreated as fast as her crewmen could sail her to safety. That night, Bacon stole into Jamestown to confer with Richard Lawrence and William Drummond. The meeting lasted till dawn, and as a new day broke, Bacon hastened to board his sloop before being detected. He was discovered, and the chase was on. Regaining his vessel, his men tried to work her up river, but she was overhauled by an armed merchantmen, the *Adam & Eve*, whose skipper, Thomas Gardiner, took Bacon prisoner and turned him over to the governor.

Jamestown was abuzz with exitement. Everyone wondered what would happen next. Would Bacon's followers try to rescue their hero? What would the governor, a man renowned for his vindictiveness, do? Berkely tipped his hand on June 9. He *pardoned* Bacon! Not only that, he restored him to the Council of State on the 10th, while promising a commission within a fortnight of the session's end. A few days later, when Bacon pleaded his wife's illness, Berkeley even gave him leave to go back to Henrico.

*   *   *

As prescribed in Berkeley's election proclamation, the Assembly convened on June 5, 1676. A different cast of characters sat in the new House of Burgesses. Five were holdovers from the old body. Of the remainder, four were without previous political experience. The rest were sitting justices of the peace, a clear indication that county magnates dictated most of the elections. So many new members and turbulent times made for an unruly House. Observers characterized the membership as "fractious and Rebellious" and full of "ill Humours." It was all of these things and worse, but it is arguable whether or not these characterizations prove the burgesses' commitment to revolutionary legislative agenda.

The session lasted for twenty days, and the members enacted twenty statutes that have come to be called "Bacon's Laws." One replaced the

Long Assembly's static defensive measures with an aggressive, and costly, plan for warring on the Indians. Two covered the Indian trade and deserted Indian lands. Another proscribed "unlawfull assemblies, routs riotts and tumults" where "ill disposed and disaffected people" gathered "in a most apparent rebellious manner." There was one to sanction Berkeley's extension of the vote to freemen. Yet another barred two Charles City justices, Edward Hill and John Stith, from office, while an act of pardon and oblivion forgave all "treasons . . . done since the first day of March last past."

The thirteen remaining "Bacon's Laws" dealt with local matters. Their clear, oft-stated intent was to lessen political tensions not related to Indian matters. Limiting officeholding to native-born Virginians or immigrants who "have bin constantly resident and abideing in the country for the space of three years" undercut the governor's power to exalt men like young Bacon. Preventing someone from being a sheriff, a clerk, and a surveyor simultaneously opened the door to a more equitable sharing of lucrative county offices. Restricting the sheriff's term to a single year guaranteed the rotation of that profitable place. Prohibiting councillors from participating in county court proceedings removed their direct interference in local affairs. Adding councillors and ministers to the tax rolls lessened the taxes of others. Lengthening the time given debtors to pay their debts eased their hardship. Allowing two justices, instead of the governor, to sign probates, eliminated a fee as well as a trip to Jamestown. In short, the June Assembly tried to content angry planters by remedying grievances that Berkeley solicited in his election proclamation. Although Charles II subsequently nullified all of Bacon's Laws, those that reformed county government were reenacted by later assemblies.

The business of the session was nearly completed by June 23. That day Bacon, at the head of 500 militia, marched into the capital and captured the government. Dispatching some of the troopers to hold key points about the town, he marched the rest of his men to the statehouse and surrounded it. Berkeley sent someone to see what he wanted. The reply came back: authority to fight the Indians, thirty blank commissions for subordinate officers, a letter justifying him to Charles II, an act of pardon, a law to displace certain persons from office, and restitution for his sloop. Nothing here suggested that Bacon contemplated overthrowing Berkeley.

Berkeley thought otherwise. *No* Virginian made demands on *him*! Bacon's actions affronted his dignity, and they were tantamount to rebellion. He angrily refused to countenance them. In a towering rage, he dashed from the statehouse and ripped open his shirt. "Here," he shouted to the soldiers, "shoot me, foregod, fair Mark, Shoot." No one moved. He turned to Bacon, calling him rebel and traitor. Reaching for his sword, he screamed, "Lett us try and end the difference singly between ourselves." "Putt it up," Bacon shot back, saying that he had no wish "to hurt a haire of your honor's head." But he adamantly insisted on his demands. "God damne my Blood," he swore, "I came for a commission, and commission I shall have before I goe." Turning toward his men, he gave the order, "Make ready and Present." The troops wheeled smartly, cocked their muskets, and aimed them at the statehouse. Terrified, the burgesses hastily acceded to Bacon, while a delegation from the Council pleaded with Berkeley to acquiesce as well. In no position to do otherwise, the old man relented.

Bacon's agenda items were all made law by June 25. When the Assembly was finishing up, the members "desiered that for the satisfaction of the people, what they had don might be publickly read." Bacon cut them off with the rejoinder, "There should be noe Laws read there, that he Would not admitt of any delays, that he came for a Commission, and would immediately have it." The job done, Berkeley dissolved the Assembly. General Bacon had his commission.

*   *   *

To date, the governor and the general had disputed the best way to fight Indians. But the contest between them was not yet settled. In the weeks and months that followed, their struggle took a turn that led the two to fight even to death for control of Virginia.

Bacon left town on June 26, amid tales of more Indian raids, this time in New Kent. For the next month scouting parties searched for Indians and then prepared to rendezvous with their general at the falls of the James. As Bacon made for the falls, he discovered that Berkeley had once more declared him a rebel. Feeling betrayed, he counter-marched eastward, determined to smash the governor.

A disgusted, exhausted man, Berkeley had quit the capital a few days after Bacon. He went to his plantation at Green Spring, and for

Sir William Berkeley (1606–1677), who served as governor of Virginia from 1642 to
1652 and from 1660 to 1677, was the redoubtable foe of the rebel Nathaniel Bacon.
Portrait by Sir Peter Lely. Virginia State Library photograph.

a time he seemed willing to leave the Indians to the general. A petition from planters in Gloucester soon shook him from his lethargy, however. In it, the Gloucestermen questioned the legality of Bacon's pressing men and supplies, which left them defenseless, and they begged for protection. Swinging into action, Berkeley invalidated Bacon's commission, declaring it was no different from a thief who took his purse and made "me owne I gave itt him freely." He rode over to Gloucester and tried to raise a troop to protect the county, but no one flocked to his standard. The Gloucester militia, as well as those in nearby Middlesex, were afraid "wee would fight Bacon," not Indians. With a few loyal followers, Berkeley retreated across Chesapeake Bay to the Eastern Shore, shocked at the realization that he could no longer command the planters' loyalties.

Bacon arrived at Middle Plantation on July 29 and spent the next two weeks trying to gain political control of the colony. He issued a "Declaration of the People" and a "Manifesto," the one a sharp indictment of Berkeley and the other a ringing vindication of his own approach to the Indian troubles. Next, he dispatched Giles Bland and William Carver to carry the fight to Berkeley's stronghold in Accomack. Then he rounded up large numbers of planters and implored them to swear to obey him and resist the governor until he could inform Charles II of the state of affairs. This move to consolidate his political base did not meet with everyone's approval. Bacon wheedled and cajoled the laggards, finally winning them over with reports of an Indian raid on the middle peninsula and of Berkeley's removal of ammunition from the Gloucester Point fort.

His rear seemingly protected, Bacon again took off for the falls of the James in pursuit of "his favourite scheme." He soon reversed his line of march and headed for the freshes of the York on the trail of a tributary nation, the Pamunkeys, who were thought to be involved in recent raids. The Pamunkeys, fearing for their safety, had earlier abandoned their villages. They found refuge in the watery lowlands between Gloucester and Middlesex counties that the English called Dragon Swamp. Finding them consumed weeks of arduous searching through the swamp. Frustrated by their task, some of Bacon's men grew weary to the point of mutiny, which compelled the general to send the conscripts among them home. At last the remaining force located the main body of the Pamunkeys and attacked. The natives offered no resistance; most ran deeper into the swamp, but eight were killed and forty-five were taken captive, together with a quantity of booty.

While Bacon chased the Pamunkeys, Sir William resolved to regain control of the Western Shore. Bland and Carver had both fallen his prisoners, so he enjoyed control of Chesapeake Bay and the rivers once more. Boarding his men on four ships and a dozen smaller vessels, he left Accomack for Jamestown, determined to retake his capital. On September 7 the flotilla arrived off the town, which was held by some 800 men. Berkeley offered pardon; the garrison accepted, and he repossessed the town the following day. Pronouncing Bacon a rebel anew, Berkeley dug in to await his enemy's certain attack.

Bacon emerged from Dragon Swamp expecting a hero's welcome for his "victory" over the Pamunkeys. He was jolted instead by the losses of the Bland-Carver expedition and his Jamestown garrison. Reinforcing his men as best he could, he crossed the York and headed for Jamestown, arriving there by the evening of September 13. He rested his men near the spot where the London Company's glass works once stood while he reconnoitered the disposition of Berkeley's defenses. These, he saw, would withstand a frontal assault, and he decided to besiege them. Berkeley tried to break the siege, but the attempt was a miserable failure. His men were less than keen to fight their fellow Virginians; they took to the ships, leaving a dejected Berkeley to slink off to his stronghold in Accomack. A victorious Bacon entered the deserted capital on September 19. After conferring with his subordinates, he ordered that the city be burned.

Torching Jamestown cost Bacon some of his appeal. His support dropped off further as he began to recruit bondsmen with the promise of freedom in return for joining him. Lacking vessels, he could not carry the fight to Berkeley in Accomack. He tried persuading the Eastern Shoremen to rise against the governor, but they would not. Having no enemy to confront, he could do no more than await Sir William's next move. As September gave way to October, the rank and file grew restless from idling in their encampment at Gloucester, and ransacking loyalist estates became their pastime. The plundering quickly spread to other regions of the colony as well. Once started, it was difficult to curb; no one was immune. Certainly not Bacon's friend William Byrd I. He "tooke such goods as best liked them" from the estate of Augustine Warner, which embittered political relations between the two for years to come.

As for Bacon, though he turned "more merceless" and "absolute" against the vandals, a more serious question loomed. Whither the revolt? Was it to fight Indians? Or Berkeley and his henchmen? Or for an independent Virginia? Or to justify himself to his king? He inclined in each of these directions at one time or another from the day he accepted command of the Southsiders. Which way would he turn next, now that the king's own redcoats were sailing toward Virginia? His answer never came because he died quite unexpectedly on October 26 1676, of what was described as the "Bloody Flux" and "Lousey Disease."

With Bacon dead, the revolt unraveled, though not without the stout resistance of his more faithful followers. Ingram and Walklett tried to fill the void, but neither man enjoyed Bacon's standing among the planters or his skills as a leader. Hearing of his enemy's death, Berkeley took the offensive, but he and his underlings were too inept to stamp out the rebellion's last flickerings unaided. Luckily for him, half a dozen armed merchantmen had recently arrived in Virginia waters, and their skippers answered his call for assistance. The captains worked their vessels up and down the York and the James in search of rebel strongholds, using their firepower to overwhelm the insurgents, though they negotiated whenever possible. One of them, Thomas Grantham, was especially adept at negotiating the rebels' surrender; he brought in both Walklett and Ingram. The skippers' help had the governor back in power by January 1677. Victorious, Berkeley and his loyalists prepared for their revenge and for the recovery of their lost property.

The rebellion's reverberations were far-reaching. Of all the participants, the tributary Indians suffered the most. Their "defeats" by Bacon's army hurried them farther along the road to extinction. They were eventually exonerated of any complicity with the Susquehannocks, but that availed them little; exoneration could not resurrect their dead or their villages. The English could count their toll less in lives and more in property and changes in their social fabric. Bacon's progress into civil war taught Virginians lessons they did not quickly forget. Everyone who joined Bacon in hopes of overturning the county magnates lost, and in defeat they were forced to admit the rule of their betters. The great men who held onto their places learned to be more attentive to those they governed. To do otherwise was to provide inspiration to future Bacons. The rebellion ended the career of Sir William Berkeley, but it did more than ruin an old man's reputation. His passing ended an era and a style of government. Virginians would never see his like again. What they got instead were chief executives determined to limit their political freedom. Unwittingly Bacon, in rebelling, handed Stuart imperialists an extraordinary opportunity to impose their idea of empire on King Charles's oldest American dominion.

5

TOWARD A NEW ORDER

Tales of events in Virginia crossed the Atlantic during the first half of 1676. As troubling as the news was, it was not entirely unwelcome in Whitehall. Bacon's revolt discredited Berkeley and reduced his influence at a court already suspicious of his methods of government. It forced royal officials to look more closely at Virginia than at any time since the fall of the London Company. Suppressing the rebellion provided them the excuse to curb Virginia to their conception of empire by hedging colonial freedom.

*   *   *

The pressing need in the fall of 1676 was to smash Bacon and restore order. To crush the rebellion, the Crown organized an expeditionary force that consisted of a regiment of a thousand regular soldiers and a squadron of assorted warships and transports. Command of the troops went to Sir Herbert Jeffreys, an experienced officer who enjoyed the confidence of James, duke of York. His naval counterpart was Sir John Berry, another Stuart loyalist of proven abilities. The task of regaining the Virginians' allegiance was also entrusted to them and to a third man, Francis Moryson, an old Virginia hand who had lately become a convert to Stuart imperialism. Together, these three constituted a commission of inquiry, charged with investigating the causes of the rebellion. They took with them orders for Berkeley to return to England and a commission for Colonel Jeffreys to replace him, as well as a royal proclamation that voided Bacon's Laws and promised pardon to all but Bacon and his chief subordinates.

To mount the expedition and to draft the commissioners' instructions took several months, but by November all seemed in readiness. On the 18th Berry and Moryson set sail for Virginia, to be joined by Jeffreys a week later. Thereafter, bad weather kept the convoy in sight of England until early December; but once the winds turned, its passage was speedy, for it anchored in Virginia waters early in February.

The worst of the rebellion was over by the first weeks of 1677, and Berkeley was well on his way to reestablishing his authority, albeit in a fashion that left a lingering, bitter aftertaste. The ringleaders, save for Bacon, who was dead, and Richard Lawrence, who escaped, were his prisoners. One by one, Bland, Carver, Cheesman, Drummond, and the others were brought before summary courts martial, tried, condemned, and executed, sometimes all in a matter of hours. These men expected no mercy. They got none. Neither did lesser actors, who might have hoped for clemency; they were hanged with equal alacrity. Those who escaped the hangman were made to pay in other ways. Berkeley first used martial law and then "An act for the releife of such loyall persons as have suffered losse by the late rebells," adopted by an obliging General Assembly, to pillage the rebels' estates. His plundering soon outdistanced that done by the rebels, and for a time there seemed to be no end to it.

None of the Virginians who knew the governor believed that he would treat the former rebels gently, nor did anyone necessarily think he should. What shocked and frightened some of them, though, was the vehemence with which he pursued his former enemies. Rather than judiciously using the executions and confiscations as terrifying examples of the fate in store for those who dared to revolt, Berkeley seemed bent on quenching a ferocious blood lust. He was.

Bacon's Rebellion was a bitter dose for a vain, arrogant man, who prided himself on his popularity and his stewardship of the king's trust. Blind to the flaws in his style of governing, Berkeley never fathomed why, after thirty-five years of what he supposed was gentle rule, *his* people turned on *him* so suddenly and so completely. Having to confront his failure, as when he wrote to Secretary of State Joseph Williamson begging to be replaced by "a more vigorous Governor," cut him to the quick. Remembrances of his submission to Bacon's demands, Jamestown's gutted ruins, and the looted remains of his beloved Green Spring were exquisite souvenirs of his humiliation. The wounds to his pride would not heal until he had revenge.

His passion for vengeance inspired his followers to settle scores of their own. Among their number were the members of the House of Burgessess in the session that met at Green Spring in February 1677 and enthusiastically adopted punitive legislation aimed at their former enemies. Others, like Augustine Warner II, vigorously hounded the late rebels in the law courts. Like Berkeley they too had suffered much at the rebels' hands, both in stolen property and in prestige. They were as determined as the governor to exact payment for their losses. Their ardor cooled, however, as they attempted to check the imperialists' efforts to undermine their places at the head of Virginia society.

*   *   *

No sooner had Jeffreys, Berry, and Moryson arrived in the colony than they discovered there was no one for the troops to fight. The army stayed in Virginia nonetheless, and its continued presence enlivened colonial politics for years to come. So long as the troops remained, the colonists were expected to pay for their sustenance, which made them all the more irritating a reminder of royalist intentions. While the soldiers idled, the commissioners went about their business. They tried to persuade the councillors and burgesses to become "the *healing Assembly*," urging the legislators to address the causes of the late discontent. Then they collected the ordinary Virginians' grievances. Much of what they got merely confirmed what they already suspected, and it formed the substance of their report to the king. The report damned the way Berkeley and his loyalists ruled. Responsibility for the revolt rested squarely with them. Furthermore, the report criticized Berkeley's methods of suppressing the rebels, and it suggested that the colony was generally too independent of the Crown's direction. It concluded with the recommendation that the powers of the General Assembly be reduced.

Predictably, Berkeley and his circle got on badly with the commission. Its very presence was an irritation. Jeffreys, Berry, and Moryson quarreled with Berkeley over their authority and his approach to dealing with ex-rebels. He would not immediately publish the king's pardon, nor would he cease exempting people from it, They insisted on the need for leniency; there was no compassion in him. He resented their meddling with the Assembly; they were angered by its refusal to countenance their proposals. Blaming the Berkeleyites for the rebellion infuriated them, and they would accept no responsibility for it; moreover, Berkeley's supporters were alarmed by such an overt play for popular support. If left unchecked, that ploy could erode their position.

Jeffreys demanded that Berkeley give the government over to him. Berkeley refused to yield, at least until he realized that a greatly annoyed Sir Herbert might throw him in irons and pack him off to London, whereupon he sailed for England in May. As a parting stroke, he left behind a letter addressed to *Lt. Governor* Jeffreys in which he accused his adversary of an "irresistable desire to rule this Country" and predicted "that the inhabitants of this Colony will quickly find a difference between your management and mine."

Berkeley's remarks were on point, though they were hardly prophetic. No politician, Jeffreys was a hard man who placed his duty to his royal masters above all others. Like other Stuart servants, he disdained colonials, and he was openly contemptuous of those who in his judgment put more value on "the Power and lawes of A few Ignorant Planters mett in An Assembly for this Government" than they did for the king's will. These "few Ignorant Planters" were of course the Berkeley loyalists. It was they who controlled Virginia's political machinery, and they were quick to oppose Jeffreys. They and he were implacable foes almost from the day he relieved Berkeley, and from that moment until Jeffreys died in December 1678, he knew little peace. He deprived his more obstreperous opponents of their seats on the Council of State, just as he drove others from their places in the House of Burgesses. Rather than cowing anyone, these dismissals redoubled the Virginians' opposition.

Their ripening resistance to Jeffreys was of a piece with a political realignment that began in the spring of 1677. All the Berkeleyites were quick to grasp how the events of recent months had altered their political landscape. Bacon's escapades revealed the depth of the planters' anger with them; moreover, their part in suppressing Bacon's men had done little to dispel that animosity. Without care, those enmities could flare into rebellion anew. The royal army stood as a constant reminder of the Crown's intentions, while Jeffreys was a forceful intruder into the colony's politics. Ludwell, Beverley, and the others recognized the dangers to their independence and the necessity of guarding their position. The question for them was how they could protect themselves from their fellow colonists and a meddlesome home government.

Forestalling future rebellions meant coming to terms with the small planters. From 1677 onwards, the great men became more solicitous of the lesser planters' interests, particularly as they grew to depend on a measure of popular support in their struggle with the Crown, and the stabilization of Virginia's internal polity began with that change. As for combating the Crown's threat, there were only two courses of action open: to rebel or to accommodate. No Virginian who opposed the Stuarts after 1677 thought of rebelling, however. Bacon's insurrection was all too obvious a monument to the risks of rebellion. Even if by some remote chance a revolt succeeded, it was folly to believe that the colony might exist independent of England. The only course was some form of accommodation with the royalists. But Jeffrey's opponents could not agree on how much of their autonomy they must surrender, and that difference of opinion divided them into three factions.

At one extreme was a group who vehemently opposed any accommodation. It consisted of men such as the Ludwell brothers, Thomas Swann, Thomas Ballard, and Robert Beverley. For the most part, these "irreconcilables" were longtime residents of Virginia, with intimate ties to Sir William Berkeley and lengthy careers in public office at every level of colonial government. They formed the core of Berkeley loyalists that Berry, Jeffreys, and Moryson called "the Green Spring faction." Until 1676 Virginia was their private domain, free of meddlesome outsiders, and they were determined to give up none of their independence. To save themselves, they rallied around Beverley and Philip Ludwell, who became the group's leading spokesmen and tacticians. They schemed to frustrate the Crown at every opportunity and so to weary their imperial opponents into forsaking their plans for controlling Virginia. Simple though it was, theirs was a perilous tactic. It cost Beverley, Ludwell, Thomas Swann, Thomas Ballard, and James Bray their offices, and it invited Jeffreys to use the army to enforce the king's wishes.

The irreconcilables' obduracy led to the formation of an opposing faction, the "trimmers." Trimmers were as experienced as irreconcilables in the ways of Virginia politics. Like Francis Moryson and Nicholas Spencer, some were nominal Berkeleyites. A few, such as Mathew Kemp, John Armistead, and Isaac Allerton, for example, were at the edges of the Green Spring faction. Others, including William Fitzhugh and Francis Page, had no link to Berkeley save for his having appointed them to the offices they held by 1677. As a group, they were never close to the old governor, so they were not as devoted to him or to his views as were the irreconcilables. In truth, before 1676 several followed Francis Moryson's example and looked toward London for favors, while still seeking Berkeley's patronage. That attitude explains the trimmers' willingness to cut their politics to fit what they saw as the new realities of the post-rebellion era. In their estimation, the relationship between Virginia and England was no longer what it had been a generation or two earlier. Like it or not, the English imperialists' view of empire was an idea whose time had come, and there were advantages in accepting it. If put into practice, it promised to stabilize Virginia as Berkeley had not. Those who supported the imperialists stood to gain in royal preferments. The trimmers were willing to swap Virginia's freedom for an ordered colony in which their positions were secure.

In the middle stood the "moderates." Moderates were survivors who could adapt to political change seemingly without appearing to trim their views to new conditions. Their political credentials were as impeccable as any in Virginia. Nathaniel Bacon, Sr., the rebel's cousin, was the quintessential moderate. In a career that spanned four decades, Bacon served the Commonwealth regime, Berkeley, and the Stuart imperialists. Younger moderates of the likes of Augustine Warner II and William Byrd I showed an equal nimbleness, even to the point of subsuming their own great dislike of one another for a larger good. In outlook, the moderates were closer to the irreconcilables than to the trimmers. They had no wish to be party to any diminution of their power or of that of the General Assembly or the county courts. Yet they were troubled by the irreconcilables' opposition to Jeffreys, just as they mistrusted the trimmers, who seemed altogether too willing to side with the Crown. Furthermore, they accepted the requirements that relations between the Crown and the colony would have to be adjusted. Given Berkeley's failure, readjustment was unavoidable, though it need not be too expensive. Seeking to minimize the costs, the moderates made an outward show of grudging support for Jeffreys while they sought ways to frustrate him, but they always stopped just short of open confrontation. In that way, they were safe from royalist suspicions, and they commanded the largest following of the councillors, burgesses, and local magistrates who comprised Virginia's political establishment after 1677. Accordingly, they were the key to post-rebellion politics.

Jeffreys never grasped these distinctions, but then his attitude toward Virginians blinded him to such shadings of opinion, and an untimely death cut short his gubernatorial tenure. His successors—Thomas, Lord Culpeper and Francis, Lord Howard of Effingham—were no more discerning than he, and neither were his masters in London. Francis Moryson would have recognized the polarities, but he had left Virginia in the summer of 1677 just as the factions were forming. Although Moryson never returned to Virginia, royalists continued to solicit his advice until he died in 1680. With or without Moryson, their understanding was clouded by the lack of sound information, which cost them an opportunity to achieve the full realization of their goal. Their heavy-handed assaults on Virginia's autonomy isolated the trimmers to the point of ineffectiveness and caused the moderates to dig in their heels.

* * *

After Jeffreys died, Sir Henry Chicheley occupied the post, pending the arrival of the new governor, Thomas, Lord Culpeper. Chicheley, "that Lump, that Mass of Dullness, that worse than Nothing," in Culpeper's pungent phrasing, was a cautious man in a tight spot. Long a resident of Virginia, he identified with its leading politicians, and he was as alarmed by the Crown's intrusion as they were. At the same time, however, he cherished his position as the colony's lieutenant governor, for it was a place of honor and profit and little responsibility, at least until Jeffrey's death. Chicheley now had to manage things until Lord Culpeper came over. He managed to keep the situation quiet even in the face of mounting concerns for continued low tobacco prices and other attendant economic difficulties, but he lacked the imagination to rein in the General Assembly that met in April 1679.

Chicheley summoned the Assembly to deal with renewed threats of

Indian raids. Solving that problem was not the only item on the members' agenda, though. This Assembly was much like its two immediate predecessors. It was dominated by irreconcilables, so it adopted several pieces of legislation that were bound to offend the Crown. Sir Henry failed to see that these laws were as inauspicious as they were inopportune. Their passage redoubled the imperialists' determination to enlarge direct royal rule at the expense of Virginia's independence. To make good on that intent, the Crown turned to Lord Culpeper.

Contemporaries depicted Thomas, Lord Culpeper, baron of Thoresway as someone who was blessed with "a singular Dexterity in making Use of all Advantages to his own Interest." A royalist who went into exile with Charles II, he returned to England in 1660 to begin the task of repairing his broken fortunes, and continued service to the king seemed the surest way to accomplish that. For a time he was captain and governor of the Isle of Wight before he took a seat on the council for foreign plantations in 1671. The council advised the Privy Council on colonial affairs, and it was there that Culpeper learned the potential value of an inheritance from his father. Culpeper *père* had left behind an interest in the Northern Neck proprietary created by Charles I in 1649, but civil war kept him and his co-proprietors from developing it.* In 1673, Culpeper *fils* used his ties with Henry Bennett, Lord Arlington to obtain the management of the Northern Neck together with a share of all Virginia's escheats[†] and quit rents[‡] for a period of thirty-one years. In 1675 he secured a reversion of the governorship upon Berkeley's death. He was sworn governor for life shortly after Sir William died in July 1677.

---

*The history of the Northern Neck proprietary is labyrinthian in its complexity, and only the late Douglas Southall Freeman came close to mastering its intricacies. His study appeared as an appendix to volume I of his *George Washington: A Biography* (New York, 1949), 447–513.

†Escheat was the reversion of land to the crown in those instances where there were no legal heirs. A person who patented the reverted land was required to pay a fee that was also called an escheat, and it was such moneys that Culpeper would collect from all Virginians who took up escheated tracts.

‡Quit rents were annual fees that all Virginia landholders owed the King as the titular owner of all land in the colony. Before Culpeper's day the quitrents were not collected with any regularity or efficiency.

At first Culpeper showed no inclination to make speed for his government. Word of Jeffreys's passing came and went, and still he tarried in England. Finally, Charles II ordered him to leave or lose his post; so, armed with new instructions, he sailed off in February 1680.

His instructions were not altogether pleasing to Culpeper, for they forced him to choose between doing his duty to the king and pursuing his private fortunes. Moreover, he suspected that his instructions would stir the colonials to even greater obstinacy. They embodied the privy councillors' latest formulations for reducing the "arrogancy of Virginia Assemblies." From now on, the Assembly would sit only at the express command of the king. The burgesses were to lose the right to initiate legislation. Henceforth, Culpeper and his councillors would draft bills and submit them for the Crown's approval before presenting them to the House for its concurrence. He was given three bills, drawn up by the Privy Council, whose adoption he was to secure along with a law to encourage the building of towns. No longer would the Assembly be permitted to take appeals from the General Court; in future such appeals would lie in the King-in-Council. Apart from these strokes, the instructions required Culpeper to repeal by proclamation statutes passed in 1677 and 1679, as well as several that had stood for a generation, all of which were seen as offending the royal prerogative.

Culpeper landed in Virginia in May 1680, amid expectations that he might be an easier man than the late, unmourned Colonel Jeffreys. The new governor was, after all, Lady Berkeley's cousin, and that was cause for optimism among the irreconcilables. Shortly after he summoned the Assembly, Culpeper appeared to send another favorable signal. He consented to the burgesses' nomination of Robert Beverley as their clerk, in spite of a royal command disqualifying the pesky Virginian from all public employment. Whatever hope he encouraged, he soon dashed it when he pressed the Assembly to enact the legislative package contained in his instructions.

Schooled well in the political arts, Culpeper skillfully wheedled the legislators into doing his bidding. Attaining passage of the town bill was easy enough, partly because the idea was popular and partly because he let Beverley craft the bill. (It was subsequently disallowed.) Then, too, he had little difficulty in securing the adoption of the Crown's draft of a law easing procedures for naturalizing foreigners. Getting the Assembly to enact the Crown's other two bills, an act of

indemnity—which would end civil litigation arising out of the
rebellion—and a law to grant the king a permanent revenue out of the
two-shilling-per-hogshead export duty on tobacco, took more than a
bit of juggling to accomplish. Culpeper got around the irreconcilables
by trading the exemption of certain former rebels for a favorable vote
on the indemnity bill. The Assembly at first rejected the revenue
measure as repugnant to its prerogatives. Culpeper called the
legislators in and gave them a sharp lecture, which he followed with
some threats and a few promises; by those means he won their
approval.

Feeling that he had done enough, Culpeper decided against challenging the Assembly over its right to take appeals from the General
Court. Nor did he choose to publish the proclamation annulling the
laws the king wanted voided. These were troubling matters that would
only anger the Virginians, and he had experienced enough of their
wrath already. Weary of matching his wits against theirs, he sum-
marily adjourned the Assembly, packed up, and left for the comforts of
England, commanding Chicheley not to call the Assembly back into
session until his return.

While his lordship partook of England's delights, the plight of the
Virginians worsened as glutted markets kept tobacco prices low.
Pressure to recall the General Assembly increased, the belief being that
it would pass a law to limit tobacco production, thereby forcing up
prices. Petitions for the Assembly circulated acress Gloucester,
Middlesex, and New Kent counties throughout the winter of
1681/1682, while several area politicians, including Robert Beverley
and Sir Henry's stepson, Ralph Wormeley II, used their influence with
Chicheley. Himself a tobacco planter, Chicheley was sympathetic to
the planters' impoverishment, but he was reluctant to go against the
explicit commands of his superior. He stalled until April 1682, when,
without consulting the Council, he ordered the legislature back into
session. As the members eagerly hastened to the capital, he got word
from Culpeper telling him not to convene the Assembly before the
governor's expected return in November.

Meeting with the burgesses on April 23, Chicheley informed them
of Culpeper's communication. Deeply dismayed by what they heard,
they pleaded with him to ignore his instructions. Chicheley would not
be dissuaded, and after four days of pointless haggling, he postponed

the Assembly until November 10. Within the week, he had a small-scale insurrection on his hands.

Their high hopes for a stay law dashed, gangs of planters in Gloucester tried to solve the problem of too much tobacco in their own way. They went from plantation to plantation and cut down tobacco seedlings as they grew in their beds. Spontaneous rioting and plant cutting soon spread to Middlesex and New Kent. Chicheley banned public meetings and turned to local militia commanders for help in containing the trouble. The cutting abated in the early months of summer, only to flare up again in August. Secretary of the Colony Nicholas Spencer put the recurrence off to too much "syder" and the planters' "itching desier" for rebellion. Whatever the case, by the time the last of the rioting was done, the plant cutters had succeeded in destroying crops on more than two hundred plantations.

But for Mathew Kemp's prompt actions and Chicheley's tolerant attitude toward the affair, things would have been worse than they were. Kemp organized patrols to range over the affected counties to prevent the cuttings and to catch what rioters they could. Most of those who were taken were released after they posted peace bonds. Among those taken into custody was Robert Beverley, whom Spencer, Kemp, and other trimmer councillors suspected of fomenting the riots. The warrant for his arrest was accompanied by an order of Council for him to surrender the records of the House of Burgesses that were in his charge. When he refused to give them up, Kemp seized them. Chicheley proclaimed the disturbance a riot, thereby absolving the participants of treason, and he issued a general pardon to all but Beverley and a few others who remained in custody pending further investigation.

Chicheley's reports to London tended to underplay the seriousness of what had happened, though he noted the baleful effects of Culpeper's prolonged absence. Bacon's account was equally low key. He too commented on the need for the governor's presence; moreover, he sought his superiors' advice and assistance. Spencer was more alarmist in his reporting, but he avoided any criticism of Culpeper, who had made him a land agent in the Northern Neck. He blamed the troubles on "the selfish purposes of some persons," and he was especially sharp in his attacks on Beverley, whose influence on the burgesses and Chicheley he found undue.

Despite their differences, the stories did not augur well for Lord Culpeper. The news of renewed rebellion in Virginia first reached London in June, and it made Culpeper's earlier triumphs over the Assembly seem hollow. It was ominous because it indicated that the colonists remained in a rebellious mood and that some of Berkeley's followers were still capable of stirring them up. It also suggested that Culpeper had not yet achieved the goal of a disciplined and orderly Virginia. On June 17, Charles II directed the governor to sail for his government no later than the first of August and to take matters in hand. The king also commanded that he not quit his post unless he received an express royal warrant to leave.

Typically, his lordship dallied until October, while he loaded HMS *Mermaid* with a cargo of goods and servants. The Assembly had been in session for more than a month before he landed in mid-December. He recessed it while he reviewed what it had done in his absence. Then, as he explained to the Privy Council, he altered almost every bill, gave the members gifts of deerskins, "rejected all things they intended for their favorite Mr. Beverley," and dissolved the Assembly with a speech against plant cutting. That done, he and the Council turned to an investigation of the plant cutters in the first weeks of 1683. He concluded that "the universal cutting up and destroying of the Tobacco-plants by force and Arms, though none killed, to Bee treason." Two men were subsequently tried and hanged. Beverley escaped prosecution for lack of evidence. Nonetheless, he was discharged from his offices and kept in custody. Culpeper confirmed Chicheley's general pardon, although, as he wrote home, he excepted Beverley "that you may proceed against him if you can."

Confident that he had put things right, Culpeper resolved "to make a steppe home this easy quiet yeare." In May, he designated Spencer president of the Council, passing over the senior councillor, Bacon, and embarked for London without royal permission. Scarcely had he landed than a thoroughly exasperated Charles deprived him of office. In his place the king put Francis, Lord Howard of Effingham.

*   *   *

Lord Howard belonged to a Protestant branch of the great Howard family whose lives and fortunes intertwined with those of sixteenth-

and seventeenth-century England. A man of modest abilities and small political accomplishment, he succeeded to the barony of Effingham in 1681. The inheritance did little to enhance his prestige or his purse; and, needing to augment his income to support a growing family, he sought preferment in the king's service. He turned to two of his kinsmen—Henry Howard, duke of Norfolk, the earl marshall of England; and Charles Mordaunt, earl of Peterborough, a privy councillor—for help in gaining an appointment. They acquainted him with the king and the duke of York, as well as that dedicated, well-informed imperial bureaucrat, William Blathwayt. York and Blathwayt were soon convinced that his loyalty and poverty suited him for a colonial post; and when the Virginia vacancy opened in August 1683, they secured Effingham's appointment to fill it.

Effingham sailed from the Kentish port of Deal in November, big with expectations of making his fortune at the expense of the Virginians. Of them, he knew little, and there was little in him that allowed him to appreciate the shadings of political differences among them. Either they were friends of the king or they were not; but supporter or foe, they were no less contemptible to him than any of his other social inferiors. He carried instructions similar to Culpeper's, and if the king and the duke wanted pliant, orderly colonists, then he would do what lay within his power to make them conform to his masters' wishes. To do less would violate the great honor and trust that had come his way. And, from that day in February 1683/84 when his ship dropped anchor in the York River until he left for home in March 1688/89, nothing—not the Virginians' stout opposition, not the death of his beloved wife, not even his own poor health—turned him from his determination to fulfill his royal charge.

On their part, the Virginians prepared to welcome their new governor with caution. A stranger to them, they knew nothing of his background or his views. Irreconcilables and moderates were of a mind to consider *any* governor an intruder instead of a friend. They still chafed from their past dealings with Jeffreys and Culpeper. Though suspicious, they could nonetheless join with the trimmers in the hope, as William Byrd I put it, that together they and Effingham could "proceed more for the countrys interest then formerly."

At first, things seemed as though they might. Leading Virginians greeted Effingham warmly, as his first weeks in the colony were filled with a whirl of social engagements. Ralph Wormeley asked him to be godfather to one of his daughters, while Philip Ludwell entertained him at Green Spring. After investigating Beverley's supposed part in the plant cutting, Effingham found the evidence insufficient to proceed, pardoned the clerk, and restored him to office. He recommissioned all of the existing county officeholders, and in one instance, he even returned a justice of the peace whom Culpeper had driven from the bench. Moreover, he reworded the sheriffs' commissions in such a way as to drop from the documents offensive wording that Culpeper had written into them.

Cracks in the façade of cordiality appeared during his first General Assembly, which he convened in April 1684. His opening speech mixed honey with gall. He struck a courteous tone toward the legislators, expressing his pleasure at being governor and reassuring his listeners of the king's regard for them. Then he outlined the heart of his remarks, his legislative proposals, which were based on his instructions. Among a long list of things, he wanted a new town law to replace the one Charles had disallowed in 1680. New regulation of the Indian trade was also needed, and the militia required "methodizing." In particular, two of his propositions were most provocative. One called for the passage of a law authorizing the governor and the councillors to levy a poll tax for "the better support of the Government." The other would require the repeal of statutes that regulated attorneys and allowed county courts to adopt their own bylaws. Effingham concluded the speech with a reminder that the Assembly should hear no appeals from the General Court.

The speech was an augury of things to come. Effingham revealed a talent for getting the Assemby to do his bidding, up to a point. All of the laws it passed in that sitting began as his proposals. He turned aside an effort by the burgesses to deny Lord Culpeper's claims for what was due him in escheats and quitrents, just as he forced them to accept the loss of their right to take appeals. But neither his sugared words nor his emphatic bullying cajoled them into giving him the town bill, the tax measure, or the repeal law. Despite those failures, the session put the Virginians on notice; he would certainly be no pushover.

Lest they need reminders, Effingham sent them two additional souvenirs. First, on May 10 he issued new commissions of the peace to all of the colony's magistrates. He accompanied those documents with a writ known as a *dedimus postestatem*, which he directed to the senior justices. The *dedimus* required them formally to swear themselves and their colleagues into office and return the writ to Effingham with their endorsement that they had complied with its contents. Anyone who failed to execute the writ was liable to lose his office. Henceforth, the commissions and the commissioning ceremonies would be renewed annually. Effingham intended that these changes, which he justified as making colonial practices more nearly congruent with those in England, would remind all local officials of their dependency on the king and on himself.

Next he confronted the Assembly's independence of the Crown. Its refusal to repeal the attorney and bylaw statute incensed him, and he would not be outdone. Nevertheless, he held his tongue and bided his time until the session was completed and he had dissolved the House of Burgesses. Then he had his revenge in a way that pointedly demonstrated how he could attack the legislature's prerogatives with impunity. On June 19 he issued a proclamation that annulled the offending laws.

His opponents could do little but seethe until the Assembly's next meeting, which did not come for a year and a half. By that time a number of events served to poison relations between the governor and the Virginians. The death of Charles II, the accession of James II, Monmouth's Rebellion, and fears of Catholic reaction stirred all sorts of rumors that agitated the colonists almost to the point of violence. They were already hostile because Effingham had raised the fees for the use of the colony's seal in land transactions. Then too, Effingham had grown more wary of Ludwell and Beverley. Ludwell and Effingham irritated each other, even though each man had been at pains to develop a correct relationship. The colonel could not accept Effingham's closeness to Secretary Spencer, who held the post he thought was rightfully his. He also despised what Effingham represented. The governor found Ludwell the most vexing of Virginians. He was the most disputatious of his councillors, he used his influence to frustrate the royal interest, and no amount of generosity seemed likely to win him over to the king. Likewise, Beverley, whom Effingham had spared and restored, never showed his benefactor due thanks or cooperation.

Francis, Lord Howard of Effingham (1643–1695), was governor of Virginia from 1683 to 1692, although resident in Virginia only for the five years from 1683 to 1689. This portrait, attributed to the school of Sir Godfrey Kneller, is in the Virginia Historical Society. Reproduced with the permission of the Society.

The death of Effingham's wife and his own nearly fatal illness had blackened his mood and sapped his energies before he met his second Assembly in November 1685.

That session was the rowdiest of any held in the seventeenth century. It began somberly. The burgesses came to Jamestown sullen and combative, fully prepared to take on the governor. When they organized the House, they nominated Beverley as their clerk and another irreconcilable, William Kendall, as speaker. Effingham, though he had not overcome his grief or his illness, rose to the occasion and got things off to a bad start by reading a short, antagonistic opening speech. His subsequent demands on the burgesses fueled their animosities. In turn, he was galled by their choice of officers, though he confirmed it, just as he was incensed at their persistent protest against his having increased the fees for use of the seal.

The centerpiece of their disagreements was a great row over what had been the agreed text of another town act. A bill to replace the law Charles II disallowed in 1680 was introduced early in the session. In due course, it was debated by the House, amended by the Council, and sent back to the House, which enacted it, ordered it engrossed, and then passed the fair copy to Effingham for his signature. When Effingham read it, he saw that it lacked the amendment which he and the Council had made, and he would not sign the act as it stood. The burgesses maintained that they had never received the amendment and claimed that the wording of the act was as it had come to them from the Council. As far as they were concerned, the act was law, and Effingham was merely trying to exercise a double veto, which no governor had ever done before. Effingham countered that argument by reminding them that no bill passed Parliament without the king's assent and neither would this one. The burgesses next held the appropriation bill to ransom, hoping to exchange it for the governor's signature. Effingham would not budge. He tried to cut a deal of his own, offering to sign all of the bills but the town act if the House passed the revenue measure. No luck. The burgesses were as obdurate as he.

Both sides were at loggerheads within a matter of days. Effingham, whose patience had stretched to the limits of its tolerance, finally forced the issue on December 12. He commanded the burgesses to wait on him, and when they appeared he assailed their intransigence and adjourned them to the following October.

The Assembly of 1685 opened a breech between the governor and the Virginians that was never bridged during the remainder of Effingham's administration. Irreconcilables had now seen their worst suspicions of the governor confirmed, and they redoubled their resolve to oppose him whenever and wherever possible. While moderate burgesses might excuse his behavior as the actions of a sick, bereaved man, even they accepted the necessity of resisting him. As for Effingham, he turned on the colonists and their leaders with a renewed determination to break them to his discipline.

His efforts proceeded along several fronts. Early in 1686, he published a proclamation overturning a number of statutes that the Assembly had refused to repeal. About this time, he also wrote a full account of the abortive session for his superiors. In separate letters that he sent to the Privy Council, Blathwayt, and James II, he sought approval for his actions and support for additional measures he now proposed. He recommended that the king signify his displeasure at the burgesses' mulishness by sending over a sharply worded dissolution order. That, he observed, "will be so great a rebuke to them." He urged that he, not the burgesses, nominate clerks of the House in the future. Finally, he asked permission to dismiss Beverley and Ludwell.

The letters were timed so that the replies would make the circuit to Virginia before the Assembly reconvened in October. When the letters reached the intended recipients, their reaction was prompt; they supported Effingham completely. James II even sent the governor a personal reply saying, "Wee doe much approve of what you have done" and telling him to act on his recommendations, but it did not reach Effingham until after the Assembly had begun.

This session was almost as stormy as its predecessor. Effingham proposed no new legislation. His primary goal was the passage of an appropriations act, but he could not forbear needling the burgesses about their behavior in what he styled "your last long ineffectual meeting." On their part, the legislators were incensed by his use of proclamations to thwart them. They sent him a memorial in which they challenged the proclamations' very legality, and the fight was on. As in 1685, Effingham again had the last word, though he waited to speak it until he got approval for the money bill. At that point, he called everybody into the Council chamber. He read James II's letter and sent them packing, remarking that this was the first time a sovereign ever had cause to dissolve an Assembly. Then he directed his scrivener to dispatch copies of the letter to all the county courts with instructions that it be read publicly at their next regular sessions so that all men might know the king's displeasure.

Effingham stripped Beverley of "all publick employments" shortly after the dissolution. Beverley pined little for his loss; he died in March 1687, though he lived long enough to see the governor also rid himself of Ludwell. The circumstances surrounding Ludwell's displacement typified the relationship between the colonel and the governor. Besides being a councillor, Ludwell was Virginia's deputy surveyor general, and as such he appointed all of the county surveyors. One of these was among the governor's more outspoken critics. Effingham ordered Ludwell to deprive the man; he did, but he filled the vacancy with one of Beverley's sons. Such impudence was intolerable, and Effingham lost no time in suspending Ludwell from all of his offices.

While what befell Ludwell and Beverley attracted the most notice, they were not the only men Effingham punished. At least half a dozen of the more vocal irreconcilables, in addition to the displaced surveyor, were removed from office or means of livelihood. Turning these men out not only nettled them, it also vexed their compatriots to see the result of too stout an opposition to a determined governor. Conversely, all of the dismissals demonstrated a fundamental truth about Effingham's position. However much he might wish it, Effingham could not drive every cheeky officeholder from his place. Any campaign of massive removals was too drastic a step. It would provoke rather than pacify, and it invited risks that were too horrible to contemplate. For the threat of deprivation to succeed, it had to be used sparingly and in concert with other, less direct, techniques of eroding the colonists' political independence. Effingham hit on the most effective of these means early in his administration.

He attacked all those customary practices in Virginia law and politics that differed sharply from what was done or thought desirable in Stuart England, insisting that they must conform to those standards. The tactic was irresistible because the colonists had no constitutional justifications to plead as arguments for their departures from English customs. Their only precedents were the passage of time and the extraordinary nature of settling in a wilderness. Such groundings were poor foundations for a case with a governor who had little knowledge of Virginia and even less regard for its colonists.

Effingham made considerable inroads during the first three years of his administration. He not only refashioned the procedures for investing local magistrates with their office but also chipped away at the militia and the church, making both more dependent on him. His taking away the use of the seal and its fees from the secretary of the colony lessened the secretary's importance. The contests with the Assembly over the business of appeals, town bills, and proclamations weakened its power. Combined with these changes, his disciplining of Beverley and the others brought obstreperous Virginians to the verge of submission, and by the spring of 1687, Effingham was preparing more incursions on their power. He informed Secretary of State Robert Spencer, earl of Sunderland, of his decision not to have "so frequent Assemblys," just as he intended to appoint the next clerk of the House. But before the year was out, Effingham's fervor for further innovations ebbed noticeably, as the governor began to think of going home to England.

Poor health and problems with his motherless children were among the personal reasons for the governor's change of heart, but there were political considerations as well. In April he became entangled in a running feud with two naval captains that lasted for more than a year. The quarrel damaged his reputation to the point where a hanger-on at Whitehall, whom he identified only as "one Hildeyard," tried to lobby him out of his post. Effingham wanted to justify his government personally to James II, whom he had not seen since 1683. It also seemed important to go back and combat the colonists' own complaints of his supposed mismanagement. In December 1687 he requested leave to come home in 1689. He received permission the following fall. On February 27 1688/89, he convened the Council to announce his imminent departure. A few weeks later, he sailed away, amid rumors of a revolution in England.

*   *   *

Neither Jeffreys nor Culpeper nor Effingham achieved the full realization of the Stuarts' vision of empire. They did, however, bring the Old

Dominion and its people under closer English supervision than either had been before 1676. Their successes compelled leading Virginians, however grudgingly, to accept that they were part of an Atlantic community whose political and economic center was England. As they did, Virginia passed another of the mileposts along the road from colonial bastion to imperial province.

6

THE MATURING OF VIRGINIA SOCIETY

The Glorious Revolution of 1688 in England, Secretary Nicholas Spencer of Virginia wrote to the Lords of Trade and Plantations in London, "had such an effect here that for some time peace and quiet were doubtful." In the mother country controversies over foreign policy, the powers of Parliament, and the royal Stuarts' preference for Catholicism had been accumulating during the later years of Charles II's reign and climaxed under his brother James II, who succeeded him in 1685. When a male heir who was certain to be raised a Catholic was born to James, the hierarchy and most of the political establishment deserted the king. Parliament invited James's Protestant daughter Mary and her husband, William, prince of Orange and stadholder of Holland, to assume the throne. William landed with his army at Torbay, England, in November 1688, and James fled in December.

In Virginia, there was a long anxious period the next spring before official proclamation of the new reign was received. When Indian hunting parties were seen crossing the Potomac River from Maryland, panic spread as excited imaginations conceived that Catholics in the sister colony had enlisted "tenn thousand Seneca" for a religious war. At the center of the alarm were the planter George Brent of Stafford County, who was a Catholic, and his law partner, William Fitzhugh, one of the wealthiest men in Virginia, who, though a Protestant, shielded him. There were baseless rumors that "most of the Cheife Magistrates" in that county and neighboring Rappahannock "were Papists." More accurate were reports to the Virginia Council that many

families were fleeing their homes and that unauthorized armed bands
were forming for defense. Most dangerous was the notion that "their
was neither King, Laws, nor Government." Governor Effingham's
abrupt departure in March 1689 left—in a delightful twist of history—
the president of the Council, Nathaniel Bacon, Sr., as acting governor.
"Matters were very pressingly leading to a rebellion," Spencer reported, but, "thank God," he, Richard Lee, Ralph and Christopher
Wormeley, and other councillors were able to move quickly to
apprehend the ringleaders. The proclamation on April 27, 1689, of the
accession of King William and Queen Mary ended any doubt about the
legitimacy of government in Virginia.

The quieting of the rumbles in northern Virginia ended almost two
decades of unrest that had often flared into much greater violence than
in 1689. The two principal instigators in Stafford, the Reverend
John Waugh and George Mason, had previously been associated with
Robert Beverley and Philip Ludwell in their confrontations with
various governors. But Beverley was dead and Ludwell was in England,
and neither Waugh nor Mason matched them in dynamism. The
resolute action of the Council at a time when external support was
unavailable was symptomatic of the emergence of a Virginia establishment, a planter elite of great wealth and estates that had firm control
of public office and the confidence to act decisively on its own.

* * *

The economic troubles that had plagued the Chesapeake since Governor Berkeley's time continued for another generation. Part of the reason
was the Navigation Acts—certainly contemporary Virginians put the
blame on them—which gave English shippers and merchants a
monopoly of the tobacco trade. But a greater cause was continued
overproduction. From about 14,000,000 pounds a year in the late
1680s, tobacco output more than doubled by 1700. Prices ranged from
as low as a ½d. a pound to 1½d., with many traumatic ups and downs
through the last twenty years of the century. Conventional wisdom at
the time was that tobacco cost at least a penny a pound to produce.

Yet obviously some planters succeeded. The reason was that
producers in general were learning how to increase productivity and
reduce costs, and some were better at their lessons than others.

Productivity in terms of the number of plants per worker advanced between sixfold and tenfold over the course of the century. The quality of the leaf improved vastly, especially in the cultivation of the sweet-scented variety. This type brought the best price in England, while the harsher Orinoco found a market in Europe. Planters mastered such techniques as prizing, or compressing, tobacco into hogsheads to take advantage of shipping rates, which were by volume rather than by weight. Larger growers could save on shipping by having sufficient cargo ready to reduce a vessel's "turn-around time" in local waters. A long wait represented an unproductive cost. The ravages of the teredo worm on wooden hulls also unnerved sea captains the longer they had to stay in the Chesapeake Bay during the summer. Greater efficiency in loading might also allow a ship to reach England in time for the higher prices of an early market. Planters often bought the crops of smaller neighbors to fill out their own, enforcing a private inspection system in the process by imposing their own mark and guarantee which could bring a premium.

Many planters diversified, putting on a merchant's hat to lay in inventories for neighborhood sale or, as in the case of the best-known example, the Byrds, for the Indian trade. Planters were also realtors. The rapid erosion tobacco caused in the soil fostered an insatiable lust for land from the beginning of the history of the crop in the Chesapeake. The craving intensified the larger plantings became and the more dependents each family had to provide for. In the absence of banks, land was an excellent form of savings, and it was the best security for credit. Often planters with large holdings assumed the role of real estate developer, actively recruiting settlers overseas. When persecution of Protestants intensified in France after the 1680s, for instance, Brent and Fitzhugh both tried to attract Huguenots to their lands in Stafford County. Only Fitzhugh was successful. Better known is the example of the 500 Huguenots whom William Byrd and others sponsored at Manakin Town in Henrico County in 1701.

The cost of English goods also steadily declined over the course of the seventeenth century as the productive capacity of the mother country improved; and with the specialization of English merchants in tobacco and the rise of outports in competition with London, commissions decreased 75 percent by 1700. The growth of English banking and insurance industries led to lower charges for those services, too.

Aggressive and enterprising entrepreneurs could thus hope to match tumbling tobacco prices with efficient management and thrive on the hairline profits that accrued.

From the beginning of tobacco culture in the colony, the key was to acquire as much of the best lands as possible and to find the labor to work them. By the last quarter of the century, the process in most instances was a case of the well off becoming better off. In addition to an initial fillip of a little capital or political and mercantile connections, many in the mid-century wave of immigration found the simple advantage of education in an age when most persons were illiterate sufficient for entry into public office and thence to wealth. Government positions were viewed as a primary road to advancement. Not only did the lucrative fees of such posts as county sheriff and secretary of the colony provide sizable income, but in the last quarter of the century one-third to three-quarters of the land patented in many counties went to political incumbents. By the turn of the century 60 percent of all estates of more than 2,000 acres in the colony belonged to families of past or present officeholders.

Of particular attraction in the 1690s was the Northern Neck between the Potomac and Rappahannock rivers, title to which after much confusion devolved upon lords Arlington and Culpeper in the 1680s. They set the tone of the proprietorship's subsequent history by obtaining a slight rewording of their charter to place the western boundary of the grant "within the heads" rather than at the "first heads or springs" of the two rivers, thereby adding the northern half of the Shenandoah Valley to their lands. Through marriage to a Culpeper heiress, Thomas, Lord Fairfax acquired the proprietorship in 1689. Until then only a relatively few grants had been made in the region, but with title finally secure, the signal flag was flown. Fairfax appointed William Fitzhugh and George Brent as his agents in Virginia, and they began a tradition carried on by Robert Carter and Thomas Lee in the early 1700s of the proprietor's representatives being their "own best customers." As the leading historian of the proprietorship remarked, "one verb told the story . . . grab, grab, grab." By the beginning of the next century throughout the colony the race had indeed gone to the swift. In each of Virginia's twenty counties one-quarter of the landholders owned half or more of the land; in five of the best tobacco counties (James City, Henrico, Charles City,

Middlesex, and King and Queen) the top quarter owned 70 percent; and in the latter county the upper 10 percent owned more than half.

* * *

Coupled with the emerging pattern in land distribution, during the decades immediately after the Restoration another trend set in, compounding the drift toward economic concentration and stratification. Population growth slowed in the mother country just before mid-century, and there were better economic times in England along with a lessening of religious and political strife. Much of the motivation that had once impelled the adventurous to test fortune in the New World disappeared. Virginia's image as one of the less healthy spots in the empire still lingered, although the most fearsome mortality rates of the early years had passed. At the same time, England's conquest and settlement of the Middle Colonies and the opening of Carolina provided enticing alternatives to any who considered migrating. As a result, the flow of indentured servants who had supplied the labor for the tobacco fields since the founding of the colony stabilized in the 1660s and 1670s and then declined just as the number of fields and their need for labor vastly increased.

Gradually planters met the need with enslaved blacks imported initially from the West Indies and then, beginning in the late 1670s and increasingly thereafter, directly from Africa. By the early 1690s in come counties blacks outnumbered whites in the work force. There was no dramatic shift of policy involved; one author calls the change an "Unthinking Decision." There just was no particular reason not to adopt slavery when it was needed. Englishmen had long been distinguished even among Europeans for their ethnocentric attitudes. From neighboring Celts and French to far-off peoples exotic to English minds, foreigners were deemed inferior in varying degrees. Though the stark difference in color gave added reason, blacks were in a sense the last in line. All other things being equal, Virginians preferred white servants. They did not threaten the ideal of a homogeneous society, and they were less expensive. The initial cost of a slave was greater than that of a servant—two or three times greater, in the last quarter of the seventeenth century—because it represented an investment in a longer period of labor. The heavier investment was also riskier since the high mortality rates affected both races. Not until the chances of survival improved after mid-century, coincidentally with the increase in need, did slavery become a viable alternative.

When the Royal African Company received the Crown's monopoly of the slave trade in 1672, it was enjoined to cater to Virginia's needs, but for the most part it concentrated on the more profitable West Indian market and left the Virginia trade to interlopers. Though this means of supply was intermittent and unreliable, by the end of the century there were probably 8,000 to 10,000 blacks in a population of about 75,000. The heaviest concentrations were on the Northern Neck and the lower peninsula between the James and York rivers. Cancellation of the monopoly of the Royal African Company in 1698 coincided with Virginia's final commitment to slave labor and unleashed private enterprise to meet the demand. A decade later, acting governor Edmund Jenings reported that practically no white servants had been brought in for several years. Just under 45,000 slaves were imported in the next half-century, by the end of which the black population stood at more than 100,000 in a total of about 250,000.

The introduction of slavery fitted the search for efficiency. The greater initial charge for slaves meant that fewer planters by about half could afford them than had owned servants a generation before. On the other hand, slavery increased productivity. Earlier in the century the predominance of white males meant a greater number of productive workers in the population than would otherwise have been the case. But as a native-born population developed and the sex ratio declined, the number of productive workers fell, since white women did not normally work in the fields. Slave women did, however, and children could be put to useful tasks as well. In fact, the larger the investment in slaves the safer, for the dangers of loss through death or lowered productivity on the part of the young, the old, and the ill could be more readily absorbed. Like the drive for land and the advantage gained by shipping and marketing in quantity, slavery facilitated the rise of giant, family-owned commercial farms, the great plantations of the eighteenth century. After the hectic pace of development earlier in the century, for a generation after 1680 the tobacco industry was settling down. The pressure was to obtain the greatest possible share of a more slowly expanding market; and in this objective a few were patently successful.

* * *

For the average white Virginian, prospects by 1700 were fading. He still was typically a small farmer, but he may not have owned his land. The only complete data on tenancy in the seventeenth century are from Surry County, in the poorer region south of the James River. There about 40 percent of the householders were tenants. Scattered evidence elsewhere suggests that the figure is not out of line. In Maryland the number of lifelong tenants jumped from about 10 percent of house-holders just after mid-century to about 30 percent at the end. Not all tenants were poor, of course. Some in the older counties along the northern bank of the James, where it had become difficult for even those with capital to find land to buy, were said to own more servants than the landlords themselves. But for the average farm in Virginia, the evidence, again fragmentary, is of a decline in the number of workers, and hence productive capacity, throughout the last quarter of the century. Older and more settled counties no longer had room for more than a small fraction of their servants once their terms were over. Although opportunities to obtain land were still greater in Virginia than in England, prospective farmers, if they remained in the East, had to look to less fertile areas farther from the easy transportation of the Tidewater rivers. Or, as a royal official informed London, they had to "goe to the Utmost bounds of the Colony . . . exposed to danger, & often times . . . Warr with the Indians." Meanwhile, in one of the richest counties, Middlesex, the bottom third of the population by 1700 owned less than 2 percent of the personal wealth, the middle three-fifths of the populace owned around a third, and 8 percent at the top, the remaining nearly two-thirds. Public expenditures for welfare in that county grew sevenfold after mid-century.

Life was hard in turn-of-the-century Virginia. The staggering death rates of the early years had receded, although from a modern perspective the effect of the decline on individual lives was infinitesi-mal. New arrivals continued to suffer heavily (one estimate is that as many as half still died soon after they landed), but the number of native-born in the white population was increasing. Birthrates were rising as the proportion of men and women became more nearly equal, and without indentures to serve, natives could marry earlier. By the

1680s and 1690s the white population was reproducing itself naturally—interestingly, just as the immigration of servants tapered off.
Yet, as everywhere in that day, childhood, especially the first three
years, remained a most exposed and dangerous time. Those who
survived to age twenty could expect to live into their forties. At
thirty-six, William Fitzhugh considered himself in his "declining
age." The effect of such demographics on family life was profound. Few
knew their grandparents; most children by their majority had lost at
least one parent, and around a third were orphans. Surviving spouses
normally remarried quickly, often as many times as death intervened.
Throughout the seventeenth century, a recent study has observed,
"From the standpoint of children, parents were ephemeral."

Most people at the end of the century still lived in quarters that were
incredibly crowded by modern standards. A recent survey of
seventeenth-century Maryland inventories suggests that about a fifth of
the families lived in one room; a third in two or fewer; and another
third in three. The average size of families in each category was four or
five. Less comprehensive studies indicate that the situation was about
the same in Virginia. Contemporaries distinguished between an
"English framed house" and "an ordinary Virginia house." The former,
if not of brick, had a brick or stone foundation and intricately
constructed members that required much skill in joinery to erect. The
latter had thinner walls, which often depended on clapboards for
structural strength, and a roof fixed atop the front and rear exterior
walls rather than joined to their top member or plate. The lighter
construction had the advantage of speed in erection, lower cost, and
thus flexibility on a rapidly expanding frontier. But it had disadvan-
tages, as one contemporary noted when he explained why Virginians
tended to expand their houses by building more rooms at ground level
rather than adding upper stories. For one reason, there was ample land,
"and now and then they are visited by high Winds, which wou'd
incommode a towering Fabrick."

An ordinary Virginia house was "earth-fast," as architects term it,
built on wooden posts or sills set in the ground. Some of the floors were
earthen; some, wooden. Clapboard for siding won out over wattle and
daub as in England because there was more wood, but often the boards
were not sealed against the wind. For the same reason roofs were
shingled, despite the cost in nails, rather than made of thatch. The

latter was difficult to obtain in the Chesapeake area, where straw-producing crops were less often grown. Few knew how to apply it, anyway. Window coverings were wooden shutters or oiled paper, with glass appearing later in the century. Chimneys were usually wattle and daub, although a trend among wealthier builders toward brick emerged later.

Most family activities—cooking, eating, sleeping—occurred in the room with the fireplace, called the "hall." Additional rooms were normally built on the side away from the fireplace rather than clustered around a central chimney, as they were in colder climates where the need to conserve heat outweighed the greater risk of fire. In Virginia additional fireplaces might eventually be built on other external walls.

Most ordinary Virginia houses were not substantial. William Fitzhugh figured that seven years was about as long as one could expect them to remain in good condition; a 1684 builder's manual optimistically promised ten or so. To be kept standing they had to be constantly repaired; one glebe dwelling, among the more solid structures of the time, was twice extensively rebuilt and three times replaced in eighty years, about one major overhaul every thirteen years. But to put this fact in perspective, ordinary Virginia houses were for the most part lower-class or middling farm dwellings, and in England, from which Virginians brought their architectural ideas, no cottage authenticated as having been built before 1700 survives.

The Maryland survey also shows that house furnishings were extraordinarily sparse. Among the poor, the master and mistress of the house might have a bed frame, but others generally had only blankets and rush-filled mattresses which they spread where they could. A table and chests for storage completed most lists; seldom were there chairs. Most homes had an iron pot and sometimes a skillet for cooking; pewterware but hardly any spoons (possibly shells served the purpose); more pressing irons than soap and tubs (clothes perhaps were boiled); and only occasionally a chamber pot (there was, after all, the great outdoors). More chamber pots, however, have been found in archaeological digs than were listed in relevant court records.

Forks were not generally used on any level of society until the eighteenth century. At mealtimes all ate solid foods with their fingers from a single dish or trencher on the table and drank from a large common vessel. Because of the use of fingers for eating, napkins were one of the first niceties that more prosperous planters allowed themselves when they could. Food generally was cooked together in a single pot, producing a "mess" or porridge that was the daily menu for most classes. The basic ingredient was field corn, as it is known today, which was boiled with beans, peas, and perhaps meat to make "hommony"; sweet corn of the type used for the table today is a later innovation. A corn bread frequently described as "heavy" was standard fare because wheat was more difficult to cultivate and more expensive. Since there were relatively few grist mills in the Tidewater, corn was often ground with a mortar and pestle, a long, tedious, arm-exhausting task. Hand mills, though expensive, were another luxury the better off allowed themselves when possible. The farther up the social scale the more often beef, pork, mutton, venison, or fowl might be at the table along with rum or wine in place of basic cider. For most, the monotonous diet was relieved only on birthdays, holidays, and other special occasions.

*   *   *

With few exceptions people seem to have used whatever wealth they acquired to improve the quality of living by obtaining more of the same kind of artifacts than by adopting a wholly new, and elegant, lifestyle. There were too many rungs in the economic ladder yet to climb for even those judged prosperous by standards of the day to think of more than one acquisition at a time. In the Maryland survey, for example, most seem to have given top priority to providing the master and mistress of the house with a feather or flock bed in place of the mattress of rushes and perhaps bedsteads for some of the others sleeping on the floor. Next, the effort seems to have been to enlarge the quarters by adding a room to which activities such as cooking, with its odors, might be consigned. Then there might be space in the hall for other furnishings such as chairs, which only about half the people had. Middling and wealthier planters moved more and more service areas outside the home to avoid the heat in summer, the danger of fire, and always the odors. With the acquisition of large numbers of laborers, especially slaves, there was also a wish to segregate the family's space as much as possible, whereas previously a few servants might have been accommodated within. The effect was misleading to outsiders, who sometimes wondered that the wealthiest homes appeared so small, not realizing that the "village," as one traveler called the cluster outside a dwelling, contained four or five more rooms that elsewhere might have been attached to the main edifice.

However many dependencies wealthier families may have had around their homes, all structures, owned by rich and poor alike, were more often than not essentially the same in construction. Archaeological evidence reveals little interest in adopting more substantial methods even when the resources were at hand. One result of insubstantial building is that only five structures from seventeenth-century Virginia have survived. All are brick: the Adam Thoroughgood house in Princess Anne County, the Warburton house in James City County, Foster's Castle in New Kent County, Fairfield in Gloucester County, and Bacon's Castle in Surry County. Originally other brick structures existed, too, but they have fallen prey to time: Governor Berkeley's Green Spring, for example, which survived long enough into the nineteenth century for the architect Benjamin Latrobe to sketch it. But the underground remains of what did not survive show that, while some middle- and upper-class house-builders experimented with brick, more simply preferred larger versions of what ordinary farmers had.

Virginians could have built in brick in the seventeenth century as well as in the eighteenth. The occasional brick structure and the advent of brick chimneys show an appreciation of the value of the material, and the cost differential between it and wood seems not to have been a major factor. The absence of interest may have stemmed from a lack of familiarity and skill. Brick was not common until late in the next century in rural English construction, where Virginians found their models. Mason's tools rarely turn up in Chesapeake inventories; and in 1687 when William Fitzhugh wrote out instructions for a friend on how to build a mansion, the first step he advised was "to get a Carpenter & Bricklayer Servants, & send them in here to serve 4 or five years." Fitzhugh thought that his friend could get "a substantial good house, at least, if not brick walls & well plaister'd," but he recommended against trying to build "either a great, or English framed house" as he had apparently done himself, "for labour is so intolerably dear & workmen so idle & negligent." Despite every effort at economy, he wrote, his own dwelling cost 300,000 pounds of tobacco (between

£1,200 and £1,300) before he was through—a third more than it would cost in London "notwithstanding we have timber for nothing." He warned of the heavy debts that could befall even those, like his friend's brother, who built a "Shell, of a house without Chimneys or partition, & not one tittle of workmanship about it more than a Tobacco house."

The design that Fitzhugh projected, should his friend ignore his warnings, boasted no esthetic pretensions; it was no conscious statement of an architectural school or style. Rather, he conceived of finer homes such as his friend sought to build as sturdier, more commodious, more luxurious versions of the average dwelling that most of his contemporaries knew. Of his own seat, which he had constructed over a decade, he wrote with obvious pride of accomplishment that it had "13 Rooms . . . four of the best of them hung [with tapestries], nine of them plentifully furnished with all things necessary & convenient . . . well furnished with brick Chimneys, four good Cellers, a Dairy, Dovecote, Stable, Barn, Hen house Kitchen & all other conveniencys . . . a large Orchard of about 2500 Apple trees . . . well fenced . . . a Garden a hundred foot square with a good Stock of Cattle hogs horses, Mares sheep &c, & necessary servants." Envisioning building as a cumulative process, much as he and others had acquired additional amenities within the home to ease the burden of life, he advised his friend to be judicious in selecting the pieces to put together initially.

Given these strictures from one of the most successful Virginians, it is not surprising that the general attitude toward housing at the time was one of indifference and resignation, of building and rebuilding as needed rather than attempting to end the process once and for all with a single major infusion of capital. The economy was in the doldrums, and only recently had Virginia's demography altered sufficiently to warrant concern about the ability of structures to survive beyond a decade or about establishing dynastic legacies. Fitzhugh and his class were newly self-made men. They had accumulated their fortunes by excelling in a stagnant market, a task they accomplished by sinking as much capital as they could into control of land and labor and by concentrating their managerial prowess on wringing the maximum out of their resources. If they were only beginning to find time away from their business to enjoy their wealth, little wonder that others less successful had not yet been emancipated.

Fitzhugh's generation was transitional. For some, at least, the worst days, in which all that could be hoped for was to survive, were over, and these few could look to improving the quality of their lives. By the end of 1670s, Fitzhugh was well on his way to his fortune; and by the mid-1680s he was toying with the idea of returning with his wealth to England, as had become the custom among the sugar barons of the West Indies. Success allowed him, like others among his peers, to gratify his social pretensions: he ordered quantities of silverware and adopted a coat of arms (though he could not agree with his brother in England on the correct form). But he was well aware that many civilities were unavailable in Virginia at any price. "Society that is good & ingenious is very scarce, & seldom to be come at except in books." As a lawyer, he was one of the mid-century immigrants who found education as valuable an asset as specie or credit for advancing in a wilderness society, and he wanted his son to have the same cultural advantages as he had. Yet in Virginia, he lamented, "Good Education of Children is almost impossible." He considered Ireland or Scotland if he could not find an estate in England until he discovered that he could not transfer his investments without greater loss than he wished to sustain. Like Robert Beverley, William Byrd I, and Ralph Wormeley among his contemporaries, he sent his son back to study instead. For themselves, the fathers found "good and ingenious" society in books, accumulating libraries that became some of the finest in the colonies. For them, if they were to find intellectual pleasure in life, it would have to be in the New World. The first corner in the maturing of Virginia culture had been turned.

* * *

In the last decades of the seventeenth century and the first of the next, there was a deep concern among well-placed Virginians and some royal officials that, after almost a century of existence, Virginia had accomplished little and was wasting its enormous potential. Among imperial authorities this concern was mainly over missed financial opportunities. Although the colony already was one of the largest

William Fitzhugh (1651–1701) was among those who became leaders of the colony in the last half of the seventeenth century and founded family dynasties. Like many others in the group he was an immigrant, arriving in the colony in 1673. Copied in 1751 by John Hesselius from a lost original and owned by the Virginia Historical Society. Reproduced by permission of the Society.

sources of royal revenue, the untold possibilities that its vast resources offered were enough to make any financial officer salivate. Among Virginians, on the other hand, concern over the colony's underdevelopment stirred interest in a variety of innovations. Economically, any exploitation of resources as yet untapped held out hope in a depressed period. Culturally, there was embarrassment among some of the newly made elite and a sense of inferiority because, despite Virginia's obvious wealth, the colony remained a rough, primitive, backward society. Among both royal officials and colonists, many agreed that government intervention at some level was the only feasible mechanism of change. What is surprising is that, among both, the objective was often to reverse the trend toward economic concentration in the colony and to redirect development toward a yeoman-urban society.

The debate runs like a thread through the politics of these decades, appearing above the warp and woof of other issues in the recurring controversy over establishing towns in Virginia. The Crown had originated the discussion: beginning with Culpeper it routinely instructed its governors to seek legislation establishing "towns on every river, and especially one at least on every great river," through which all imports and exports were to flow. Siphoning all trade through a few points, it was believed, would greatly facilitate collecting customs and enforcing the Navigation Acts. But some Virginians thought that towns could have other advantages less congenial to imperial interests—developing manufactures, for example. It was because of these add-ons that the bill that Robert Beverley introduced in 1680 at Culpeper's request was disallowed when it reached London. Beverley tried again in 1684 with the same result. After his death, others made another attempt in 1691 and a final effort in 1706, with no different outcome.

In the legislation encouraging the founding of towns, in a number of government reports, and in several publications by Virginia residents between the 1680s and the 1720s, the same theme appears: the rise of the plantation economy was regretted. Only occasionally did writers acknowledge that profit in a volatile international staple market came from the economies of concentration. Robert Beverley vaguely alluded in his original bill to "laying ready all tobaccoes for exportation" in the towns he proposed in order to offset the "continued lownes of the price." Otherwise the campaign for towns suggested urban, artisan, middle-class values at variance with trends in Chesapeake society. Since all plans called for some degree of government coercion or subvention, most advocates realized that towns were not natural to the colony. Virginians would not give up exclusively planting tobacco, Beverley warned in his preamble, "if the same be not by all prudentiall meanes and wayes prevented." The implication repeatedly was that socially and culturally Virginia had to be made right; sometimes (though not by Beverley) specific reference was made to the superior virtues of town-centered New England.

Politically the rise of a plantation system, in the opinion of royal officials, explained the power of the Virginia elite which, ever since Bacon's Rebellion, they had been trying to tame. Two of the most vigorous exponents of this premise were the longtime commissioner of customs in America, Edward Randolph, and his successor after 1703, Colonel Robert Quary. From the two emanated a steady stream of reports to London during the 1690s and the first years of the eighteenth century recounting the myriad violations of the Navigation Acts and other abuses they had uncovered. In 1692 Randolph reiterated that towns at "2 or 3 places in every trading River" would expedite regulation. He blamed the slow population growth in Virginia on abuses of the headright system, which he said allowed a relatively small number of individuals—"on every River . . . ten to thirty," Quary later estimated—to accumulate vast tracts of land and hold them off the market for speculation. Potential settlers heard that little land was left for them if they came, Randolph contended. White immigration fell off, and Virginia failed to expand to the utmost.

Worse, Randolph continued, the king was defrauded of his quitrents. While most Virginia leaders conceded the monarch's right to collect annually 2s. on every hundred acres as a vestige of medieval feudal dues, they firmly maintained that the rents should be collected only on productive lands and not on those held for future tobacco fields or speculation. Clerks allowed planters, in effect, to take options on lands by not registering titles on which rents would become due until the claimants were ready to exploit the tracts. To curtail such abuses, Randolph called for, first, a vigorous campaign either to collect arrears or to recover the lands, and then, a limitation of future grants to 500 acres per individual. In his view, the Crown would be better served by a large number of moderately sized tobacco farms than by a few giant plantations. Eight years later Quary underscored the political danger of the latter when he pointed out that all leaders of the opposition to governors over the past quarter-century had been great landowners. Continuation of their arrogance and pretensions, he warned, "if not timely prevented, will have a very ill consequence."

Another report in 1697, written this time by colonists, was equally critical of the trend toward concentration, which it blamed for the general backwardness of the colony. Henry Hartwell, a prosperous lawyer and twenty-odd-year member of the Council in Virginia, James Blair, commissary of the bishop of London in the colony, and Edward Chilton, until recently attorney general, were all in London on separate missions when the Board of Trade called on them to submit a joint account of the state of the Old Dominion. "The first and eldest of the English *Plantations* in America," they wrote, Virginia "looks all like a wild Desart." Like the customs commissioners, the three authors laid the cause to abuses of the headright system, at which they charged governors, councillors, and burgesses alike connived. The wealthy monopolized the land, white immigration declined, and Virginia failed to measure up to expectations, they concluded.

What was different from Randolph's and Quary's reports was the embarrassment that the three Virginians felt at cataloguing the shortcomings of their colony. They were mortified to report that the primitive hoe remained the principal agricultural implement in Virginia. So great was the rage for tobacco, they observed, that trees were merely girdled and the crop planted among the stumps, which prevented the use of plows and the introduction of cereal grains that are sown broadcast. Only corn could be hoed like tobacco. Because the latter required work only in the summer, they stated, the people "acquire great Habits of Idleness all the rest of the Year." Unacquainted with any craft, Virginians had to import their manufactured goods. In contrast to New England, which the authors compared most favorably, Virginia lacked towns and their amenities, including "Trades and Manufactures . . . well educated Children . . . [and] industrious and thriving people." The three colonists concurred with royal officials that change had to come from London because most of the General Assembly, "having never seen a Town . . . cannot therefore imagine the Benefit of it."

The spate of criticism from the generation that spanned 1700 continued eight years later when Beverley's son and namesake published *The History and Present State of Virginia, in Four Parts* (1705). He, too, lamented that the form of settlement in the colony was "Country Seats, without Towns." Despite ample resources, he reported, "to the Eternal Reproach of their Laziness," Virginians bought all their manufactured goods from Great Britain. Like Hartwell, Blair, and Chilton, Beverley was "asham'd to publish this slothful Indolence of my Countrymen, but that I hope it will rouse them out of their Lethargy." Unlike the three coauthors, however, young Beverley did not denounce the Virginia method of land distribution. His family was too much a beneficiary of the pattern of large landholding that resulted.

Almost twenty more years passed before the tone of such publications began to change, ever so slightly. Beverley's second edition in 1722 omitted the worst diatribes against every governor since Berkeley for opposing economic diversification and thwarting attempts to establish towns. At the same time, Beverley retained arguments in the revised text that were calculated to reverse the decline of white immigration and increase the chance of a yeoman society. Virginia was "the best poor Man's Country in the World," he boasted, where no one was ever reduced to begging. The terrible mortality of the early years was over, he told his readers, because of the introduction of quinine. Furthermore, he confidently attested, the large number of slaves did not depress the conditions of white labor, for "Slaves are not worked so hard, nor so many Hours in a Day, as the Husbandman, and Day-Labourers in *England*."

Two years later an English parson who had recently decided to settle permanently in the colony published his version of *The Present State of Virginia* (1724) to bring earlier accounts up to date. The Reverend Hugh Jones was decidedly more upbeat in his evaluation than his predecessors. For one thing, he was more appreciative of the natural environment; "The whole country is a perfect forest, except where the woods are cleared for plantations." He repeated Beverley's assurances regarding quinine and reiterated that Virginia slaves were better off than "Wood-cutters in England." Of the absence of a work ethic, which others found so dismaying, he was more tolerant and perhaps even a little admiring: "The common planters leading easy lives don't much admire labour, or any manly exercise, except horse-racing, nor diversion, except cock-fighting." But "No people can entertain their friends with better cheer and welcome."

Jones had a better appreciation of the economic forces at work in Virginia than earlier writers had. Personally he would have preferred to see the introduction of cereal crops and production of naval stores, iron, and silk, but the truth was, he wrote, that Virginians were not attracted to manufacturing "because of the . . . uncertain prospect of gain." He sensed that the model of New England–style towns was not right for the colony. Actually, he pointed out, a Virginia plantation was "a little market," serving a function that villages might provide elsewhere. Indeed, if the results of the survey of Maryland inventories hold for Virginia, whatever crafts were developing were at the center of the managerial revolution on the plantations. Inventories from middling and lower classes disclose few craft tools at all. The capital-less and the less enterprising, when they had the money to buy, were the ones left with little recourse for the most mundane items except the British market.

By the end of the first quarter of the new century, the economic and social pattern of Virginia's future was fixed. Gradually colonists began to perceive that the longing for cultural identity would be fulfilled in the elegance of "Country Seats" rather than the artisanship of bustling towns. Nonetheless, ideas died slowly. Three years after Jones's book appeared, someone, most likely James Blair himself, had the old Hartwell, Blair, and Chilton report to the Board of Trade published with a little updating under the title *The Present State of Virginia, and the College* (1727). Blair, who was often at odds with Jones politically, may not have wished the parson to have the last word.

7

THE ERA OF THE COUNCIL

Virginia's plantation society took shape during the generation that overlapped 1700. Economically, the system sought the efficiency and savings of concentration. Socially, it gave rise to a planter elite, and politically that elite found expression in the Council. The twelve-member board was its command post in the running battle with Crown officials who would have checked the rising power of the tobacco establishment if they could. The Council was a habitat of powerful personalities. The fierce competitiveness and individualism its members exhibited reflected qualities necessary for success in the turn-of-the-century economic environment. With only slight exaggeration Colonel Quary observed that councillors regarded themselves "almost . . . upon equal Terms with . . . the House of Lords."

Two issues were the focus of the political struggle with the Crown. One was land policy. Governors had instructions to change it in order to cultivate a class of middling farmers. But in the face of threatened French encroachment, large patents often seemed an easier way to encourage settlement, even to royal executives. The other matter, which kept cropping up to trip unwary governors, was the founding of a college. No one was really opposed to the idea, least of all royal representatives, but some Virginians were more intent on it than others and expected the same degree of commitment from everyone. The cause of the college made the political career of the Reverend James Blair, the dominant personality of the age. He was the president of the college and the most forceful leader of the Church of England in Virginia. Driving relentlessly for the advancement of both institutions, but especially of the college, he brought down three executives who appeared to him to stand in his way.

*   *   *

Blair's political strength was a product of the Glorious Revolution in England. He was a minister of the Church of Scotland who had been deprived of his parish in the early 1680s for refusing to endorse the Catholic succession to the Scottish and English thrones. Finding employment in London in the Rolls Office, which its chaplain Gilbert Burnet turned into a refuge for persecuted Protestant clergy, Blair was eventually recruited by Henry Compton, bishop of London, to serve in Virginia. Since the founding of Jamestown, Compton's predecessors had been charged with oversight of the church in the colonies, but he was the most active in fulfilling the responsibility. Blair could not have been more fortunate in his selection of sponsors. Burnet, a leading opponent of papist influence, later became bishop of Salisbury, and Compton, beloved tutor of James II's Protestant daughters, Mary and Anne, was one of the primary instigators of the decision to replace James with Mary and her husband, William. Arriving in Virginia in 1685, Blair obtained a frontier parish at Varina in Henrico County, and two years later married Sarah, daughter of the powerful Harrison family of Surry County. With the success of the revolution in England, Compton was for the moment at the highest level of the new regime; and in December 1689 he named his protégé as his commissary, or personal representative, in Virginia.

At the time of Blair's arrival in the colony, the church in Virginia had only half enough ministers for its needs, and the living conditions offered by scattered parishes in the colonial wilds did not attract the best candidates. Immediately upon receipt of his appointment as commissary, Blair called a convocation of the clergy in July 1690 to institute reform. Though the extent of the bishop of London's own power in America was unclear, Blair was intent on stretching to the maximum the authority in his commission to exercise whatever power "pertains and belongs, or ought to pertain and belong, to the office of Commissary." The alacrity with which he plunged into the cause of reform is indicative of the passion that ruled his career for over half a century in Virginia: a determination to establish his own authority and through it that of the church at a level that no bishop enjoyed in England.

The decree that emanated from the July 1690 convocation could hardly have excited most of the clergy or churchgoers of the day. It directed the creation of ecclesiastical courts to discipline clerics and laity alike. It also appeared indifferent to current opinion in the mother country by implying suppression of dissenters, at least of Quakers and more "enthusiastic" sects. The year before, Parliament had enacted the Toleration Act. Blair was behind the Council's resolution in July 1690 calling for stricter enforcement of ecclesiastical laws and the governor's announcement of a county-by-county visitation by the commissary the next spring. Ecclesiastical courts, however, had been dreaded by Englishmen since Tudor and early Stuart times, and the first House of Burgesses under the new monarchs William and Mary, which met in April 1691, ignored the proposal. Although the commissary continued to argue that moral offenses should be under his jurisdiction rather than the county courts, he never again mustered the level of support for the idea that briefly developed during his first months in office.

* * *

Blair was more successful with his other idea, the founding of a college. It caught the imagination of most leaders of the day, for it promised a remedy for one of the major shortcomings that so many contemporaries found in Virginia. "Considering the bad Circumstances of the Country for want of Education for their Youth" and aware that there "should be a Seminary for the breeding of good Ministers," sponsors led by Blair had presented a formal proposal in 1689. "If Towns go forwards," the commissary jotted down in his notes, a college would make possible "that a Schoolmaster be maintained in every town at least for teaching English & writing." But no official action had been feasible until the post-revolutionary government was settled. Then, at the April 1691 Assembly, the plan received unanimous endorsement and offers of support and service from every shade of political opinion.

The time was propitious. The new regime in England, desirous of consolidating support, was proving unusually conciliatory on colonial matters. Philip Ludwell, whom the Assembly had sent to England to

The Rev. James Blair (1655–1743), the founder of the College of William and Mary, Commissary of the Bishop of London, Rector of Bruton Parish Church, a member of the Council of the colony—all in all, one of the most powerful men in early eighteenth-century Virginia. This portrait, in the possession of the College, probably by Charles Bridges, was painted when Blair was nearly 80. Colonial Williamsburg photograph.

present the colony's grievances against Governor Effingham, reported that the new king and the Lords of Trade were responding more sympathetically than could have been expected under James II. The lords tried to compromise the dispute with Effingham. They upheld him on one issue, declaring that a law that he wanted was in force but strongly recommending that it be repealed because it was so unpopular in the colony. On another matter, they rescinded fees that the governor had imposed for use of the colony's seal and for recording surveys. Then Effingham, who had come to England to defend himself, decided to remain in the mother country for his health. The lords left him the title of governor and dispatched a deputy, Francis Nicholson, in his stead.

Virginians applauded the choice of successor. Although coming from service as lieutenant governor under James II's much-despised Dominion of New England, Nicholson won wide approval at his new post during his first, relatively short, administration from May 1690 to February 1692. He quickly developed friendly relations with Virginia leaders, generously entertaining them in his rented accommodations in Jamestown or in local taverns because the governor's house had not yet been rebuilt. He made common cause with Blair, whose commission as commissary he brought across the ocean. Devoted himself throughout his career to the Anglican church and a special patron of its educational endeavors, he readily became an enthusiastic supporter of the college. Immediately upon his arrival he toured the frontiers for a personal assessment of the Indian threat that had seemed so fearful while the revolution in England was in progress. He reorganized the militia and negotiated an understanding on cooperative defense with Maryland. Convening his first Assembly on April 16, 1691, he offered prizes in conjunction with its meeting for "Riding, Running, Shooting, Wrestling, and Broadsword" in the hope of inaugurating a regular series of "Olympic Games." Nicholson was acting cynically, however. Simultaneously he was confiding to the Lords of Trade that, with the aftermath of the revolution still unsettled in many colonies, he thought it wise to avoid antagonizing "the Mob" in Virginia.

Blair sailed for England in June 1691 to secure a charter for the college. When he arrived in the mother country in early fall, he found his old acquaintances at the Rolls Office in an ideal position to assist him in his quest. The lobby he put together was of formidable ecclesiastical and political power. Besides Compton and Burnet, now bishop of Salisbury, the group included William Lloyd, bishop of St. Asaph; the renowned preacher Edward Stillingfleet, bishop of Worcester; and most important, John Tillotson, the new archbishop of Canterbury. In addition, Blair called for aid from Governor Effingham and the great tobacco merchant, Micajah Perry, who often acted as the colony's agent and who agreed on this occasion to serve as the college's treasurer in England. Through Tillotson in particular, Blair won the enthusiastic support of Queen Mary and, through her, the positive personal commitment of the king.

The process nonetheless took eighteen months before the royal charter was finally issued on February 8, 1693. Since William's accession the country had been at war with France, with which the new king had already been contending in his former role as prince of Orange and stadtholder of Holland. Often the monarch and his chief advisers lacked the time to attend to other matters.

And complications arose. To complete the application Blair had to write back to Nicholson to have the legislature nominate a candidate for the presidency; he modestly hinted that he was available. The governor whisked the recommendation through the legislature. Some English officials also vigorously resisted William's pledge of nearly £2,000 from the royal quitrents in Virginia because more pressing, unforeseen demands could easily arise in wartime. Blair and his friends prevailed, and the college obtained the £2,000. It was also given the proceeds of the office of surveyor general in Virginia; a penny-a-pound levy on tobacco shipped from Maryland and Virginia anywhere in the empire outside the mother country; 10,000 acres of its choice on Pamunkey Neck in King William County; and 10,000 more south of Blackwater Swamp in Surry and Isle of Wight counties on the Southside. Blair sought private subscriptions, too. Among the gifts, for example, he and his patrons persuaded the executors of the estate of Robert Boyle, the world-famous chemist, to endow an Indian school at the college, which came to be known as The Brafferton after the manor in Yorkshire dedicated to the purpose. Blair and his supporters also intervened in what appeared to be an otherwise hopeless legal case to obtain a donation for the fund. On condition that £300 go to the college, they played on the king's personal liking for the institution to help three pirates who had been pardoned under an amnesty recover

The Sir Christopher Wren Building (restored) was the principal structure of the colonial College of William and Mary, housing classrooms, commons, chapel, and rooms for students and faculty. Colonial Williamsburg photograph.

stolen goods that the government had confiscated when they were captured. About £2,500 were also raised in Virginia for the college.

*   *   *

Meanwhile, in the colony, Nicholson's appointment brought a euphoric lull to Virginia politics. During the legislative session in the spring of 1691, the burgesses frequently invited conferences with the Council in advance of enacting legislation, and Nicholson was willing to overlook many of his instructions to let the legislators have their way. The cooperation resulted in, among other things, long-sought measures to encourage the production of hemp and flax in the colony and the creation of a new office of treasurer under the legislature to take charge of income raised by acts of the Assembly as distinct from royal revenues. When the burgesses revived a town plan calling for 20 ports as in the 1680 bill, the Council first insisted on only 12, then compromised on 20, with 5 restricted to retail trade and only 15 to be ports of entry. Though the Crown still objected to the number and to the encouragement of artisans that the bill provided, the governor approved the statute, leaving to the Privy Council the task of blocking the legislation.

By the time Blair returned to Virginia in the fall of 1693, the political situation in the colony had changed significantly. Nicholson had been transferred to Maryland, and his successor in Virginia was Sir Edmund Andros. The new appointee, like Nicholson, was a military man, an old imperial hand who had long been associated with the Crown's attempt since the Restoration to strengthen its control over the empire. He had served as governor in New York following its conquest from the Dutch and had been governor, and Nicholson's superior, in the Dominion of New England. Neither he nor Nicholson had made careers of pandering to local interests. But like Nicholson, Andros's experience during the overthrow of the Dominion—he had been imprisoned in Boston while Nicholson had to flee New York— left him cautious. He initially followed his predecessor's example of accommodation, equivocating at first on the question of ports, for example. Indeed, until the commissary arrived, Andros could report to London, seconded by Edward Randolph, who was passing through, that Virginia, in Randolph's words, wore "the face of peace."

Gradually tension built between Andros and the burgesses. First, there was the town act of 1691 which went into effect the month he arrived. Initially he did nothing about it, waiting for the royal bureaucracy to act. When no word arrived, he was forced to take a stand. As speculators began to buy land at the designated locations, smaller farmers, fearing the impending restrictions on their freedom to trade (often illegally), disrupted surveys, particularly in King and Queen County. Ship captains, unable to determine where to land, at planters' wharves or at the new sites, sailed on to Maryland. Ultimately, in the spring of 1693 Andros persuaded the Assembly to suspend implementation. Meanwhile, English tobacco merchants were organizing. Although they did not object to "Towns on a Modest Account," as Micajah Perry put it, the sites were not to give birth to manufacturing. On this mercantilistic policy the new regime had little quarrel with its predecessor, and once again the Privy Council vetoed the plan unless the number of towns was reduced and support for crafts eliminated. The Crown also demanded that the Assembly prohibit the exportation of bulk tobacco because it could be more easily smuggled than tobacco in hogsheads. When the burgesses refused both mandates, the governor dissolved the Assembly. Throughout the remainder of his administration Andros continued to push for a more narrowly defined statute on towns, but, although the Council occasionally would listen, the burgesses would not.

On other issues there was more room for maneuver. Andros avoided any attempt to reform the system of land distribution, as his instructions required, for fear of the outburst it would provoke, and in his campaign for revisions in the town act he allowed some encouragement of diversification. In 1693, as part of overall imperial strategy, he sent a £600 subsidy to New York, which royal authorities considered the principal American theater in the war with France. As usual, the burgesses objected to providing money out of provincial revenues for imperial defense in other colonies when funds from the quitrents were available. Nonetheless, they did agree to another £500 in 1695. Andros went along with the new office of treasurer until the burgesses tried to expend funds without the governor's warrant. Then he refused to submit the records or let them hold any more elections for the office. In the final year of his administration, when he was ill and under fire from several sides, another flare-up over the burgesses' refusal to enact the legislation his instructions demanded caused him to dissolve them twice.

*   *   *

Throughout the heightening confrontation, the sharpest burr for the governor was James Blair, for whom as always the central issue was the college. Friction between the two was probably unavoidable, if for no other reason than that Blair's brilliant tour de force in obtaining the charter established him as a rival arbiter of Virginia politics, a competing line of communication to high places in England. The governor could foresee the potential undermining of his authority in the Crown's decision to place Blair on the Council, as Nicholson had recommended but Andros had not. The commissary took his seat in the summer of 1694.

Although personalities provided color and volatility, the antagonism between the leaders had political roots that stretched back to England. Blair's success on behalf of the college raised questions of imperial policy, though that result was far from his intention. He was no supporter of excessive autonomy for a planter elite with whom he often quarrelled, and he had no aversion to royal intervention in the colony if it was for a purpose he approved. But appeals to royal authority were double-edged. While capitalizing on his Whig connections to obtain his charter, he crossed some in England who thought that in endowing the college William and Mary had gone too far. In particular, the secretary to the Lords of Trade, William Blathwayt, whose survival in office since the 1660s reflects the essential continuity of imperial policy despite internal conflict and revolution, saw a principle of long standing in danger—and Andros was his man. Since early in his career Blathwayt had striven to reserve royal quitrents in Virginia for contingencies that might arise anywhere in the American empire. He shortly persuaded William, for example, to commit an additional war subsidy to New York. But at the moment William had also given almost £2,000 to Virginia's new college, and Blair had inveigled Queen Mary to allot another £800 for clerical salaries.

Imperial officials were able to have the king postpone the latter grant for three years. One result certain to cause difficulty was that Blair did not receive a salary as commissary until 1695. William planted other seeds of trouble by decreeing that the funds should be used as the queen desired if it turned out that the governor and Council did not need them. From Blair's perspective, Andros did everything he could to ensure that there would be no surplus, though as a sign that the story had two sides, one of the expenditures to which Blair objected was the subsidy the king himself ordered for New York. (Much of the existing evidence about Andros's administration, it should be remembered, comes from the testimony of Blair and other opponents of the governor.)

Concerning the college, the real trouble was the depression brought on by the French war. Fewer than half the ships needed to move the tobacco crop to market were available because the navy could not furnish sufficient convoys. As a result, the penny-a-pound duty produced little. Quite likely the depression was also the main reason why little of the £2,500 privately pledged to the college materialized (only £500 by 1697). The incumbent surveyor general refused to give up his office, too, so nothing came from that source until he died in 1695.

Blair, however, blamed the governor. At first Andros had been most cooperative in locating the college at Middle Plantation, midway on the peninsula between the James and York rivers. He also helped enact an export duty on hides and furs for its endowment. But when squatters and speculators (one of the largest of whom was Ralph Wormeley at Pamunkey Neck) kept the college from realizing the benefit of the lands it received, Blair felt that Andros could have done more to oust them. The commissary complained that Andros and other great men set a bad example for the populace by not meeting their pledges to the college. Blair was especially angry with the governor for not supplying the bricks Andros had promised for the college building. Andros's defenders retorted that what really turned donors away was the fact that from 1694 on Blair took a salary as president from the collections even though only the grammar school was in session. Construction of the college building did not begin until 1695 and was not complete until 1700; and only then did a search for a faculty commence. Unquestionably the governor was less ardent in his support for the college than his predecessor, his dislike for whom, Blair observed, led him to avoid "everything that looks like an imitation of Governor Nicholson." To Andros's chagrin Nicholson had been appointed a college trustee and frequently returned from Maryland for meetings. On one visit Andros quarrelled with him and tried to arrest him for his insulting language—just to intimidate him from coming again, Blair averred. For his part, Blair did not help his cause by threatening to institute suits for the pledges and reputedly preaching that those who did not contribute "would be damned."

The explosion came in a Council meeting on April 19, 1695. Andros gave the members advance notice of a speech he planned for the House of Burgesses. He announced, among other things, the assistance for New York and a raise in pay for frontier rangers. Meanwhile, clerical salaries (which, being paid in tobacco, were actually declining because of falling prices) were to remain the same. According to the minutes, Blair responded with "severall Undecent reflections reiterated and asserted with passion," for which it was "the Unanimouse Opinion of the Council" that he ought to be expelled "till directions therin," that is, until they called him back. After the meeting, Blair added "some other reflections" about the governor. When the commissary, unrepentant, appeared at the next Council meeting on the 26th, the Council again expelled him, "Mr. Blair Not Shewing any reason for any his Unjust reflections nor so much as Extenuating the same." Because of the added "reflections," Andros at that point intervened to suspend Blair permanently from membership.

Blair remained off the Council for over a year, until he could appeal to his friends in England and obtain an order from the king restoring him in August 1696. But that same year Parliament enacted a law "for Preventing Frauds . . . in the Plantation Trade." Because, the act alleged, these frauds were "committed by Scotch Men and others," among the statute's provisions was one forbidding anyone to serve as an officer of a court who was not a native-born Englishman or colonist. On April 20, 1697, Blair himself raised the question of whether the statute applied to him, since the Council functioned as a court in Virginia; and his fellow members and the governor lost no time in excluding him again. The motive for their haste is not immediately apparent, for it had been known for some time that Blair was to leave for England within a few days. At the least it was poor strategy. Publicly the reason for Blair's trip was to lobby for increased clerical salaries and to set things right with the Boyle executors. News of the governor's purported attitude toward the college (he was alleged to have said, "Pish, it will come to nothing") had led the executors to delay the grant to the college for fear of wasting it. Privately Blair had corresponded with Nicholson about the possibility of having his old friend succeed Andros. Now, the commissary had an issue of abuse of power to press with his patrons.

*   *   *

To Blair's good fortune—or perhaps it was a knack—he was able to hitch his cause to a major affair of state. When he arrived in England that summer the government was in the midst of a complete revamping of the imperial administration. Since Charles II's reign, responsibility for the colonies had resided in a standing committee of the Privy Council (consisting in fact by the 1690s of the whole council) known as the Lords of Trade, of which Blathwayt was secretary and principal administrator. The French war had brought to the fore a basic weakness in the system; namely, that the lords, being privy councillors, were too often otherwise involved to afford the attention an expanding empire demanded. More to the point, Blathwayt, now secretary at war, was too often on the Continent with William, who directed the campaign in person. In the face of heavy losses to French marauders and an increase in piracy, the merchant community insisted that Parliament institute reform. At the same time, the surveyor general of customs, Edward Randolph, after a tour of the American colonies, presented a report documenting that the somewhat more relaxed administration since William's accession had led to frauds and abuses everywhere in the enforcement of the acts of trade.

The outcome was the creation of a new committee, the Lords Commissioners of Trade and Plantations, known for short as the Board of Trade. Its members were not to be on the Privy Council but to be advisory to it, and were for the most part administrative experts in imperial affairs and trade. Parliament also enacted a new Navigation Act, closing many of the loopholes that Randolph had uncovered. For continuity, Blathwayt moved from secretary to full membership on the new board, but a rival was also named, the philosopher John Locke, whose friend and associate Lord Somers was currently chief minister to William. Because Blathwayt continued to be diverted by his duties as war minister, Locke exercised a strong influence over the board in its initial years.

Once more, Blair's connections within the Whig coalition that overthrew James II were his avenue to success. Through them he met Locke, who he found had his own reasons for looking into the numerous complaints that Randolph, Blair, and others lodged against the government of Virginia. The larger issue was Locke's fundamental disagreement with Blathwayt over the proper means of administering the empire. Arguing essentially for government of laws not of men, he rejected Blathwayt's tried-and-true method of controlling the colonies by dispensing patronage to bind local politicians to the Crown's interest. Blathwayt was, as one biographer has called him, the "imperial fixer" par excellence.

In contrast, as befit the philosopher of the Glorious Revolution, Locke was wary of concentration of power in the executive, preferring instead a system of divided, and hence restricted, authority. Yet it should be noted that he yielded nothing to Blathwayt in his determination to maintain and advance the mother country's dominance over the empire. He apparently expected that wise and just application of mercantilistic policy would be perceived by both sides as mutually beneficial and would be no less effective than Blathwayt's influence peddling in assuring the central government's control of imperial trade. "The flourishing of the plantations under their due & just regulations being that which I do & shall always aim at whilst I have the honour to sit at the board," was the way he explained his administrative goal to Blair in response to a letter thanking him for his assistance. Locke's stand reveals the consistency of imperial policy from Cromwell through Charles and James to William. After a brief let-up to establish the revolution, William's rule in colonial matters differed from his predecessors' only in seeking, through the Navigation Act of 1696, to become more effective. The split between Locke and Blathwayt, however, was all Blair needed to undo Edmund Andros.

*   *   *

The first case to come before the new board involved an appeal of two creditors from a Virginia law that exempted councillors from prosecution for debt. It afforded an opportunity to open the whole question of abuses in the colony's government as Randolph's report alleged. Locke closely interrogated Blair for almost a week toward the end of the summer of 1697, and on the basis of the interviews composed a set of questions that the board officially put to the commissary and to two other Virginia officials, Edward Chilton and Henry Hartwell, who happened to be in London. The written answers were highly detrimental to Andros. The three Virginians corroborated Randolph's allegations that every governor since Bacon's Rebellion had connived at a land system that kept vast reaches off the market and retarded the development of the colony. The scramble for grants had corrupted the Council, and sometimes the burgesses, the three asserted, and had permitted each governor since Berkeley to indulge in "arbitrary Proceedings."

The board's own concern was naturally more imperial than colonial, although, as Locke maintained, either interest suffered from poor rule. "In the administration of the Government of Virginia," the majority report found, "all things are made so entirely dependent on the Governor's single will and pleasure that, if there happen to be an ill man in that post, it cannot reasonably be expected that any person, and least of all Councillors, should oppose him or advise the King of his miscarriages." The stark contrast, too, between the optimism of Randolph's report in 1693 and his indictment in 1696 could hardly have helped Andros. Whatever the reason, the imperial interest was plainly not faring well under the governor's administration. Having reached its conclusion, however, the board took no further action during the winter of 1697–1698 because Locke, an asthmatic, always fled the oppressive atmosphere and smoke of London during the colder months.

In that interim, Blair completed the destruction of his rival at a hearing before the archbishop of Canterbury and the bishop of London at the latter's residence, Lambeth Palace, in December. The issue was Blair's castigation of Andros and his minions as "no real friends to the Clergy." Blair's brother-in-law, Benjamin Harrison III, was there to support him, while Blathwayt's cousin, John Povey, and William Byrd II, who just concluded his law studies at Middle Temple, defended Andros. Byrd struggled to show that it was the issue of Blair's salary before college classes were in session that discouraged collections. He pointed to the fact that Andros had personally pledged support for the

college. (Byrd even promised to see that the bricks were delivered.) As
for clerical salaries, Andros had initially not implemented his instructions to increase them because of the difficult economic times, but
eventually (and reluctantly, though Byrd did not say that) had raised
them to 16,000 pounds of tobacco a year. The defense, however, was
overwhelmed by the massively detailed complaints that Blair and
Harrison presented. In March Andros, who was elderly, ill, and
demoralized, and had recently been injured in a fall from his horse,
resigned. Shortly, Blair joyfully reported, the board named in the
former governor's stead, the "person, whom of all others" Andros "had
the least kindness for": Francis Nicholson.

*   *   *

When Locke returned to London in the summer of 1698, the struggle
with Blathwayt was resumed over the instructions to be issued to
Nicholson. Locke intended to base them on his report on Virginia the
year before, while Blathwayt vowed that "I should think it a sin while
I take the king's money to agree to it." For the most part Locke had his
way in the final draft adopted in September 1698. The governor's
ability to build a following in the Council was sharply curtailed.
Implicitly the restriction meant new freedom for the Council, but it
also left that body a less likely mechanism for enhancing members'
fortunes. A governor always had to report his reasons for suspending a
councillor to London. Now he had to send the defendant's replies to his
charges as well—a requirement simultaneously imposed on Maryland
and on five other colonies soon afterward.

At the same time, the Council's freedom of debate was somewhat
broadened. Whereas councillors had formerly been accorded that
freedom "in all affairs of public concern that may be debated in the
council," the wording now read in "all things to be debated of in
council." Councillors became subject to prosecution for debt and could
not serve as customs collectors or naval officers (the latter, despite the
title, were civilian officials keeping track of the colony's imports and
exports), in order not to be in the position of auditing their own
accounts in Council, as had been the case. Tobacco received by
collectors had to be sold at auction to avoid any suspicion, which had
been common before, that councillors bought it below market price. In

addition, along with their usual oaths as councillors, members had to take one more as judges binding themselves to be impartial to all.

The constraints on the governor's use of patronage and the built-in certainty of antagonism between him and the Council as he began to put the reforms into effect did not augur well for imperial authority in the colony. Yet the board's clear anticipation in the instructions was that the changes would markedly improve the care of England's interests in Virginia. As Randolph recommended, there were to be surveys of landholdings in each county to facilitate collection of arrears in the payment of quitrents, with a special report on the legal basis of grants over 20,000 acres. A new scheme for land distribution designed to prevent large holdings for speculation was to be instituted, and there was to be a general revision of the laws.

Although Blair obtained a judgment that the recent Navigation Act did not exclude Scots from the Council, he was not reinstated at the change of administration. The reason was that Daniel Parke, who had been feuding with Blair and Nicholson for several years and at one point had physically pulled Sarah Harrison Blair from a pew in Bruton Parish Church to which he claimed she had no right, testified that Blair and his friend Benjamin Harrison were smuggling tobacco to Scotland. (The same day Harrison testified that it was Andros and the secretary of the colony Ralph Wormeley who were in league with smugglers. They probably all were.) Parke also pointed out that the new policy to avoid conflicts of interest in auditing tax collections would be violated by the commissary's appointment, because as president of the college he received the proceeds of the two-penny-a-pound levy on tobacco. The Board of Trade took the matter under advisement. Blair had to wait.

* * *

Once again, the incoming administration enjoyed a honeymoon. Blair returned home with the new governor's credentials in time for Nicholson to assume office early in December 1698. The commissary looked forward to "Halcyon days" and over a year later wrote to the archbishop of Canterbury of "this Country enjoying Great peace & quietness." At the same time the governor was impressing on that prelate the need to restore Blair to the Council as soon as possible. For both leaders the first order of business was to pick up the projects on which they had previously cooperated where they had left them nearly a decade before.

Probably because of the short-term boom in tobacco prices during the closing years of the century, Blair could report that the pledges to the college "come in apace." He and the governor, moreover, saw in building the college an opportunity to achieve the most sought-after goal of recent decades, the founding of a town. With the burning for the third time of the statehouse at Jamestown in October 1698, the public was ready for a change. In a well-orchestrated promotional event, Nicholson adjourned the first general Assembly of his administration in April 1699 to Middle Plantation, where on May Day five of the college's new students were shown off in a series of speeches carefully tailored to inform the legislators why they should set the new capital there.

Town and gown "will be mutually assistant to one Another" was the theme. Participation in the town's life, particularly in the workings of the body politic at its vital center, it was argued, would draw scholars out of their isolation. With scholarship and teaching fueled by such integration, "the Nations of America" would soon acclaim the college "the Mansion house of virtue, the Parnassus of the Muses, and a Seminary of excellent men." On the other side, "the chief difficulty in making a Town," one young social analyst observed, was "bringing a considerable number of Inhabitants to it." The college would provide a population base. Crafts and markets would develop to supply it, and business would expand because parents and friends would come to see the students. Clinching the argument for a generation feeling pangs of inferiority about its accomplishments was the assurance that the new town "may equal if not outdo Boston, New York, Philadelphia, Charlestown, and Annapolis." Moreover, the expense would be no more than it would cost to rebuild the statehouse. What politician could resist? The burgesses had the principal speech summing up the argument read a second time and voted to move the capital to the site, renaming it Williamsburg.

The founding of Williamsburg was the cultural fillip to their society that so many Virginians desired. It brought the latest intellectual currents of the Enlightenment to eighteenth-century Virginia. Governor Nicholson already had thought extensively about a site plan for the new town. The burning of most of central London in 1666 had provided the opportunity for Sir Christopher Wren and John Evelyn, whom the king commissioned to direct the reconstruction, to introduce Renaissance architectural principles well known on the Continent. Chief among these were the focusing of attention on important buildings or monuments by means of wide avenues terminating in spacious squares and the basing of the overall plan on principles of mathematical symmetry. Nicholson's army assignments around Europe had introduced him to numerous examples of these principles, and there is reason to think that, when he returned briefly to England in 1693–1694 after planning the college with Blair, he sought out Evelyn and possibly Wren himself for advice. Nicholson had already had an opportunity to practice city planning in Maryland when the legislature there voted to move the capital from St. Mary's City to Annapolis because the center of population was shifting farther up Chesapeake Bay. Although the evidence is not completely certain, Nicholson was probably the major influence in producing the plan for the new site: radial streets leading to two broad squares surrounding the statehouse and the church.

Within five years Nicholson had another chance to practice his art at Williamsburg, for which the evidence is clear that he was the primary designer. At the time the only structures in the area were the college building, nearing completion at the western end of the land set aside for the new capital, and, dotted along a road running to the east, Bruton Parish Church and half a dozen or so residences and dependencies that the colony purchased from John Page. Originally the road snaked along the crest dividing the drainage basins—and the deep ravines—running south and north towards the James and York rivers. Nicholson's plan was to tear down some of the residential buildings to straighten the road (but still have it run along the crest) for one mile due east of the college past the church. The new avenue was named Duke of Gloucester Street after William and Mary's son and heir apparent, who died in 1700.

Along this axis the governor laid out two sections, the relative measurements of which reveal the fascination with symmetry that was the vogue of the day. The section on the west was a square a half mile on each side with the church at the center. The second, on the east, was half as wide. The distance from the church to the proposed capitol on the east was as great as the width of the western section, and extending the road beyond the capitol made the eastern section three-quarters as long as the other. In keeping with contemporary architectural guidelines, the road directed attention to the three main attractions of the town. Large open areas or plazas surrounded two of these, the college and the capitol, and a third open area provided a marketplace a little to the east of the center of town. Within this framework, half-acre lots were offered for sale conditional on construction of a house and fenced yard within two years. To ensure a regular appearance houses were to front within six feet of the street. Several contemporaries also said that Nicholson meant the town's roads to form the initials W and M, but he apparently never carried out this idea; or if he did, as a nineteenth-century wit remarked, "he made his letter[s] very badly."

*   *   *

Just as a decade before, both governor and commissary remained deeply troubled about the state of religion in Virginia and once more assigned reform high priority. Nicholson convened a conference of clergy in April 1700, at which he admonished them to "be more careful as to your morals & diligent in your several Parochial duties," promising to prosecute them if they were not. Although Blair later complained that Nicholson called the meeting without consulting him, he cooperated at the time, taking over after the governor's introduction to examine the participants' credentials and to lead a probing discussion of church affairs.

The previous year, as his instructions specified, the governor had charged the General Assembly with revising the colony's laws, including the statutes pertaining to religion. At the request of the committee on revisal, Blair submitted a plan calling for significant alterations in church policy. Once again, he proposed reviving ecclesiastical courts to oversee the clergy. (This time, no mention was made of jurisdiction over the laity.) In addition, he called for consolidation of parishes to pool resources and simultaneously the imposition of a tithe of 40 pounds of tobacco to allow graduated clerical salaries up to 32,000 pounds a year, double the current level. He would also routinely supply five slaves and a herd of seven or eight cows. Finally,

These two buildings, the H-shaped reconstruction of the Capitol in Williamsburg (above), built in 1701–1705 and rebuilt after a fire in 1751–1753, and Christ Church, Lancaster County (below), probably the finest Greek-cruciform colonial church in Virginia, completed in 1732, illustrate the development of public architecture in Virginia in the first half of the eighteenth century. Virginia State Library photograph.

Blair asked for a tighter nomination schedule that would expedite filling church vacancies and conferring permanent tenure on ministers.

As before, the commissary found little interest in so extensive a reform. The revision of the laws was not completed until 1705, and it made no mention of the recommended changes. Had Blair's proposals been adopted, ministers would have been elevated to the socioeconomic level of some of the most substantial planters in the community, well above the situation of the vast majority of their flocks. Along with the reluctance of vestries to yield control of the clergy by making permanent appointments and the old fear of ecclesiastical courts, legislators were understandably hesitant to confer such an economic boon on the ministry before the improvement in reputation the raises were supposed to ensure occurred.

*   *   *

Nicholson's instructions assured that the "Halcyon days" would not last forever. The reforms that Locke envisioned as instituting ideas of balanced and restricted government may have advanced the imperial interest by curtailing the Council along with the governor, but they were bound to alienate the oligarchy that was restrained. The most important object of the change was the land system. Hartwell, Blair, and Chilton, along with Edward Randolph, had revealed to the Board of Trade how no one in authority cared if ships' crews claimed headrights every time they entered the country, or if captains then claimed the same crewmen as if they had imported them as servants, or if claimants just paid clerks in the secretary of the colony's office—"a constant Mint of these Rights"—one to five shillings an entry. As for the requirement that each fifty-acre lot be "seated" within three years by building a house, planting a crop, and keeping cattle or swine for a year, either constructing "an Hog-House" *or* "planting and tending one Acre . . . no Matter how badly" usually sufficed. Besides, if nothing was done, the land never reverted to the Crown.

Nicholson immediately ended one abuse in April 1699: the claiming of headrights for imported slaves, which in view of current trends would soon have been a cornucopia. Otherwise he was unsuccessful in replacing the system of headrights and treasury rights, as he was directed, with grants of 100 acres for "each laboring person" actually settled on the land within three years of the patent. Since the proposal required legislative action, the Council frustrated it by never putting it on its agenda. A decade later the Board of Trade gave up and withdrew the instruction. The old system survived.

The hope of major reform thwarted, Nicholson tried for at least a partial victory by exercising his administrative control over the sale of treasury rights. These were claims sold directly to anyone who could pay 5*s.* for a 50-acre lot. The governor forbade surveyors and county clerks to register patents for more than 1,000 acres without his signature. The effect was minimal, but it gave birth to the Council's repeated assertion that the governor was circumventing its authority, since normally it authorized all patents. Nicholson also sidestepped the Council's traditional control of the nomination of sheriffs, who were crucial to any hope of enforcing the land law. He began to appoint candidates without consulting the board; by 1703, not a single confirmation of a sheriff's appointment appeared in the Council's minutes. The governor also insisted on the right of the secretary of the colony to appoint clerks of county courts without reference to the Council, a point on which the Board of Trade eventually upheld him.

Of plural officeholding, which Nicholson was instructed to check, the most glaring example was the Council itself. Most of its members held, in addition to their seats, appointments as customs collectors or as naval officers. Within a few months of his arrival Nicholson had forced Robert Carter to resign as naval officer in order to accept a seat on the Council and had displaced eight councillors from collectorships. The ex-collectors' first reaction was to demand some form of compensation for the loss of fees. But eventually the complaint assumed constitutional proportions, for "Naval officers are put in and turned out at pleasure without any advice of the Council."

The most serious confrontation was with the Byrds, who had supported Andros and might have become allies. Nicholson was specifically directed to separate the offices of receiver general and auditor general of customs, which the elder Byrd had held simultaneously since 1687. Nicholson failed to effect any change until Byrd died in 1704. By then the victory was hollow, for it was Nicholson's successor who bestowed the receiver generalship alone upon the son. Nicholson was also wont to talk about the possibility of creating an intercolonial joint stock company, through which the government would regulate the Indian trade in which the Byrds were heavily involved. He also spoke of the need for the Crown to buy out the Fairfaxes, for whom Robert Carter had just become agent. In neither case did his suggestion win support for his cause.

The growing tension between the governor and the councillors became public in 1702, when Nicholson opened the Blackwater Swamp area in the Southside to settlement. Because of the shortage of available acreage in older established areas, the move had been looked forward to for some time. One of Blair's complaints against Governor Andros, for example, had been that Andros had been too dilatory in making it possible for the college to dispose of its endowment lands in that region. Now the college had its opportunity. As opening day approached, a land rush was in the offing. The Harrisons, however, connived with the surveyor Thomas Swann to take up all the choice sections before he unlocked his doors to the public. The ensuing outcry of fraud from smaller planters forced Nicholson to close the region once more to settlement pending an investigation, thereby infuriating the Harrisons and, for a double reason, son-in-law Blair.

*   *   *

Despite the rising opposition, Nicholson did have notable success achieving the most important of the Board of Trade's objectives: increasing royal revenues. From the collection of quitrents he built a reserve of £4,100 by 1703 and more than £5,700 by the end of his administration two years later. He was the first governor to institute suits for the collection of quitrents, although his term in office was not long enough to bring any to conclusion. More important, Nicholson required a survey to be conducted in 1704 that resulted in the only quitrent roll for the entire colony outside of the northern proprietary. It is a major source of historians' knowledge of the size and composition of the population.

Nicholson's success as a collector, however, worked havoc with his defense policy, for Virginians could not see why they had to raise money to be spent outside the colony when the Crown had funds of its own. At the outset of his second administration Nicholson once more reviewed the colony's military posture. He found the few coastal forts so delapidated that he concluded, "it is more dangerous . . . to have

Such Fortifications, than to be without them," since they were so exposed to capture. He ordered them abandoned. Although pirates plagued the coast during those days, only one small royal navy ship, HMS *Shoreham*, was stationed in Chesapeake Bay, and its commander was reluctant to challenge marauders. In April 1700 Nicholson gained local notoriety when he boarded the *Shoreham* and forced the captain to chase a pirate ship, which they captured. Then the governor had a long wrangle with the House of Burgesses over whether they should pay the £420 it cost to send the captives to England for trial. In the end they took the sum out of the funds designated for the governor's house in the new capital at Williamsburg.

The need to coordinate colonial defense became urgent when another war with France (known as Queen Anne's War) broke out in 1702 after a five-year truce. As before, imperial strategy in America centered on New York. Imperial authorities assigned quotas to other colonies to help in its defense. Virginia's was the largest: £900 and 240 men. Virginians, however, concluded that operations hundreds of miles away helped New York's fur trade more than they helped Virginia's defense. On this issue the burgesses were more stubborn than the Council; and in the August 1701 session they refused to meet the quota or even to amend the militia law to provide better training for local defense. William Byrd I, Benjamin Harrison, and a group of other speculators put through compromise legislation setting aside tracts of 10,000 to 30,000 acres on the frontier free of quitrents for settlers who would undertake to maintain a fort in the area at their own expense. The plan was to subvert Nicholson's hopes of land reform as much as to achieve dependable defense.

* * *

Except for the defense issue, the governor achieved a significant following among the burgesses and other groups outside the Council. With the break between the governor and most of the councillors in the open, the two sides challenged each other in the burgesses' elections of 1702, the first since those routinely held four years before upon the appointment of the new executive. The governor generally did well in frontier counties, still the strongholds of the smaller planter. But for overall results, the evidence is sparse. The most that can be said is that

Robert Carter, a critic of the governor, referred to the outcome as "bad" and wrote to fellow councillor Philip Ludwell that "twas very nigh impossible to stem the Tide with the Strongest Arm." Opponents of the governor, he thought, had not managed the campaign well.

The governor also consistently did well among the clergy, largely because of the antipathy most had toward the commissary. Considering the ministers' reputation at the time, few could have felt much affection for the censorious Scot who was constantly trying to subject them to ecclesiastical courts and law. In 1700 Nicholson informed the archbishop of Canterbury that there were six to eight vacancies available but the people did not want any more Scots to fill them. The animosity toward Blair was despite the fact that he did raise the clergy's salaries and improve the quality of their lives. Had his plan of 1699 succeeded, Virginia's ministers would have been hard pressed not to have acclaimed him their champion.

Over the next three years, however, Blair reversed himself on a key component of his plan, induction of ministers. Because there was no bishop in Virginia and no aristocratic patrons, as in England, who might have claimed the power to appoint ministers for local churches, parish vestries alone exercised that authority through the seventeenth century. Canonically a vestry had six months in which to "present" or recommend a candidate to the governor who, after examining credentials, would "induct" or appoint the person permanently. In view of the caliber of seventeenth-century recruits, vestries preferred annual contracts instead. Since the lack of security only lessened the appeal of Virginia to better qualified personnel, imperial authorities had for some time instructed governors to "collate" or appoint ministers on their own if vestries did not act within the stipulated period. No governor in the seventeenth century did so. From the time of his appointment as commissary Blair had been eager to try, but Andros declined.

Nicholson was more willing to take up the challenge. Upon his arrival he called for a legal opinion on his authority from the attorney general of England, Sir Edward Northey. Then, when an opinion supporting the governor arrived in 1703, Blair changed his mind and advised vestries to ignore it. His reason is not clear—perhaps to solidify his strength with the Council, or perhaps because he had concluded that the vestries' control was the better method of disciplining clergy.

At least half of the clergy in Virginia wrote in outrage to the bishop of London, and in the conflict with the Council threw their support to the governor. The battle nonetheless was hopeless, for in the end the vestries still levied the tithe on which the clergy's sustenance depended, and recourse to legal action was futile since vestries and county courts greatly overlapped in personnel. During the year following publication of Northey's ruling, five vestries accepted it, thirty-nine refused, and seven did not bother to respond.

Nicholson thus had significant resources in the contest with the Council, had he not been his own worst enemy. He had a violent temper and, what was worse, did not always keep barracks manners out of the drawing room. The extent of his cursing and alleged lewdness, and of his frequent threats of bodily harm, even in Council and General Court sessions, are difficult to assess because most of the descriptions are by antagonists. But of his temper his most stalwart defender conceded, "this perhaps is a great truth," and the reaction of his friend Micajah Perry in England was that "the charge rings so of you." From the number of times the story was repeated, he must at least once have allowed that his term of duty among the Moors in Tangier taught him how to handle Virginians. Having fallen hopelessly in love with young Lucy Burwell, he frantically pursued her after she spurned him for Edmund Berkeley. His denunciations of her family and of Berkeley and other supposed rivals in 1701 and 1702, however embellished in the telling, made him a laughingstock in both the colony and England. Whatever the truth of the stories, the image that grew, as one sympathizer pointed out to him, rendered it exceedingly difficult for his friends to protect him. "I beseech you," he was implored, "do not force us to hang our tails, as . . . Mr. Perry terms it."

Once more Commissary Blair emerged at the center of the opposition. Although Nicholson and he worked well together for several years, each was convinced that he had made the political fortune of the other: Blair because he secured the governorship for Nicholson; and the governor because he obtained the nomination for the college presidency for Blair. It may have been that, when the Board of Trade finally restored Blair to the Council in June 1701, he more directly experienced Nicholson's highhandedness. Certainly, after the capital moved to Williamsburg, the two were constantly under each other's feet, for until the capitol building was sufficiently completed in 1704

Nicholson had to maintain his office and hold legislative sessions at the college. He also had to live in college property after quarreling with Blair's father-in-law, Benjamin Harrison, for asking what the governor considered too high a rent for the only other available dwelling in town.

Although Blair, who had criticized the planter elite in 1697, now joined it in opposition to Nicholson, the pattern of the commissary's politics had not changed. The consistency in his career was his total devotion to the projects that he considered his own: the church in Virginia and the college. He brooked no excuse for anything less than 100 percent commitment from others. Despite the fact that Nicholson had been a charter sponsor of the college, the scandal at Blackwater Swamp forced him to halt the sale of college lands, along with others. He was unable to push construction of the capitol and a residence for the governor rapidly enough to relieve the college of the burden of state tenants; and although he wrote urgently to the archbishop of Canterbury for a divinity professor to inaugurate college classes, none came, presumably because his influence or his effort was insufficient. Throughout his administration only the grammar school was in operation. Above all, from Blair's many references to Nicholson's profanity and sexual habits—the commissary said he could not bring himself to describe the latter in writing—he formed an aversion to the governor and concluded that Nicholson's service to the church was a sham: "I do really believe, since Oliver Cromwell, there never was a man that deceived so many with a shew of religion, which is now turned into a mixture of the grossest hypocrisy & lewdness & Prophaneness, that can be imagined."

The first public conflict between the two came in May 1702 at a lavish celebration of the accession of Queen Anne. The occasion cost Nicholson £500. It included an elaborate parade and fireworks display and succeeded, according to critics, in "making a great number of men drunk." The falling-out between the old friends had political over-tones, for it occurred over a commemorative oration that Blair delivered for William III. Outwardly, the commissary's condemnation of the tyranny of Charles II and James II in contrast to the beneficence of William was a post-revolutionary political cliché. Nicholson took offense at what he perceived (probably correctly) as an implication that his administration suffered in a similar comparison. Worse politically for the governor, in complaining about Blair's supposed insult, he fell into a defense of the Tory monarchs to Thomas Tenison, then archbishop of Canterbury, who with Burnet and Compton had helped to overthrow James.

In the ensuing candid exchange of opinions, Nicholson baldly told Blair that whatever the commissary had done for him had served Blair's own ends. He taunted the commissary that he, Nicholson, had likewise "made a tool" of Blair. Indeed he had—and he thereby laid the mine that destroyed him. A protégé of Blathwayt like Andros, Nicholson had become the latter's bitter rival and used Blair's Whiggish connections to outmaneuver Blathwayt and snatch the governorship from Andros. Thus when the confrontation with Blair arose, a friend who was close to Henry Compton put it simply, "my Lord of London told me . . . that he verily believes a great man in plantation affairs lies at lurch for some such occasion to do your business."

* * *

Nicholson's staunchest supporter did not help either. When the first complaints reached London, the authorities asked Robert Quary to investigate. He arrived in Virginia in September 1703 and was immediately named to the Council. Shortly he was penning a whitewash. Nicholson's opponents, he charged, had "Commonwealth Principles" and were not to be taken seriously. "This Government was never under better or happyer circumstances." As for Blair, Quary wrote, he was too well known by the Board of Trade for anyone to fear "his cuning and malice."

Quary's report confirmed another waverer, Robert Beverley II, in support of the opposition. Although never a proponent of Andros as Byrd had been, Beverley was no admirer of Blair: "few people had abused and reflected upon one another so much as they had done," Nicholson stated. Beverley blamed the move of the capital to Williamsburg, which depreciated the value of land in Jamestown in which he had invested, largely on the commissary. In London during the winter of 1703–1704, where he was writing *The History of Virginia* to promote the colony's virtues, Beverley was aghast at the credence that Quary's report enjoyed. Beverley composed a narrative of recent events, separate from his history, that he circulated privately. "I thought when old Randolph was dead, his Place could not have been filled with another such Pest to mankind, but here's his Successor ten times worse." Beverley charged that, rather than the governor's opponents being Cromwellian, the danger of subversion was from the other side, that Quary and Nicholson only raised the specter of the Commonwealth and rebellion to have an army sent to the colonies and the governor appointed commanding general. When a copy of Beverley's manuscript fell into the governor's hands the next year, he suspended the author from his post as clerk of the Council.

*   *   *

In May 1703 six councillors—Blair, Robert Carter, Benjamin Harrison, John Lightfoot, Philip Ludwell, and Matthew Page—petitioned the queen to remove Nicholson. In July Blair set sail for England to reinforce the written word. Although the evidence is circumstantial, the strategy seems to have been to catch Nicholson unawares. At the time Blair left, the governor was completely confident that he was doing the Board of Trade's bidding and had no doubt that it would fully support him. Indeed, politically the councillors were in the weak position of asking the board to repudiate its carefully designed instructions to the governor. The petitioners seem to have decided to focus instead on the accusation that Nicholson's personality did not befit a representative of the queen. The key was to overwhelm their audience with innumerable illustrations of Nicholson's temperament and to force him to answer endless details of their indictment before he could counterattack. The hope was to prevent him from responding for as long as possible, so that their allegations would have time to sink in and, more important, so that he could not raise questions of imperial policy in his defense. In the governor's words, not theirs, "Fling dirt enough and some will stick."

Thinking that Blair was going mainly to state his side of the quarrel over church matters, such as the dispute over induction, Nicholson obtained a supportive resolution from the clerical conference in August. Over the next year and a half, he also secured strong support from the Council minority, the burgesses, and such organs of public opinion as a grand jury and militia companies, and he had a letter from the William and Mary grammar school master, Mongo Ingles, critical of Blair's presidency. He challenged the Council itself to state whether they knew of any complaints about his governorship, but the members said nothing officially.

Meanwhile, Blair in England delayed presenting the petition to the Board of Trade until March 1704, after the tobacco fleet on which news might have leaked to Nicholson had sailed. In the interim he was "affidaviting," as one of the governor's followers said, assembling massive documentation from, among others, Beverley and the other five "Memorial Gentlemen"—the governor's label for the petitioners— and three lengthy affidavits from himself. Repetitive language in a number of the papers reveals the coordination behind the effort.

Nicholson relied for his defense on the colony's agent, John Thrale (whose appointment without the Council's consent was one of the charges against the governor), but the man knew little about Virginia affairs and died during the hearing. The president of the Council, Edmund Jenings, who was in England on family business and from whom Nicholson expected some aid, carefully remained away from the hearings. Upon Thrale's death the Board of Trade called for reply directly from the governor. The delay meant that Nicholson did not learn the scope of the charges until December 1704, again too late to reply via the fleet returning to England that fall. Nicholson's answer in March 1705, as the opposition probably foresaw, became mired in detailed refutations and countercharges equally as personal as the original, without rising to the level of policy. Still unsuspecting, the governor remained completely confident of victory.

The queen's notice of dismissal dated April 1705 in favor of Colonel Edward Nott crossed Nicholson's reply at sea. With the French war calling for all of the Crown's attention, royal authorities could no longer wait to calm the colonial tempest. The queen's secretary, writing to soften the blow, unwittingly confirmed the shrewdness of the opposition's tactics; "it is not on account of any information against you, of any displeasure H.M. has taken against you, that she has recalled you, but that she thinks it to be for her service at this time." As a sign of her continued confidence, a few years later, after he had led the expedition that captured Port Royal, she appointed him governor of her new colony, Nova Scotia. In the next reign he became the first royal governor of South Carolina.

*   *   *

Governor Edward Nott reached Virginia in August 1705. Although addressed as governor, he technically ranked as lieutenant governor. His appointment signaled a new policy that prevailed for the next sixty-three years. The governorship was bestowed on a high-ranking figure who remained in Britain while a deputy was sent to the colony for a share of the fees. In this case the governor was George Hamilton, earl of Orkney, one of the ablest generals serving under the duke of Marlborough, England's great commander during the wars with France. Orkney held the Virginia post until his death in 1737. Nott was the first of five Virginia lieutenant governors who served with Orkney under Marlborough. A professional soldier from Berwick in northern England, Nott had thrown his lot with William III early in the revolution. In the 1690s, serving in the same regiment as his brother-in-law, Nathaniel Blakiston, later governor of Maryland, he achieved a good record in the West Indies during the first war with France. Initially Nott was rewarded with the deputy governorship of Berwick. Then, upon Thrale's death, Blakiston became the agent for Virginia and doubtless assisted in the decision of Orkney and Marlborough, now the queen's trusted adviser, to assign Nott to the vacancy in the colony.

Despite the beneficial effects of quinine that the younger Beverley touted in his history, Nott died during his second summer in Williamsburg in 1706. His short administration fulfilled Blair's prediction on the eve of his appointment: the new governor would be all that opponents of Nicholson could want. A mild-mannered man, Nott let the establishment have much of its own way. Once more, for example, the Board of Trade instructed him to have a small number of ports established for the tobacco trade, and once more the burgesses tried to capitalize by accepting a bill sponsored by Beverley providing tax exemptions and other incentives for artisans who moved into towns. After some debate, Nott signed the bill in 1706; and once more the Board of Trade recommended disallowance for the usual reasons four years later. With that final rebuff the Assembly did not return to the issue again.

The mandatory election after the accession of a new governor resulted in the defeat of many of Nicholson's followers, although their replacements were not in every case adherents of the opposite faction. Benjamin Harrison ousted the Nicholsonian Peter Beverley as Speaker of the burgesses, but after Beverley's defeat, he was given the chair of the crucial Committee on Propositions and Grievances. Another of Nicholson's supporters, Miles Cary, headed the Committee on Public Claims. Nott's goal, and apparently that of most members of the session, was the restoration of harmony. Nott blocked an effort to purge the naval-officer lists of Nicholson partisans; and an attempt to deprive the secretary of the colony, Edmund Jenings, of the power to appoint county-court clerks as punishment for being too friendly to Nicholson expired in conference.

The governor also vetoed a bill forbidding the executive to appoint justices of the peace without the Council's consent, as Nicholson had done, but neither Nott nor his successors followed Nicholson's precedent. Nott did agree to a requirement that sheriffs be justices of the peace appointed on the recommendation of their fellow magistrates, and he acquiesced in the novel proposition of the Council that its oath to conform to the governor's instructions bound it only in its executive capacity, not in its role as part of the legislature. Nott also accepted, in place of Nicholson's land reform (which he still had instructions to pursue), a limitation on grants to 4,000 acres apiece. The statute did not restrict the number of grants an individual could have, however. The legislature at last obliged the governor by endorsing the revision of the laws that had been lingering for two years and that included a provision for a new house in Williamsburg for him. At his death the assembly erected a monument to him in Bruton Parish graveyard.

After Nott's demise the Council was at the acme of its power. For four years it ruled Virginia without either a governor or a House of Burgesses. Its president, Edmund Jenings, served as acting governor. Although the Crown quickly named another of Orkney's officers, Robert Hunter, to succeed Nott, he was captured by the French on the way over and, when released, was reassigned to New York. Because there was no precedent for an incumbent governor's death, the consensus was that no authority existed to call the Assembly—and the colony did without one. That it was able to do so is indicative of the extent to which the county courts and vestries handled almost all of the affairs of government that were vital to everyday living. Once in power, the Council ignored completely the instructions regarding land reform and restored the old system without qualification. It voluminously explained to the Board of Trade why the traditional procedures were superior, and in the end persuaded the board, many of whose members had taken their seats since the original policy was adopted, if not that reform was unnecessary, that it was unenforceable. The board omitted the relevant section from subsequent governors' instructions. The Virginia establishment had won.

8

GOVERNOR ALEXANDER SPOTSWOOD

The tobacco fleet that sailed in September 1706, Robert Quary wrote to the Board of Trade, was "the greatest fleet that ever went from the tobacco Plantations, near 300 sails." The fleet was twice as large as any before Nicholson's second administration. A brief boom in the tobacco market between the end of King William's War in 1697 and the outbreak of Queen Anne's War in 1702 saw prices more than double from the wartime low of 1d. a pound to 2½d. The already rapid expansion of Virginia investment in land and slaves vastly accelerated, mostly on credit from English merchants eager to lend because of the promising market. More than a million acres were patented and about 3,000 slaves imported during those years. But with the renewal of warfare and the loss once more of French and Spanish markets to English suppliers, prices began to slide. Nonetheless, for several years Virginia reaction was even heavier investment. From just over 28,000 hogsheads in the first year of Nicholson's second term, tobacco shipments climbed to 40,000 in 1706, an increase of more than 40 percent. Although the huge fleet lost 30 vessels and 15,000 hogsheads to Atlantic storms and French privateers, the remainder so glutted the market that merchants shut tight the spigot of credit and desperately began recalling their loans. The Chesapeake colonies plunged into deep depression for the rest of the war.

The industry's problems were manifold. The closing of Continental markets to the English during the renewed war was a windfall for competitors. Dutch production ballooned from 10 million pounds in

1700 to 27 million in 1706. The growing popularity of snuff lessened the emphasis on quality, because cheaper tobacco could be pulverized and disguised under the heavy flavoring that came into fashion. For the moment, the success of French privateers satisfied whatever lingering taste there was on the Continent for the "Best Virginia." As prices fell, wartime transportation and insurance charges rose until it was no longer worthwhile to move the crop to market. In 1711 the fleet comprised only twenty vessels. Compounding the misery, the corn crop failed disastrously in 1709–1710, forcing the Council to impose an embargo. With amazing insensitivity British customs officials in 1711 began demanding immediate payment of tobacco duties on landing rather than waiting, as was customary, until sales were consummated and funds became available. Merchants were forced to dump their inventories at any price to raise the capital for the payments. Parliament was prevailed on to restore the former practice three years later, but by then merchants and planters alike had lost heavily.

*   *   *

The bleak times clouded the arrival of another of the earl of Orkney's subalterns as lieutenant governor in June 1710. Born in Tangier, where his father had been an army surgeon, Alexander Spotswood had continued his family's tradition of military service. During the War of the Spanish Succession (as Queen Anne's War was called in Europe) he had attracted the duke of Marlborough's attention and served well in several important posts. His reward was Virginia. After four years of strong but legally ill-defined Council rule, Virginians welcomed the new governor. For one thing, his presence meant that they could have their House of Burgesses back. Although the first election under the new administration resulted in a House with only eighteen of the fifty-one members who had served under Nicholson, the difference was more cosmetic than real. For the most part, the same families were represented. Fourteen of the eighteen returnees were appointed to standing committees, and Peter Beverley was brought back as Speaker by a vote of 21 to 16 over a newcomer, John Holloway, of King and Queen County.

The initial reaction of the aristocratic soldier-governor was dismay at the quality of the burgesses that the first election cast up. He ordered another within two years, but was no better pleased with the outcome. Repeatedly he wrote in his letters to Britain that "the Mob of this Country" chose "only persons of mean figure and character," whom he sarcastically excused for pandering to public emotions since they "had scarce any other merit to qualify them for the People's Choice." His first impulse was to see if there was any chance of changing the suffrage laws. The Council quickly and decisively informed him that the present system was "suitable to the Circumstances of this Country." Upon that advice the governor accepted the inevitable and set about finding the means of putting the House to work for him.

It was not that Spotswood was at constant loggerheads with the burgesses in these early years, but that because of the depression they measured all issues by one standard: economy. Soon after Spotswood arrived at his post, for example, a rebellion threatened his counterpart Edward Hyde in North Carolina. Spotswood sent a militia detachment to help secure peace. The next year, 1712, when some Tuscarora Indians attacked the Carolinians, the Virginia governor again intervened with a show of force that dissuaded the remaining members of the tribe from going to war and brought them over to the government's side. The experience led Spotswood to inaugurate a policy, which he followed for the rest of his administration, of signing defense pacts with nearby friendly tribes to act as buffers against more distant enemies. The Virginia Assembly praised the policy, but the burgesses refused to pay for either the campaign or the cost of the client relationships on the ground that the Assembly had not authorized them beforehand.

Instead, the lower house insisted on appropriating £20,000 for an all-out war against the Tuscarora. The move, the Council pointed out, was hardly consistent with the drive for economy. Anyway, the Crown was certain to veto the taxes enacted since they were mostly on imported British manufactures. The feeling in Virginia, as well as in South Carolina, which had also been asked to aid, was that the North Carolinians, who had a reputation for lawlessness in the early eighteenth century, were the main cause of their own troubles by failing to curb the worst abuses against the Indians. In the end, the issue in Virginia bogged down in a quarrel between the houses. The governor had to carry on a much-reduced campaign with private subscriptions and quitrent revenues. Eventually Spotswood at least gained some political capital out of the situation. When he finally obtained £1,000 for 300 men from the legislature, it was too late. Because of the delay most of the burden for assisting North Carolina fell on its sister colony to the south, whose forces finally defeated the Tuscarora in March 1713. The upshot was that Spotswood established a name for economy with the Virginia Assembly by returning £700 of the £1,000 appropriated.

Five years later Spotswood again came to the rescue in Carolina, this time against the pirate Edward Teach, the notorious "Blackbeard." The years of King William's War and Queen Anne's War and shortly thereafter were the heyday of piracy in the western Atlantic. Spotswood reported that at one point in 1717 Blackbeard virtually ended trade off the Virginia coast. The next year the governor heard that the pirate chief intended to fortify Ocracoke Sound and turn it into a permanent pirates' haven. The North Carolina government was apparently unable, or perhaps unwilling, to resist. (The secretary of the colony and possibly Governor Eden himself were thought to be "fencing" Blackbeard's loot.) In November 1718 Spotswood organized an expedition under royal navy lieutenant Robert Maynard with sailors from two men-of-war stationed in Chesapeake Bay. Maynard took two light sloops, with which he was able to cross the sand bars guarding the entrance to Ocracoke Sound. When the battle began, the pirates boarded Maynard's vessel in swashbuckling style. Blackbeard and Maynard engaged in a hand-to-hand duel with swords until Maynard's men finally gunned the pirate commander down. Despite Governor Eden's protest that the expedition violated Carolina territory, Maynard, with Blackbeard's head hanging from his bowsprit, took fifteen captives back to Williamsburg. Thirteen were convicted and executed; two were pardoned. The glory days of piracy were over.

* * *

Apart from the Indian wars in Carolina, few points of contention arose between Spotswood and the Virginia legislature during the early years of his administration. He started off with the good news that Parliament had extended the right of habeas corpus to the colonies and that the Crown had abandoned its instructions to its governors to reform the land system in Virginia. Spotswood did request a statute, which the Assembly passed, requiring the seating of three acres in every fifty and decreeing forfeiture of title for failure to pay quitrents. But the legislators took advantage of the new executive's wish for the law to confirm grants that the Council had issued on doubtful legal grounds during the period of its rule. It also provided that forfeiture would not occur unless someone else petitioned to take up the land in question, a recourse that legislators could be confident few Virginians would resort to against one another. A subsequent act in 1712 further softened the impact of the governor's bill by scaling the definition of "seating" a tract to fit the quality of the land involved.

In other areas the governor's pleas for increasing the requirements of militia duty and upgrading coastal defenses went unheeded because of the expense. Governor and Council backed away from a potentially dangerous dispute when, in answer to petitions that had been ignored for several years, they tentatively proposed redrawing the boundaries of several older counties in a more rational way. Spotswood also diverged from the spirit of his instructions to let stand with only mild protest an extension of the 1705 duty on imported slaves that British slave-trading interests opposed. The original rate of £1 a head was raised to £5. Purporting to raise a revenue for the governor's new residence in Williamsburg, the act was also designed to curtail the output of tobacco in these lean years by reducing the available work force. Since the extension was embedded in an omnibus appropriations bill, the governor had to accede or lose the bill entirely.

This indifferent legislative record led Spotswood to try to remedy a persistent weakness in the governorship during the first half of the eighteenth century: the ebbing of its patronage. The continued drain was in two directions. On one side, the increasing strength of Virginia political institutions gradually extended colonial control over many local appointments. On the other, Robert Walpole and other British ministers of the period relied on an insatiable network of patronage to line up the votes they themselves needed in Parliament. More and more, they made appointments in the colony to satisfy a British political need rather than a Virginian one. Aspirants quickly learned to look abroad for sponsors other than the governor. Spotswood decided to halt the shrinkage by creating patronage of his own and to generate it in conjunction with innovative and daring solutions to two of

Virginia's most pressing troubles: the tobacco glut and defense against the Indians.

His first proposal, the tobacco plan, Spotswood set forth in 1713. Part of the colony's economic problem, it was generally recognized, was that, although larger producers tried to assure the quality of their cargoes, enough trash tobacco slipped through to injure the overall reputation of the colony's product. In addition, since tobacco was legal tender in Virginia, some planters deliberately cultivated inferior crops or, after harvesting the prime leaves, salvaged "seconds" for use in exchange for goods or payment of debts. An effort to impose fines for the use of seconds in 1706 proved difficult to enforce. Spotswood consequently proposed a system of public warehouses where all tobacco for export or use as commodity money would be inspected and bonded. The governor was quite proud of the scheme, for which he claimed sole authorship. He considered the final statute "the most Extraordinary one that ever pass'd a Virginia Assembly" and asked that "no one . . . envy me the honour of the Project."

Instead of "honour" came protest from all sides. Royal officials concerned about customs revenues which were based on volume traditionally resisted any limitation of production, and small Virginia planters always feared that, aside from losing a chance for smuggling, with their limited resources it was more likely to be their crops that would be rejected at inspection. To the officials Spotswood stressed the tighter regulation of the industry that his system would provide and, once quality was assured, the possibility of increased demand and thus production and revenue. To the planters he wasted no tears on the fate of smaller farmers, but advanced the usual arguments for concentration: control of production, improvement of quality, and reduction of shipping costs.

The argument that won the most votes, however, was unspoken: the proposed system generated about forty inspectorships, each estimated to be worth £250 a year. Twenty-nine of the fifty-one burgesses, and close relatives of four others, received public appointments from the governor. Spotswood also gained leverage from the fact that four times during these years the membership of the Council fell below nine, the magic number at which his instructions permitted him to appoint new members without reference to London. His bill went through.

* * *

The following year Spotswood rode the wave of victory to propose a reform of the Indian trade as part of his strategy for western defense. Since the Tuscarora War, he had been hoping to erect permanent buffers of tributary Indians to the south of the James River to protect the colony against the more hostile tribes of North Carolina. Winning the confidence of a number of smaller tribes who had in common a fear of the Tuscarora, he persuaded them to gather around Fort Christanna on the Meherrin River and to send their leaders' children as hostages to study at William and Mary. The number of children who came exceeded the ability of the Boyle bequest to support them. When the assembly refused to augment the fund, the governor was forced to seek private contributions and to appeal for aid from the Anglican church's Society for the Propagation of the Gospel in Foreign Parts and from the bishop of London. Success in these measures allowed Spotswood to advance his standing as an economizer with the cost-conscious legislature by announcing a reduction of approximately one-third in the cost of guarding the frontier when the tributary Indians replaced the rangers formerly employed on the Southside.

The savings also allowed Spotswood, without asking for additional funds, to found a similar outpost at Germanna on the Rappahannock River to protect the colony to the northwest. At the governor's request, the Assembly rescinded all fees and taxes for seven years to encourage settlement there. Spotswood had already been in correspondence with Baron Christoph de Graffenried, who had been trying for several years to establish a colony of Germans from the mining areas of Switzerland in the American South. At the same time, Spotswood petitioned the Board of Trade to allow the smelting of iron that had been found at the Rappahannock site into unworked bars. These, he argued, would not violate the mercantilistic prohibition against crafts and industries in the colonies because they could be sent to Britain as ballast on tobacco ships at so low a cost that Virginians would never be tempted to turn them into finished products. The board was not persuaded and declined to encourage any mining except of precious metals. Nonetheless, without public announcement, miners arrived at Spotswood's expense in the spring of 1714. After a brief search for silver, they turned to iron. By the 1720s, despite the governor's assurances to his superiors, "backs and frames for Chymnies, Potts, doggs [andirons], frying, stewing, and baking pans" were for sale in Williamsburg "some at 2*d* a pound, others at 3*d*." Although his successors were more candid with the Board of Trade, they minimized the fledgling industry in their reports and succeeded in staving off any attempt to curb it through mid-century.

The capstone to Spotswood's defense plan was creation of the Virginia Indian Company, a quasi-public joint-stock corporation, to which was granted a twenty-year monopoly of the Indian trade south of the James River. Unlike the company that Nicholson had sketched out but had not formally proposed, Spotswood's was not intercolonial. His object was to bring the Indian trade under some kind of order to control the worst abuses against the Indians, rendering them less likely, he hoped, to resort to war. In addition, as part of his cost-sharing policy, the company in return for its monopoly was to assume responsibility for Fort Christanna and its garrison after two years. The company was also to maintain a school for Indian children at the fort and contribute to the construction of a public magazine at Williamsburg. Initially Spotswood expected Indian traders to be the principal purchasers of the company's stock. But the general unhappiness of that class with the idea of regulation, and a fear among the broader investing public that the company had too many obligations forced on it, resulted in no sales for three months. Spotswood then apparently put pressure on new appointees to the Council and other prominent politicians to buy shares. Once organized, the company seems to have worked as anticipated. It took responsibility for the fort on schedule, its school had more than seventy students enrolled, and it began payments toward the public magazine.

Unfortunately for Spotswood, the times were not ripe for reform. The peace of Utrecht in 1713 did not produce the boom in the tobacco market that had followed the treaty of Ryswick sixteen years before. Although markets were restored with the war's end and shipping costs declined, the unfavorable customs regulations stifled the renewal of trade until they were rescinded in 1714. Several consecutive years of bad weather curtailed production and, moreover, produced crops with exceptionally high percentages of trash tobacco. Implementation of the warehouse act in November 1714 bore out the worst fears of small farmers about the impact of an inspection system on them. In a better year Spotswood might have been able to persuade more people of the virtues of concentration, but not this year. Even larger planters, who might have been expected to heed such arguments, found fault with their inability to operate from their own wharves. While no serious violence broke out, passage of an act that fall making it a crime to burn public warehouses shows how far the administration thought the opposition might go. To compound the crisis, the corn crop failed once again, forcing the imposition of another embargo.

However statesmanlike Spotswood may have considered his objectives, the methods he used to attain them gave the opposition an unanswerable rallying cry: he had bought the legislature. He might nonetheless have ridden out the onslaught had not Queen Anne's death in August 1714 automatically terminated the Assembly with which he had such good relations. Then, the outbreak of the Yamasee War in the Carolinas in March 1715 compelled him to call a new election earlier than he had expected. The campaign was bitter and, in many cases, rough and tumble; one defeated incumbent was cited in the House for having "Assaulted beaten, and very much wounded" his successful opponent. Only sixteen incumbents out of fifty-one survived. Of these only one was an inspector. All the other returnees had opposed the act and had been passed over by Spotswood in distributing his largess. Only five burgesses whom he had not rewarded were not reelected or succeeded by their sons. Only one of the newcomers was an inspector. Speaker Peter Beverley was defeated in his home county of Gloucester, and when he was subsequently elected by the college, was ousted by a vote of the full House in an interpretation of the rules.* His successor as Speaker was a freshman, Daniel McCarty of Westmoreland. The opposition's floor leaders were old foes of the governor, both personal and political. Gawin Corbin of King and Queen County Spotswood had

---

*The college attempted to exercise its right to elect a burgess for the first time with the selection of Beverley. Because a faculty had not yet been appointed and by terms of the charter control still remained with the trustees, the anti-Spotswood majority ruled that Beverley could not be seated. The majority permitted the anti-Spotswood John Parke Custis to sit for the college in 1718, however, and Thomas Jones represented it in 1720. George Nicholas was the first burgess elected in strict accord with the charter in 1730, after the newly appointed faculty assumed control the year before.

dismissed as naval officer on charges of corruption; George Marable of James City County had lost his position as county justice and had been censured by the earlier House for the language he used in opposing the tobacco act; and Edwin Conway of Lancaster County, who had also resisted the act, the governor singled out as a particularly bitter enemy.

Although Spotswood had been soundly defeated in a landslide, the new House was inexperienced and ineffective. The opposition had petitions from twenty-three of the colony's twenty-five counties protesting the tobacco law, yet they became entangled in a time-consuming constitutional debate with the governor over whether they could enquire into why a few pro-Spotswood county justices had held back others. They tried to force Spotswood to accept repeal of the tobacco act by attaching it to an appropriations bill for the Indian war, handing the Council a simple excuse for rejecting it: it was not relevant to the appropriation. They even failed to agree among themselves on bills barring salaried officials from sitting in the House and requiring elections every three years that would have been to their partisan interest. A bill intended to bankrupt the Virginia Indian Company by heaping added expenses on it, including responsibility for defense of the colony against "all Indians whatsoever," failed in the Council.

So poor was the burgesses' performance that it revived all of Spotswood's earlier contempt for the kind of representative Virginian elections produced. In dissolving the Assembly he yielded to the temptation of dismissing it with a speech that, while undoubtedly personally gratifying, was a serious political mistake. It was grossly and unnecessarily insulting. He began by announcing to the delegates that he would not ask the Speaker for the usual summary of the session's activities "as I question whether you have truly Considered what you have been doing" and so would "Spare you the Confusion of telling your own Actions."

A formal communication from the House he characterized as "a Composition of indefinite Sentences." The chairman of two standing committees, he said, could not "Spell *English* or Write Common Sense." His ultimate taunt was that "'tis Strange that you have not been able to fall upon any Just Measures to Redress the mighty Grievances you came fraughted with." So intemperate was the address that the Board of Trade pointed out to him that, however understand-able his feelings, it was self-defeating to incense the "Electors to such a Degree as may require considerable time before the People are brought to Temper again." They only hoped, they told Spotswood, "that by your prudent Management no future Assemblies will deserve such a Reprimand."

* * *

Meanwhile, in spite of the low priority the burgesses assigned intercolonial defense, Spotswood had been doing all that he could to assist South Carolina in the Yamasee War. The Indians had struck swiftly and unexpectedly along the Carolina frontier in the spring of 1715 and had driven back settlement to within thirty miles of Charleston. Reports were that South Carolina could muster only 1,500 troops, whereas the Indians numbered 8,000 (a considerable exaggeration), and that the French were behind the attack. Spotswood immediately wrote to other governors urging joint action, but he received no offers. He and the Council authorized 160 muskets for the southern colony and agreed to recruit 300 men, provided that South Carolina paid their wages and sent an equal number of slaves to take their place in Virginia's work force. No slaves ever came, and the troops wrote back that they were ill-treated. The result was that a second appeal from South Carolina for more men in the fall went unanswered. When the burgesses tied the war appropriation of £450 to repeal of the tobacco act, Spotswood resorted again to royal revenues. The Virginia troops who did go played an important role in finally defeating the Indians, but governmental relations between the two colonies were at the nadir. Personally Spotswood emerged from the episode with an added reputation for vision. The Board of Trade commended him for being one of the few in the colonies to perceive the strategic implication of the Indian war and the need for intercolonial cooperation to counteract it.

The next year Spotswood's concern for imperial strategy and his flair for the dramatic led him on the much-heralded expedition of the Knights of the Golden Horseshoe. Having learned that rangers had discovered a way over the Blue Ridge, he organized a troop of 63 horsemen for an expedition. It comprised fourteen rangers, four Indians, and a dozen gentlemen with their servants. Among them was the historian Beverley and a young Huguenot British army officer,

John Fontaine, who kept a diary of the trip. Although the riding was hard and encounters with a bear and some rattlesnakes were frightening, the general mood was jovial. The weather was good and the hunting excellent. Leaving Germanna on August 29, the party followed the Rapidan River and its southern branch, then crossed the mountains through Swift Run Gap to the Shenandoah River. Fording the latter on September 6, the group spent a happy day on the west bank, which they claimed for King George I. The festivities concluded, Fontaine recorded, with "a good dinner" and a ceremony in which volleys were fired and the healths of the king, the several members of the royal family, and the governor drunk, each in a different beverage. By Fontaine's count, they had "Virginia red wine and white wine, Irish usquebaugh, brandy, shrub, two sorts of rum, champagne, canary, cherry, punch, water, cider, &c." While the rangers remained behind to explore farther, the main body returned to Germanna on September 10. Later the governor awarded a golden keepsake in the shape of a small horseshoe to everyone who had drunk the king's health at the mountain pass. Besides an amiable two-week vacation, Spotswood's purpose was to stage a public-relations event to dramatize for Virginians the opening of the West and the urgency of securing it before the French did. He succeeded.

*   *   *

Elsewhere in the firmament, Spotswood's star was shining less brightly. Having alienated the burgesses, he was beginning to have difficulties with the Council, which until then had supported him. Receiver General William Byrd II was already aggrieved because the Indian Company infringed on his family's Indian trade and because he of all the old traders was not allowed to participate in it. He and Auditor General Philip Ludwell, with whom Spotswood was locked in a court case over the boundary of Governor's Land at Jamestown, were further incensed by Spotswood's administrative reform of the system for collecting quitrents. Since his first years in the colony the governor had sought to regularize accounting methods and require frequent surveys of the lands subject to rent. Ideally he preferred to take the collections out of the hands of the sheriffs, who were notoriously negligent, and centralize them. First, he had unsuccessfully tried to transfer responsibility to the county surveyors, and then he offered a discount if planters paid their rents directly to the receiver general.

Byrd and Ludwell had two objections to the scheme. If the governor's calculations proved wrong and their total receipts did not rise, the discount reduced their commissions. More broadly, for the receiver general to become an active collector instead of just processing sheriffs' accounts increased the pressure to maintain better records and to distinguish between the public and private funds in the possession of the two supervisory officials. Neither was engaged in fraud, but it was common, both in Britain and in the colonies, for officeholders to use public monies in their trust as collateral for private loans or as a source of interest-free loans to themselves. The upshot was that Byrd resigned his post; and when Ludwell refused to abide by the new regulations, Spotswood dismissed him and would have suspended him from the Council had not Ludwell's relatives comprised a near majority that could have blocked the move.

Byrd took his case to England, but made no headway on the issue of quitrent collections. He did find, however, that a few years' experience with the tobacco act had turned many of the influential merchants against it, affording an opportunity for revenge. With his own dislike of the Indian Company, he had the ingredients for a coalition against all of Spotswood's programs. The principal argument against both the tobacco and the Indian trade acts was that they were monopolies in restraint of trade, which was quite damning in government circles because it meant that they diminished the Crown's potential revenue. Working against the tobacco act, too, was the fact that it was not as effective as it should have been, for merchants were able to testify that unacceptable quantities of trash tobacco were still coming through. Although Spotswood tried to marshall counterarguments from long distance, Byrd had the advantage, and the Privy Council disallowed both acts in July 1717.

* * *

The issue of quitrent collections affected only the two councillors involved. What stirred the others was the question of appointments to the new courts of jail delivery or, as they were known, oyer and terminer. Spotswood's instructions authorized creation of the courts.

The meeting place of the House of Burgesses (above), the lower house of the colonial Virginia legislature, and the Council Chamber (below), where the smaller, more aristocratic Council met as the upper house of the legislature, in the Capitol at Williamsburg. The visual contrast between the two rooms effectively captures the character of the two bodies. Colonial Williamsburg photographs.

No one disputed the need for them, for as the colony grew, the normal meetings of the General Court twice a year in April and October were too few to keep up with the volume of criminal cases referred to it. What was challenged was whether the governor could appoint anyone other than councillors to the new bench, for in certain circumstances it exercised power as a supreme court and could become a competitor of the Council.

In 1712 Spotswood tried to divide the houses on the court issue by appointing Speaker Peter Beverley and two other burgesses to the new posts. When the Council objected, the matter was sent to the Board of Trade, where it remained in abeyance for four years. A decision supporting Spotswood in 1716 only produced another standoff, for the Council refused to accede, fearing that its independence was at stake. The governor in turn declined to preside over a General Court that questioned the royal prerogative. The case returned once more to Great Britain, where in December 1717 Attorney General Edward Northey handed down a delphic opinion. The law was with Spotswood, he ruled, but he advised that only councillors be appointed except in emergencies. Behind the scenes William Byrd had been at work. He was at Northey's "chambers day after day," he wrote to a friend. "I thought it expedient to fea the attorney pretty handsomely, that his Report might be as favourable as possible."

Spotswood kept up the debate for a while longer, but eventually he yielded. He and his successors followed Northey's advice, rendering the court of oyer and terminer indistinguishable from the General Court. When its meeting times were routinely set in January and June, it was as if the General Court held four sessions a year.

* * *

Spotswood was finally forced to call another election in the spring of 1718 because the disallowance of the Indian Company act left his defense policy in tatters. He may have hoped that time had healed old wounds, for the economy was enjoying a resurgence. For a number of years after Queen Anne's War crops had been short as a result of the weather, while demand continued to rise. Prices were slow to respond, but by mid-decade they began to climb. In 1718 they reached $2d.$ to $2\frac{1}{2}d.$ a pound. By then the volume shipped surpassed 50,000 hogsheads. As a sign of prosperity the surplus in the treasury from the tobacco levy exceeded £10,000 sterling.

If the governor thought that many minds had been changed, he was wrong. Disaffection because of the quitrent regulations had spread well beyond Byrd and Ludwell, and revenue that year dropped to half the normal return. Since the attorney general's opinion had not yet arrived, councillors were soon on the lists expounding their view of the oyer and terminer appointments. And Spotswood's announced intention of seeking compensation for the Indian Company for its expenditures at Fort Christanna and its contributions toward the Williamsburg magazine provoked outraged cries that the governor's "Creatures and favourites" were being rewarded.

Faced with opposition, Spotswood's condescension once again got the better of him. He circulated one of the earliest campaign documents in Virginia history, advising voters "to choose men of Estates & Familys of moderation and dutiful to their superiors." The document was a gift to the other side. Shortly a reply to the "Rascaly paper" appeared by an author Spotswood identified as "a Member of the Council," probably Ludwell. It charged that it would cost "100,000 Pounds of Tobacco" a year to assume the company's responsibility for Christanna, which was "useless" anyway, and that the "very Considerable Bank of money" in the treasury would disappear "if a Court party has the fingering of it." Reminding readers "how the last Assembly was abused for their Just services to the Country," it concluded with the peroration, "Surely no freeholder will give his vote for any man" who would "Screen a Tottering Governour."

The exchange is significant, for it reflected the slow drift of the political center of gravity in the colony toward the lower house. With increasing frequency under Nicholson and Spotswood, both sides in the quarrels between governor and Council appealed to the burgesses for support. Despite Spotswood's contempt for the burgesses, by dispensing patronage among them and contesting the polls in 1718, he, along with his opponents, acknowledged the lower house as arbiter.

When the poll of 1718 was over, most of the previous House had been returned. Speaker McCarty was reelected. Worse for Spotswood, among the seventeen new faces in the chamber were several even more rabidly opposed to him than their predecessors had been. The commissary's brother Archibald, Ludwell's partner in a store in

Williamsburg whom the governor had denied a seat on the Council, replaced John Clayton of Jamestown, a lawyer who had played a moderating role in the previous session. Also John Parke Custis, who accused Spotswood of stealing wood from his land, succeeded Peter Beverley as the college representative.

Emerging as the floor leader of the anti-Spotswood faction was John Grymes, Ludwell's son-in-law, whom William Blathwayt had selected to succeed Ludwell as auditor general. If Grymes had not already been alienated, he quickly became so when the governor kept him waiting for more than four months before he accepted his credentials and swore him into office. Largely as a result of Byrd's adroit defense of Ludwell, the Board of Trade, while acquiescing in the auditor general's removal, decided to keep the office in the family and let the accusations of malfeasance against the former holder lie dormant. Grymes saw that word went back to Blathwayt that the governor "is not only very angry with you, but the Lords of Trade & the Treasury have as much incurr'd his displeasure." Spotswood had said, Grymes recounted, that he would "lett his Majesty know how they serve him" for responding so adversely to the charges against Ludwell.

Spotswood had no success at all with this Assembly. His opening address was conciliatory enough, showing that he was trying to heed the Board of Trade's advice about his approach to the legislature. The burgesses, however, were not to be swayed from their refusal to compensate the Indian Company or to assume the cost of defense. In response to his request for his own expenses in negotiating Indian policy, they resolved that "thanks be given" but "the Sallary he received by his Majesty's favour is a recompense for the Same." A crisis erupted when the burgesses attempted to appoint William Byrd their official agent and pay him £300. Since they planned to petition the king against Spotswood, they wanted a sympathetic person to address the court. Blakiston adhered too closely to Spotswood's views. When the governor vetoed the bill unless Byrd's instructions were routed through him, the burgesses appointed Byrd without pay. The House was also angry that, when Peter Beverley lost the Speaker's chair, the governor did not transfer the treasurership, which normally went to the Speaker, to his successor, McCarty. The tax surplus aggravated the problem. To keep so much sterling out of the marketplace seriously weakened the chronically specie-starved economy, but instead of having the treasurer loan it out, the burgesses proposed to divide £8,000 between him and the private merchant Archibald Blair to invest. Spotswood's reaction was such that the burgesses did not bother to send the bill to his desk. Eventually they let Beverley alone place £10,000 at interest.

In this frustrating situation Spotswood adjourned the Assembly for five months. During the interval the tide began to shift in his favor. Already some of the opposition had become concerned, as was he, that the partisanship was injuring the colony. Many had opposed him because of his now-defunct policies rather than out of loyalty to his personal enemies; and when word came that Byrd was pressing his candidacy as Spotswood's successor, there were second thoughts. Nathaniel Harrison, whom Byrd had left in his place as deputy receiver general, wrote to Philip Ludwell that he was considering "the consequences if Collo. Byrd should ever obtain his end and come over Govr." During the legislative session Harrison floated the idea of a truce, to which Spotswood responded by inviting the whole Council to his house for a drink. But after much negotiation, in which, for one thing, Spotswood agreed to acknowledge that he had lost the battle over the oyer and terminer appointments, the effort at accommodation fell through.

Emotions were still too heated in the spring of 1718 for peace. Dissident councillors staged a rival bonfire on the night the governor held an open party for the king's birthday, and the burgesses appointed his worst enemies to a committee to see how construction of his residence was coming. He refused to receive them and complained, as he did on numerous occasions during these years, that his opponents did not even treat him "with decent good manners." As a sine qua non in the negotiations he demanded more respect and common courtesy in their attitudes toward him. By November, when the legislature reassembled, the mood was different. Of the fourteen complaints in the draft petition for Byrd to present to the Crown, eight were eliminated on the floor, as was the explicit, though not the implicit, request for the governor's removal.

*   *   *

While the Assembly was in adjournment, Spotswood had decided to go on the offensive. First he asked the Board of Trade to replace Blair,

Byrd, Ludwell, and John Smith on the Council with Peter Beverley and others of the governor's choosing. Byrd was especially vulnerable because he had been in England, away from his Council duties, for three years and did not yet seem ready to return. Instantly he was converted from a candidate for the governorship to a politician desperately scrambling to avoid complete exclusion from power. The earl of Orkney endorsed Spotswood's implied ultimatum. He testified before the board that Spotswood had put the government of Virginia "on a much better foot . . . than it had formerly been," but acknowledged that to avoid deadlock either the governor or the councillors had to go. The board waited until March 1719 to recommend to the king that Byrd be relieved because of his long absence, but it decided against a wholesale purge. Instead, it seized on three vacancies that had developed to appoint Peter Beverley and two other of Spotswood's nominees to the Council. By furious politicking Byrd persuaded the Privy Council to let him retain his post, provided that he return home immediately and work for peace.

The second prong of Spotswood's attack did not succeed as well. In line with his longstanding advocacy of the royal prerogative, he decided to pursue the policy that both his immediate predecessors and Commissary Blair had been advocating: the right of the governor to collate and induct a minister if a vestry failed to present a candidate within six months of a vacancy. Spotswood went further, however, to argue that as representative of the king, who he claimed was patron of all the parishes in Virginia, the governor could appoint a minister without reference to the vestry. In England wealthy patrons who paid for, or whose predecessors had paid for, a parish church enjoyed this right. Blair argued in reply that, since Virginia parishes paid for their own churches, the vestries as representatives of the parishes were the patrons. The right of collation, he held, devolved on the governor only when a vestry allowed its right to lapse by not acting within the proper time.

In opposing Spotswood on this score, Blair had the vestries solidly behind him, although they did not endorse Blair's own idea that in certain circumstances the right of collation lapsed to the governor. The clergy, on the other hand, at a conference in April 1719, strongly backed Spotswood's interpretation and took the attack to Blair by requesting that the Crown look into the legitimacy of his Scottish ordination. Leading them was Hugh Jones, who had been appointed professor of mathematics at the college through Spotswood's influence over Blair's objections. Each side obtained official legal opinions from Britain supporting its cause, forcing—though only after much heat had been expended—an agreement to refer the matter to the General Court. There it remained without resolution for the rest of Spotswood's administration.

The agreement to disagree over the question of collation was part of a general truce formally inscribed in the Council journal at the opening of the next session of the General Court in April 1720. When the governor rebuffed Byrd's initial attempts at reconciliation in accord with the terms of Byrd's reinstatement by the Privy Council, factionalism had threatened to continue full-blown. Then in the middle of a Council meeting on April 29, during which "there passed abundance of hard words . . . for about two hours," according to Byrd, "of a sudden the clouds cleared away and we began to be perfectly good friends." The written terms were that, if disputes recurred, each side would prepare "a fair and impartial State of the Case" to be sent to the Board of Trade for adjudication, but that neither side would attempt any other politicking to influence the outcome in Britain. Similarly, the ecclesiastical dispute, being "a matter of Law," was to go before the General Court. With that, the governor invited everyone to dinner and an evening concert, and had ceremonial volleys discharged and the city of Williamsburg illuminated in celebration. "The governor kissed us all round," Byrd recalled, and "everybody expressed great joy."

The basis for the reconciliation was an agreement, not to stop arguing, but to keep the argument as much as possible within Virginia. The key to that understanding was Spotswood's decision to become a Virginian. He apparently announced his intention in the Council meeting and, as proof of his sincerity, offered to adopt the Virginian point of view on land policy because, like almost every other Virginia planter, he planned to become a speculator.

*   *   *

The result was not so much a lessening of partisanship as a change in tone. In the elections for the Assembly that fall Byrd showed no compunction about campaigning against the governor, and if his critics are to be believed, Spotswood continued dispensing patronage to his advantage. There also were many who were not included in the arrangement, especially anti-Spotswood leaders in the burgesses who felt betrayed by their allies in the Council. Contests in many areas thus ran along the same lines as before. Several opposition leaders— Marable, Conway, and Speaker McCarty—lost, while the governor's close friend Robert Beverley won. But Spotswood's opponents retained a narrow lead and elected John Holloway the new Speaker. Nonetheless, Spotswood entered the session in fine humor and in his opening remarks publicly confirmed his plan to become a permanent resident of the colony.

The usual squabbling broke out during the session over reform of the militia and the governor's expenses in negotiating with the Indians, neither of which the burgesses approved, and over the cost of his house, to which they again reluctantly made another contribution. But it was the governor who presented the main agenda for the session. The centerpiece was a new land law that more than fulfilled his contention that the interest of colony and empire could be made compatible. "I look upon Virginia as a rib taken from Britain's side," he told the Assembly. "If a conscientious discharge of our duty engages us Governors to be specially mindful for Great Britain's interest, yet I cannot see why that may not go hand in hand with the prosperity of these plantations."

Spotswood's proposal was to create two new counties to command the "northern" and the "southern pass" (Swift Run and Rockfish gaps) over the mountains. One county to the south, running roughly from the Roanoke to the North Anna River (the boundaries were left largely to "the direction of the governour with consent of the Council"), was named Brunswick after the new ruling family of Great Britain; the other, between the North Anna and the Rappahannock rivers, was called Spotsylvania. The justification for the new counties was the same as had been advanced for Christanna and Germanna before: the constant encroachment of the French and their native allies and the need to build buffers against them. To encourage settlement the bill rescinded all "publick levies" in the area for ten years, provided £1,000 for military supplies, and allotted £500 for each county to build "a church, court house, prison, pillory, and stocks." The definition of "seating" land was relaxed. The governor petitioned the Crown to forgo quitrents in the area for the ten-year period and to build and man a fort at each of the passes. Without doubt it was strategically wise to secure the mountain passes if Virginia and Britain intended to contest France for the region. At the same time, the policy permitted speculators to reserve large tracts with almost no immediate expense (even payment of treasury fees was postponed) until settlers appeared to buy. On the last day of the session the Council approved awards totaling 100,000 acres in Spotsylvania, 40,000 of which were for the governor.

Spotswood was ebullient. He boasted in his report to the Board of Trade that at this session "more business has been done than in all the Sessions since 1714," and in justification of his land policy he cited to his superiors the same rationale that he advanced to the Assembly: "the growing power of the French on the Mississippi." He also carefully pointed out to the board that, although the current House of Burgesses included "a great many of the same members who composed the last," their present Address to me was unanimous." Their earlier complaints against him, he concluded, were more from "humour than reason." Their most recent statement expressed joy to "see a late unhappy division so unexpectedly united" and pleasure at being "under the administration of so just a Governor." The board, however, probably noted the other source of the burgesses' "joy" in the full copy of the address that Spotswood enclosed, the conclusion that the country was "in so prosperous and flourishing a condition as to want no supplies from us."

*   *   *

Spotswood found equal pleasure in the remaining two years of his administration. Old antagonisms occasionally flared up, as in 1721, when the burgesses attempted to appoint William Byrd, who was returning to England, as their agent at a salary of £400. Spotswood blocked the measure by insisting again that he sign Byrd's instructions and that Byrd post a bond not to exceed those instructions. But the next year the governor did not oppose the appointment at a fee of £300. The reason was probably that, since Blakiston had died, Byrd stood a good chance of becoming the regular agent anyway. Through these years Spotswood and the Council kept up the train of land grants under the generous provisions of the statute creating the new western counties. Their way became easier when, at the death of the secretary of the colony, William Cooke, in the fall of 1721, Spotswood assumed personal responsibility for registering land titles. Eventually he recorded tens of thousands more acres for himself.

Spotswood and the burgesses also finally composed their differences over Indian affairs. Spotswood had traveled to Philadelphia and New York in 1717 to stop the Iroquois from passing through Virginia and upsetting the delicate tribal balances of the area on their way to attack their traditional enemies, the Catawba, in Carolina. The Iroquois had earlier allied with the Tuscarora during their war; and they often sided with the Meherrin and Nottoway, who, like the Tuscarora, were Iroquoian peoples, against the Saponi, who with the Catawba were of Siouan stock. A raid on the Saponi at Fort Christanna in 1717 was the immediate stimulus for the governor's trip north. There he had no greater success arranging intercolonial cooperation for defense than in his own Assembly, with which he only embroiled himself in one more wrangle over whether to reimburse his expenses since the Assembly had not authorized the trip. Believing the New York negotiators insufficiently attuned to Virginia interests, he proposed that a fort be established in Swift Run Gap as an alternative to Albany as the official center of contact with the Iroquois. Unlike the New York town, however, the new rendezvous point had yet to be built. Both the Iroquois and the New Yorkers rejected the idea; and the Board of Trade obviously considered the suggestion just an obeisance to local Virginia pride that further threatened what little intercolonial cooperation had already been achieved. It told Spotswood to be content with the normal channel of communication through Albany and "to wave the Ceremonial provided the essential Part can be obtained."

Spotswood's insistence eventually did persuade the New Yorkers that the Iroquois must be kept from traveling through the settled parts of the East rather than just promising not to attack the English and their Indian allies. In 1721 the Iroquois at last agreed that they would remain north of the Potomac River and west of the Blue Ridge, provided that Virginia's tributary tribes stayed south and east of that line. This time the burgesses concurred with the governor that he and a representative of each chamber ought to go to Albany to ratify the pact. They appropriated £1,000 for the trip, along with £300 for the previous one. Although the basic agreements had been reached in preliminary talks before Spotswood arrived, he considered that his firmness towards the Indians at the conference set a good example for the New Yorkers, whom he deemed much too lenient.

*   *   *

Adding the results of the conference to the turn of domestic events, Spotswood congratulated himself that his twelve-year administration was a success on every count. Yet when he arrived home in October 1722, he found that he had been out of office for almost a month. In his place was a relatively inexperienced soldier-diplomat, Hugh Drysdale, whom the new chief minister of Great Britain, Robert Walpole, had personally recommended for the position. The actual politics of the change have been lost to historians in the recesses of British bureaucracy. Suffice it to say that James Blair, who had been in London since the spring of 1721, returned on the same vessel as Drysdale, and the word was that the churchman would be the next governor's "Prime Minister."

The conciliar truce of 1720 had done little to reconcile the commissary and Spotswood. The college trustees had suspended Blair's salary as president at the end of Nicholson's administration in 1705, in answer to the criticism that classes were not yet in session (doubtless trustee Nicholson jumped at the opportunity). As yet, the stipend had not been reinstated—one of the official reasons for the commissary's fourth trip to Britain. Referral of the dispute over collation to the General Court served him poorly, too. Whether the court ruled for Spotswood or the vestries, he lost. The decision under which as commissary he could expect to wield the maximum influence was that the right of appointment lay in the vestries but lapsed to the governor if they did not act in time. Spotswood himself did not hide the continued ill feeling between the two. When Blair routinely inquired if he could be of service while in London, the governor retorted that "I shall be contented with his not offering to do me any Disservice."

Most likely, Blair was able once again to capitalize on the political situation he found in Great Britain, where a significant number of concerns about Spotswood's governorship had been accumulating. Since most of Blair's contacts in the mother country were gone, he assiduously recultivated influence with the current bishop of London,

John Robinson, whose commissary he continued to be. Robinson's family had a long association with Virginia. His brother Christopher had been secretary of the colony, and a nephew John had just been appointed to the Council. The bishop, however, had been a high-ranking diplomat under the Tory administration at the end of Queen Anne's reign, and he was out of favor with the Whig ministries that followed the accession of King George I in 1714.

Aside from Robinson, Blair probably took advantage of the Walpole administration's constant hunger for patronage, although why the great minister should have favored Drysdale remains unclear. The new governor fit the mold of recent appointees in that he had a good war record under Marlborough and Orkney, but he had not risen as high in their service as his predecessors had. In another area, Walpole's brother Horace, who had succeeded Blathwayt as auditor general and surveyor general of the royal revenue in the colonies (two more of the great bureaucrat's many posts), was sharply critical of Spotswood's recent land policies as barely disguised land-grabbing. Furthermore, William Byrd II, who was also in London, called to the surveyor general's attention the iron mines that Spotswood operated in Germanna in violation of the spirit of mercantilism if not the letter of the law. Spotswood himself always blamed his dismissal on the earl of Orkney, who may have come to fear that the controversies his deputy repeatedly stirred jeopardized his own governorship. Or Orkney may just have sensed which way the wind was blowing. Certainly before Spotswood left for New York in the summer of 1722 he had intimations that he was in trouble, for he significantly accelerated the pace of land grants in the county named for him. Indeed, his land acquisitions ever since the truce with the Council in 1720 smack of the proverbial putting something aside for a rainy day.

9

THE GOLDEN AGE
OF COLONIAL VIRGINIA

As Alexander Spotswood departed from office, the Chesapeake economy was on the verge of another take-off, which would last until the American Revolution. Virginia was entering a golden age. With increasing wealth, the province culturally came into its own. The planter elite found themselves participants in the British Enlightenment to a greater extent than anyone in the colonial wilderness had envisioned just a few decades before. In architecture especially, Virginians brought a genre representative of the age on both sides of the Atlantic—the country house—nearer to perfection than anywhere else outside the mother country. Less obvious until a crisis occurred in a later generation was the evolution of strains of inherited thought in Virginia into an ideology of self-government and individual liberty. In time this ideology challenged both the colony's commitment to the empire and the social structure of the plantation society itself.

The rate of growth in colonial tobacco production, which had been tenfold in the half-century before 1675, had slowed to a mere doubling by 1700 and then had become relatively stagnant. In the half-century to come the volume would more than triple, from about 30 million pounds a year to about 100 million, of which about 70 percent was from Virginia. Expansion of the Continental market, particularly the French, accounted for most of the growth. In France the sale of tobacco was a royal monopoly franchised to various companies and finally to the United General Farms, or the farmers-general as they were known, who bid for the privilege of administering this royal prerogative. The

numerous captures of English merchantmen during the wars at the turn
of the century were a long-term bonanza, for they developed a taste in
France for the American weed. More important, the French government sought to encourage the purchase of tobacco from as few sources
as possible. To take advantage of the French economic strategy, the
British, especially the Scots, responded with a degree of concentration
in marketing that far outdistanced what the great planters had achieved
before.

The production of tobacco was already highly specialized. The
lighter, sweet-scented leaf from the Yorktown and Rappahannock River
areas had long brought higher prices on the English market. By the
eighteenth century that outlet was relatively satiated. Growth occurred
elsewhere, as the output of sweet-scented tobacco dropped from just
under two-thirds of the total at the beginning of the century to less than
a third at the Revolution. The newer Continental demand was met in
the Potomac and James river areas (including the Southside), where
newly opened lands kept production costs low. The cheaper Orinoco of
these areas, although stronger tasting, could be diluted and flavored in
the production of snuff, which constituted most of the French market.
The Upper and Lower James River naval districts accounted for just over
half the total output of Virginia by the time of Independence.

Tidewater planters traditionally marketed their tobacco by consignment. Each endeavored to establish correspondence with a British
merchant who undertook to receive the tobacco and sell it on
commission, handling all of the considerable red tape and payment of
duties in the interim. Often the merchant also acted as jobber for the
planter, putting together a return cargo of manufactured items for use
or sale in America. Already a significant amount of concentration had
taken place in this system, for the advantage was with the planter who
had the credit or contacts to establish a correspondence. Given the
distance involved and the poor communications, the relationships had
to be entirely personal. Because honor and trust were the only cement,
each participant wanted to know with whom he was dealing. These
connections were fundamental in fostering the rise of a class of great
planters who acted as wholesalers in the imperial market for most of the
Tidewater and the eastern Piedmont. As their operations grew in size,
these planters took advantage of economies of scale, reducing shipping
and distribution costs and using the quality and quantity of the tobacco

they controlled to gain an edge in meeting the rising demands of the market.

Although Scots were involved in the tobacco trade before the eighteenth century, their right to participate remained in dispute until the Act of Union of 1707. That act, which joined the kingdoms of England and Scotland, bestowed on them the status of full-fledged nationals under the terms of the Navigation Acts. Their entrance in force into the tobacco market coincided with the expansion into the Piedmont under Spotswood's tutelage. The region became their particular province, though they had dealings throughout Virginia. Their role in Maryland was much less. In essence they prospered by reversing the techniques of the English merchant, not waiting for the tobacco to come to them but sending their own agents or factors, as they were called, to buy it in the field. The purchases were often paid for in commodities which they had stockpiled in stores around the countryside. Small farmers on the newly opened frontier much preferred this method, for they did not have the capital or credit to wait two years or more for the proceeds of a crop to return from overseas.

In turn, the Scots reaped the advantages of concentration, such as assembling cargoes in advance to reduce shipping costs and turn-around time, to a far greater extent than even the largest planter. Moreover, Glasgow, on the west coast of Scotland, is closer to Virginia across the North Atlantic via the Great Circle Route, as it is termed today, than is London or Bristol. From ports in the south of England ships following the trade winds sailed down the coast of Europe to the Azores and the Madeira Islands before turning west through the Sargasso Sea—a route that inflated insurance rates because of the frequent wars with France and Spain and the danger of Caribbean pirates.

Interestingly, it was the Scots who finally achieved the dream of urban development in Virginia. They needed no legislative mandate, for in the process of funneling their purchases and laying in inventories, particularly at Norfolk, which became the home of many chief factors, they supplied the natural roots of urban growth. Norfolk joined Jamestown and Williamsburg as an incorporated city in 1736. In the third quarter of the century the Scots captured about 50 percent of the trade. By then, three giant firms had emerged, under the leadership of William Cunninghame, John Glassford, and Alexander Speirs, which could treat with the farmers-general as equals, offering long-term contracts for enormous quantities of leaf. As a result, the French bought about 40 percent of all the tobacco the Scots proffered and only about 10 to 12 percent of the tobacco sold by the English.

Ironically, at the same time Virginia was beginning to wean itself from dependence on tobacco. Unlike the British plantation colonies of the West Indies, the Old Dominion, after the early starving times, had been able to feed its own population and to produce a small surplus of foodstuffs for sale. In the last half of the seventeenth century a trade developed, primarily with New England vessels that stopped to pick up cargoes on their way to the Caribbean. Eighteenth-century changes in the North Atlantic economy slowly expanded the demand on America for grain, a trend that began to affect Virginia significantly in the 1720s and 1730s. First, the population of the British Caribbean continued to grow as new areas, such as the interior of Jamaica, were opened. More important, the nations on the northern littoral of the Mediterranean Sea experienced increasing difficulty supporting their people. At the same time, Britain, which had previously helped to supply these areas, began to withdraw from the market because of its own industrialization and urbanization, until it became an importer of food late in the century. The slack in the world food trade was taken up first by Pennsylvania and Delaware, via Philadelphia, in the later 1600s and early 1700s; then by Maryland, the Eastern Shore, and the Northern Neck, which also shipped through Philadelphia and the new port of Baltimore, founded in 1729. Finally, after mid-century, the shift moved southward through the Tidewater as lands became worn out from tobacco plantings. Although for the rest of the colonial period almost four-fifths of Virginia's income from exports still came from tobacco, the dominion was so vast that it also became the largest colonial producer of corn; and while still well behind the leader, Pennsylvania, it almost caught up with New York in the production of wheat.

*   *   *

One of the anomalies of colonial American history is that, although Virginia was the wealthiest of the British mainland colonies, it was also the most heavily in debt. Eventually Virginians owed British merchants almost as much as the rest of the mainland colonies combined, well over a million pounds sterling. Yet from a British viewpoint the investment was generally good business, for tobacco was one of the few North American commodities with a guaranteed market in Europe. Indeed, merchants normally competed intensely to advance credit to planters, in order to secure as much of their product for resale as possible. Much of the million-pound indebtedness was in fact incurred by the smaller planters of the Piedmont after the Scots entered the trade and forced up the bidding.

Some Virginians worried about the problem. Thomas Jefferson later lamented how the debts went on "from father to son for many generations." Critics looked at the luxurious mansions along Virginia rivers and concluded that the cause was the planters' spendthrift ways. It was, in part, but the reason was more complicated than simply that. Because Chesapeake tobacco was one of the largest generators of capital in the imperial economy, the debts in a sense reflected British reinvestment in future production. They funded the purchases of land, equipment, and slaves that fueled expansion. But there was no banking system outside of the British Isles to service the process. Extensions of commerical credit appeared on the books as no different from personal consumer loans. The usual procedure was for planters to draw bills of exchange on their accounts with British correspondents in anticipation of the sale of their crops. These bills might circulate through many hands before they were presented for payment in Britain. Poor communications and vast distances aggravated the problem. Like farmers of any age, tobacco planters needed funds to tide them over between crops. In their case that period might extend for several years after the initial sowing. The temptation to overdraw was difficult to control, for once merchants were in the trade, they found it hard to cut back on the credit they extended lest they lose their sources of supply. A cycle, vicious or not depending on the point of view, had begun.

A related problem was that the domestic monetary system in all the colonies, including Virginia, was woefully inadequate for the rapidly growing American economy. There were no mines in British North America to supply gold and silver for minting coins, and British mercantilism forbade the shipment of bullion from the mother country for the purpose. Most coins in circulation derived from the trade with the foreign West Indian islands, but they quickly passed on to Great Britain because of the need for specie to pay debts there. One by one, from the 1690s on, mainland colonies remedied the problem by issuing paper currency, often to meet an immediate need to pay troops and buy supplies in the frequent colonial wars with France. The method was a form of deficit financing, for the issues were usually redeemable in payment of future taxes. Inevitably the issues depreciated to varying extents relative to sterling because the latter was so much more in demand for payments to the mother country. Virginia avoided this resort until the onset of the French and Indian War in 1755. Until then the colony's valuable weed provided an entirely acceptable alternative in the form of commodity money. The usual practice in retail trade was to carry accounts in sterling on the books until the requisite amount of tobacco or other goods or services was presented to clear them, sometimes months or years later. The result was that practically everyone owed everyone else. The Chesapeake economy was an enormous iceberg of indebtedness, of which the encumbrances to Great Britain were only the most visible evidence.

*   *   *

The great upsurge in tobacco production in the 1700s was possible only because of the torrent of black migration into the colony in the first half of the century. With it the white population was able to capitalize on the expanding market to a vastly greater extent than it could have otherwise. Without it the Virginia economy would hardly have fallen into a state of destitution or bare self-sufficiency, but it would have expanded at a significantly lower rate. It must be remembered that the achievements of the golden age, with all that they meant for the American Revolution, were products of massive, systematic exploitation of the labor force. The rates of importation of blacks, temporarily high just at the turn of the century, subsequently slackened because of bad times. Then they climbed from around 1,000 a year in 1715 to 1,700–1,800 by the 1740s. From the beginning of the century to mid-point, in all at least 45,000 slaves came. (Official records exist for only about three-quarters of the legal trade, let alone for any other.) Because the demand became greater than could be supplied from the West Indies, through which most earlier blacks had passed, after 1720 virtually all came directly from Africa. Then, with the increase in native births among blacks, the need for importation tapered off. By the 1740s the percentage of blacks in the total population from all sources was approaching 30, while in the Tidewater counties between the James and York rivers it exceeded 50.

The lot of the new immigrants was far worse than that of any white in the deadliest days of the seventeenth century. About 20 percent of the Africans died from the rigors of the ocean voyage—the infamous Middle Passage, during which they were packed for weeks between decks too close for standing. Another 5 percent were so ill they expired shortly after landing; and probably 25 percent more died during seasoning. Survivors found little to ameliorate their condition in the New World, to the extent that life can in any way be ameliorated under slavery. Family life was uncommon, for as might be expected among persons selected for heavy labor, males predominated by more than two to one. Nor was there much companionship of any sort for many. Although almost two-thirds came from the same region of Africa, the Bight of Biafra, there were still, in Hugh Jones's words, so many "harsh jargons" among them that many were foreigners to each other. Judging from the complaints of buyers, loneliness, despair, and related ailments were the reaction of many new arrivals to their fate.

During the first years of contact with large numbers of Africans the array of tribal customs and the babel of languages struck Anglo-Virginians as "outlandish" and the talk not "sensible." The experience fixed in white minds for generations the stereotypes of childlike dependence, ineptitude, and laziness on the part of the new immigrants. To modern eyes the debilities were more likely a shrewd form of resistance. William Byrd II once romanticized about how he could stroll through his domain "like one of the Patriarchs," taking pride in "my flocks and my herds, my bondmen, and bond-women." But he had responsibilities, too, he quickly added: "I must take care to keep all my people to their duty, to set all the springs in motion, and to make every one draw his equal share to carry the machine forward." However idyllic his fantasy, Byrd remained well aware that slavery rested on brutality and force. With the inevitable fear of all slaveholders, he suspected that, childlike or not, the oppressed were biding their time, particularly as their numbers grew. One "unhappy effect of owning many Negroes," he warned, "is the necessity of being severe. Numbers make them insolent, and then foul means must do, what fair will not." Virginia experienced no serious slave revolt until the turn of the next century because blacks never attained the majorities they had in South Carolina and the West Indies. Moreover, they were often dispersed on scattered quarters since, even on the largest plantations, tobacco had to be cultivated in relatively small plots. Nonetheless, the litany of complaints in the diaries of eighteenth-century planters like Byrd and Landon Carter attest to the trouble "the Patriarchs" had making their "bondsmen, and bond-women" do their bidding.

The constant replenishment of the black population with freshly arrived Africans until the mid-1700s prevented much change in the slaves' condition before then. Gradually a creole population formed, in which sex ratios evened out and in which native women, in comparison with those who experienced the Middle Passage, were healthier and more fertile. The black population may have begun to reproduce itself as early as the 1710s and 1720s and certainly was doing so by the 1730s. Blacks living on plantations with ten or more slaves were the more apt to form families and to experience a social life beyond the watchful eye of the master. Most slaves, however, lived on farms with fewer than that number through mid-century. After that, the average size of the quarters on which slaves lived in the Tidewater crept upward, until by the end of the American Revolution perhaps three-fourths of the slaves in that area lived in communities of critical mass.

The increase in slave births also lessened the whites' dependence on Africa for labor. Most arrivals who might have felt the strangeness of foreigners thereafter went to the Piedmont. The increasing use of English afforded a cultural bond among creoles, as did conversions to Christianity, which occurred in significant numbers for the first time during the Great Awakening from the 1740s to the 1770s. Separate black congregations were forming by the time of the Revolution.

Historians must rely largely on white sources for evidence of patterns within this cultural development. From the complaints of white preachers about the lack of orthodoxy, for example, black interpretation of Christianity obviously differed from that of the masters. Belief in magic and witches remained important ingredients much longer among blacks than it did among Europeans. The heavy dependence of nonliterate societies on oral and musical transference of cultural values was another origin of stereotypes about blacks. (Lower literacy rates also caused whites to depend more on oral and musical transfer in the seventeenth and eighteenth centuries than later.) But the condescen-

The Old Plantation, a watercolor by an unknown artist (c. 1800). It was found in South Carolina and in the judgment of Rhys Isaac may depict a wedding. It provides a graphic representation of black social life in the slave quarters. The original is in the Abby Aldrich Rockefeller Folk Art Center, Williamsburg. Colonial Williamsburg photograph.

sion of contemporary white observers toward black music and dancing—"Rude and uncultivated . . . violent . . . and grotesque" was the way one described them—documents the emergence of separate communities.

Demographic changes made possible the first signs of Afro-American culture about the third quarter of the eighteenth century. The extent to which the process was not just simple acculturation remains controversial. Most recent researchers, however, have come to view the end product as being the blacks' own, created out of the two major cultural influences, African and Anglo-American, to which they were exposed.

*   *   *

Behind both the surge in tobacco production and the rise of the grain trade was the settlement of the Piedmont and the Valley. The county that Spotswood organized and named for himself in 1721 was Virginia's twenty-eighth, and the first beyond the Tidewater. By 1750 sixteen more had been created. The first burst of expansion came in the salient along the Rappahannock River, into which Spotswood led the way. Not far behind was the movement westward along the Potomac in the Fairfax proprietary and, farther south, along the James, where the Randolphs, Jeffersons, Walkers, and Cabells, among others, pushed out to present Albemarle County by the 1740s. Well before mid-century settlers had also scattered through the Valley of Virginia. Most were German and Scotch-Irish from Pennsylvania, but a significant third were settlers of English descent who had crossed the Blue Ridge from eastern Virginia. The bulk of that regions's early trade in hemp, grain, cattle, and horses went back along the Great Wagon Road to Pennsylvania. Then two more wagon routes were opened: one from the lower valley, where the elevations were less, to Alexandria and Fredericksburg in the 1740s; the other, from Staunton to Fredericksburg a decade later. In 1748 a settlement at Draper's Meadow near modern Blacksburg was the first beyond the Valley in the Allegheny Mountains. Two years later the surveyor Dr. Thomas Walker and his party discovered Cumberland Gap at the point where the modern states of Virginia, Kentucky, and North Carolina converge. The group were the first Englishmen to penetrate the mountains onto the Allegheny Plateau.

South of the James River, William Byrd II tried to help prepare the way in 1728 for a similar round of settlement by joining a survey of the long-disputed boundary with North Carolina. Determining the border was a necessity if valid titles were to be secured. On that score, the expedition was successful. In addition, Byrd laid the groundwork for a literary reputation by keeping a journal of the trip for publication. He drafted two versions, "The History of the Dividing Line" and, more candid and humorous, "The Secret History of the Dividing Line"; but, despite the urging of literary friends in London, he withheld both from the printer. The first did not appear until 1841; the second, until 1929. During the trip Byrd also acquired 20,000 acres on the Dan River, and later added 100,000 more, which he called his Eden. Again, on a trip to inspect his holdings, he prepared a diary entitled "A Journey to the Land of Eden," which would have added to his artistic luster had he brought himself to release it for publication. He should not have been inhibited, for modern critics compare his writing favorably with that of some of the best British stylists of the day.

As an economic venture, however, the expedition to lay out the dividing line was less of an accomplishment. Byrd's own plan to attract immigrants from Switzerland to Eden failed. Generally, despite determination of the boundary, the land to the south of the James proved not as appealing to settlers as did that to the north. Settlement lagged by at least a generation. Most of the region drains into the Roanoke River, which flows through North Carolina into Albemarle Sound. Ocean vessels had difficulty entering the sound because of barrier reefs. Settlers moving westward from Virginia had no water route to follow, as they had in areas to the north of the James, and no ease of access to the sea, which was so essential for a tobacco economy to prosper.

*   *   *

The rapid expansion to the west was encouraged by a new philosophy of land grants. Before, under the headright system, grants were made—at least, according to the law—after settlers arrived in Virginia to whoever paid their passage over. Now, beginning under Nicholson and becoming standard under Spotswood and his successors, the policy was to accelerate settlement by issuing grants before the settlers came, theoretically conditioning title upon the seating of a certain number of persons within a specified time. Few grants, however, ever reverted because of noncompliance. From tens of thousands of acres, grants escalated to more than 100,000 for Joist Hite and Robert McKey near modern Winchester in 1731 and to almost 120,000 for William Beverley near modern Staunton later in the decade. Faced with the threat of encroachment, Thomas, Lord Fairfax came in person to Virginia in 1735 to defend his claims and succeeded in reconfirming his 6,000,000 acres. Though as yet not quite as handsome, the stakes for resident Virginians continued to rise. James Patton received 200,000 acres on the New River in 1743, and two years later a syndicate of Tidewater speculators called the Greenbriar Company obtained 100,000 acres on the river of that name. In 1749 the Ohio Company, composed mostly of Northern Neck planters, received 200,000 acres and an option on 300,000 more in modern West Virginia; while the Loyal Land Company, of mainly Albemarle men, acquired 800,000 acres around Cumberland Gap. Throughout, the justification for the headlong rush to the West was as Spotswood had enunciated: the need to fend off the French from the area. From that perspective, at least, the policy achieved its goal.

The policy also carried the plantation system into most corners of the colony, continuing and spreading the trend toward social stratification that had begun in the previous century. A study of tax lists at the end of the American Revolution shows that by then only about half of all white adult males in Virginia were landowners and that about a tenth held half of the land and almost as much of the personal property. Among the other half of the males, most (about a third of all) were agricultural laborers and the remainder (15 to 20 percent) were tenants. Some of those recorded as landless may have been relatives of landowners, and some tenants may have held titles elsewhere. But the fact remains that the bulk of the land was not widely held. Although data for the earlier period are scattered both chronologically and geographically, those that are available suggest that the postwar statistics were not out of line with what had been emerging. In Middlesex County, during the first half of the century, the proportion of personal wealth held by the wealthiest third more than doubled.

Whereas those at the pinnacle of the county's elite were almost fifty times better off than the poorest in 1700, they were more than a hundred times better off fifty years later.

As settlement progressed, the familar plantation model of the Tidewater was barely a generation behind. Particularly in areas where land had been distributed in large tracts, the rate of tenancy rose through the century as late arrivals found no other way to settle. The highest figures were from the Northern Neck, where, in some counties after the War for Independence, up to 75 percent lacked title to land. There the plantation system may be said to have reached its fullest bloom. By mid-century, in the Piedmont north of the James River, where larger grants were also the rule, the pattern in the areas of initial settlement along the fall line was the same, though the level of tenancy was not quite so high. Later in 1768, farther west in Albemarle County, Thomas Jefferson began to build his new home, Monticello, which differed little as a social symbol from the mansions of the East. The virtue of the cloning was that, as the tobacco economy expanded, newly settled areas were relatively easily assimilated to the old, enabling Virginia to escape the worst of the East-West conflicts that disrupted so many sister provinces.

* * *

Still, the "husbandman," about whom many throughout American history, beginning with Jefferson, have theorized as the ideal citizen, simultaneously staged a comeback. At first, the introduction of slavery had pressed hard on smaller farmers who could not afford the more costly blacks as easily as they could afford indentured servants. The number of households without a servant or slave increased through the end of the seventeenth century. Then, with the slackening of white immigration, fewer farmers were just beginning to eke out a living. Most who were able to acquire land at all did better. The number of farms dependent mainly on the labor of the head of the household declined again. With the exhaustion of tobacco land and the introduction of grain, the average size of estates in the long-established Tidewater dropped by a fifth over the first half of the eighteenth century, and the number of householders increased by two-thirds, more and more of them holding slaves. Significantly, more of the estates proved in court during that period had values of more than £100. While the rich were becoming very rich, some of the less well off (though not the least) were becoming better off than before.

The fact is that, despite the great plantations, most white Virginians in the eighteenth century were small farmers. Read another way, the data above mean that at the conclusion of the Revolution 40 percent of the white males owned half of the land and another 15 to 20 percent had access to the soil as tenants. The figures probably had not varied much over the previous generation. These small landholders were the people whom contemporaries considered the backbone of society. Legislation in 1705 and 1736 progressively tightened the requirements for the suffrage. The first act codified the seventeenth-century practice that the voter should be a freeholder, and not a black, woman, or Catholic recusant, but left the definition of a freehold open. The second specified that a voter should own or hold in life tenancy at least 100 acres of unimproved land or 25 "with a house and plantation." Comparable requirements were enacted for the few town dwellers. With the inclusion of life tenants, it is estimated that under these rules at mid-century probably 55 to 60 percent of white adult males possessed the franchise and that about two-thirds of those who had the privilege regularly exercised it. The result was hardly a broad-based democracy by modern standards. No more than one in five or six of the potential electorate, white or black, male or female, had a voice in government. But the question is relative. Landholding was more widely distributed in Virginia than in the mother country, and two to three times as many persons by percentage of population had the vote in the colony as in contemporary Britain.

Officeholding was another matter. It was much more restricted than the franchise. Although it was technically open to anyone who possessed the vote, the smaller the farmer the more content he apparently was to leave higher office to his betters, not only because of their social position and education but also because they had more laborers to care for their fields while they served. Although all voters were members of the establishment, part of the planter elite, it contained gradations and the gaps were wide. At one end were the great planters, like the Wormeleys of Middlesex, whose marriages, political contacts, and business affairs spanned many counties and, indeed, were even international in scope. At the other were simple farmers whose lives and horizons remained nearer home. The best estimates place the proportion of literacy among white males in the middle of the eighteenth century, for example, at around two-thirds, close to the percentage believed to have qualified for the vote. While the two categories do not precisely overlap, most voters clearly were literate. But in the case of some, it must be remembered, the definition of literacy in these studies is merely the ability to sign one's name.

* * *

The only elections at the time were for the House of Burgesses. These were usually festive occasions, serving a widely dispersed rural population—along with militia musters, plantation balls, and church services—as a chance for social gathering. Although by the law of 1705 candidates were not supposed to treat electors in return for support, voters expected the prohibition to be widely ignored—an anticipation that only the wealthy could satisfy. Frequent examples of long terms in office, and the passing of offices within families from one generation to the next as if by inheritance, measure the extent of deference in the society. The exceptional durability did not have to be, however, for occasionally voters measured up to the romantic ideal of the independent landowner, which most of them were, to turn out incumbents when the issue warranted, as Spotswood discovered in 1715.

As that election and the one three years later reveal, the political significance of the House of Burgesses was increasing during the early decades of the eighteenth century despite the outward dominance of the Council. As mentioned before, the frequent confrontations between governors and Council enhanced the lower chamber's standing and bolstered its political self-confidence as both sides bid for its support. Basically what was happening was that the advance of settlement and growth of population were outrunning the Council. A twelve-member board could not satisfy all the political ambitions that were emerging. As a practical matter, the Council's advisory role to the governor confined its membership to eastern Virginia, within relatively easy traveling distance of the capital in Williamsburg. Inevitably the Council had to give way as the primary reflector of public opinion to the more expandable lower house.

The shift was gradual, the product not of a master plan or campaign but of pragmatic, ad hoc decisions with regard to specific issues over a long time. Seldom did the chambers come into conflict over the matter. The lower house slowly gained the institutional mechanisms to advance from a role largely limited to periodically reviewing and restraining executive initiatives to one of formulating and implementing decisions itself. In most cases the model was Parliament, which was gaining similar ground in Great Britain. In view of the implications, it is interesting that royal officials as well as colonists seem to have accepted the logic of the imitation. Almost from its beginning early in the seventeenth century, the House of Burgesses had the power to establish electoral districts, to judge disputed elections, to expel members, and to set suffrage requirements. But, despite a few attempts, it was never able to assume the right to determine the frequency of its elections or of its own sessions. The right to appoint the Speaker, which the House of Commons obtained in 1679, the burgesses firmly secured a decade later. After the Glorious Revolution it was never questioned that, as in Britain, the lower house alone should introduce appropriation bills, although it normally allowed the Council to participate fully in their preparation. In the 1680s the Crown reclaimed the power to appoint the chamber's clerk (as it still did that of the House of Commons), but governors traditionally named only persons acceptable to the burgesses who paid the clerks' salaries. From its origin the legislature exercised the power to create county courts, whereas the governor appointed the justices. Although the lower chamber lost its right to hear appeals in 1682 and the Council alone continued as the supreme court, the burgesses frequently enacted statutes regulating the latter, with only sporadic objections from the Crown. In 1728 the House formed a standing committee on courts of justice.

The appointment of subordinate provincial officials such as collectors and naval officers remained the prerogative of the governor and Council throughout the colonial period. In 1691, however, the burgesses gained the right to have a treasurer to audit provincial revenues, and the office eventually extended its investigative authority over most executive functions. The burgesses had set surveyors' fees since 1624; and by the end of the seventeenth century they had enlarged their control to include the assessments of the colonial secretary, clerks of county courts, and sheriffs. In 1699 they added the fees of collectors and naval officers, and in 1718 coroners and constables. By the middle of the eighteenth century the House also controlled the fees of the governor, the attorney general, and all officers of the chamber itself. Although for almost seventy-five years governors' instructions allowed them to set fees with the advice of the Council, none attempted to do so before 1750. In 1726 Spotswood's successor suggested that in order to enforce their own decrees the burgesses ought to have a sergeant at arms whom the governor would appoint but who, like the clerk, would be paid by the House. In 1732 the colony became the first in the South to have a public printer. The lower chamber invited William Parks to come from Maryland to fill the post. Four years later he founded the colony's first newspaper, the *Virginia Gazette*, in Williamsburg.

Actually the rise of the burgesses, despite their earlier beginning, was not as rapid as in the case of lower houses in some other colonies because politics were less confrontational in Virginia. For the most part, Spotswood's successors preferred tact and diplomacy to head-on collisions in their dealings with the legislative branch. Only occasionally did the Council clash with its junior partner, among whose members sat many councillors' sons and siblings. Among the burgesses themselves, organized factions were more the exception than the rule compared with other colonies. Rivalries and disagreements arose, but they did not become systematic. Councillors and burgesses represented essentially the same constituents: tobacco and grain farmers who, despite great discrepancies in size of operation, had to face imperial authorities and the international marketplace together; landholders, large and small, who were dependent on maintenance of traditional land policies; and whites in an increasingly biracial society. Whatever their differences, on the major issues all had more in common than not.

*   *   *

The Golden Age was everything that a Virginian concerned about the cultural contribution of his homeland could have wished for. Within a generation the upper class in the older settled areas of the colony turned from provincial frontier barons into close replicas of the eighteenth-century British country gentry. There were differences—the British were not dependent on slavery and a single staple for their wealth, and their aristocratic traditions were grayer with age—but there were enough similarities for Virginians to believe that they were conforming to the mold.

Imitation of the British gentry rationalized the political and social structure that had evolved from the cultivation of tobacco in the colony. For centuries in the mother country, newly acquired wealth had achieved social status through the acquisition of land. The same pattern worked well in the colony, where it provided an inspirational model for success in an otherwise tough, competitive milieu. Larger landholders in Great Britain played patriotic, paternalistic roles in their counties, roles that also suited the Virginia scene; and tillers of the soil in eighteenth-century literature enjoyed a reputation as conservators of what was good from the past. Although often at odds intellectually and politically with London, whose more sophisticated lifestyle many in Britain and America deemed corrupt, the British country gentry were not cultural hermits. Their country houses were a significant genre in the architectural revival of the Enlightenment. It was the country house, a symbol of regional power and cultural achievement, on which the Virginia elite lavished their energies and brought to a degree of perfection unsurpassed anywhere in the empire outside the mother nation.

The British Enlightenment reached its height in the eighteenth century, and Virginia shared tangentially in its triumphs. The age was characterized by a confident assurance that its intellectual attainments were matched in Western civilization only by those of the ancient world. Knowledge of the classics became the first step in education. Every cultivated person was comfortable with copious classical allusions and pithy quotations from Greek and Roman authors in his reading, writing, and public speaking. Every study of history, politics, or the arts commenced with a review of the accomplishments of the ancients. The most common cliché among eighteenth-century thinkers was that civilization had fallen from the eminence of ancient times into the "ignorance and superstition" of the medieval "Dark Ages." Only in their own era had enlightenment returned.

A chauvinistic offshoot of this view of history peculiar to the English was that the mother country had enjoyed a golden age in antiquity also. Tribal councils known as *witans*, which the Roman historian Tacitus described among Germanic peoples, were seen as instruments of representative government analogous to the Roman Senate and the later

Shirley, one of the great James River plantation houses, built between 1720 and 1740. Colonial Williamsburg photograph.

English Parliament and were believed to have been imported into England by the Anglo-Saxons in the fifth and sixth centuries. In contrast, the rest of Europe appeared to have been weighted down by feudalism and absolute monarchy. Neither of these evils, it was held, had come to England until its conquest by the Norman French in 1066. Until then, too, the Saxons were supposed to have resisted the encroachments of the papacy, to which was generally ascribed most of the backwardness of the medieval period. Anglo-Saxon England, in other words, was Protestant in spirit, and perhaps in fact as well. For that reason and others, the Enlightenment in England had less of an antireligious bias than it had on the Continent, which had suffered more from Catholics and Protestants alike during the religious wars of the early seventeenth century. Englishmen were more apt to see the Reformation as the first light in the medieval darkness than as another example of medieval superstition.

To a surprising extent, in view of the popular image of the rollicking, fun-loving cavalier, eighteenth-century Virginia intellectuals were concerned with religion. Virginia libraries whose contents are known contained more books on that subject than on any other. Most were works on piety and morality rather than on theological disputation. Virginians responded to the rationalistic attacks of the day more by not raising questions than by attempting to resolve them.

Of greater interest was the construction of a code of behavior by which gentlemen should live, for violence was not far beneath the surface in colonial Virginia. Even the Tidewater was relatively close to the frontier, where the next tobacco fields were to be opened, and most gentlemen were slaveholders. As yet, culture was a little thin: "Virginians being naturally of good parts. . . . neither require nor admire as much learning, as we do in Britain," was the way Hugh Jones put it. The eighteenth-century elite were sons and grandsons of self-made men. They were commercial farmers and international traders; they were capitalists, the fittest who had survived in a fiercely competitive economy. The drive to excel sometimes led to the wager of an entire fortune on a cock fight, a horse race, or a roll of the dice; the code of honor that made them gentlemen could require a duel. Strong egos were part of the definition of Virginian. The problem for would-be gentry was to distinguish themselves from the eye-gouging frontiersmen and farm laborers, to establish communitarian values in a violently individualistic society.

The most popular answer was Roman Stoicism, as expounded by Cicero, Seneca, and the emperor Marcus Aurelius. It emphasized acceptance of fate and unflinching devotion to duty, a philosophy quite compatible, for those who were concerned about a parallel, with the view of life implied in Christian teachings on the virtue of fortitude. Stoicism held significant political implications, too. Honor and duty explain the many hours that planters spent in what was virtually volunteer work on the vestry, the county court, the House of Burgesses, or the Council. It also generated constant watchfulness for, and consequently frequent discovery of, corruption in government. A favorite pseudonym for letters to the editor was "Cato," the name of one Roman Senator famous for his chastisement of contemporaries for moral and civic failings and of another who had heroically and tragically died defending the Roman Republic against the emperor Caesar. A popular play in George Washington's youth was *Cato* by Joseph Addison, which told the story of the second senator, and the best-known commentary on contemporary British politics was a series of sharply critical essays signed "Cato" by two British journalists, John Trenchard and Thomas Gordon.

The enlightenment on which British prided themselves extended to the modern age as well as the ancient. The long-drawn-out revolutions of the seventeenth century had evoked widespread speculation in the mother country on the nature of government and the feasibility of popular self-rule. Answers ranged from proclamations of democratic leveling to ardent defenses of absolutism, whether based on divine right or on sheer power. Since there had been no really pertinent examples of popular rule for more than a millennium and a half, writers repeatedly referred to fifth-century Greece and the Roman Republic, or to such odd contemporary illustrations as the elected monarchy of Poland, for their typology. Inevitably they turned to Caesar's empire for descriptions of what happened to popular government if the people were not eternally vigilant. When the English uprisings of the seventeenth century led to a compromise between monarchy and popular representation, at least of the upper classes, the result was lionized as an ideal mixture, seemingly in perfect balance with the harmonies of nature. A book in 1748, *The Spirit of the Laws*, ended every doubt. The author, baron de Montesquieu, was a subject of the nation with which Britain was at war during much of the century. After studying all the constitutions of the past and present that he could find, this Frenchman pronounced the British constitution the best in history. It masterfully blended in the king, lords, and commons, he wrote, the three fundamental forms of government defined by the ancients: monarchy, aristocracy, and democracy. It skillfully divided the fearsome power of sovereignty between its executive, legislative, and judicial components, so that each would check the excesses of the others. The work understandably was quickly translated and became standard reading on both shores of the British empire.

The test of any human endeavor at the time was conformity to the dictates of science; it was the moving force of the Enlightenment. The moderns—Francis Bacon, Isaac Newton, and John Locke—who in Jefferson's estimation were worthy of being added to the pantheon of ancients, were all known for their advancement of rationalistic, empirical epistemology. Their insistence on observation of nature and inductive reasoning raised serious challenges to ideas of innate charac-teristics, such as the Christian doctrine of Original Sin, and to accounts of miracles, such as providential intervention in history and the mystery of the Trinity. Astronomical observations from Copernicus to Newton emphasized the awesome inevitability of the Laws of Motion that governed the universe. At the same time, the positing of such laws raised the hopeful possibility that, by studying and understanding them, men could avoid the "ignorance and superstition" of their ancestors, whether in science, ethics, or government. Predictions of the actual limit to which progress might go varied widely with each philosopher. By modern standards, advances in the quality of life on either side of the Atlantic remained discouragingly few. But some advances had occurred, compared with the past, and more could confidently be anticipated.

The vogue of science propelled Virginians and other Americans more rapidly ahead in international intellectual circles than might otherwise have been the case for a frontier society. They had at their doorsteps the best laboratory available in which to observe nature, the colonial wilderness. "In the beginning all the world was America," John Locke wrote. Collecting and shipping specimens unknown in Europe brought

Americans into correspondence with such Continental giants as Carl Linnaeus of Sweden and John Frederick Gronovius of Leyden. The president of the British Royal Society, Sir Hans Sloane, and others of the British natural history circle financed John Banister's trip to Virginia, which led to the publication of *Historia Plantarum* in 1686. Mark Catesby, whom biographers have named "the eighteenth-century Audubon" because of his beautiful paintings of birds, spent several years in Virginia early in the century. (Later the British natural history circle backed a second trip farther south, which he recorded in his famous *Natural History of Carolina, Florida, and the Bahama Islands* [1731–1743].) The same group sought a parish for Hugh Jones in the Chesapeake Bay region to have him as their observer on the scene because of his interest in botany.

The linchpin of British-American scientific correspondence was the Quaker merchant in London, Peter Collinson, who had far-flung contacts throughout the empire. One of his intimates was John Parke Custis of Williamsburg. Custis developed a magnificent specimen garden, about which he corresponded with Collinson for fifteen years. But Collinson's most famous Virginia correspondent was the clerk of the Gloucester County Court, John Clayton, who collaborated with Gronovius in the publication of *Flora Virginica* in 1739, with a second edition in 1762. It earned Clayton election to the Royal Society of Sweden. In Urbanna, Dr. John Mitchell, a physician and fellow of the British Royal Society who had been trained at the universities of Edinburgh and Leyden, won praise from Linnaeus for his corrections of the Swede's classification system. Mitchell also wrote a paper for the Royal Society on the odd creature, the opossum; and it was his map of French and British North America that was used in the peace negotiations of the American Revolutionary War. These men were only the most visible of many such figures, for the model planter was, among his many avocations, an amateur scientist. William Byrd's garden was as renowned for the number of rare species it contained as his library was for the size of its collection, one of the largest in British America. John Page contributed to the observations of the two transits of Venus in the 1760s; and, with Governor Francis Fauquier, himself a member of the Royal Society, he helped found the Virginia Society for the Promotion of Useful Knowledge, of which Clayton was the first president, in the 1770s.

William Byrd II (1647–1744), planter, Councillor, diarist, owner of the largest library in the Colony, and builder of Westover, among the most famous of the great eighteenth-century Virginia plantation houses, was perhaps the most prominent figure of the "Golden Age" of Virginia culture. Artist unknown. Photograph by Colonial Williamsburg, which owns the original.

Evelyn Byrd (1707–1737) was the daughter of William Byrd II, whose stern refusal to permit her to marry an English baronet in 1723 suggests the patriarchal quality of family life among the Virginia gentry. Artist unknown. Photograph by Colonial Williamsburg, which owns the orginal.

The Virginia Enlightenment was a quiet echo of the British. Fashions and styles often peaked in the mother country ten to twenty years before they appeared in the colony. Culturally Virginians would have foundered without the British to follow. Their accomplishment is that they were able to follow. During the first half of the eighteenth century the virgin wilderness was still only fifty to a few hundred miles away. Within a short generation Virginians produced a self-confident upper class that believed (whatever the British may have thought) that it could hobnob, if it chose, with the gentry "at home." The cost was high. Two-fifths of Virginia's people at mid-century were enslaved, and the concentration of capital required for the elite to meet the cultural challenges left many of the remaining three-fifths socially and economically far below the leaders.

*   *   *

The most obvious sign of the golden era into which colonial Virginians emerged with much pain and sweat for the majority was the building of the famed Georgian mansions along the rivers of the Tidewater. Awe-inspiring in their magnificence, they were symbols of the great planters' wealth, signs of their political and social hegemony. They were also intellectual statements, conscious testimony that the colony's leaders were abreast of the latest current of ideas in the Western world, that culturally Virginia need apologize to none. "Country Seats," as the younger Beverley grudgingly had to admit, were the core of eighteenth-century Virginia life. Yet, ironically, the ideas that the Georgian mansions reflected were first introduced to the colony through the building of a town, the only one that the campaign for urban growth succeeded in founding.

Williamsburg's buildings, Hugh Jones declared, "are justly reputed the best in all the English America, and are exceeded by few of their kind in England." At one end of the city stood "the Capitol, a noble, beautiful, and commodious pile," most likely designed by Francis Nicholson, the city's planner. The remaining public structures were paeans to Jones's patron, Alexander Spotswood. Across town from the capitol was the college, "beautiful and commodious, being first modelled by Sir Christopher Wren [and] adapted to the nature of the country." The building had burned in the fall of 1705 and had been

rebuilt "by the ingenious . . . Governor Spotswood." In between lay
other examples of that governor's conception: Bruton Parish Church,
"adorned as the best churches in London"; the Public Magazine, "a
large octagon tower"; and the debtors' prison, whose flat roof was an
architectural first in Virginia. The pièce de résistance was, as Jones
described it, "the Palace or Governor's House, a magnificent structure
. . . beautified with gates, fine gardens, offices, walks, a fine canal,
orchards, etc. . . . by . . . the most accomplished Colonel Spotswood."

The style that Williamsburg brought to the colony derived from
principles inherited from the ancient world and expounded during the
Renaissance by such authors as the Italian Andrea Palladio. Inigo Jones
introduced it to England during the first half of the seventeenth
century; and Sir Christopher Wren, given the tragic opportunity of the
Great Fire of London, converted Restoration England to its belief.
Nicholas Hawksmore, John Vanbrugh, and many others became its
high priests in the next generation. By the beginning of the eighteenth
century the new look totally dominated the construction of public
buildings and fine residences in Britain, providing the models that first
Francis Nicholson and then Alexander Spotswood taught the Virginia
upper class to emulate.

Buildings in the new style followed rules of mathematical symmetry, reflecting both classical taste and the cult of science that
characterized the seventeenth- and eighteenth-century Enlightenment.
When the Bruton Parish vestry decided in 1710, for example, that
their old brick church was becoming too costly to maintain, planning
a replacement gave Spotswood a chance to display his skill in geometry.
The overall height of the building he designed is half its length, the
width of the transept is a third the length of the nave, and the
transept's length forms the altitude of an equilateral triangle based on
the length of the nave. Similarly, when an armory was needed for some
arms that Queen Anne presented the colony in 1714, Spotswood called
on the legislature to take the opportunity to provide "an Estate of
Inheritance." He proposed an octagonal structure, the walls and roof of
which are equal in height. The distance from ground to rooftop equals
the diagonal of a square, each of whose sides equals the width of the
building—a ratio that mathematicians term the Golden Section.

The most pronounced effect of the new style in Virginia was the
construction of buildings that, as Hugh Jones repeated almost by rote

in description after description, were more "commodious" than before. The archetype was Spotswood's masterpiece, the governor's residence. It had been begun before he arrived. Partly in celebration of Nicholson's departure, the Assembly in 1705, after years of nudging by the Crown, had appropriated £3,000 for Governor Nott to commence construction. The funds were from a tax on liquors and imported slaves, which had the added effect in the troubled times of reducing the rate of expansion of tobacco production. Construction lagged, however, because of Nott's untimely death. Another £400 became necessary, and then £200 more. Yet when Spotswood arrived, no money was left for the roof; and the structure had to be temporarily boarded over for protection against the elements.

During the early, more pleasant, days of the new governor's administration, he obtained the Assembly's approval for another £1,560 to complete the house and its dependencies, and £635 for furnishings and landscaping. The funds were for "a Court-yard . . . a brick wall four foot high, with balustrades of wood . . . a Garden of the length of two hundred fifty-four foot and of the breadth of one hundred forty foot . . . and . . . handsome gates." Two years later, Spotswood was back for £900 more, which he again received from the liquor and slave tax. Because of the economic decline, however, he was unable to realize sufficient revenue, and the Assembly extended the levy. This time it placed no limit on the amount he could spend from it.

At that point, with the controversy over the tobacco inspection law and the Indian Company raging, councillors began making sarcastic remarks about Spotswood's "Palace." The petition for his removal in 1718 contained a complaint about the extravagance of the construction. One of the costs objected to was doubtless the billiard room; another, the overawing display of weaponry affixed to the walls of the entrance hall. Still another focus of complaint was probably the six-foot wall Spotswood built around the courtyard instead of the four-foot one that was authorized. He also annoyed some by his elegant solution to the problem of the deep ravines that plagued Williamsburg landscapers by terracing the one to the west of the dwelling and featuring a "canal" or pond at the bottom. Such canals, usually stocked with carp and graced with oriental-style bridges and balustrades, were a frequent motif in Britain, an outgrowth of the empire's expanding trade with Asia. The main gardens north of the Palace were formally geometric in

The reconstructed Governor's Palace in Williamsburg, originally begun in 1705 and completed under Governor Alexander Spotswood in 1720 except for the addition of a ballroom in 1751. As the residence of the chief official in the colony and the most impressive house in the capital town, it symbolized royal authority for colonists. Colonial Williamsburg photograph.

the prevailing mode. Spotswood, however, seems also to have been aware of the avant-garde trend in the mother country toward less patterned extensions of gardens into the surrounding countryside to bring the natural terrain into view. He became involved in a bitter quarrel with Councillor John Parke Custis, whose Queen's Creek estate lay to the north of the Palace, for cutting down too much good timber to improve the "vista."

Spotswood's response to the criticism was that, from the time he received the carte blanche, he had spent "but little more" than £1,200, which he thought a colony with a £10,000 surplus in its treasury could afford. Moreover, it should be noted in his defense, the legislature from the beginning clearly intended the dwelling to be among the most elegant in the colonies. The original statute called for a brick structure fifty-four feet long by forty-eight feet wide, two and a half stories high, with new-style sash windows instead of the old-fashioned casement. The building was to have a leaded, slate roof, a feature practically unknown in the colonies. Aside from the cost and difficulty of importing the stone unbroken, the roof created the problem for a time of finding someone who knew how to build it. After the governor and the Council were reconciled in 1720, a committee found that £521 14s. 4½ d. were needed to complete the project. The total cost was slightly more than £7,000, roughly the equivalent, at the average of a penny a pound, of 1,800,000 pounds of tobacco, or the output of more than 1,800 people for a year.

The scale and magnificence of the Palace and its grounds, and the founding of Williamsburg generally, revolutionized architectural thinking in Virginia. Within a decade and a half after the Palace was completed, a number of the colony's grandest residences rose to challenge it. Robert Carter I remodeled Corotoman in Lancaster County and built Christ Church to imitate and outshine Bruton. The cruciform design of the latter was peculiarly Virginian; in England Wren did not favor it. Only in Virginia, of all the colonies, did that floor plan become the norm in church building for the rest of the colonial period. In Charles City County, Benjamin Harrison IV's Berkeley and William Byrd II's Westover appeared; in Westmoreland, Thomas Lee's Stratford Hall and Robert Carter II's Nomini Hall; in Chesterfield, Henry Cary's Ampthill (Cary's father was the contractor for the Capitol and the first stage of the Palace); and in Richmond

County, Landon Carter's Sabine Hall. Virginia's great planters were not to be put to shame by a British governor, whether he had become naturalized or not. Mann Page's Rosewell in Gloucester County was the largest residence ever built in a British American colony, and more grand buildings were constructed in the Georgian mode in Virginia than in any other colony. Paneled and pilastered walls, parquet floors, molded ceilings, marble fireplaces, and grand staircases adorned interiors where the practical and mundane had sufficed before. The imitation of the Palace was not slavish. With professional assistance beyond the level of skilled carpenter-contractors unavailable, an amateur expertise in architecture became a mark of a cultivated man. A thriving market in handbooks from Great Britain from 1720 on offered a potpourri of elements within the classical rubric from which each housebuilder could assemble a unique package to express his individual taste and personality. What was common was an opulence and a grandeur that not only broadcast the fact of enormous economic success but also satisfied a desire to bring Virginia out of a cultural backwater into the intellectual mainstream of the Western world.

10

THE POLITICS OF ACCOMMODATION: GOVERNORS HUGH DRYSDALE AND WILLIAM GOOCH

With the arrival of the little-known Hugh Drysdale in September 1722 Virginia entered the final phase of its colonial development. Under the new governor the tone of politics dramatically altered, for the Board of Trade had sought out an appointee who would avoid the kind of trouble Spotswood generated. The economic situation remained grave for a while longer, but within a decade a period of sustained growth commenced. By mid-century, among the planter class, it was difficult not to be proud to be a Virginian. Economically successful and politically well governed, the foremost among them were as cultivated as any other subjects of the empire.

Serendipitously, Drysdale's mission of harmony benefited immediately from events in the colony that established his popularity. Landing just as a slave conspiracy was uncovered, he gained public approval by energetically prosecuting those involved, but as his investigation convinced him that the plot was "foolish" and "impracticable," he was able to quiet public opinion and avoid overreaction. The alarm allowed him to push through the Assembly militia reforms that had eluded his predecessors: new oaths, new fines for nonattendance, and a requirement that anyone who was exempt from service must furnish a substitute with a horse. Drysdale's experience with the trials also led him to obtain an act that better defined procedures for trying slaves on capital charges. With this beginning, his executive style set the precedent for the next generation. He worked amicably with the local establishment and brought closer to reality the goal that many governors espoused but never achieved: the melding of colonial and imperial interests.

On the discouraging side, Drysdale's arrival coincided with a deepening downturn in the economy. Booming tobacco production over the past several years finally caught up with demand just as Western Europe was struck by one of the most severe financial shocks of the century. The lure of fabulous profits in the New World had so captivated the investing publics of Britain and France after the recent war that virtually identical get-rich-quick schemes ran wild in each country. At the center of the schemes were speculating companies—the French Mississippi Company and the British South Sea Company—that gained government monopolies over important areas of colonial trade in return for promises of painless payment of national debts. Speculation was out of control until finally the South Sea Bubble, as it was known in Britain, burst in the summer of 1720 with reverberations around the world. So distracted by the craze were British merchants that too few ships came to transport the near-record tobacco output of the Chesapeake that year. By the time the next fleet arrived prices had tumbled to half, and in two years some quotations fell beneath $\frac{1}{2}d$. a pound, as the trade spiraled into a decade-long depression.

The result was renewed attempts by Virginians to curb production. The efforts led to clashes with royal authorities and, because Drysdale supported the colony's plans, enhanced his stature with the planters. One resort was an old standby, a tax on imported slaves and liquors. Drysdale approved it, he explained to the Board of Trade, because the board itself had allowed a similar act before. Besides, the new legislation imposed a levy of only £2 a slave, whereas the earlier act had set £5. Despite the lower rate, the Royal African Company and other slave-trading interests lobbied more aggressively than before and succeeded in persuading the board to reject the measure. An attempt to tax imported slaves alone in 1728 suffered similarly.

The other economic therapy was a stint act passed in the spring of 1723 to limit production for three years to 10,000 plants a year for each householder or 6,000 for each tithable, if there were more than one on a farm. Lowered capacity improved quality, the argument ran.

This time, Drysdale excused his sanction of the act to the Board of Trade on the ground that the measure did not take effect for a year, permitting ample time for the board's review. Although the board let the statute stand, it is difficult to tell what effect the act had. A drought in 1724 reduced production, and then a storm, which John Parke Custis thought brought more rain than had fallen at one time "since the universal deluge," destroyed 34,000 hogsheads of what had been harvested, by Drysdale's count. The succeeding year produced a "small cropp" as well. Nonetheless, the act was renewed in 1728 and not repealed until 1730.

One area in which the new governor did not win enthusiastic backing in Virginia was his investigation of his predecessor's land grants. Only Commissary Blair, whose man Drysdale was generally considered to be, and Receiver General John Grymes endorsed the inquiry. Most large landholders had too much to lose themselves if Spotswood's land policies were overturned. One outcome of the investigation was that the Board of Trade finally accepted Spotswood's argument that settlement of the West should be hastened in order to check the French. In 1723 it approved his exemption of newly patented lands from quitrents for seven years. At the same time, it limited the amount any individual could claim to 1,000 acres. A series of reports from Drysdale and Grymes laid bare the extent of the grants Spotswood had made to himself (86,000 acres) and the many violations of procedure he had permitted. The former governor conceded that there had been "certain formalities ommitted in passing of patents," but once more advanced in his defense the threat of the French. He also noted his service to the Crown and the colony and the vindictive nature of his enemies' attacks. Returning to England for six years in the spring of 1724, Spotswood skillfully raised legal issue after legal issue before the Board of Trade until, whether from exhaustion or conviction, it resolved all questions in his favor.

After Drysdale's first Assembly in the spring of 1723, which he called to deal with the economic crisis, he summoned only one other. He explained that, since another session would have little to do, he did not want to burden the people with unnecessary expenses in such dire times. He was correct. When he finally convened a second session of the legislature in May 1726, it found only a few matters to occupy its time. The most important of these was the creation, at Drysdale's urging, of the post of sergeant at arms to enforce the burgesses' own regulations—one more acknowledgement of their emerging power. Establishment of the post was one of the governor's last official acts. Having been ill for several weeks, he first announced his return to Britain for treatment, then changed his mind because, he said, he had found a physician in Virginia "who gives me hopes of a perfect cure." He died two weeks later.

*   *   *

The Council did little while awaiting Drysdale's successor. The contrast to its vigor after Nott's demise is an indication of the political decline that was setting in. One reason for the lethargy, perhaps, was that it had already won its major battles with Spotswood and earlier governors. Still, it could have addressed economic issues. Undoubtedly another cause was the advanced age of many members. Robert Carter had to replace Edmund Jenings as president when the latter became senile, but Carter himself was ill and would not come to Williamsburg during the summer. Blair was seventy-three. Philip Ludwell and Nathaniel Harrison died shortly after Drysdale. Only John Grymes, appointed in 1725, had the old fire. Councillors also had less time for politics because of the ever-increasing volume of other business with which they dealt. Having forced the governor to appoint them to the courts of oyer and terminer, they were spending several months a year on judicial matters alone. A political vacuum was forming that the chamber in the other wing of the capitol was prepared and eager to fill.

The next governor, William Gooch, the fifth appointee in a row to have served under Marlborough and Orkney, arrived in Williamsburg in September 1727. Gooch was the ablest politician of the five. Ever tactful and charming, the new executive was a master diplomat who found, for example, that the answer to the continuing problem of Commissary Blair, "a very vile old fellow" who had been the ruin of so many of his predecessors, was "to kill him with kindness." The tactic worked, for Gooch's administration lasted twenty-two years, seventeen during the remaining years of Blair's long lifetime.

During his first few years in office Gooch seemed content with the usual planter response to hard times. There had been a slight revival of prices around mid-decade because bad weather earlier in the 1720s had cut production by about a fifth. But the respite was brief, and the stint law notwithstanding, the colony's answer to the continuing downturn was once again to invest additional capital. More than 10,000 slaves were imported and almost a million new acres patented, mostly in the Piedmont, by 1730. By then previous losses in production had been more than recouped; former record levels of output were exceeded by 20 percent.

Compounding the colony's woes, tobacco consignment merchants, whom Scottish factors were beginning to outdistance, organized and aggressively sought ways of improving their competitive position. They attempted to increase their income by imposing new charges such as shipping fees for supplies bound for the colonies. Manufactured items had traditionally been carried free to America as a business incentive, because their volume was minuscule compared with the bulk of eastward-bound crops and because ships had to make the voyage anyway. Planters' resistance nullified most of the new rates within a few years, with the exception of a ½ of 1 percent commission for negotiating bills of exchange that became standard. Meanwhile, the added costs did not help recovery.

Parliament, too, under the leadership of the new and powerful prime minister, Robert Walpole, inaugurated reforms to recapture some of the customs revenue the government believed was slipping away. Scottish dealers, in particular, had acquired a reputation for flagrant violations of trade regulations, and tighter controls were imposed in 1723 to end their clandestine activities. In the long run, the reforms proved a boon to Virginians, for in an effort both to encourage expansion of trade and to curtail smuggling, Walpole decided to rebate all duties on tobacco reexported from the mother country. The new policy was a major stimulus in the enormous development of tobacco markets on the European continent that underlay the sustained growth of Chesapeake production over the next half-century. At the moment, the provision that fell most heavily on tobacco growers was the prohibition of stripping stems from plants before shipping, as was the custom with sweet-scented tobacco. The premise behind the decree was an instinctive worry of customs commissioners that stemming reduced bulk and therefore revenue. Little heed was given the Virginia argument that stemming improved quality.

The colony that Gooch took over was most dispirited. There seemed to be no way to alleviate the depression. As was customary for new governors, Gooch held an election shortly after his arrival. It was heatedly, and in some areas violently, contested. Half of the incumbents were displaced, yet no single issue other than general frustration appears to have been at stake. Gooch himself offered only a few platitudes for guidance in his maiden address to the Assembly, and although the body worked busily for several sessions turning out laws, the effect was negligible. The solution adopted for the economic crisis was reenactment of the stint law early in 1728 and another import duty on slaves. The main focus of the delegates was on obtaining repeal of the parliamentary prohibition of stemming, for which they sent one of their number, John Randolph, to London. When at last he succeeded in 1729, they voted him a generous £1,000 in expenses as his reward. He was unable to save the duty on slaves, however.

*   *   *

As a consequence, Virginia planters were desperate when Gooch proposed the legislation that became his hallmark, the tobacco inspection act of 1730. Basically the same as Spotswood's law, which had caused an uproar fifteen years before, Gooch's bill called for the inspection and bonding at public warehouses of all tobacco shipped abroad; for the destruction of all unacceptable tobacco; for standardization of the size of hogsheads at 36 inches by 48 inches; for maintenance of detailed records to prevent smuggling; and for circulation of warehouse receipts as legal tender in lieu of tobacco itself, which had been used as commodity money until then. The idea differed from Spotswood's mainly in the matter of patronage. Appointments were to be made jointly by the governor and the Council, and the duties of inspector were defined to preclude anyone holding the office while serving as burgess.

Gooch prepared the bill's political path well. He began a letterwriting campaign to the mother country as early as February 1729 to neutralize the expected opposition from British merchants and the imperial bureaucracy. He scored an important initial victory in obtaining the approval of Micajah Perry before the bill was introduced. In the hope of securing similar regulation in Maryland, Gooch kept the governor of that colony so well informed of the plan that a copy was

A view of the town of York, Virginia, from the River.

A view of Yorktown, Virginia, in 1755, by an unknown artist. The small size of the port, even though it was a major shipping center for tobacco planters on the York River and its tributaries, is indicative of the rural character of the colony. Courtesy of the Mariners' Museum, Newport News, Virginia.

presented to the Maryland assembly the day before it was filed in Virginia. The sister colony did not follow Virginia's example until 1747, however.

Gooch introduced the measure in a forceful address at the opening of the May 1730 session of the Virginia Assembly. In this and other speeches he relied heavily on the astute advice, and possibly the ghostwriting, of his brother Thomas, then master of Gonville and Caius College, Cambridge, and later bishop first of Norwich and then Ely. As anticipated, the proposal generated vigorous opposition from large planters, who resented disruption of the merchandising methods they had perfected, and from small planters, who feared that their crops would be the most likely to be judged substandard.

Unfortunately for historians, the records on the course of the debate are scanty. The main leader of the opposition in the House of Burgesses was Edwin Conway of Lancaster County, a relatively well-off planter who, however, presented the small farmer's view. Once, a key provision survived only on the casting vote of Speaker John Holloway, on whose lands near Williamsburg two inspection warehouses were built. At least six other burgesses obtained warehouses on their lands, and five more subsequently resigned their House seats to become inspectors. Gooch acknowledged, moreover, that he wined and dined all the burgesses at the Palace "very fairly the length of the session."

Yet in the end a major consideration in passing the legislation was the governor's willingness to relinquish whatever patronage might have permanently accrued to his office. To keep the burgesses "in good Humour," he said, he agreed to a place bill that forbade any sheriff or member of the House to hold "any Office of Profit in the Colony." He also agreed to shift the burden of the legislators' stipends from the counties to the provincial treasury through another increase in the imported liquor tax. The final vote in the house, 46 to 5, did not reflect the intensity of the struggle.

The contest was as difficult in the Council. Again the records are thin, and the story depends largely on the report of a firm opponent, John Parke Custis. Despite his partisanship, Custis credited the ultimate success of the bill entirely to the governor: "it would never had passed. . . . had it not bin spirited up by all the artful means imaginable." Although the Assembly did make a number of changes in the final act, none fundamentally altered Gooch's original proposal.

The battle then shifted to London, where again Gooch displayed his acuity in maneuvering the proposal through the political maze. A major obstacle was the opposition of a bitter personal enemy, the surveyor general of the customs in the southern colonies, Richard Fitzwilliams, who had just returned to the mother country from Virginia. Although Fitzwilliams had come to the colony only thirteen years before, powerful political friends quickly brought him the post of collector of customs in the lower James River district and then his current position as surveyor general and elevation to the Council in 1725. One of the few people with whom Gooch could not get along (doubtless because it was well known that Fitzwilliams had his sights on the governorship), the customs official had a record of opposing the governor on virtually every issue.

Fitzwilliams's greatest influence was naturally with his employers, the Board of Customs Commissioners, from whom he secured an adverse opinion that normally would have ended the life of a colonial statute. Ordinarily the Board of Trade automatically followed the commissioners' wishes on questions of revenue. In this case, the colonial agent, Peter Leheup, persuaded the board not to heed the commissioners' opinion until Gooch was able to send over a memorial answering their objections.

The memorial arrived in May 1731, and its masterful argument won the day. Gooch brilliantly upended the commissioners' chief concern by arguing that, far from limiting production, the act would actually increase it. Higher prices would entice farmers to plant more, and better quality would win a larger share of the foreign market for Great Britain than it had enjoyed to date. On the other hand, he warned, to reject the statute risked new stint laws to curtail production and lower prices that could drive colonists into manufacturing. Convinced by these impeccably mercantilistic arguments, the Board of Trade approved the act for a four-year trial, but told Gooch that his reputation was on the line.

Official announcement of the Crown's consent did not arrive in Virginia until months after the date for implementation of the act, August 1, 1731. The delay encouraged opponents to regroup. They spread the word not to obey the act since it would soon be disallowed. Gooch himself delayed preparations for enforcement until well into the spring, hoping every day for favorable word from London. When the time came, some warehouses were not ready. In some areas scales and mechanisms for prizing hogsheads were unavailable. Some inspectors turned out to be corrupt or incompetent. Smaller planters were especially angered by the requirement in the original act forbidding cargo vessels to use their own crews and boats to load. The purpose was to force ships to load only at public warehouses, but the restriction meant that planters who did not own boats to move their tobacco to the warehouses had to hire them. Even nature seemed in league with Gooch's opponents, for heavy rains reduced the 1731 crop to the smallest in ten years, seemingly obviating the need for the act. Inspectors found themselves in the position of destroying tobacco for which ship captains returning to Britain with partially empty holds were willing to pay at least a small amount.

Riots broke out in March 1732. On March 7, Gooch reported to the Board of Trade, "malicious and evil dispos'd persons" burned the warehouses at Deep Creek, Lancaster County, and Coan, Northumberland. He had expected trouble because he had had the legislature declare warehouse arson a felony the session before. When the outbreaks occurred, Gooch and the Council immediately offered a £100 reward for apprehension of the culprits. A week later, after a "Tumultuous and unlawful" meeting, "a Number of the meaner Sort of People" destroyed the facilities at Quantico, Prince William County. The same group may have been responsible for a fire at Gibson's in King George County as well. Gooch called out the militia from the Northern Neck and the counties just south of the Rappahannock River, but in the end seems to have pardoned most of the offenders. Why the violence centered in the Northern Neck is unclear. The region produced the poorer quality, lower-priced Orinoco tobacco, and the higher percentage of tenancy in the area may have meant that more persons had immediately pressing payments to meet. Available evidence is that most of those involved were farmers with fewer than 100 acres and estates of less than £100.

The uprisings strengthened the governor's hand. They frightened opponents of the act, like John Parke Custis and Robert Carter, into publicly calling for acquiescence. When Gooch summoned the legislature in May, despite his initial uneasiness that it might work against him, it rallied to his side. In just six days it modified the provision regarding ships' crews loading tobacco; it fended off a barrage of petitions calling for repeal, mostly from the Northern Neck; and it easily defeated a move to substitute another stint act. The burning of a fifth warehouse at Falmouth, King George County, in June further aroused the burgesses until Gooch quieted them with the report that "there is some ground to believe it burnt by Accident." The final outbreak of violence occurred in October 1732, when a militia muster in Lancaster County became unruly because of alleged abuses by the inspector, Joseph Carter, at Corotoman Creek. In that and similar, though less threatening, episodes involving charges of malfeasance among inspectors, Gooch moved quickly to investigate and apparently established a record of fairness and justice in his decisions.

For his own part, Gooch once more met the crisis with an impressive demonstration of his polemical skill. He published a pamphlet whose clarity and punch its wordy title belied: *A Dialogue Between Thomas Sweet-Scented, William Orinoco, Planters, both men of good Understanding, and Justice Love-Country, who can speak for himself* (1732). It proved immediately popular, going through three printings in a year. In the format of a play, two planters question an all-knowing justice of the peace, who masterfully explains in easy-to-understand language the anticipated benefits of the inspection system. Gooch particularly sought to deal with the dismay of small planters at the sight of some of their crop going up in flames. The improved quality of the rest, the author assured them, meant higher prices that would sustain their incomes. Apparently the tract was extraordinarily effective. In reporting the uprisings and their aftermath, the *Pennsylvania Gazette* remarked that "some Papers having been since published, wherein the People are better informed as to the Design of the Law, Things seem now to grow more quiet and settled."

Fortunately for Gooch, the short crops that year and the next, which seemed initially to favor his opponents, turned to his advantage. Prices pushed upward to between $2d$. and $2\frac{1}{2}d$. a pound by 1733, for which public opinion gave the inspection act full credit. A handbook for justices of the peace that George Webb published in 1736 declared in print for the rest of the century to read that "Notwithstanding all Objections and Clamours to the contrary, it must be acknowledged" that the act "produced a good Effect, and considerable advance of the Market, both here and Abroad." The statute was on the law books to stay, and the governor's reputation was preserved.

* * *

For Gooch, the inspection act was a prime example of how the regulation of trade could work simultaneously for the benefit of colony and empire. He successfully promoted the statute in Britain as part of the trade reforms aimed at control of smuggling that his political patron, Robert Walpole, had undertaken. That approach projected Virginia onto the main stage of British politics, for not only did the prime minister concur in Gooch's interpretation, but he looked to Virginia for important assistance in his broader campaign to reform the British tax system.

For the better part of a decade Walpole had been considering as the ultimate step in his innovations a fundamental shift in the method of obtaining revenue from imports. He proposed the abolition of the heavy duties currently assessed on tobacco and other staples in favor of a more easily enforceable excise on imported goods retailed in Great Britain. Since the effect would be to transfer to the British buying public the taxes currently paid by Virginia planters—and because of chronically low prices seldom passed on—the idea appealed to tobaccomen. In fact, there is evidence that Walpole may have schemed with Gooch as early as 1728 or 1729 to have it look as if the stimulus for an excise came from Virginia.

Whoever planned it, the opportunity Walpole wanted did come from the Old Dominion. British merchants continued to try to enhance their business advantage at the expense of tobacco growers. A perennial quarrel springing from the vast amount of credit extended to the colony was over how to collect debts that were in default. Because the original evidence of the debt was in the form of simple entries by creditor and debtor in books three thousand miles apart, disagreements were constant over not only the amounts involved but also the rate of interest, when precisely the interest began, and countless other details. In English law such "book debts" became legally binding only when a court certified them after considering the evidence of both parties. English law also forbade encumbering real estate for business debts unless a mortgage had been given. In 1732, however, London and Bristol merchants successfully lobbied in Parliament for a different procedure in the colonies that allowed creditors to prove book debts merely on their own oaths and to attach both real estate and slaves to secure them. Upon learning of the new policy, which they regarded as blatantly discriminatory, the House of Burgesses in June 1732, with the strong support of the governor and the Council, resolved to petition the ministry "to put tobacco under an Excise." John Randolph, who had just returned from lobbying against the prohibition on stemming in the mother country, was sent back to see the new plan through.

Walpole introduced his Excise Bill in March 1733. Rumors of the impending submission had been rife in Britain for six months or more; it became virtually the sole topic of political discussion. Both sides were ready for the contest when the day came. In addition to the issue of bilking the British public, which was ready-made for the opposition, the merchant community unanimously rejected the idea. Consignment merchants disliked it because duties were normally among the charges on which they based their commissions. Scottish and other direct purchase merchants were opposed, it was widely suspected, because, as the government intended, an excise would interfere with their smuggling. (Englishmen and Virginians generally refused to believe that the Scots could have expanded their share of the market as rapidly as they did by fair means. Gooch, for example, cited their unfair competition, which supposedly undercut prices, as his standard explanation of the tobacco depression for British officials.)

The struggle over the excise in Britain was intense, and the newly arrived Virginia agent John Randolph was at the center. His major contribution was a pamphlet entitled *The Case of the Planters of Tobacco in Virginia, As Presented by Themselves; Signed by the President of the Council and Speaker of the House of Burgesses. To which is added a Vindication of the said Representation* (1733). The publication consisted of the June petition of the General Assembly in favor of an excise plan plus a *Vindication* written by Randolph himself to disprove the insistence of Micajah Perry and other merchants that Walpole and not the Virginians had originated the scheme. The overlap of material between the *Vindication* and Walpole's writings and speeches suggests a closer cooperation than was publicly admitted. The pamphlet had a significant impact in British political circles; and in gratitude Walpole had Randolph named to the knighthood, the only colonial Virginian to be so honored. But the intervention could not halt the tide. In office for thirteen years at this point, Walpole had made many enemies and had raised many issues for which the excise became a symbol. The theme of popular exploitation was a cause over which the opposition could forget its differences and rally against him. Seeing that he could not carry the bill, the minister withdrew it before it was defeated and his whole administration undermined.

*　　*　　*

Whether because of the inspection law or the remarkable broadening of the market in Europe, tobacco prices by the mid-1730s entered a twenty-year upcycle that provided the most powerful answer to Gooch's critics. When he called an election in 1736, the campaign evoked some of the worst namecalling, "treating" of voters, and intimidation in Virginia's history. The issue was repeal of the inspection act, and 70 percent of the burgesses who had voted for it were replaced. Under the guidance of the familiar opposition leader Edwin Conway, the new House rammed through an act of repeal by a comfortable margin, only to have the Council reject the bill. There is reason to believe that many burgesses hoped for that outcome. They had voted for repeal to assuage popular anger with the expectation that the upper house would block the measure. When the opposition brought in another stint act to salvage what they could from the loss, the burgesses declined to endorse it. This session is also the one that raised the qualifications for voting by redefining the freehold. The suffrage revision further permitted voters who owned the requisite land to cast ballots in as many counties as they were qualified in, a practice that had been forbidden in 1705. Whether there was any connection between the near miss on repeal and the restructuring of the franchise is unclear. The new Assembly at the same time further extended the place bill by excluding tobacco officials from political activity.

When most of the same burgesses returned for their second session two years later, the political scene was markedly different. The former Speaker, Sir John Randolph, had died; and in the first action of the session the members decisively elected John Robinson, Jr., of Middlesex County over Edwin Conway to fill the post. Son of a powerful member of the Council and nephew of a bishop of London, Robinson had only entered the House at the last election. His skill in legislative management quickly thrust him to the fore and kept him in the chair until his death twenty-eight years later. Gooch had called the session to extend the inspection act, which was about to expire; and under Robinson's direction the opposition, led by Conway and Gawin Corbin, had little chance. The Speaker and his ally, Isham Randolph of Goochland County, worked for delegates sympathetic to the act in nine by-elections, and Robinson prevented any vote on the question of extension except in the fullest possible House. While Conway maintained his strength of about thirty votes, which had been enough to pass repeal in the previous session, he was in the minority each time the inspection act came up in this session. Three years later the act was extended again, with no opposition at all.

Gooch summoned two additional sessions of the legislature in 1740 to deal with the outbreak of King George's War. For the first time in the long series of struggles with France since William III's accession, Virginians were called to participate in a meaningful way. Like Walpole's excise, the war turned them into participants rather than onlookers in a major event of the empire. When the British announced a campaign against Cartagena (in modern Colombia) for the summer of 1740, former governor Spotswood suggested raising an intercolonial expeditionary force of 3,000 men. Virginia's quota was 400. (It is interesting that this unit was the first to be referred to by both British officials and colonists as "American.") Spotswood received a commission as major general to direct the recruiting, but died in Annapolis in June. Many of the gentry eagerly heeded the call to wartime glory. Gooch left the colony in the care of the Council to assume command, while younger Virginians competed intently for commissions as captains. One of the successful was George Washington's older half-brother, Lawrence, who later named his residence after the commander in chief of the expedition, Admiral Edward Vernon. Outside the elite, however, enthusiasm for the plan, was noticeably less, and recruiters were forced to fill the lower ranks largely with convict laborers. Bureaucratic delays kept the force from sailing until fall and from reaching its objective until the following March. Despite Vernon's warnings to hurry, army commanders did not begin the attack until the Spanish were well entrenched and the rainy and yellow-fever season had come. The ensuing campaign was a fiasco; half of the colonists lost their lives, mainly to disease. Gooch himself was struck by a cannon ball in the ankle and partially crippled for life.

During the governor's absence, though in keeping with his desire to hold elections as frequently as in Britain, the Council dissolved the Assembly. Gooch called new elections in the fall of 1741, but because of his wound and the illness and death of his only son, he postponed a meeting until May 1742. As a result of these personal setbacks, Gooch was not his vigorous self again for the rest of his term. No outstanding issue marked the 1741 campaign; and when the legislature met, Robinson easily beat off an attempt by Northern Neck representatives to elect Henry Fitzhugh in his stead. Gooch found the burgesses happily pliant on matters that he suggested, such as a bill "for the effectual suppression of vice." Almost by instinct, however, they rejected his proposals for expenditures on defense until the French and Indian threat spread closer in their direction. They voted a gift of £200 for the Iroquois after the Treaty of Lancaster in 1744, when the Indians ceded most of western Maryland and Pennsylvania and agreed to aid the British in the war. Finally, an emergency session in July 1746 appropriated £4,000 toward a British expedition in New York against French Canada. Gooch secured passage of the grant by consenting, probably because of the deterioration of his health, to a major precedent in the burgesses' rise to power: he agreed to allow a committee of the House to disburse the funds. The governor's frequent absences from the Council also often brought its president, the Speaker's father, John Robinson, Sr., to the chair.

In these years the placidity of Virginia politics was pervasive. There were some tensions: Northern Neck leaders increasingly resented the dominance of the Robinson-Randolph clique, whose orientation was toward western expansion along the James River Valley instead of the Potomac; and Robinson himself was continually at odds with his neighbor from Middlesex County, Gawin Corbin. But these were minor tempests during a period of prosperity, when the large and middling tobacco growers who elected the burgesses were assured that their representatives looked after their interests as well as any could.

The worst upset that occurred in Gooch's later years concerned an issue on which middle- and lower-peninsula burgesses and those from the adjacent Piedmont, all of whom usually supported the Speaker, were not united. In 1747 the Capitol in Williamsburg burned, necessitating another emergency session of the Assembly and creating an opportunity to consider whether it was not time to move the colonial capital elsewhere. As settlement spread west and north, the population center moved farther and farther from Williamsburg. For example, just shifting the capital to New Kent or Hanover County, as some proposed, would save many burgesses a day or more of travel. Others wanted the capital at Bermuda Hundred or West Point. First the burgesses voted to build a city on the Pamunkey River in New Kent, then at Newcastle in Hanover, and then on the Pamunkey again. The Council, most of whose members lived near Williamsburg and did not want to move, rejected all suggestions. The burgesses tried to appoint a study commission, which the Council also blocked; and Gooch called another election to end the stalemate.

It did not. New faces meant new suggestions. In the fall of 1746 the House decided on yet another site in Hanover. At one point emotions ran so high that Councillor John Blair accosted Speaker Robinson on the street and denounced him for the "Hellish scheme" of moving. An enraged lower house demanded an apology, and to avoid an irreconcilable split, the Council reprimanded Blair. As suddenly as the House had decided to move, it reversed itself and ordered the Capitol rebuilt—though with the proviso that doing so did "not fix the Seat of Government in Williamsburg." The next spring the burgesses opted again for Newcastle, but the Council once more demurred. Then, after one final effort three years later, the burgesses let the issue lapse, and the capital remained in Williamsburg for another generation. With less fanfare but more significance, the Assembly in 1748 also enacted a revision of the laws that had been several years in the writing.

Another issue that chronically flared up between the burgesses and the Council with little advance notice was the demand for reform of the vestries. In 1740 the burgesses overturned a committee recommendation on the floor—itself an almost unheard-of procedure—to vote overwhelmingly for the election of vestrymen by parishioners. The council, as usual, preserved tradition. Two years later the exact scenario was repeated, with the addition that the burgesses rejected the Council's alternative suggestion that a few reforms in the current system of self-appointed boards were enough. Renewed efforts by the burgesses in 1744 and 1746 shared the same fate. What seems to have been at stake was less philosophical objection to the self-perpetuation of vestries than the fact that vestrymen were not performing their duties in some parishes. Areas with declining populations or too few

Anglicans and too many dissenters in the neighborhood often could not provide a sufficient roster of reliable candidates. A repeated demand in petitions was to redefine how many members were needed for a vestry to act. At any rate, despite the lopsidedness of the votes, the burgesses never became too incensed at the Council's vetoes, perhaps even counting on them to spare them hard decisions in this as in other delicate political situations.

In 1747 William Stith, rector of Henrico parish and former professor of the College of William and Mary, published *The History of the First Discovery and Settlement of Virginia*. The work affords an insight into how educated Virginians viewed themselves and their province at mid-century. Stith intended the volume as the first of "a General History of the Colony," but the rest were never written. The work was good history and found many readers, though, as Thomas Jefferson later observed, it had "no taste in style." The interpretation it propounded of the early years of the colony remained standard until well into the twentieth century. Stith placed particular emphasis on the founding of the House of Burgesses in 1619, describing how "by the Introduction of the British Form of Government, by Way of Parliament or Assembly, the people were again restored to their Birthright, the Enjoyment of British Liberty." "By the Royal Charters, and by all other Law and Reason," he declared, "the English, transplanted hither, had a Right to all the Liberties and Privileges of English subjects." Stith took particular offense at the recently published ruling of a New York judge that in the colonies, unlike Britain, the king "governs by his PREROGATIVE." Stith appended the texts of the three original Virginia charters of 1606, 1609, and 1612, of which only a handful of manuscript copies then existed in the colony, to prove that colonists had "a Right to all the Liberties, Franchises, and Immunities of Englishmen."

Just as exciting as the past Stith described was what readers might infer from the study lay ahead. For any Virginian with his eyes on lands across the Appalachian Mountains, multiple printed copies of the early charters now documented how Virginia's borders ran "West, and Northwest" and "Sea to Sea." To whet appetites news came in the spring of 1749 that the Privy Council had confirmed the enormous grant to the Ohio Company, which for the first time lay directly athwart French claims to the Ohio River Valley. Although Gooch, wearied by his years in office and aching from his wartime wound, had been planning to retire the following June, he delayed his departure until August. He now considered himself free to convey grants to the Loyal Land Company and others that he had refrained from issuing before for fear of renewing the war with France.

The Virginia establishment obviously felt good at the midway point in the eighteenth century. The Treaty of Aix-la-Chapelle had just ended a war in which for the first time they had played a significant role in imperial affairs, and they were prosperous. Ignoring the 1713 Treaty of Utrecht, in which Britain had acknowledged Spanish claims beyond the Mississippi (not too many Virginians at the time knew where the river was), President of the Council Thomas Lee, organizer of the Ohio Company and interim governor until Gooch's successor appeared, wrote in his annual report to London in 1750, "Virginia is Bounded by the Great Atlantic Ocean to the East, by North Carolina to the South, by Maryland and Pennsylvania to the North, and by the South Sea to the West including California." He and his fellow colonists, he declared, would shortly make the Ohio Valley "the strongest frontier that is to any of the King's Dominions in America; since the Lands are rich on the Aligany and Ohio [rivers] where I am told more People may conveniently settle than at this time inhabit Pennsylvania, the Jerseys and New York." Virginians were ready for the French and for the future.

11

THE TROUBLED WORLD
OF MID-CENTURY VIRGINIA

For all the confidence, energy, and sense of fulfillment Virginians seemed to display as the second half of the eighteenth century began, they faced a less certain future than such outward optimism suggested. The decades of the 1730s and 1740s indeed marked the culmination of a long maturation of the colony. The burgeoning prosperity, the high degree of social harmony among the free inhabitants of Virginia, the stability and skill of its leadership, and the quality of its cultural life continue to impress us. In other respects, however, the world of mid-eighteenth-century Virginia was far less stable and potentially more volatile than we have often believed. The two decades that had just passed were, in the longer view of Virginia's history, more exceptional than typical. A remarkable, uncharacteristic indifference to colonial affairs on the part of British politicians left the colony's leadership freer from the customary political tug-of-war with imperial officials than at any time since the end of Bacon's Rebellion. As black population grew by natural increase and to a lesser extent by continued importation of Africans, slaveholding spread among larger numbers of planters, strengthening an identity of racial and economic interest among whites. A rapid expansion of settlement to interior regions of the colony—Piedmont lands along the major river systems, the Valley, and finally the Southside—drew much of the energies of Virginians and also created new opportunities for landownership. The result was to lessen or at least postpone the probability of social disruption or political confrontation even as expansion created new, sometimes unstable areas and more diverse populations that had to be absorbed into the life of the colony. For that matter, the years from 1720 to 1750 had not passed without sometimes divisive battles—Sir William Gooch's tobacco inspection plan was a good example—but a spirit of compromise had been more representative of the times.

Just as the exceptional stability of the era could not blot out all political controversy, neither could it altogether displace longer-range, underlying elements of stress in the social order. The enslavement of blacks, who now numbered almost half the total population of the colony, and exceeded that proportion in parts of Tidewater, united whites more closely in many respects but sometimes produced, too, a deep sense of uneasiness. Nor could the spread of slave ownership among a larger percentage of freemen entirely compensate for economic disparity between larger and smaller slaveholders or between landed and landless Virginians. Finally, that closely knit circle of elite leaders who dominated society and government could never rest entirely secure in their authority. Not even the conciliatory spirit of a William Gooch could make its members forget that they were in the end colonials and provincials, social and political inferiors in that larger transatlantic world of which they so much aspired to be a part. Inside Virginia the narrow base of leadership, confined to a small number of families concentrated in the central portions of the older Tidewater region, could hardly fail to be a source of some difficulty in a growing, dynamic colony.

Indeed, that dynamism—marked by the closely interrelated phenomena of rapid increase in population, expansion of the limits of settled territory, and economic growth—may have been especially critical in the gathering threat to stability. A population that had numbered roughly 115,000 in 1730 grew to perhaps 180,000 by 1740 and increased again to approximately 340,000 by 1760. The growth continued until the outbreak of the Revolutionary War. By then the total had reached as much as a half million, but as a consequence of the struggle with the French and the Indians on the frontier the western limits of settlement had not expanded greatly after 1750. By 1760, however, it was possible to count 22 new counties that the Assembly had created since 1730—an increase of 70 percent in a combined total of 52. Accompanying economic growth had begun by the 1720s after a long cycle of stagnation and continued with only occasional disruptions until 1760. Tobacco prices on the British market, the size of the export crop, the value of imports, the amount of available credit, and per capita income had all registered long-term increases over the forty-year cycle, although real income for individuals rose only in the fifteen years after 1745. If such prosperity was unlikely to stir the kind of discontent born of hard times, the very growth—economic, geographic, and demographic alike—placed other strains on the social and political fabric, sometimes threatening to outdistance that recently established order in the colony. Inevitably it played a part, too, by visibly enhancing the economic value of the colony to Britain, in fundamentally altering the relationship between the Virginia colony and the empire of which it was a member. By 1750, perhaps a few years earlier, the first signs of a series of crises in the life of the colony in which these underlying circumstances almost certainly played some part began to appear.

Initially the most clearly perceived aspect of the crisis occurred in imperial affairs in reaction to a tightening web of British controls over the government and economy of the colonies. The impetus for new policies arose from a heightened sense of the value of the empire, but without specific reference to Virginia. Most of the other colonies, in fact, shared the phenomenal growth that the Old Dominion had been experiencing, although it remained the largest and most populous, by far the most valuable to British interests of those located on the North American mainland. From much lower percentages at the beginning of the eighteenth century the combined volume of colonial exports to, and imports from, Britain had grown to something more than a third of all British trade. With continuing population increase there was every reason to expect those markets to go on expanding. The outbreak of a new round of European wars in 1739, in which a significant part of the military and naval activity took place in the American colonies of England, France, and Spain, also began to bring home the strategic importance of America; the end of the first of these wars in 1748 afforded the English government a freer hand to deal with the American question. In the preceding year a significant alteration had also taken place in British domestic politics, one that brought to an end a long period of administration by shifting coalitions of politicians who lacked the capacity to carry out concerted policies of any sort and who found it especially easy to allow colonial affairs to drift without sustained direction. The change established the clear dominance of leaders able for a time to pursue consistent policies without fear of upsetting delicate political combinations. Finally, a series of colonial disturbances, especially in Massachusetts and some of the West Indian islands (but not in Virginia, where Gooch had governed in so conciliatory a manner) reinforced the concern of imperial officials.

Perhaps the first manifestation of such a revision in colonial policy occurred in the attempted reinvigoration of the principal imperial administrative body, the Board of Trade, now headed by the earl of Halifax. His efforts at greater regulation of commerce, improved communications, and even coercion of recalcitrant colonial governments, were sporadic, local, and not in the end especially effective, but the board nonetheless between 1748 and 1756 achieved, as Jack P. Greene has observed, a "major reversal in the tone and quality of imperial behavior toward the colonies." Too, its failure to secure more substantial results only stimulated officials to seek even stronger measures at the first opportunity.

If affairs in Virginia had not necessarily been a direct influence on the new policies, the changed political climate inevitably affected the colony, as evidenced especially by three major controversies that began in that same period in which the Board of Trade stepped up its activities: a dispute over imperial review of the 1748 revision of the Virginia law code, the Pistole Fee Controversy, and the Parsons' Cause.

The first of the three originated in the enactment by the Virginia Assembly of a full-scale overhaul of the colony's laws during the sessions of 1748 and 1749. The laborious and time-consuming work, though perhaps long overdue, was a routine recodification, including the reenactment of many older statutes, not an effort to introduce sweeping reforms. By British law, however, all statutes enacted by the Assembly, provided the governor approved them, had to be submitted to the Board of Trade for review before they could remain in force. Usually the board simply recommended to the Crown that legislation be permitted to stand—from the colonists' perspective no news was good news. Two other actions were possible. In cases where the board had objections to a new law, its members might propose disallowance, a decision that would be ratified by an order of the Privy Council with the consequence that once the decision was known in the colony, the law ceased to have legal force. Rarely the board also called for formal confirmation of a law by an Order in Council, which meant that it remained in force but that subsequent revisions had to contain a suspending clause delaying the effective date of the new legislation until it had been reviewed and approved in England. Theoretically any law that repealed an existing law or that was to remain in effect for less than two years also required inclusion of a suspending clause. Although colonial assemblies therefore already seemed to be severely restricted in the amount of legislation they could put in force before the review of the Board of Trade had been completed, in practice most legislation had been routinely allowed to stand without the more formal action of confirmation or insistence on a suspending clause. Disallowance occurred, but not with great frequency.

In the present instance, however, the board took even more time than usual in completing its review. When it finally responded in 1751, it acted in the new spirit of closer supervision, even of those statutes that had long been in force. The result was that the members disallowed ten laws, retroactively at that, rather than simply from the time the order of disallowance reached the colony; formally confirmed fifty-seven; assigned seven probationary status; and referred three to the treasury for further consideration. Several of the decisions to disallow rested on the lack of suspending clauses. The confirmation of the majority of the new statutes was, if anything, more ominous, for the net effect was to require that virtually all new legislation passed thereafter by the Assembly would have to contain a suspending clause and could not take effect for two years or more after its enactment. All in all, the actions of the board constituted an unprecedented degree of interference in the ordinary legislative processes of the empire's oldest colonial assembly.

When the Board of Trade's decision reached Williamsburg, the laws had long since been printed and placed in force. The leaders of the colony faced the necessity of resurrecting at least temporarily the old laws, fearing that judicial decisions already made by the General Court under the new statutes would be jeopardized. They also saw their legislative independence seriously restricted for the future. Although the burgesses adopted an address to the king, appointed a new agent to represent them in London, and appealed to the Board·of Trade to rescind its actions, they gained few concessions. The episode and its unsuccessful outcome had served notice of the far-reaching impact of changing imperial policies.

At almost the same time Virginians became embroiled in a second controversy, one that the royal governor had instigated on his own authority but which nonetheless raised a second and even more sensitive issue of imperial domination. The popular, long-term governor Sir William Gooch returned to England in 1749, to be replaced in 1751 by Robert Dinwiddie, a Scottish businessman who had served in the British customs service. A former member of the Council in Virginia while surveyor general of customs in the Southern colonies, Dinwiddie was a typical colonial bureaucrat, a man much more disposed to press the Crown's interest than Gooch had been. Like most of the Virginia governors in the eighteenth century, who were in reality lieutenant governors subsisting on only a portion of the salary while an absentee governor pocketed the remainder, he was also desirous of increasing his income in any way possible.

Viewing the large number of patents for grants of new land in western Virginia that were awaiting his approval by affixing the seal of the colony, Dinwiddie thought he saw a lucrative source of money if he charged a new fee for validating the patents. He also, it must be said, thought he saw an opportunity to regulate the whole land patent system more effectively and to force speculators to pay quit rents on their lands. He decided the sum of one pistole, a Spanish coin worth 18s. 6d. in English money and widely circulated in the colony, would be appropriate. Equivalent modern values for colonial currency are difficult to determine, but one might think of the sum at the time as roughly the purchase price of a cow—not a small amount of money, especially when many of the patents had been filed by active land speculators who had a number of such applications pending. Moreover, many patentees were active leaders in the provincial government, members of Dinwiddie's Council, representatives in the House of Burgesses, or their associates, who were not likely to accept the costs they would incur without a fight.

At first opportunity—Dinwiddie waited as long as he dared before calling a session of the Assembly in 1754—the House of Burgesses attacked his actions in language that differed little from the rhetoric that would dominate the Revolutionary crisis a few years hence. The pistole fee, they charged, was not only unprecedented and harmful to the spread of settlement to the west but also an infringement on the rights of the people, even a seizure of their property and a tax levied without consent. It therefore violated the constitution, and anyone who paid the fee was "a betrayer of the rights of the people." It was the kind of thing, the senior burgess Richard Bland warned, "which like a small spark if not extinguished in the beginning will soon gain ground and at last blaze out into an irresistible flame."

For a time Dinwiddie stood his ground, even at some risk to support for the new colonial war that had broken out, since the burgesses did not hesitate to withhold military appropriations in the hope of pressuring him to surrender. Finally, both sides took their case to the Privy Council, Dinwiddie by a written statement of his position and the House of Burgesses by the dispatch of the attorney general of the colony as its special agent. In the end the Privy Council resolved the conflict by upholding the theoretical right of the governor to collect the pistole fee, but with so many exceptions to its application as to limit drastically its practical effect. In keeping with the new tone of imperial policy, however, the Crown officials avoided the surrender as a matter of right of a power claimed by an imperial official, and Virginians were quick to recall the controversy when they became embroiled in the larger one that broke out a decade later.

Soon a third dispute, the Parsons' Cause, further inflamed the relationship between Virginians and imperial authorities. At issue was the response by many of the Anglican clergy in Virginia and officials in England to two measures, the so-called Twopenny Acts, passed by the Virginia Assembly in 1755 and 1758, respectively, to relieve taxpayers of the customary obligation of paying their taxes in tobacco during two years of short crops and abnormally high prices. Both laws permitted the commutation of such payments at a rate of two pence per pound of tobacco—well below its market value at the time. The 1755 law was to remain in effect for only ten months; the 1758 law, for twelve. Among the obligations affected were the salaries paid from public funds to the clergy of the legally established Anglican church, which had been fixed at 16,000 pounds of tobacco yearly by one of the 1748 laws that had been confirmed by the Crown. The legislature omitted the suspending clause from both acts, even though both the temporary duration of the laws and their amendment of an earlier confirmed act should have required it. To have done so, defenders of the measures later pointed out, would have defeated the whole purpose of the legislation by preventing its taking effect in sufficient time. The new lieutenant governor, Francis Fauquier, realized that he was violating his instructions in assenting to the 1758 measure, but he readily approved it and allowed it to go into operation, because his predecessor's approval of the 1755 law had produced no repercussions.

Passage of the 1758 act immediately evoked strong opposition from many of the clergy, for had the law not been enacted, the higher-priced tobacco would have meant a substantial addition to their income. To avoid the loss, a number, though not all, of the ministers determined to resist its enforcement. The Reverend John Camm, professor of divinity at the College of William and Mary and rector of Yorkhampton Parish in nearby York County, emerged as their principal spokesman. In late 1758 or early 1759 Camm sailed for England to seek the intervention of the home government. What Camm wanted was not the customary disallowance of the law, for by the time the official news of that decision could reach Williamsburg the law would long since have fulfilled its purpose and expired. Instead, Camm asked in a memorial he presented to the Privy Council on behalf of the clergy that both Twopenny Acts be declared null and void from the moment of their passage, which would, if granted, presumably open the way for recovery of the full value of the clerical salaries.

On August 10, 1759, however, after full hearings before the Board of Trade and before one of its own committees, the Privy Council declined to do more than disallow the law in conventional terms. In a sense the Assembly won its point. As a practical matter the smaller salaries would stand. The Privy Council went on, however, to couple its disallowance with criticism of the Assembly and a tart instruction to Governor Fauquier threatening that he would face recall if he failed in the future to observe his original instructions by insisting on the inclusion of a suspending clause where legally required. The Assembly responded in a "Humble Representation of the Council and Burgesses of Virginia," prepared in October 1760. The sixteenth article of the governor's instructions had not been observed for a long time, the Assembly observed, and its enforcement now would "involve the Colony in the most insuperable Difficulties."

There matters hung for the moment, with neither side satisfied by the outcome. After his return from England, Camm and at least four of his colleagues determined to sue for recovery of the additional salary. Camm also circulated within the colony a letter written by the bishop of London to the Board of Trade in support of the clerical request for retroactive nullification of the Twopenny Acts. Fauquier was so incensed by Camm's conduct that in an explosive incident he committed a supreme insult in the culture of colonial Virginia by pointing the cleric out to his slaves and ordering them never again to admit him beyond the gates of the Governor's Palace. For their part the provincial leaders moved in the Assembly before the end of 1759 to support the Yorkhampton vestry in their defense against Camm's suit; and two veteran pamphleteers, Landon Carter and Richard Bland, responded to the bishop's letter and to Camm's action. Within a few years Virginians had been presented with a concrete example of the effects of the Board of Trade's sweeping response to the 1748 law revision, and they did not like what they saw.

* * *

None of the three issues—the Board of Trade's action on the law revision, the Pistole Fee Controversy, or the Parson's Cause—had produced a sustained confrontation between colonists and imperial officials. The reaction had so far occurred in conventional political channels. Yet neither had any of the three been truly resolved. Rather, all were for the time being subsumed in the necessity for cooperation between Britain and the colonies in the new war that had begun in America in 1754 and on the European continent two years later. The Seven Years' War, appropriately renamed by Lawrence H. Gipson the Great War for the Empire, was a worldwide struggle between England on the one hand and France and her Spanish allies on the other. A principal stake was domination of the vast interior of the eastern North American continent, especially Canada and the Ohio country that stretched from western Pennsylvania through present-day Ohio, Illinois, and Indiana to the Mississippi River.

The interests of the Virginia colony, or more strictly those of small but prominent groups of her inhabitants who were investors and speculators in western lands, loomed large in the outbreak of the North American phase of the war. By the mid-1740s, with much of the land of the colony already patented as far west as the Allegheny Mountains on the far side of the Great Valley, several groups of land speculators, one of them including the Speaker of the House of Burgesses and some of his associates and another the attorney general of the colony, had received grants of 100,000 acres and more in the trans-Allegheny region. On a single day in July 1749 the Virginia Council, with Governor Gooch's acquiesence, had issued grants totaling more than a million acres. Many of the grants lay along the Greenbrier, Kanawha, and New rivers in the southwestern part of the colony or in present-day West Virginia. Another such combination, organized in 1747 by Thomas Lee, the president of the Council at the time, and named the Ohio Company, had, however, secured a grant of 200,000 acres on the Ohio River, with rights to an additional 300,000 acres if the company maintained a fort and settled a hundred families within seven years. Lee's fellow members of the company were, like him, predominantly from the Northern Neck region of the colony. They eventually included George Washington, Richard Henry Lee, George Mason, and other prominent figures, together with English investors and Governor Dinwiddie. The Ohio Company grant occupied a strategic region, for it included the land around the forks of the Monongahela and the Allegheny rivers, where the Ohio River formed. It also brought the group into conflict for effective possession of the region with rival Pennsylvania speculators, with Indians, and soon with the French, who reasserted an interest in the Ohio country after peace was concluded in 1748.

The Ohio Company group moved quickly to begin the exploitation of their grant, first establishing a trading post and fort at Wills Creek on the site of Cumberland, Maryland, an important location on the best route to the Ohio region. The French reacted no less rapidly, first sending a 1749 expedition under the command of Céloron de Blainville on a circular march from Lake Erie and back, burying along the way lead plates on which French claims to the region were recorded. A later expedition destroyed an English trading post near Lake Erie and erected a series of three forts extending south from the lake into northwestern Pennsylvania. The forts both established a French military occupation of the Ohio country and served as a base from which to win many of the Indians in the area, including tribes formerly allied with the British, to their side.

The French moves aroused alarm in Britain and directly affected colonies such as Pennsylvania and Virginia—in the latter case the degree of concern distinctly lessened beyond the immediate circle of Ohio Company investors. No one had military forces with which to challenge the French, although by 1753 Governor Dinwiddie had secured permission to begin preparations to resist the French penetration in the Ohio region. Late in 1753 the governor first sent a diplomatic mission, headed by the twenty-one-year-old George Washington, to issue a warning to the French that was promptly ignored, although the publication of his journal of the expedition in 1754 set him on the road to fame.

By now in the midst of his fight with the Assembly over the pistole fee, Dinwiddie next managed to equip a small expedition that constructed a fort at the junction of the Ohio, only to be driven off without hostilities by the French, who finished it as Fort Duquesne and established the location as a pivotal point in the ensuing war. A little later Washington set out on his second trip, with ill-equipped reinforcements for the earlier expedition. On May 28, 1754, with a detachment of his own force and a group of Indian allies, he skirmished near the Great Meadows with a small French expedition commanded by Joseph Coulon, Sieur de Jumonville, who fell with nine of his men. Since the French carried diplomatic credentials and Britain and France were not yet officially at war, Washington's conduct stirred a diplomatic incident, and the propriety of his action remains a controversial question. Washington then built a rough fortification at Fort Necessity, and there was forced to surrender to a larger French force in July. The fiasco left the French in effective control of the Ohio region, but the young, inexperienced Virginian had led the first combat of the Seven Years' War.

Those hasty, ill-prepared moves had, moreover, proved Virginia's inability to recover the region on its own and had merged the conflict into the larger international war that was developing. While not formally at war with France until 1756, the British themselves now assumed overall leadership. The war went no better. Their first response was the dispatch of General Edward Braddock with two regiments of British regular troops. Landing at Alexandria and reinforcing his small force with colonials, including Virginia forces commanded by Washington, Braddock undertook an expedition to the Ohio that ended in his crushing defeat and death near Fort Duquesne on July 9, 1755. For the next three years the British continued to suffer reverses all along the frontier, opening the outmost settlements in colonies such as Virginia to repeated Indian attacks.

In some respects the war effort in Virginia was a dreary story, yet by its own lights the colony put forth a strong and costly effort. The Assembly continued to bicker with Dinwiddie but in the end voted more funds than its resources really permitted, making up the difference by two substantial issues of paper money. The British pressed for ever more financial and military support, but the colony's militia law and the state of readiness of the militiamen were wholly unequal to the task of highest priority, defending the colony's frontier, let alone to supplementing British forces. The Assembly tightened the militia law and raised a Virginia regiment, which George Washington, commissioned a provincial colonel, commanded from August 15, 1755. Hostile Indians had earlier begun attacking the long and exposed frontier of the colony. Settlers suffered a number of casualties, especially in the lands along the New and Holston rivers to the southwest. In one battle at Draper's Meadows, Colonel James Patton, the leader of settlement in that region, fell. By late 1755 Winchester, a major town to the north in the lower Valley and the site of Washington's headquarters, was threatened. Although the Assembly attempted to strengthen frontier military forces further in the spring of 1756, the war with the Indians remained essentially defensive, dependent on the maintenance of a chain of forts that were far too scattered and too poorly manned to be entirely effective. In 1757, when the frontier was admittedly somewhat quieter, Washington had no more than four hundred men to guard a frontier line that stretched for three hundred and fifty miles.

By 1758 the war began to turn in favor of the British, and the political bickering at Williamsburg largely ended with the departure of Dinwiddie. John Blair, a Virginian and president of the Council, served as acting governor pending the arrival of the new governor, Francis Fauquier, who proved much more popular than his predecessor. With the prospect of a new attack on Fort Duquesne led by General John Forbes, the Assembly moved to create a second provincial regiment under the command of William Byrd III and to authorize its use wherever needed. The Virginians, Washington particularly, were disappointed that Forbes took his expedition through rival Pennsylvania and not, like Braddock, along the route from Virginia. But on

George Washington as painted by Charles Willson Peale in 1772. Although Washington was 40 at the time, the artist depicted him as a younger man in the uniform of the First Virginia Regiment in the Seven Years' war. Courtesy of the Washington/Custis/Lee Collection, Washington and Lee University, Virginia.

November 24, 1758, Forbes recaptured the post at the forks of the
Ohio, renaming it Fort Pitt and establishing British dominance of the
Ohio region. Victories elsewhere, notably on the Plains of Abraham
outside Quebec, led to the fall of French Canada.

The war with the French thus had receded from the Virginia
frontier, and the war effort slackened in the colony, as it did in others.
Washington had resigned his command and had gone home to take a
seat in the Assembly, which was increasingly reluctant to continue
voting funds for the war. The colony had a heavy debt in the form of
the paper money that had to be retired from future payment of taxes,
and the private economy was suffering as well. Yet turning back the
French threat had not ended all Indian warfare, for toward the end of
1759 the Cherokees took up arms along the southern frontier,
extending as far north as Virginia. Although two Virginia expeditions
into eastern Tennessee proved ineffective, attacks farther to the south
by British regulars and South Carolina forces reduced the Indians by
the end of 1761. The colony, though still maintaining a regiment,
could look forward to the final peace that was concluded at Paris in
1763. The terms of the treaty were definitive, unlike those of 1748. It
stripped France of its North American mainland possessions and left
the British for the first time in complete control of all of the continent
east of the Mississippi.

The war was a complex event, the first military struggle of such
magnitude in which Virginians had been so closely involved. On the
surface its prosecution seemed to set an example of close cooperation
between mother country and colonies, to the advantage of both. The
home government made a strong and costly commitment to the
security of the colonies and, if the peace terms were an indication,
opened the way for additional growth and prosperity in America. As
George Washington wrote in early May 1763 from Williamsburg,
where he had gone to take his seat in the forthcoming session of the
Assembly, "The signing of the Definitive Treaty seems to be the only
piece of News w'ch prevails here at present, and diffuses general Joy."
Yet he went on in the same letter to complain that he and the other
burgesses faced the principal task of dealing with the protests of British
merchants and officials against the paper currency that the colony had
authorized to help finance the war. The issue, he complained, was "ill
timed" and calculated to "set the whole Country in Flames." Indeed

the session, as he had predicted, proved to be as acerbic as those that had dealt with the pistole fee or the Parsons' Cause, the latter still very much a live dispute.

In truth, the experience of the war brought England and Virginia into a closer relationship, which in the end antagonized them both. It provided not so much an interruption in or resolution of the controversies that had arisen on the eve of the war as a crucial link in a steadily deteriorating relationship. For all its worldwide scope, Virginians always viewed the conflict from a narrower perspective, confined to their immediate objectives of securing the Ohio country and stabilizing their own Indian frontier. However much events in Canada, or in other, more remote American frontiers, or even in Europe, might affect the successful achievement of such objectives, the colony responded willingly with men and money only to its direct interests, which now seemed satisfied. Yet Virginians were convinced that they had done so generously, making financial contributions totaling about £120,000 sterling.* Raising troops had been a more serious problem, for the war had little popular support. On at least two occasions, one at Fredericksburg and the other at Petersburg, recruitment efforts stirred riots. Washington complained in 1754, "You may with equal success attempt to raise the dead to life again as the force of this country." Eventually, of course, the colony put two provincial regiments in the field, and the militia of the western counties participated in frontier defense, but willingly only if they remained close to home.

For the British, however, the contributions never seemed enough. For one thing, Virginians received a bad press from their governor. In the face of his ongoing difficulties with the House of Burgesses, Dinwiddie seldom missed an opportunity in his reports to the home government to denigrate the legislature's efforts on behalf of the war. Virginia in particular appeared to many Britons as a wealthy colony, its gentry living on a scale that approximated that of many of the country gentry at home. The British pressed all the colonies for stronger contributions of money and fighting men and bridled at the extent of illicit trade that many colonists conducted with the French West

---

*Jack P. Greene's calculations conclude that Virginia's unreimbursed contributions to the war were 19.1 percent of such support, second only to Massachusetts but fifth among the colonies in per capita contributions.

Indian islands throughout the war. Everything that had happened only
reinforced the sense that better regulation of the colonies was more
necessary than ever.

Virginians resented British criticism and remained convinced that
they had done their share. As the war drew to an end, not only was the
public treasury overextended but the private economy was in shambles
from a credit crisis and from the first pronounced depression in the
tobacco market since the early 1740s. Moreover, the experience of
dealing with British officials, civilian and military, had not been
pleasant, driving home that sense of being treated as distinct inferiors.
It had been particularly disquieting for those who came in direct
contact with officers of the British army. The regulars looked with
condescension on colonial fighting men and insisted that any colonial
officer, regardless of rank, should take precedence after the most junior
British officer. George Washington provided a classic example. His
service as a provincial officer on Braddock's staff during the first
expedition to the Ohio had been frustrating. His experience in dealing
with Governor Dinwiddie while commanding the Virginia regiment
had destroyed the earlier friendship between the two men. On a long
trip to Boston to seek a regular commission in the British army he had
met a cold reception. The Great War for the Empire had not only
launched his military career but almost certainly had something to do
with the alacrity with which he became an outspoken Patriot in the
Revolution.

In the early 1760s such hostility was hardly fixed. It would be too
much to argue that the full-scale colonial revolt that followed so
quickly was now irreversible. Customary political channels remained
open, and the colonists still expected to work through them. Yet,
given the strength of feeling on both sides, it was hardly conceivable
that the imperial world would not continue to be marked by the same
tensions and disagreements that had already appeared before and
during the war—or that Virginians would not be principal actors in
whatever disputes might occur.

*   *   *

The sense of crisis that had begun to affect the lives of the Virginia
colonists is not, however, to be measured exclusively by the response to

great public events, which often touched the lives of many only indirectly. Virginians displayed increasing signs as well of strain in their personal lives, if not in the whole social fabric. The evidence is often tentative and circumstantial, its full implications elusive, but the recent work of several scholars suggests a number of elements of this internal crisis. Perhaps, then, a significant number of colonists were no more at ease with themselves and their society than were their leaders with the larger world of Anglo-American affairs.[*]

Some of the strongest, most pervasive expressions of these concerns occurred, in fact, among the very members of the gentry who were most recently aware of changing imperial relations. In their private letters and diaries, in their more public and signed writings, in anonymous essays and letters in The *Virginia Gazette* (an especially noticeable number seemed to appear in the early 1750s), members of the class did not address specific issues but instead generally lamented the spirit of the times as increasingly "Infatuated and Abandoned," fixing most pointedly on the decline of their own class. Instead of a spirit of independence, freedom from slavish attachments to party or faction, and possession of virtue, they found vice and weakness increasingly prevalent in the lives of too many leaders of the colony. All those values for which they expressed such high regard carried relatively precise meaning for men of the eighteenth century. They equated independence with the possession of enough property to assure an ability to act according to one's best and most responsible judgment in public affairs without obligation to, or dependence on, others. Those whose estates were heavily indebted might be as lacking in independence as those who possessed little or no property in the first place and were equally unqualified for leadership. Any political combination for the pursuit of self-interest, whether in the form of a more permanent and fixed "party" or a more shifting, unstable "faction," likewise subverted the capacity of leaders to act with an impartial sense of the public interest. Virtue, frequently especially identified as "public virtue," was the

---

[*]The discussion that follows in the remainder of this chapter relies heavily at one point or another on work by Jack P. Greene, Rhys Isaac, Gordon Wood, Daniel B. Smith, T. H. Breen, A. G. Roeber, and Richard Beeman as cited in the bibliographical essay at the end of the volume, although the final conclusion is not one to which any of them might necessarily subscribe completely.

quality that gave leaders a sense of honor, high responsibility, and concern for the common good—virtue summed up all the moral qualities that made one the right sort of leader. The forces that many feared were undermining these qualities included a disturbing growth of luxury and extravagance that led planters to spend beyond their means and fall into debt and an accompanying propensity for idleness and vice, typified by excess gambling, swearing, and drinking.

Clergymen, Anglican and dissenter alike, obviously found such excesses abominable and certain to invoke divine wrath upon Virginia, if indeed they had not already done so. Members of the elite deplored, as one did, the "damned situation our Country is in" with, he added, "no money to be got but at Horceraces & Gaming Tables & that not sufficient to open the Eyes of the People who frequent those places." A York County blacksmith and poet, Charles Hansford, in his 1752 poem "My Country's Worth" might ask, "Who can but love the place that hath brought forth/Such men of virtue, merit, honor, worth?" and yet in the same poem lament the decline that had taken place:

> I well remember, fifty years ago
> This wretched practice scarcely then was known.
> Then if a gentleman had lost a crown
> At gleek or at backgammon, 'twere a wonder
> And rumbled through the neighborhood like thunder.
> But many now do win and lose pistoles
> By fifties—nay, by hundreds. In what shoals
> Our gentry to the gaming tables run!

The cumulative effect was disastrous, for as one *Virginia Gazette* writer warned, "Luxury poisons a whole Nation" and "all Conditions and Ranks of Men are confounded." Who, he continued, could reverse the decline "unless the Great Men should prove to be so much of Philosophers, as to set an Example of Moderation themselves, and so, to put out of Countenance all those, who love a pompous Expence"? But many thought the colony already too corrupted and the title of gentleman so debased that it might be no longer possible "to preserve it in its original Reputation." Some, like the Richmond County leader and diarist Landon Carter, talked of retiring altogether from public affairs (a decision that the voters in time made for him) and relying only on the achievement of "inward satisfaction" as a goal in life. Carter was notoriously irascible and cantankerous, the very sort of person one might expect to become a minority of one, but the frequent lamentations and complaints in his copious diary were not atypical, only more numerous and quotable.

Another and very different but equally classic example of dismay at the decline of public virtue in the Old Dominion was a dramatic farce, *The Candidates, or, the Humours of a Virginia Election*, written about 1770 by Robert Munford, a legislator younger than Carter who represented a county in the more recently settled Southside region. *The Candidates* is often noticed more for its broad humor and accurate description of the detailed procedures under which Virginia elections were conducted. Yet Munford clearly intended a biting satire on the deteriorating quality of candidates for public office and their subversion of proper electoral practices, and perhaps beyond that a lament for the decline of society generally. In the play Worthy, a burgess of the old school possessed of virtue and honor, has determined not to stand for reelection. Along with Wou'dbe, a responsible though less outstanding man than Worthy, three far less deserving men have declared. One, Sir John Toddy, is an idle, dissipated man; another, Smallhopes, is chiefly interested in horses; and a third, Strutabout, is a conceited pretender who has promised to repeal taxes, "make the rivers navigable, and bring the tides over the tops of the hills" in order to gain votes. The fawning, servile cultivation of the voters that the three display stands in complete contrast to the independence of Worthy. In the end Worthy reenters the contest and with Wou'dbe saves the day, but the ending was so contrived that Munford's true intent was almost certainly to condemn what he believed to be the growing corruption of the electoral process and the election of unqualified men.

Although Munford apparently had in mind specific individuals and events in his own Southside—allusions that might have been recognized by an audience if we had any evidence that the play was ever performed at the time—he, like the other critics, did not name the corrupt and unworthy men or the issues and interests they sought to advance. Since almost all the cries of alarm remained couched so exclusively in such vaguely moralistic terms, it has been tempting to treat them as simply stylized rhetoric, if not the outcry of a few eccentrics like Landon Carter. Maintaining, however, that such "frenzied rhetoric could spring only from the most severe sorts of social strain," Gordon Wood has concluded: "Contrary to the impression of confidence and stability that the Virginia gentry have historically acquired, they seemed to have been in very uneasy circumstances in the years before the Revolution." It may be important, nevertheless, not to lose sight of the degree to which the leaders who expressed such deep concerns about their society were still in most of their actions a confident group, engaged all the while in opposing Dinwiddie on the pistole fee or imperial officials on the new regulations and restrictions in the manner they had always done, not demonstrating many signs of retreating from their accustomed sense of public responsibility. It may capture their mood somewhat more precisely to say that they "faced the future with an uncertain blend of anxiety and confidence."

What were the issues, problems, or conflicts that might have been capable of stirring such deep apprehensions among the outwardly confident Virginia gentry? One ought not, in the first place, rule out the rising imperial crisis itself as an important source of inner tension among provincial leaders in the colony. They lived, as many others did not, within the transatlantic world of the empire, not only because of political relationships but also intellectually and culturally, deriving their models of education and taste from Britain, and economically, as a consequence of their large-scale, direct participation in the tobacco export market. Defensive about their provincial status, yet proud and driven at times to exaggerated claims of colonial superiority, the Virginia elite also sought to emulate their perhaps idealized view of the English gentry, to be recognized for their own attainments, but in countless ways they were constantly reminded of their inferiority. Often they seemed to walk a tight psychological rope. Outwardly in their public rhetoric they continued to "glory in" their "Dependence upon Great Britain" as their "greatest Happiness and only Security." Nevertheless, the recent experience in the war had brought many a humiliating reminder of the status of provincials like themselves. There was a singular coincidence, too, between some of the public lamentations of decline and the recent political controversies with imperial officials. The extent to which those issues had at their base an effort to limit legislative independence of the Assembly directly attacked what was perhaps the single most important symbol of authority for the gentry. Yet the Virginia leaders could not, or did not, bring themselves to the point of making a direct link between their sense of crisis and the increasingly troubled state of imperial relations.

Members of the gentry appeared equally unwilling to attribute the malaise of moral decay explicitly to the appearance of the fateful disease of faction in their own ranks. Since the journals of the House of Burgesses failed to record either votes or the substance of debate—in itself perhaps a significant omission that testified how little the body operated on a basis of sharp division or narrowly won votes—evidence of consistent alignments in provincial politics is all but nonexistent. At the most, there had emerged by the 1740s or 1750s "two poorly delineated but recognizable postures or style of leadership." One emphasized a strongly moral stance and maximum independence of the electorate, whose role was confined to choosing the most impartial and virtuous men to act in their best interest. Such men advocated a "responsible" style, admittedly sometimes more in theory than in practice. The second group, dominated by many of the inner circle of provincial leaders, gave somewhat more emphasis to practical political maneuvers and greater attention to the will of one's constituents. Theirs has been termed a "representative" style, although it hardly precluded great independence of action and certainly never invited the antics of a Strutabout. One can also detect a tendency for leaders from the Northern Neck, an area of large landholdings but the most remote of the Tidewater peninsulas from the capital, to predominate among "responsibles," whereas the "representative" group centered somewhat more closely on counties nearer Williamsburg. Almost the only recent issue on which the alignment seemed somewhat clearly drawn was that of support for the Seven Years' War, when the responsible group had taken a stronger stand in favor of appropriations to prosecute it. Although these same alignments would reappear in the 1760s, they remained extremely loose and few men fitted either model exactly.

Other areas increasingly concerned the gentry, however. For one thing, there was the matter of tobacco, their principal means of livelihood and beyond that a potent cultural symbol. Tobacco not only provided the direct means of achieving the independence they valued so highly but also evoked images of their status as gentlemen planters occupying their country seats, attended by servants and slaves. A crop of recognized quality might help determine a sense of self-worth. At the same time, it had become increasingly apparent that an obvious disillusion with tobacco had set in, perhaps most of all among the larger planters. Even before the long-term cycle of prosperity had begun to draw to a close after 1760, many felt caught inescapably in debt as purchases on credit constantly outran the income realized from tobacco. Recent increases in tobacco production in the colony were entirely the result of the expansion of production in the newer Piedmont regions, while the tobacco economy of Tidewater had stagnated. By the end of the colonial period only about 25 percent of the total exports of tobacco were shipped to consignment merchants with whom larger Tidewater planters dealt. All of the recent increases in tobacco production were, in effect, the consequence of the opening of new lands in the Piedmont. A particularly graphic example was that of the York River customs district, which accounted for 36 percent of Chesapeake tobacco exports in 1727 and only 14 percent in 1768. Some tobacco growers, especially in the Northern Neck, had already begun to convert to the cultivation of wheat, one example being George Washington, who had despaired of producing good marketable tobacco at Mount Vernon. Sold through merchants in the colony, primarily exported to Ireland, southern Europe, or the West Indies rather than to Britain, and dependent on local sources of credit, wheat promised in many respects to reorganize the economy and alter relationships with British capital and markets. Larger planters who moved to wheat cultivation might farm the same lands with the same labor force, but an older symbolic world, in which tobacco, social status, and even the political culture were linked, would disappear. Certainly the process had not gone very far at all before 1760; and tobacco still dominated Virginia exports at any time before 1776. Yet planters could no longer be completely optimistic about a world based fundamentally on tobacco.

The county court system, the cornerstone of local government in the colony, also appeared to be experiencing difficulty. Even with the creation of new counties, population growth tended to place a heavier burden on the courts, with the result that the effectiveness of the justices sometimes came under question. In some part justices seemed to respond to a heavier load of cases by refusing to attend or to sit for the full time that sessions now required. The rise of a group of trained lawyers, formally licensed after 1732 and admitted to practice before the county courts as well as the General Court, brought in its wake criticism of untrained gentlemen judges for their lack of the same technical knowledge of law and legal procedures that the attorneys displayed. Such complaints seemed to come mostly from the lawyers themselves and were as yet muted, for the leading attorneys were members of the same planter elite, often members of the Assembly, and scarcely a well-defined professional class with distinct interests apart from those of the old elite.

The increase in population and its spread over a much larger area placed other, more fundamental strains on the social and political structure of the colony. In Virginia there was far less resistance than in any other royal colony except Massachusetts to bringing newly settled regions fully into the political system in an equitable manner. As the number of new counties created in the years after 1730 might suggest, Virginia leaders demonstrated remarkable willingness to extend county organization freely, thereby making the vital services of the county courts accessible to the larger body of inhabitants and expanding opportunities for leadership among new local elites as justices and burgesses. Nevertheless, that leadership in the newer counties of the Valley and Southside, to which few members of the old elite or their families migrated, was likely to be very different from that of Tidewater counties or even that in parts of the Piedmont to which members of older families often moved. In areas like Southside most were first-generation leaders, not the sons and grandsons of an older ruling group. Although men of prominence in the new counties, they had less education and wealth on the average and less taste for the more cultivated life style of the Tidewater elite. If it is possible to generalize from the most closely studied of the new counties, Lunenburg in the Southside region, the panel of justices there in the beginning met infrequently, experienced a high turnover, and had difficulty in organizing an Anglican parish in the county. While the elite demonstrated signs of greater stability after the 1750s, at no time before the Revolution had the county achieved the sort of economic development that could endow its social elite with a maturity and stability comparable to that of leaders in most of the older counties in the east. Yet another telling indication of the unsettled quality of leadership in Southside was the frequency with which contested elections from such counties as Lunenburg or Halifax, an even newer Southside county, reached the Committee on Privileges and Elections of the Burgesses.

The Hanover County Courthouse, built about 1733, is typical in design of the small, rural courthouses that were centers of local government for the scattered populations of colonial Virginia counties. Colonial Williamsburg photograph.

In the private, family life of the established elite other changes were also beginning to take place. "Inside the great house," Daniel Blake Smith has noted, the maturation of plantation society in the early decades of the eighteenth century had strengthened the family ties that were somewhat weakened by the mortality and early age of death in the first years of the colony and brought with it an elaboration of the networks of kin, embracing more family members in a widening circle of more distantly related family members. That development had likewise reinforced within the family that same authority and power that the head of such a family enjoyed in the larger, public world. Sons were expected to follow obediently their fathers' plans for education and career, and both sons and daughters could expect their fathers to exercise a strong control over their marriages. If the circle of both family and close friends was a wide and sociable one, the private world of the planter and his family was patriarchal and authoritarian, duplicating in many ways the characteristics of that external, public world in which the planter also moved. A marked shift was, however, settling in by the middle of the century, not becoming easily apparent until perhaps the final three decades of the century. The change may well have owed a great deal to the appearance by the 1760s of a generation born after 1720 who lacked direct experience with the hardships that had been common in the years before their birth.

In the course of that evolution family relationships became "more openly affectionate," with less of the previous discipline and paternal control. A planter's children—in no small part because of the slave labor that set them free—grew up with more choice and autonomy, greater intimacy with members of the immediate family, and in the end more control over their own marriages. That seemingly warmer, more open relationship occurred within a shrinking circle of family and close friends and amid greater privacy. Strong family ties and patriarchal authority hardly disappeared, however, in a society that remained so predominantly rural, agricultural, and enmeshed in slaveholding. Virginia experienced this revolution in family life less completely than many colonies did. Yet as this change, however confined, was set in motion, it seemed possible that the erosion of paternal authority in the planter-stateman's world might have begun to have a subtly corrosive effect on his sense of public authority.

It is possible to read quite differently the precise weight of these various signs of change in the structure of family, society, and political order, even to reject one or more of them out of hand. Collectively, however, they add a degree of substance to the sometimes formless but nonetheless deeply felt sense of moral decline and political failure expressed by so many of the elite. Those apprehensions may, on the other hand, have owed less to true decline than to unsettling change. For if anything seemed unmistakably present in mid-eighteenth-century Virginia, it was evidence of dynamic growth that was almost certain to have consequences for the narrowly based political elite who had been governing the colony. The old leadership found itself caught between a more aggressive group of imperial officials and a new, untested group of leaders presiding over a volatile, unstable social order in newer regions within the colony. One consequence was a pervasive sense of crisis among the gentry of the colony—as yet internalized, primarily intellectual and psychological in character, not fully focused, even with the presence of the several specific issues that the imperial relationship had already generated, and not accompanied by a demonstrable loss of confidence in their ability to conduct the affairs of the colony.

*   *   *

To conclude that such a crisis existed is to leave still unanswered the fundamental question of how far into the lower and middle ranks of the society of colonial Virginia it might have extended. In a political world in which elections turned most often on personality and seldom on openly debated issues, manifestations of more popular discontent have not been easy to find—at least until the recent work of the historian Rhys Isaac found a possible focus for the apprehensions and grievances of more ordinary Virginians in the rise of religious dissent within the colony after the 1740s.

With a constant shortage of clergy, with parishes of such great extent that many people lived far from the nearest church building, and with a formalism in its services that many found unappealing, the established Anglican church experienced increasing difficulty in reaching a growing, more diverse population. Nor did the members of the gentry themselves, however much they believed the established church to be a necessary and beneficial institution in society, set an example of strong commitment to its beliefs and practices. Many colonists, left with only the most nominal connection to the church, increasingly came under the sway of dissenting sects, often through the particular influence of itinerant evangelical preachers who traveled widely through the colonies in the course of the revival known as the Great Awakening. A sizable Quaker minority already lived in Virginia; and by the 1740s Presbyterianism had caught hold rapidly, both from the missionary activities of New Light ministers who were part of the Great Awakening and from the influx of more traditional Scotch-Irish Presbyterians into the newly settled western areas of the colony. Smaller numbers of German groups came as well, mostly Lutheran or Reformed but with a leaven of more pietistic sects like the Mennonites. These earlier dissenting groups likewise included some Baptists. By the 1760s, however, a newer and more pronounced upsurge of revivalism occurred with the appearance of the strongly evangelical Separate Baptists. By 1775 their churches were perhaps as numerous as those of the Anglican establishment and slightly exceeded those of the Presbyterians—each had close to a hundred churches in the colony by that date. Although the laws of the colony, as the courts generally interpreted them, permitted the existence of dissenting churches, such congregations had to be licensed under various restrictions, and their members were still liable for the payment of taxes to support the established church.

For a number of reasons the Separate Baptists had particularly strong effects on the religious and social life of the colony. With their success, dissenting groups as a whole probably came to outnumber Anglicans. The Baptists were, moreover, far less compromising than most of the earlier dissenters, unwilling to conform to the legal requirements of licensing their ministers to preach only at fixed locations and more determined to confront the error and immorality they believed to exist among Anglican clergy and laity. The Baptist movement posed not simply a religious challenge—though it was that in a profound way—but a wider social and cultural challenge, nothing less than a repudiation of the entire world of the planter elite, of which an easygoing Anglicanism was only one feature.

Certainly in their evangelical fervor, calls for strict personal morality, reliance on the experience of sudden, emotional conversion, and preference for ministers who had felt a divine call to preach rather than for clergymen who had been formally educated and ordained by prescribed liturgical forms, the Baptists offered a sweeping religious contrast with Anglicanism. And the two conflicting systems of belief also reflected totally divergent styles of life. On the one hand, the gentry were sensitive about personal honor and set great store on physical prowess and self-assertiveness. They were proud, a characteristic that expressed itself in their very bearing and sometimes condescending treatment of inferiors. They sat according to rank in the parish church. On court days they attended in positions of dominance, presiding over the court and receiving respectful treatment from lesser men. They enjoyed a social life that turned on drinking, dancing, and gambling both in the privacy of their great houses and on more public occasions, and the Anglican church did not ordinarily condemn them for it. Lesser colonists, apart from the Quakers, had long enjoyed similar social rituals, incorporating the same cultural values, whether at their own distinct gatherings or by making the most of their participation in such public occasions as court day, elections, and militia musters. They accepted disparity in social rank, though not without expecting a certain civility and recognition from the gentry and sometimes denying their votes on election day to the excessively haughty.

The Baptists, on the other hand, created a very different social and cultural world—egalitarian, solemn, austere. The flock forsook gambling, swearing, and drinking and were censured within the congregation for transgressing, in the process displacing the county court to some extent as the body that determined the moral standards of the community. They would not condone force or permit physical aggressiveness. Forming a close, supportive fellowship, they called into question by their example and by their convictions much about the old order, not only its religious faith but also its cultural values and even the very sources of authority. In its logical end the Separate Baptist movement was the antithesis of all that the planter world represented.

As Isaac remarked, the Baptists contended for neighborhood, farm, and slave quarter, not at first for the great house or for political control. Their phenomenal success bespoke their wide appeal, even a mounting dissatisfaction with the old ordered, traditional society. After the 1760s the confrontation between the two worlds was occasionally violent, especially in areas that had experienced little of the earlier activity of dissenters. Angry supporters of the status quo sometimes broke up meetings of the Baptists and physically assaulted their preachers, all to little avail. As strongly as the Baptists began to catch on, there was, however, a distinct geographical pattern in their earliest successes. If one drew a line from north to south through the colony, running from Alexandria through Fredericksburg, Richmond, Petersburg, and south to the North Carolina boundary—that is, roughly dividing Virginia into the Tidewater section to the east that had been settled before 1700 and the newer western areas that had been settled at a later date—only scattered Baptist congregations existed in the east as late as 1775, except for a pocket of pronounced strength in Caroline, Essex, and King and Queen counties. The greatest concentration lay in two areas, one group of counties in the Piedmont to the west of Alexandria and Fredericksburg and another in the newer parts of the Southside along the North Carolina border. To some extent the strength of the early Baptist movement was concentrated in areas of the colony that had experienced the most recent population growth and the greatest difficulty in establishing political order and stable leadership. Yet the social and cultural contrast between the Baptists and the old order was in every sense striking, even though the movement had only begun to establish itself in Virginia as the Revolutionary crisis commenced.

There remained one other distinct and numerous group within the society of colonial Virginia—the vast body of blacks, all but a tiny number held in slavery. Even though slavery had spread into the Piedmont, the concentration of blacks in many of the older Tidewater counties, where they sometimes outnumbered whites, was still marked. The preservation of a somewhat distinct culture, blending African survivals with adaptations from white culture, and the ability to preserve a degree of independence in such areas of personal life as marriage, relations with kin, and social life was more characteristic of the slaves' behavior than outright rebellion, although running away was a common form of resistance and individual acts of violence against whites an occasional one. Even among the largest slave owners blacks customarily lived in smaller groups on separate quarters and plantations rather than in the larger concentrations more characteristic of Low Country South Carolina, but the amount of more-or-less-secret com-

Mill Creek or Mauck's Meeting House, said to date from the colonial era. Although possibly erected in the Shenandoah Valley by German rather than Separate Baptists, it offers in its simplicity, as Rhys Isaac suggests, a striking contrast between the evangelical churches of the Great Awakening and those built by the established Anglican Church, as illustrated by Christ Church, Lancaster County (shown on page 159). Virginia State Library photograph.

munication among neighboring groups of blacks was obviously extensive.

By the middle of the eighteenth century white Virginians displayed an increasing concern about the presence in society of black slaves in such large numbers. Efforts to discourage further importation of new slaves directly from Africa, often by imposing import duties, were frequent, and resentment emerged at British objection to such restrictive measures in order to protect the interests of English slave traders. The principal objection of whites was less a fear of outright rebellion, though that concern also acted on them in subtle ways, than a feeling that slavery had become another manifestation of the moral crisis with which leading Virginians seemed so preoccupied, for they perceived in the absolute control that masters had over a large group of dependent laborers a principal temptation to the idleness, luxury, and vice that undermined those qualities of virtue and self-control on which society and government depended. Not only in their view did slavery destroy industry and respect for labor, but purchase of slaves consumed the resources of the colony. "One of the first Signs of the Decay, and perhaps the primary Cause of the Destruction of the most flourishing Government that ever existed," George Mason had written in 1765 of ancient Rome, "was the Introduction of great Numbers of Slaves—an Evil very pathetically described by the Roman historians." Slavery was, a *Virginia Gazette* contributor had noted, for Virginia "an internal Weakness, or Distemper." Almost no one conceived abolition as possible, but the colonists were to some extent obsessed with what they saw as the insidious influence of slavery.

But what of the slaves themselves? In the three or four years following the end of the war in 1763 an unusually intense wave of slave crimes erupted in Caroline County. In that time twelve trials for felonies, including murder, illegal administration of medicine, and arson, had taken place. The courts of oyer and terminer that heard the cases convicted eleven of the twelve, ordering the execution of nine and allowing two to be released under the customary plea of benefit of clergy, while acquitting only one. Perhaps more widely characteristic, however, of a certain resistance to slavery by blacks was their enthusiastic response to evangelical religious groups, Presbyterians, older Baptist groups, and Separate Baptists alike. The early Baptists in particular made few racial distinctions, welcoming black converts and generally opposing the ownership of slaves among their adherents. Blacks, moreover, molded the new faith to their own culture, not prohibiting dancing, as did white evangelicals, but converting it in part into a religious ritual, giving more emphasis to the communal features of the religion than their white counterparts and following in many cases their own black preachers. The consequence in many respects was to reinforce and strengthen the existing Afro-American culture rather than to offer a direct challenge to slavery, although clearly evangelical successes among blacks added another source of strength to the secret, independent, and sometimes defiant life of the slave quarter.

*   *   *

To examine Virginia at the middle of the eighteenth century in the knowledge that it, like the other American colonies, stood on the threshold of the Revolution all too easily invites the discovery of a provincial society in the grip of a degree of turmoil that made the struggle inevitable, or finds portentous meaning in every hint of the kind of stress or tension that exists in almost every society. It seems hardly likely, however, that any Virginian of the time, however prescient, could have understood that a revolution was imminent—at least to the best of our knowledge not one did. Yet it was also true that an unusual number of changes were beginning to occur in both the imperial and provincial worlds in which Virginians lived, changes which gave substance to the apprehensions that seemed to have affected so many. The new, more restrictive attitude toward the colonies by British officials was clearly the most obvious, having already stirred a number of open controversies and colored the prosecution of the recent war.

Too, life in some of the more recently settled portions of the colony exhibited a fluid, unsettled quality, often typical of recent frontiers, marked in this instance by such signs as an unusual frequency in disputed elections for the burgesses, less effective county courts, and a leadership that lacked wealth, experience, or family connections equivalent to those of the more established leaders in older sections of the Tidewater. To a marked extent the initial successes of the evangelical revival were concentrated in such areas. Because some parts of the Piedmont were settled as extensions of Tidewater society and because many older leaders accepted a Scottish, Scotch-Irish, and

German dominance of the Valley, the Southside emerged as the principal battleground between the old and the new order.

Perhaps far more apparent to the old elite and more clearly related to its apprehensive mood were elements of weakness in the established order itself. In particular, slavery had come to arouse increasing concern, not out of regard for the condition of blacks themselves but from a sense that its effect on white society was deleterious. Moreover, the tobacco economy seemed to be not simply in a temporary depression, though at the beginning of the 1760s it was, but in a more permanent decline. While less obvious, the private world of the gentry was perhaps altering, too, in ways that reduced the patriarchal role of fathers. And the effects of the new imperial policies perhaps extended beyond the visible issues they raised in public life, disturbing the self-perception of an elite with a deep attachment to the transatlantic culture of the empire.

The world—or rather the two worlds, imperial and provincial—that Virginians inhabited was in a state of flux. The nature of the earliest response to these changes had been at once formless and deeply felt. Collectively, however, the potential effects of virtually all the changes converged in one direction: a weakening of the various bases of authority—personal, moral, social, political—of the leadership of the colony. The tumultuous public life of the Southside revealed the weakness of traditional forms of political authority in such an area, not so much because they had been consciously rejected as from a lack of time in which they might fully mature. The recent imperial measures all aimed at reducing the legislative independence of the Virginia Assembly, the very bulwark of the public authority of the provincial leadership. If evangelicals had begun to reprove the gentry for a loss of moral authority, its members may have arrived at the same disturbing conclusion on their own, as evidenced by their lamentations over excess and immorality in their lives and the hostility they turned against the Anglican clergy. Slavery subverted, or was thought to subvert, the energy and sense of responsibility of the elite, and the decline of tobacco threatened the essential economic base for the personal independence that was essential to leadership. Thus, in many ways the elements were in place for a crisis in leadership, one not altogether separable from a crisis in the whole society but one, nevertheless, that at mid-century remained embryonic and unformed.

12

THE STAMP ACT CRISIS:
THE REVOLUTION BEGINS

If many Virginians felt anger and frustration at the end of the Seven Years' War, the mood of Britons was no better. Despite the magnificence of the triumph, even because of it, the nation faced problems that no government could long evade. For one thing, the war had left behind a national debt of record proportions, one that had grown from over £72 million in 1755 to more than £122 million in 1763 and was still rising from accumulating interest. Much of it in the British view had been incurred in direct defense of the American colonies, whose own assemblies proved reluctant to vote adequate sums for a war in which they had so much at stake. The newly acquired territories—Canada, Florida, and the vast Ohio region—were, moreover, thinly settled and poorly developed. Whatever their strategic value, they would not add to the wealth of the empire for a long time but would only add to the burden of maintaining it. Too, the new lands, inhabited by nationals and former Indian allies of the defeated powers, left imperial authorities with a staggering political problem of organizing and administering so vast a region. Nor, despite the extent of its defeat, was it possible to count France out of the European balance of power or of attempts to regain its American possessions. Finally, the impact of the war and its outcome—news of great battles in a heretofore remote North American wilderness, realization of the extent of British commitment on that distant continent, need for enough knowledge of the region to determine what territories Spain and France must yield—united to call more attention to the sprawling empire already in being.

Such concerns, added to the determination the British had already begun to display to strengthen control over the older colonies, all but inexorably led political leaders of varying stripes to build on those policies that Halifax and others had already initiated. Indeed, the war years had brought no real break in the pursuit of such restrictive policies, except perhaps a brief interruption in the first years of the war as the precarious military situation and the need for securing maximum support from the colonies preoccupied the British. By about 1759, as soon as the war had turned decisively in Britain's favor, officials edged toward the resumption and elaboration of the prewar regulatory measure without waiting for the formalities of peace.

Once the Treaty of Paris was concluded, the process moved forward more steadily, aided by the significant changes in the composition of the group of politicians who made up the ministry. With his accession to the throne in 1760, the young monarch George III had begun a reshuffling of the key cabinet posts. By the end of the war in 1763 the man who emerged as the chief minister and principal architect of imperial policy was George Grenville, chancellor of the exchequer. Aptly described as a man with a "tidy mind," Grenville was someone to whom the idea of tightening control over the colonies would have appealed in any event simply because it bore the stamp of order and efficiency. He almost certainly came to power without fixed ideas about colonial policy or any comprehensive scheme for effecting them. Such proposals abounded at the time among past and present colonial governors and other colonial "experts," but the very spirit of British politics, pragmatic, local-minded, occupied with bargaining among all sorts of factions and interests, militated against broad, theoretical conceptions of policy. But establishment of a tighter colonial policy was, of course, already in progress; and the new pressures of war debt, the vast new territory to be organized, the desires of various interest groups in England, and a sense of dissatisfaction with the conduct of the colonies all reinforced the objective. Nor was George Grenville the sort of man to evade the tasks that the times forced on him. Step by step he and his associates moved to meet each exigency with a series of administrative orders and acts of Parliament. Over a brief span of two years an unprecedented variety of colonial regulatory measures unfolded.

Grenville inherited more than one decision made by his predecessors, in particular that of keeping a military force of about 7,500 regulars in North America—a little more than double the number of troops stationed there before the outbreak of war. That it was part of a general defense against possible French resurgence has been the accepted reason for the somewhat chance decision, although a few officials apparently saw it frankly as a means of keeping the colonies under control. At any rate, the forces would remain for the most part on the frontier or in the newly acquired colonies—for the moment no one thought of stationing soldiers in the older centers of population along the seaboard. The general expectation was, however, that the colonists must help with the considerable expense of maintaining these garrisons.

Grenville took over, too, in the face of a new crisis that made the presence of an army in North America seem fortunate. In May 1763 a full-scale Indian uprising under the leadership of the Ottawa chieftain Pontiac erupted in the region near Detroit and spread quickly eastward as far as the frontiers of Pennsylvania and Virginia. Although virtually every western post fell except Detroit and Fort Pitt, both of which were besieged, British forces under Colonel Henry Bouquet were able to relieve Fort Pitt by August and force the Indians to raise their siege of Detroit. The unrest placed greater urgency on the task of organizing civil government and evolving Indian and land policies for the newly secured territories. The result was the King's Proclamation of October 7, 1763, which established several new British colonial governments, including Quebec. It also excluded from both Quebec and the older seaboard colonies all of the vast region between a line drawn roughly along the crest of the Alleghenies and the Mississippi River, closed it to white settlers, and "for the present, and until our further pleasure be known" reserved it to the Indians who lived there. The competing interest on one side or the other of the question—those of the Indians themselves, Indian traders, colonial and military officials, land speculators from England and various colonies—were unusually complex, but it was the speculators who saw their ambitions particularly thwarted by the establishment of the Proclamation Line.

Grenville also moved to stem the widely recognized evasion by American shippers of the customs duties and trade regulations, to keep

the benefits of commerce within the empire, and to meet a larger share
of the high administrative costs of the customs service from duties. In
the beginning he sought no legislation, relying instead on a series of
administrative orders for absentee customs officers to go to the colonies
and discharge the responsibilities of their posts, for royal governors to
take a more active hand in reporting violations, and for additional naval
vessels to patrol American waters. Grenville knew, however, that even
when properly enforced the customs regulations would return little
revenue, for most duties were primarily intended to make illicit trade
financially prohibitive, not to encourage extensive collections. So,
having issued the initial orders, he began to prepare legislation that
would turn the customs duties into a source of revenue and further
improve their administration. He proposed adding new duties and
revising others downward, especially the import duty on foreign
molasses, so that they would cease to be prohibitory and might actually
be paid with frequency. He also added to the customs regulations an
elaborate series of bonds that clearly listed a vessel's cargo and ports of
call, transferred trials of violators out of sympathetic colonial courts
and into admiralty courts that sat without juries under Crown-
appointed judges, and granted customs officers immunity from damage
suits when they failed to obtain convictions. Parliament lost no time in
enacting his recommendations into law as the American Revenue Act,
or, more popularly, the Sugar Act of 1764.

The ministry also took the occasion of the annual renewal of the
army appropriation to include a system of requisitions whereby the
commanding officers of troops stationed in the American colonies could
call on the colonial governments to provide quarters and certain basic
supplies for their men. The Quartering Act of 1765, as Americans
called the measure, was in its own way a revenue measure, too, since
colonial governments would presumably have to pass along the costs of
compliance to taxpayers. Caught up in their determination to bring the
colonies under every necessary regulation, imperial officials were
likewise no longer willing to ask provincial assemblies to cease
objectionable practices—they demanded it by law. Tired of haggling
with the Virginia Assembly and one or two others over their issuance
of paper money, Parliament now disposed of the matter by enacting the
Currency Act of 1764, which prohibited future issues of paper money

anywhere in the colonies as legal tender in the payment of private debts, although it left existing issues in circulation.

To Grenville and others these measures were still not adequate, above all where the question of revenue to help in meeting the costs of imperial administration was concerned. In working out the details of the Sugar Act, he had reached the conclusion that customs duties alone would never be sufficient, so he had included in the law an additional resolution stating somewhat cryptically that "towards further defraying the said Expenses, it may be proper to charge certain Stamp Duties in the said Colonies and Plantations." In effect, he served notice that Parliament might at some future date be asked to enact a system of excise taxes on newspapers, legal documents, and similar paper instruments, an exaction that had been frequently levied on Britons at home. Grenville went to work so quickly on the complicated details of such a scheme that he apparently had had it in mind all along. Before the end of 1764 the colonists understood that the measure—a much more explicit taxation of colonists by the home government than the customs duties of the Sugar Act—was under consideration, and they moved through their respective colonial agents and by legislative resolutions and addresses to try to head it off.

However much these actions of 1763 and 1764 were a series of specific responses to a variety of problems imposed by the recent war, they also carried forward in sometimes dramatic ways the movement toward a more carefully regulated empire that Grenville's predecessors had begun. The ministers, too, responded to the strong desires of substantial groups and interests in Britain, among them both the country gentry opposed to higher taxes at home and mercantile interests concerned with safeguarding their investment in colonial markets. The measures had overwhelming support from virtually every powerful political bloc in Britain. In the end they made a logical whole despite their piecemeal preparation, each step following upon the preceding in a way that comprised a consistent, sweeping "program," though hardly the dark conspiracy that many colonists would come to make of it.

*   *   *

News of each law or decree reached the colonies gradually, with the consequence that early reactions varied from colony to colony. Often the initial opposition was halting and sporadic, although it began to mount after news of the Sugar Act, especially in colonies with strong groups of local merchants. The reaction in Virginia gathered slowly indeed. Not all of the Grenville measures affected the colony with the same force. The Currency Act, however, was another, final step in an ongoing controversy, aimed squarely at Virginia. The prohibition on further western settlement in 1763 had immediate implications for several powerful groups of land speculators in the colony, especially those who were members of the Ohio Company. The Sugar Act and stricter customs enforcement, on the other hand, had little direct effect, unless in the new duty on a favorite solace of the gentry, madeira wine. The tobacco trade, as far as anyone knew, operated comfortably within the imperial system, among other reasons because of its dependence on British credit and markets. Virginia would, however, bear with all the colonies the burden of stamp duties if the new act were passed.

After more than a decade of disputes with the home government it may seem surprising that the Virginia response should now seem so mild and should occur in such traditional, almost ritualistic forms. For one thing, none of the new imperial measures passed before the end of 1764 directly affected the larger number of Virginians. In contrast, in the continuing dispute over the Parsons' Cause, a series of clerical suits for additional salary had reached several county courts, where numbers of more ordinary colonists might follow them as jurymen or simple spectators and might personally confront what they regarded as clerical arrogance. Certainly the Parsons' Cause played a significant part in launching the political career of Patrick Henry, for his powerful plea before a Hanover County jury in the case of the Reverend James Maury first brought him to prominence. Henry entered the case after Maury had already won a favorable judgment and a jury had been convened to determine the amount of compensation to which he was entitled. Maury's lawyer had objected to the selection of jurors of low status, including dissenters, but Henry had defended them as "honest men" and they had been sworn. Henry's subsequent plea justified both the utility and legality of the Twopenny act, labeling the king a tyrant who had forfeited any constitutional claim to obedience by annulling it. Henry went on, with the obvious approbation of the jurymen, to denounce the clergy as "enemies of the community" for refusing to accept the law. In the end he secured a verdict of one penny in damages, although Maury should have received almost £300. Henry had misread or ignored the fact that it was not Crown disallowance but the Hanover Court's eccentric reasoning that the Twopenny Act had been retroactively void which produced the original decision in Maury's favor, but he had made the issue a popular cause and turned it as much against the king as the clergy.

For the first but hardly the last time the style and tone of the old leadership's response differed drastically from Henry's. They, too, had continued their opposition to the clergy in the Parsons' Cause but by following more conventional political and legal channels. In the case of the Grenville measures, news of which were beginning to reach the colony while the Parsons' Cause still raged, the response of the leadership was similarly measured. No one seemed disposed to fight over the restriction on western land grants that the Proclamation of 1763 imposed. Even those who were active in the Ohio Company appeared to conclude that they had more to gain from political maneuver under the aegis of British investors in the company. Although the Currency Act capped an issue on which the burgesses had been contending with the home government and the mercantile lobby for months, they directed their anger principally against the "Machinations of those very Merchants who draw their Subsistence, as it were from our very Vitals." If anything, there was a stronger feeling of relief that by failing to do more than prohibit future issues and demand retirement of existing currency on schedule, Parliament had not gone as far as the merchants wanted. Consequently, paper money would circulate for a few years yet, and leaders of the colony evidently concluded they could live with the act. While the Sugar Act was being debated in London, Virginia interests had "made no figure at all." Charles Steuart, a future customs official and Scottish merchant with Norfolk connections, taunted Virginians with the observation that "Mr. G[renvill]e cut your throats with a feather."

On the other hand, when the full text of the act reached the colony, sometime at the end of April or the beginning of May 1764, the leadership was quick to fix on the single vague provision regarding a future stamp act and to follow with concern the additional information that the Virginia agent, Edward Montague, began to supply. From the first, they viewed it as evidence of "a resolution, to oppress North

Patrick Henry as depicted in a posthumous portrait by Thomas Sully that is almost certainly an idealized interpretation of the great orator and popular leader of the Revolution in Virginia. Colonial Williamsburg photograph.

America with the iron hand of power, unrestrained by any sentiment, drawn from reason, the liberty of mankind, or the genius of their own government." The words were those of Richard Henry Lee, a leader of the Northern Neck gentry, a member of one of the most prominent families in the colony, and a burgess for his home county of Westmoreland. Virginians fastened so exclusively on the proposed taxation as evidence of an intent to bring the colonies under complete subjection that the issue displaced their opposition to any other measures. Because the next session of the Assembly would not open until October 30, they moved in the interim to record their opposition and try to find out more from George Grenville about the alternatives for furnishing the needed revenue that he had declared himself willing to consider. At least twice during the summer the standing committee of correspondence of the House of Burgesses, appointed to handle communications with the Virginia agent, assembled in Williamsburg to send advice and instructions. The principal recommendations of the group, composed of Speaker John Robinson, Attorney General Randolph, several other prominent burgesses, and the members of the Governor's Council residing in Williamsburg, were to accept the trade regulations of the Sugar Act as they were already enacted but to impress on Montague the need to use his "whole weight and Influence" in opposing the impending stamp legislation, while offering to meet any reasonable request for funds raised by the Assembly itself.

When the Assembly convened later in the fall, the burgesses turned rapidly to the preparation of separate addresses to king, lords, and Commons against passage of the stamp act. Of the eight-man committee appointed to prepare the statements, four senior members of the inner circle of the leadership—the attorney general, Richard Henry Lee, Landon Carter, and George Wythe—seem to have been particularly influential, and Edmund Pendleton, a young lawyer and protégé of Randolph, perhaps equally so. The committee reported its drafts within two weeks, and the full membership of the lower house quickly approved. An unusual decision to seek the concurrence of the Council resulted in agreement on an amended version by both houses on December 18. Governor Fauquier reported that while the original draft was "warm and indecent," he had been informed "by some Gentlemen of the Committee . . . that their whole Study has been to endeavor to mollify them."

In their final form all of the addresses nonetheless made strong statements of constitutional principle against Parliamentary taxation. Two advanced without qualification the fundamental claim from which Americans never deviated: that the colonies enjoyed the "ancient and inestimable Right of being governed by such Laws respecting their internal Polity and Taxation as are derived from their own Consent." In contrast, the proposed duties were "subversive . . . of that Freedom which all men, especially those who derive their Constitution from Britain, have a Right to enjoy." These strong assertions of right lay embedded, however, in long, reasoned texts that opened with traditional expressions of humility and respect toward king and Parliament. They were not brief, peremptory resolutions of the kind that would dominate many subsequent protests. Looking back on them many years later, Edmund Pendleton emphasized that they had attacked the taxation power of Parliament "with Manly but decent language," contrasting them with Patrick Henry's "pepered resolutions" of the next year, an action he recalled as marked by too much "warmth of temper."

Much about these protests indeed bears out Pendleton's later characterization. Their tone was as restrained as he said. They made no effort to spell out a line of future conduct, should Parliament and Grenville persist in the taxation measure. In fact, during the month preceding their passage Peyton Randolph, while serving on the committee that framed the protests, had in his capacity as attorney general readily supplied Governor Fauquier with a list of the kinds of legal writs and forms customarily used in Virginia, so that he might forward it for the use of officials who were drafting the stamp legislation. Yet on the matter of constitutional right the Assembly had been uncompromising, and behind their formal statements lay a clear recognition of the central problem that the Stamp Act would present. Unlike most of the prior regulatory measures, the Stamp Act raised the specter of the use of the taxation power and the revenues it would generate to establish stronger internal control over the colonies and to further weaken the power of the Assembly; and it did so on the constitutional premise that Parliament's authority was absolute.

Although the respected senior burgess Richard Bland seems not to have been involved actively in the preparation of the legislative protests, he contributed an important and far-reaching statement challenging Parliament's complete authority over the colonies in a pamphlet published three days before the October 30, 1774, session of the Assembly opened. *The Colonel Dismounted* was in the first instance Bland's final argument against the stand of the clergy in the Parsons' Cause. Upon hearing of the proposed stamp duties he broadened it to deny that either royal instructions or acts of Parliament had legal force in matters affecting the "INTERNAL Government" of a colony. Although Bland couched his argument in characteristically restrained and moderate language, he had, even at this early stage of the controversy, already unequivocally asserted the American claim to autonomy in the internal affairs of each colony.

At the same time the modest action taken revealed a group of men who still saw those ultimate consequences of the stamp duties as abstract and theoretical, who had not yet had their deepest passions aroused, and who still seemed to regard the issue as one of ordinary political maneuver and accommodation. Whatever the evidence that they might have begun to feel their political position threatened, they acted in this instance with a sense of security and confidence that they had made their protest and that it would be heard. These were men who were still comfortable with the transatlantic politics of the empire, used to playing the game according to well-understood, if tacit, rules.

* * *

Nothing had, in sum, prepared the old leadership for the extent to which they would see that complacency shaken, indeed all but destroyed, by the rush of events in the two years following the passage of George Grenville's Stamp Act in March of 1765. By the time this first, formative period of the Revolution had ended, it had exposed a deeper gulf in the imperial world than anyone on either side of the Atlantic could have foreseen and had served as a catalyst to draw into sharper focus some of those underlying pressures that had begun to operate against the political order within the colony.

The political events of 1765 and 1766 were played out, moreover, against a background of the recent sharp economic depression. In the economic sphere no less than the political, a long period of relatively steady development was giving way to one of marked fluctuation and instability. As the Seven Years' War drew to an end, both tobacco exports from the colony and imports of British goods, underwritten by rapid expansion of British credit, reached record highs in 1759 and again in 1760. Then, with the market glutted, tobacco prices began a drastic decline, while British merchants proceeded to restrict new credit, to demand settlement of outstanding debts, and to reduce further exports. Another year of record tobacco exports and somewhat increased exports in 1763 served only to intensify a depression which, by 1764, seemed deeply entrenched. Resentment mounted against merchants when they pressed in person or in the courts for payment and when they were perceived as the architects of the new Currency Act that could only add to the fiscal crisis. In the summer of 1764 William Allason, a Scottish merchant who operated on the Rappahannock River, ordered a pair of pistols, explaining that "it is sometimes Dangerous in Travelling through our wooden Country, Particularly at this time when the Planters are pressed for old Ballances."

Yet the year 1765 began quietly enough. Their work completed the previous December, the members of the Assembly adjourned, leaving the committee of correspondence the task of sending their addresses against the Stamp Act proposal to Edward Montague for delivery. Then, in February, George Grenville dropped the other shoe and introduced the stamp legislation. While Montague had found an opposition member of Parliament who was willing to introduce the Virginia petition, in the end the House of Commons refused to receive any of the American statements, Virginia's included, partly on the grounds that they called into question the authority of Parliament but also on the strength of a general custom against hearing petitions on money bills. The stamp duties passed rapidly through Parliament and received the king's signature on March 22. Grenville sought to make the measure more palatable by indicating that he would appoint Americans as stamp distributors in each of the colonies and by assuring that the proceeds of the tax would be spent in America, primarily to help in supporting the military forces that had remained after the end of the Seven Years' War. He was too astute to expect Americans to like the Stamp Act, but evidently he believed that they would in the end comply, an impression which gained support from the number of colonists who sought appointments as distributors.

News of the passage of the Stamp Act began to reach the colonies by mid-April. The *Virginia Gazette*, the colony's only newspaper, published a table of the duties in the April 26 issue but declined to print an introductory comment critical of the high cost of the duties. The author, John Mercer, whose son George would shortly be revealed as the chief distributor of stamps for Virginia, thereupon sent copies of his statement to several of those who were preparing to attend the session of the Assembly that would open on May 1.

The leaders of the Assembly, however, faced a dilemma, for they clearly had other matters on their mind. Uppermost was a proposal for a provincial loan office, to be funded from a loan of £240,000 sterling from British merchants to be used in part to retire the old paper currency still outstanding and in part for making loans to private individuals at interest in the forms of bills of credit that might circulate as a new form of currency backed by the funds held in the treasury of the colony. The loan office idea stood to accomplish several objectives. It might overcome the restraints of the Currency Act and afford indebted planters a means of relief from the depression. It perhaps promised, too, to solve a pressing political problem, for by retiring the existing paper money the old leaders might put to rest persistent rumors that their principal spokesman, the Speaker of the House and treasurer of the colony, John Robinson, had been making illegal loans from the treasury to his associates. Such charges against a figure as powerful as Robinson provided an early sign that political insurgency within the colony might become as critical an issue as the state of the economy and the new policies of imperial regulation.

Since Crown approval would be indispensable for the loan office legislation, the burgesses could not easily advance that objective and at the same time defiantly oppose the Stamp Act. They seemed to have made their choice, for while the journals of the first weeks of the session made no reference to the Stamp Act, a group of resolutions outlining the loan office plan passed the lower house, only to fail in a more skeptical Council. With the defeat, many of the old leaders, rather than turn now to imperial policy, began drifting away toward their homes. By May 30 hardly more than a third of the full membership of the lower house was still in attendance. Years later Edmund Pendleton, one of those who departed early, argued that he and others had done so without knowing the Stamp Act had passed, owing to the belated arrival of a letter from the Virginia agent. Clearly, however, they had had other and earlier sources of information—and other priorities. A letter written from New York later in the summer of 1765 suggested that those who left did so because they did not know what to do next. For the moment in the spring of 1765 the old leadership had hesitated, and the question of whether Virginia would resist the Stamp Act seemed to hang in the balance.

Resistance did not collapse, but the initiative in organizing it passed to a new burgess attending his first session, the recent hero of the Parsons' Cause, Patrick Henry. It had been common knowledge, apparently discussed before many of the members began to leave, that Henry and half a dozen or so of his associates—including George Johnson of Fairfax in the Northern Neck, John Fleming of the Piedmont county of Cumberland, and Robert Munford and Paul Carrington, both from Southside counties—had already begun to prepare a set of resolutions opposing the Stamp Act. Then on May 29, on George Johnson's motion seconded by Henry, the House agreed unanimously to go into committee of the whole to discuss the resolutions that the group had composed. Peyton Randolph was in the chair in place of the absent Speaker, and the number of delegates still present was very close to the minimum for a quorum.

After a day of debate in the committee of the whole and another in regular session, Henry narrowly carried on May 30 five resolves from a total list of seven, the fifth by a margin of one vote. The passage of the fifth reportedly moved Peyton Randolph to declare, "By God, I would have given one hundred guineas for a single vote!" Then Henry or one of his supporters departed, and on the last day of the month the remaining members voted to rescind one resolution so that the official journals of the House recorded only four, omitting in particular the two strongest from the original list. Within the next few weeks, however, texts that included the two appeared in the newspapers of several other colonies. Thus in other parts of America the action of the Virginia delegates seemed both more extreme and more unanimous than it had actually been and had a marked effect in crystallizing legislative opposition elsewhere in America. The Massachusetts Patriot Oxenbridge Thacher had roused from his deathbed long enough to say of the Virginians, "They are men!"

Whether Henry himself had actually written the resolutions is unclear. They have been attributed at times to John Fleming, who led the floor fight for their adoption, while another of Henry's group, Paul Carrington, later professed not to recall who had actually "held the pen." The four that remained in the House journals essentially restated in briefer form what the old leaders had argued the preceding fall, the conventional constitutional wisdom of the day in America: that colonists lived under the British constitution and continued, by virtue of their charters or the condition of their original settlement, to enjoy the customary rights of British subjects, including that of being governed in their internal affairs—"internal polity"—only by their elected representatives. Of the three that did not appear (one of which had, of course, been rescinded and the other two not adopted, though not necessarily brought to a vote), the fifth declared that any recognition of the principle that the power of taxation belonged to any body other than the assembly of a colony had "a manifest Tendency to destroy British as well as American Freedom." The sixth and seventh, however, went further in declaring that the people of the colony owed no obedience to any tax law not passed by the Assembly of the colony and that any person who upheld the authority of Parliament should be branded an enemy of Virginia. They were, in effect, a call for defiance of the Stamp Act.

The adoption of the Stamp Act Resolves, in some part at least over the objections of the old leadership of the burgesses, has become at once the best known and most elusive event of the Revolution in Virginia, "clear in legend but cloudy in history," as Edmund S. Morgan has noted. The debate, the second episode in the elevation of Henry to heroic stature, was the occasion for his "Caesar-Brutus" speech in which Henry appeared, by citing the examples of Julius Caesar and King Charles I, to invite the assassination or execution of George III— only to have the hall of the burgesses ring out with cries of treason. The apocryphal version of that dramatic moment concluded with Henry looking his hearers in the eye and, after suggesting that George might profit from their example, declaring, "If this be treason, make the most of it!" A contemporary account, left by a French traveler who happened to be in Williamsburg and attended the debate, reported Henry as having immediately backed down, begging the pardon of his audience and declaring himself as loyal a servant of the king as any he had. The

Frenchman's version, in fact, took nothing away from the drama of the moment.

The significant question surrounding that intense debate of May 1765 is not, however, whether Henry apologized for remarks made in such heat but why the leadership opposed him so bitterly and what his victory meant. The four resolutions that remained in the journals obviously raised no issue of principle, though perhaps one of tactics. Another possibility has always seemed to be the traditional dislike of the senior legislator for the upstart newcomer. Henry and most of those who gave him his strongest support were indeed freshman burgesses, four of them from new counties, and their opponents largely veterans. Governor Fauquier had also called Henry's group the "young, hot, and giddy" members, yet it was true as well that the burgesses paid rather less attention to seniority than do most modern legislative bodies. Henry himself, though arriving late for his first session, nonetheless immediately received an important committee assignment, something often denied longtime members of more modest ability.

Edmund Randolph, nephew of Peyton and later a prominent political figure, had a further suggestion in a history of Virginia which he wrote but never published. As the colony grew and new counties were created, Randolph claimed to detect the appearance, gradually and at first almost unconsciously, of a new group of legislators, who were by his description less wealthy and less aristocratic than the delegates from the older counties. When he went on to discuss the issues that their presence raised in Virginia politics, he could name only one. The old and the new men, he wrote, diverged in their views about "granting public money": "While one would pay a public servant upon a strict calculation of the labor to be performed, the other would augment the stipend for the sake of dignity." Contained in that issue, however, is a differing style of politics, one which reinforced that vague division between "representative" and "responsible" legislators.

The men around Speaker Robinson and Attorney General Randolph not only were concerned about the dignity of office but also responded to matters of policy in a manner conditioned by past experience, by the leverage they had often obtained on royal officials in the colony, and by the ready assumption that they possessed the influence to bring about a revision of British policy. Living mostly in the Tidewater, many were used to dealing with the colony's agent in London, with leading consignment merchants, and with others able to exercise some direct influence in British politics. It was perhaps too early to see the Stamp Act as representing an all but fatal blow to this system of imperial politics, and the hesitation of these men in the spring of 1765 was in many ways a reaffirmation of the "spirit of 1764."

Henry and his backers, on the other hand, were not simply new men from the upcountry sections of the colony who had only recently been brought actively into provincial politics. They were men for whom the empire was more remote: if their acquaintance with provincial politics was recent, that with imperial politics was still more slight. In economic matters they and their constituents were more likely to deal with resident factors at Scottish stores in their own neighborhoods and in a relationship based more on suspicion than on longtime confidence. When they became concerned with imperial issues, their response stood to be quick, direct, and not especially subtle.

That explanation of the contest between the two groups gains additional confirmation from what seemed in the final analysis to be the fundamental difference in the debate; namely, the likelihood that it focused not on constitutional principle at all, not on resentment of Henry alone, but on the strategy for action contained in the last two resolves, which were among the three kept off the official record. By denying that the colonists were obligated to obey the Stamp Act and by branding its supporters as traitors, they appeared to incite overt resistance. In an especially revealing observation the Frenchman had recorded that "the whole house was for Entering resolves on the records but they Differed much with regard [to] the Contents or purport thereof." In even more telling fashion Edmund Randolph's account, noting the defeat of the two strongest resolutions, added that the "rest . . . being more correspondent with the general sentiment were by the severance of those two, better guarantees of a stable opposition to Parliament."

Yet the difference was hardly as minor as Randolph perhaps attempted to make it. For at this initial stage of the Revolution Patrick Henry had opened the possibility of a major transformation of both the imperial and domestic politics of Virginia, one that would in many ways have responded to a number of aspects of the underlying crisis in the colony, perhaps confirming the worst apprehensions of the old leadership. In their own uncertainty they had given him an opening,

John Robinson (1704–1766), who held the offices of Speaker of the House of Burgesses and Treasurer of the Colony for nearly 30 years, epitomized the power and influence of the leaders of the Virginia legislature in the eighteenth century. His death and the attendant disclosure of illegal loans he had made from the Treasury funds touched off a significant political crisis in the colony. Colonial Williamsburg photograph. Portrait by John Wollaston.

and characteristically he had seized it. For the imperial world the complete version of Henry's resolves, with both the stronger and rejected articles included, posed the choice between another effort at accommodation by relying on traditional lines of communication or overt defiance of a British law. The potential effect on the domestic order was perhaps as great. Henry had worked with a tiny bloc of delegates in a very thin House, and his victory—partial at best—was no guarantee of success in a fully attended session. In the end the opposition had staved off what they objected too most strongly, though they clearly did not regard it as a great triumph. But Henry had once again, as in the Parsons' Cause, become a popular and powerful symbol, aptly described by Rhys Isaac as the political counterpart of the evangelical preacher, bringing a similar extemporaneous, emotional style and moral fervor to politics. He had laid bare two competing styles of politics and all that they represented in the wider social order of Virginia.

*   *   *

The possibilities for which Henry stood had merely been revealed, however, not achieved. On June 1, Fauquier sent the remaining burgesses home by dissolving the Assembly. The Virginia resolves and those of a similar nature from other colonial assemblies were, if anything, less likely to deter British officials from proceeding with the Stamp Act, now that it has been passed, than had the burgesses' appeals in 1764. In England George Grenville completed the appointment of distributors for each colony, provided the necessary supply of stamped paper, and made other preparations, while in Virginia Fauquier, aware of what he termed "general discontent," did what he could to suppress it by keeping the text of Henry's resolves out of the *Virginia Gazette* and by postponing the next scheduled session of the Assembly. The latter step had the added benefit from his standpoint of preventing Virginia from electing delegates to an intercolonial Stamp Act Congress in New York.

So the opposition was left to fester and develop at a more local level, particularly under the leadership of Richard Henry Lee and his family in the Northern Neck region, which emerged as the most important center of opposition to the Stamp Act in the colony. Unlike the section from which much of Henry's circle had come, the older parts of the Northern Neck lay within the Tidewater. Although they shared its economic and social organization to a considerable degree, they remained somewhat on the periphery of provincial politics, furnishing a smaller percentage of the inner circle of leaders of the colony and displaying somewhat different interests, including an early commitment to a more diversified economy that might achieve greater economic independence than tobacco afforded.

One important manifestation of these activities was a series of local demonstrations against the Stamp Act in Prince William County, Loudoun County, and Lee's home county of Westmoreland. At the Westmoreland demonstration on September 24 and 25, 1765, events began on the first day with a procession headed by two of Richard Henry Lee's slaves wearing the livery of the English political radical John Wilkes, followed by a crowd of both blacks and whites. Behind them came effigies of George Mercer, who was by now known to have been appointed stamp distributor for his native colony, and of George Grenville. The two effigies were guarded by more of Lee's slaves, apparently unclothed and playing the parts of jailors, sheriffs, and hangmen, while Mercer's effigy held placards reading, "Money is my God," and "Slavery I love." Lee himself and the rest of the crowd followed. The day ended with the hanging of the effigies, which on the next day were again hanged and then burned after Lee had read a satirical "dying speech of George Mercer."

At the same time, the Westmoreland justices notified the governor and the Council that they intended to close the court once the Stamp Act took effect rather than use stamped paper and "become Instrumental in the Destruction of Our Country's Right and Liberties." The idea gained currency everywhere, and it became apparent that most of the Virginia court system would cease to function on November 1.

As that date approached, George Mercer still had not arrived with the first consignment of stamps for Virginia. At last, on October 29, he landed at Hampton. Met by an angry crowd that finally dispersed, he went on the next day to Williamsburg, where the General Court of the colony was in session and the town consequently crowded. There another large gathering awaited him near the capitol, followed him into the nearby open area known as the Exchange, and dispersed only when the governor himself escorted Mercer to his residence. Fauquier recounted the anger of the assembled crowd, whom, he added, "I should call a Mob, did I not know that it was chiefly, if not altogether composed of, Gentlemen of property in the Colony." Characteristically Edmund Pendleton remembered it, in contrast, as an occasion "when a Number of grave and respectable Gentlemen assembled, without the smallest appearance of a Mob, and required his resignation."

Mercer's resignation and the closing of the General Court itself were the only two things really attainable at the provincial level, given Fauquier's intention to keep the Assembly adjourned, and both were accomplished by November 1. Before returning to England, however, Mercer secretly stored his supply of stamped paper aboard a British vessel assigned to Virginia waters and provided for their sale should conditions improve. The *Gazette* also suspended publication; and trade, apart from clearances to the West Indies, largely came to a standstill, although Fauquier was willing to issue clearance papers stating that the required stamped forms were unavailable in order to protect ships against customs seizure.

Except for the events at the end of October, the pattern of opposition remained overwhelmingly local in character. A few of the county courts, beginning with that of Northampton on February 11, 1766, declared the Stamp Act unconstitutional and began to sit without using stamps for legal documents. Two more incidents of mob action took place, now involving threats to actual individuals, not to effigies. In late February, upon hearing that the Tappahannock merchant Archibald Ritchie, a Scot who had long lived in the colony, had declared he would clear his vessels on stamped papers, a Westmoreland County group met at Leedstown, adopted resolutions attacking the Stamp Act and those who supported it, and joined with others from the Tappahannock region to force Ritchie to recant. Estimates of the number of marchers ranged between four and six hundred—it was no minor event. Lee's incoming correspondence reveals the extent of his involvement, and Fauquier also made it clear in his reports home that he held the Lee family as principally responsible. About a month later a comparable incident took place in Norfolk. There the opponents of the Stamp Act organized formally as the Sons of Liberty and adopted resolutions similar to those of the Leedstown associators. They also seized a ship captain, William Smith, whom they suspected of having informed against an accused smuggler, tarred and feathered him, and twice threw him in the river, where he narrowly escaped drowning.

Except for the access that some of the Northern Neck leaders had to the *Maryland Gazette*, Virginia continued to lack a press during the period of opposition to the Stamp Act. By the time the printers elsewhere had resumed publication without stamps, Joseph Royle had died, leaving Williamsburg without a printer. In the spring of 1776, however, some of those whom Fauquier called "the hot Burgesses" had invited William Rind to come from Maryland and establish a more independent newspaper, while Royle's old foreman, Alexander Purdie, had already resumed the original *Gazette* in March and also sought to win the support of the leaders of the colony. So in the end, the Stamp Act controversy had given Williamsburg rival *Virginia Gazettes*, both more independent of the governor's influence than the earlier paper had been.

The lack of a press for some months had deprived the colony of the same kind of political comment and reporting of acts of defiance that had helped to keep up the opposition elsewhere. Belatedly, in 1766, when the Williamsburg presses were again operating, the veteran burgess and pamphleteer Richard Bland published through Alexander Purdie the only extant Stamp Act pamphlet from the colony, *An Inquiry Into the Rights of the Colonies*. Bland's essay, apart from a vote of thanks from the Norfolk Sons of Liberty, received no great notice, but once again, as he had done in *The Colonel Dismounted*, he clearly identified the logical end of opposition to Parliamentary control of taxation and the internal polity of the colonies; that is, the claim to complete autonomy in internal affairs.

It is difficult to know everything that transpired during the months in which the Stamp Act was in effect. The governor himself sent conflicting reports to his superiors. In his letter of December 11, 1765, he questioned whether "in the present Temper of the People" it would be advisable to call an Assembly and concluded that he would probably postpone it until the following November—which would mean sixteen months would pass without a session. In particular, Fauquier doubted that a fully attended session would reverse the Henry resolves. In March of 1766 he reported, on the other hand, that some merchants had applied to him for passes for trade to the Mediterranean on stamped paper and expressed the opinion that "the more enlightened and sensible Men of the Colony" would quietly accept enforcement of the Stamp Act. But the next month he had to provide a full account of the savage attack on Captain William Smith in Norfolk. On balance, Fauquier's judgment in his gloomier moods seemed to be the more correct, as when he wrote in a private letter on February 3: "You should be informed that the Articles you may have seen in some of the public papers, that Business goes on as usual in this Colony: is entirely without foundation, the Contrary being true, that the Courts of justice are shut up and all Business at a Stand."

Fauquier had particular reference, of course, to commerce and the legal business related to it, but Virginia appeared in many other respects as well to be virtually paralyzed by opposition to the Stamp Act for a period of a year or more. From his own point of view the governor was no doubt well advised to keep the Assembly from meeting, although that course almost certainly served to perpetuate the dilemma in which the old leadership of the colony found itself in May of 1765 and to further the political tendencies that had been unleashed in the last session. To earlier lack of a plan of action by the provincial leaders was now added a lack of opportunity to come together and do anything decisive. In local politics, moreover, interruption of the civil jurisdiction of the county courts and the extent to which—at least in an area such as the Northern Neck—alternative and more popular forms of political response had evolved were striking innovations.

By the early spring of 1766 colonists, including those in Virginia, knew that Parliament had repeal of the Stamp Act under consideration, primarily because of the pressure of those British merchants who had been badly hurt by the dislocation of trade. Then, at least by early May, the reports of repeal were firm. From late May through June both *Virginia Gazettes* recorded a seemingly endless round of public celebrations—toasts, balls, illuminations, bonfires, addresses, divine services, and the like. If one took it all at face value, bitter feeling over the Stamp Act seemed to have dissipated almost overnight. Councillor William Nelson's letter of July 25 to his friend and mercantile correspondent John Norton observed that "Repeal . . . hath put us into a good Humour: it hath taken away the hatefull Cause of Disgust and ill blood between the Mother Country and the Colonies." In printing "An Ode Occasioned by the Repeal of the Stamp-Act, and the Present Freedom of the Press," the *Gazette* of August 15 was moved to publish some of its typically atrocious poetry. Fauquier noted, too, that he had received a petition to call the Assembly into session sooner than it was scheduled so that the members might demonstrate their gratitude for repeal, but he told the petitioners he would first require every assurance that the Assembly would not adopt "another set of seditious resolutions" and thereby "cut its throat."

As it turned out, Fauquier's caution was well taken. The *Gazette* almost immediately began to carry letters critical of those who had asked for the earlier session, attacking them for not waiting until Parliament had completed other legislation affecting the colonies and asking why they had not been equally vigilant in seeking a session in time to have elected delegates to the Stamp Act Congress the preceding year. When the Assembly finally did meet in November, as Fauquier had planned, its response was still far from what he had hoped. The customary addresses of loyalty and gratitude were given, but their tone was not what the governor desired. The address of the burgesses to the governor, he complained, showed "great Weakness and want of Judgment, but much Heat in the Composers." Its "Spirit of justification of their former proceedings" also bothered him, and he confessed to the secretary of state that he had a difficult time framing his response. Finally he "picked and culled such parts" as seemed least objectionable and addressed his reply to them. Governor Fauquier had a distinctly unrepentant colony on his hands.

In the end the British seemed to retreat by repealing the Stamp Act—although not without first reasserting in the Declaratory Act of 1766 Parliament's complete legislative authority over the colonies. Repeal had glossed over, more than resolved, the fundamental issue of colonial autonomy that threatened to tear the empire asunder. The two years during which the Stamp Act was proposed, passed, and nullified left a legacy of mutual distrust, a precedent for colonial defiance, and a shaken faith in old patterns of accommodating conflicting interests that drew Virginia and the other colonies all but inescapably toward revolt.

13

THE FORMATION OF
THE REVOLUTIONARY COALITION

The inability of the established Virginia leaders to bring about modification or withdrawal of the proposed Stamp Act or to place themselves at the head of the opposition after its passage had two important consequences. First, it seriously weakened the traditional, informal system of imperial politics in which they had participated for more than a century. Second, it challenged the effectiveness of their political style, if not the substance of their power in provincial politics. They were as yet embattled, not displaced, but their ordeal had not ended. A series of domestic controversies that erupted in the aftermath of the Stamp Act crisis and then a renewal of the imperial conflict, when a new round of regulatory measures began to unfold after 1767, put them to a further test.

Lingering resentment against the British was hardly the sole reason for the tumultuous nature of the 1766 Assembly session, as Governor Fauquier accurately sensed when he predicted that "Party feuds" would run high during the meeting. The business of the Assembly combined with a group of related events to produce an explosive domestic political controversy all but unprecedented in the history of the colony. When William Nelson revised his optimistic forecast of the previous summer and now wrote John Norton of battles that were "too numerous and scurrilous to merit your attention," he was perhaps correct as to their number but wrong in his appraisal of their significance.

On May 11, 1766, not quite six months earlier, John Robinson,

Speaker of the burgesses and treasurer of the colony for more than twenty-five years and the undisputed leader of the old elite, had died. The loss would have been a blow to the members of the group in any event, but when it became quickly apparent that earlier rumors were correct and his treasury accounts were as much as £100,000 in arrears, they faced political embarrassment as well as personal loss. The circumstances of the shortage were complicated, but in effect Robinson had been receiving Virginia paper currency from the two wartime issues; and rather than retiring the notes from circulation as required by law, he had put them back into circulation in the form of loans to friends and political associates. Although Robinson had not benefited personally, the list of leading Virginians who had received at least small amounts was lengthy. Nor was there any way of replacing the missing funds on short notice.

It was no longer possible to bury the issue, as the late Speaker's allies had done when Richard Henry Lee sought to press it in previous sessions of the Assembly. Accounts of the shortage, though couched in delicate terms respectful of the late Speaker's great "generosity" with friends, appeared in newspapers. Moreover, the news complicated what otherwise would probably have been an easy accession of Attorney General Peyton Randolph to the two most powerful offices in the gift of the colonial leaders. The issue now became one not only of rival candidates for the two offices but of separating them for the future as well, to prevent so great a concentration of power in the hands of one person. The old leadership rallied behind Randolph and determined to support his candidacy for both offices. Robert Carter Nicholas, a Williamsburg lawyer, a man as conservative as Randolph but nonetheless a personal rival, a leader of the "responsible" persuasion, announced for treasurer, while Richard Bland and the ever-ambitious Richard Henry Lee both sought the speakership.

No election for Speaker had been held for more than a quarter of a century, and never before had one been marked by open campaigning through debate in the *Gazette* and letters of solicitation such as were sent to members of the November 1766 Assembly, where the matter would be decided. Nor had the election ever taken place against a background of scandal. Again the signs pointed to a marked alteration in the character of Virginia politics; and, rather like the Henry resolves, the outcome was at least a partial victory for the insurgents.

Amid the lingering recriminations of the summer campaign the House agreed to separate the two offices, electing Nicholas to the treasurer's post but at the same time confirming Randolph in the speakership. It could be seen as still another contest between the "moralist" and "political" wings of the Assembly in the terms Edmund Randolph had employed in describing the Stamp Act fight, or between the "representative" and "responsible" coalitions. The more public character of the contest, its presentation in some part as a moral issue, and the necessity for the old leadership to yield one of the offices were telling developments.

Richard Henry Lee's unsuccessful bid for the post of Speaker, meanwhile, spawned still another public controversy. It related more directly to the Stamp Act and perhaps complicated more than it clarified political alignments within the colony, but in the end it made its own contribution to the roiled political climate. Lee was an outspoken "moralist" and frequent critic of the late Speaker, as well as a strong advocate for Northern Neck interests who felt somewhat excluded from a position of major influence by the Robinson group. Lee also cast himself as an early and uncompromising opponent of the Stamp Act, although he had not attended the May 1765 Assembly. He had been associated particularly with the popular demonstrations in Westmoreland and Essex counties and had been especially savage in his ridicule of the Virginia stamp distributor George Mercer.

The Mercer family—George, his father John, and his brother James—already had ties to Lee's political opponents and were angered all the more by the sharpness of Lee's attack. Somewhere, perhaps from John Robinson before his death, George Mercer discovered that Lee had himself been an applicant for the stamp distributor's post, leaving him open to the charge that he was more a frustrated jobseeker than a principled opponent of the Stamp Act. The three Mercers determined to use the evidence not so much to vindicate the hapless Mercer as to block Lee's quest for the speakership by branding him a man of uncontrollable ambition. Lee probably had small chance of success anyway, but he had in the end to throw his support to Bland, who even so lost to Randolph. Lee survived as a major leader of the Revolutionary movement, however, while Mercer remained discredited and ultimately became mentally disturbed. Still, the attack hit home, and the long exchanges in both editions of the *Virginia Gazette* further emphasized the vituperative, personal nature of the fight over the election of a new Speaker and treasurer.

It became apparent, too, that the presence of two newspapers, each with an editor more independent than their immediate predecessor, began to play its part in a more open debate of issues like the Robinson scandal or the fight between Lee and Mercer, issues that in former days might have been joined in a much more covert fashion. Nor had the editors run out of other lively stories to stir their readers and sharpen the politics of the day, for at the same time that the other disputes were in full swing, readers were treated to a murder scandal, involving still another prominent member of the political establishment. The murder had occurred in June 1766 in a tavern at Cumberland Courthouse, to the west of Richmond. The culprit was Colonel John Chiswell, a former member of the burgesses. He had married into the Randolph family, was the father-in-law of the recently deceased John Robinson, and became a partner with Robinson, William Byrd, and others in a lead mine in southwestern Virginia. He was nonetheless insolvent. On the day of the murder, witnesses testified to his loudness and profane speech. Chiswell had fallen into a dispute with a Prince Edward County merchant, Robert Routledge, who had spent the whole day at the tavern and was obviously intoxicated. In his rage Chiswell first tried to hurl various objects—a bowl of bumbo punch, candlesticks, and fire tongs—at Routledge and finally had called on his servant for his sword. Sober but highly overwrought, Chiswell stabbed his victim through the heart and then boldly defended his act, calling for a bowl of toddy to celebrate. Examined in Cumberland Court and charged with murder, he was remanded to jail without bail. Since felonies committed by free persons could only be tried in the General Court, the sheriff of the county a week later transported Chiswell to Williamsburg to be delivered to the Public Gaol. When he arrived at Williamsburg, however, three judges of the General Court, including the president of the Council, John Blair, and William Byrd, Chiswell's business associate, upon the legal advice of George Wythe and two other lawyers released him on bail without an examination of the Cumberland evidence.

The *Gazette* was not long in printing letters that rehearsed the crime in its gory details and called into question the propriety of Chiswell's admission to bail. Although some of the argument concerned technical points of law, critics also argued that the accused's connection with Attorney General Randolph—who was not yet the new Speaker—would affect the case. Nor was Chiswell's relationship to John Robinson overlooked. Chiswell left Williamsburg for a time, but the dispute raged on until he returned in September to prepare for his November trial, obviously agitated and, as one account noted, suffering an "uneasiness of mind." Then the affair ended in mid-October when he was found dead, a victim either of suicide or, perhaps, of hypertension.

All these controversies pointed in one way or another to the inner circle of leaders of the colony—as collaborators in and beneficiaries of Speaker Robinson's improprieties, as instigators of the attack on Richard Henry Lee, as associates of John Chiswell who were willing to make exceptions in the law for his benefit. All the issues, moreover, given the free and public examination to which they were subjected in the columns of the rival *Virginia Gazettes* (neither editor was identified with one side in any of the disputes), raised the prospect of a vastly different, more openly combative style of politics, possibly a full-scale assault on the entrenched position of the old leaders.

The most significant outcome of these crises was a compromise that left Peyton Randolph in possession of the powerful office of Speaker and his brother John confirmed in Peyton's former position of attorney general. The new treasurer, Robert Carter Nicholas, whatever the differences in personality and style between him and the new Speaker, was scarcely a newcomer to the elite. Related to the Carters through his mother, married into the Cary family, an intimate business correspondent of the powerful consignment merchant John Norton, Nicholas had served in the burgesses since 1756 and had already been appointed interim treasurer after Robinson's death. In fact, other than the phenomenal rise of Patrick Henry, not without a few family connections of his own, the recent disputes more nearly divided the old leadership a little more sharply into its "responsible" and "representative" wings than it brought new leaders to prominence in the Assembly. The preferred style of the old leadership had always been one of accommodation and flexibility. It had not abandoned its claim to a sense of public responsibility, for Robinson's executors, with Edmund Pendleton taking the lead, succeeded in shoring up their late colleague's finances and eventually discharging his obligation to the treasury. Nor had there ever been any doubt of their opposition to those aspects of British policy that seriously challenged their own position. Denied a favorable resolution of the imperial difficulties, they had turned to compromise with the forces within, though without giving much ground in the process. They had passed through their dark night of despair, had perhaps learned a few lessons for the future, and had survived.

*   *   *

The resolution that the old leadership achieved might have been less certain had the British not, within a few months of the Stamp Act repeal, resumed their policies of taxation and regulation. Repeal, the work of a new ministry that replaced Grenville's, came in spite of, not because of, American opposition, a result of pressure from the powerful colonial mercantile lobby that did not want further disruption of its trade. None of the fiscal problems at home had abated, nor had the determination of most political leaders to bring the colonies under stricter control.

After still another reshuffling of the cabinet, one of its dominant figures, chancellor of the Exchequer Charles Townshend, came forward in 1767 with a new series of revenue-producing colonial import duties that followed the more successful model of the Sugar Act, with which, as amended in 1766, the colonists had quietly begun to comply. The so-called Townshend duties nevertheless again raised the critical taxation issue, for Townshend made no claim whatsoever that any regulation of trade was intended—he simply wanted revenue. While the Townshend taxes bore the major brunt of renewed American opposition, they were, in fact, accompanied by a series of other objectionable laws and administrative orders and also by the somewhat ominous removal of many of the British military forces in America from the frontier, where they were expensive to maintain, to urban centers such as New York and Boston (their presence in the latter produced in 1770 the military-civilian clash we know as the Boston Massacre). Relocation of the troops brought an attempt to enforce the terms of the Quartering Act through the requisition of supplies and barracks from the New York provincial government. Although the legislature resisted at first, the 1767 New York Restraining Act, which

Peyton Randolph (ca. 1721–1775), attorney general of Virginia from 1748 until 1766 when he succeeded John Robinson as Speaker of the House of Burgesses. He also served as President of the Continental Congress in 1774 and 1775. The portrait by John Wollaston is at the Virginia Historical Society and is reproduced with its permission.

threatened to suspend the Assembly if it did not comply, brought its members to heel. New moves also tightened administration of the customs regulations further by establishing new vice-admiralty courts and by appointing an American Board of Customs Commissioners to reside in America and give overall supervision to enforcement efforts. In addition, the ministry moved to forbid enlargement of representation in colonial assemblies for the future without approval, which in a larger colony like Virginia promised to make it impossible to continue the policy of creating new counties as populations grew and settlement spread.

No one of these controversies, not even the Townshend Acts, had the dramatic impact of the Stamp Act, but collectively they had an escalating effect, especially as the British followed with efforts to intimidate the colonial assemblies and to enforce the customs regulations rigorously, at times almost capriciously. The disputes did not fundamentally alter the terms of the debate, which remained generally the same from 1764 until the eve of independence, but the tone grew sharper. Colonial claims of complete legislative autonomy in internal affairs moved to the fore, and the single question of taxation receded. Too, in these years American distrust and suspicion of the British became deeper and more nearly irrevocable. Leaders of colonial opposition perfected a variety of techniques and means of opposition. The result was not a reprise of the Stamp Act controversy but a profound intensification of the conflict, one somewhat obscured by a second British retreat and by the collapse of much of the colonial opposition after 1770.

At times the response in Virginia seemed almost perfunctory, the colony taking its cues from elsewhere in America rather than forming part of the vanguard as it had in 1765. That reaction was more a consequence of unanimity, however, than apathy. For an interim after Governor Fauquier's death in early 1768 no British governor was resident in Williamsburg, and the compliant and aged president of the council, John Blair, served as acting governor. With his acquiescence the Assembly of 1768 unanimously adopted a new set of addresses to king and Parliament and a letter to other colonial assemblies that responded to a circular letter from the Massachusetts General Court. Then, before the end of the year, a new governor, Norborne Berkeley, baron de Botetourt, arrived, bearing a commission not as lieutenant governor but as governor in chief, the first such appointment since the beginning of the eighteenth century. Even in so difficult a time Botetourt was able to remain personally popular during his brief governorship. He was a man of charm and affability, very much mourned and buried with high style in the chapel at William and Mary upon his death in the fall of 1770. It was no doubt indicative of his tact and ability to get along that he was able to obscure from the provincial leaders the exact terms of his instructions, which demanded far more than those of his predecessors that he hold a tight rein on the provincial government and bring about a thorough subjection of the colony to the will of imperial government. It cannot be said, however, that he succeeded by either diplomacy or force in achieving that objective. Calling his first Assembly in the fall of 1769, he opened it as befitted a governor in chief with unusual pomp, meant no doubt to give the colonists a stirring show as well as to impress on them the power and position of the Crown and its chief representative. If so, the effect was lost, for the burgesses proceeded within a matter of days to adopt still another set of resolutions protesting the various British actions of recent months. Botetourt promptly dissolved the session, telling the burgesses after calling them into his presence that "I have heard your resolutions and I augur their ill effects."

Despite a personal regard for Botetourt, members of the burgesses had been ready for him. Resentful of his postponement of the Assembly session for some months after his arrival, they also discovered he was under instructions to deliver an opening speech written for him in England that denounced the addresses adopted the previous year and demanded acceptance of the Declaratory Act. In the meantime they also received the news of a Parliamentary proposal to bring American leaders to England for trial under the treason statute of Henry VIII. Botetourt suppressed his prepared remarks in favor of harmless generalities, but the burgesses proceeded with their new resolutions, three reasserting the colonial view on taxation, the right to petition the king, and the right to join with other colonies in protests, and the fourth branding treason trials in England as a violation of the right to jury trial and the right to summon witnesses. They also ordered a copy sent to all the other colonial assemblies and printed in the *Virginia Gazette.*

Botetourt's dissolution of the Assembly was in itself a new measure for Virginia, since Fauquier had sent the rump of the 1765 Assembly home only when it was more than ready to go. The response of the legislators was equally unprecedented but made almost instinctively. Most of the members reassembled across the street from the capitol at the Raleigh Tavern in an extralegal meeting and took the first steps toward associating Virginia with a nonimportation agreement that had spread from the New England colonies southward. The agreement, a voluntary one, pledged those who signed it not to import a long list of commodities from England, especially those that bore duties under the Townshend Act or those that were luxuries, not to import slaves from overseas, and to favor where possible products made by Virginia artisans.

Although parts of the agreement were modeled on the one adopted in Philadelphia, many of the underlying ideas and assumptions about nonimportation and nonconsumption had a history of their own in Virginia, one intimately related to the growing apprehension that mounting debt and the worsening tobacco economy of the Tidewater were part of a general moral and economic decline and loss of independence that threatened the colony. To an increasing number of Virginians, the answer lay in reducing private debt, restricting consumption of needless luxuries, and achieving economic independence by diversifying crops and breaking the stranglehold of tobacco and the British merchants who controlled its marketing. The appeal was in part to enlightened self-interest, in part to achieving the kind of personal independence that would assure political liberty and virtue.

Such ideas of economic reform gained their strongest following not so much among the main group of Tidewater planters as among those from the Northern Neck, men like Richard Henry Lee, George Mason, and George Washington. With the depression of the 1760s the program grew in appeal. Many of those who favored it also tended to press for stronger opposition to the Stamp Act, opposed such easy credit schemes as the loan office, and generally stood against John Robinson and Peyton Randolph. Some efforts to carry out nonimportation were made in 1765, but with the passage of the Townshend duties the movement took on greater force. The ideas behind it gained even more popularity when the *Virginia Gazette* republished John Dickinson's *Letters From a Farmer in Pennsylvania* in early 1768 in tandem with a supporting Virginia statement, the "Monitor" letters of

Richard Henry Lee's brother Arthur. When the extralegal session of Virginia legislators adopted the 1769 nonimportation agreement, Northern Neck spokesmen again took the lead, because Washington introduced the specific proposals, which were based on statements earlier prepared by Mason.

The Virginia nonimportation agreement was in difficulty from the moment the informal meeting at the Raleigh Tavern put it into effect. Few merchants joined the agreement, and those who did sign ignored it. Nor were many of the planters any more diligent in observing its terms—the combined total value of imports into the two Chesapeake colonies of Maryland and Virginia totaled almost £500,000 during 1769. By the time news of the partial repeal of the Townshend duties reached the colony in 1770, the agreement was in an advanced state of disintegration. Some lamented that it was so "soon forgotten, so basely deserted, and both the letter and spirit of it kicked out of doors," but the tendency was to make merchants the villains of the piece rather than to engage in recriminations against planter violators. Virginians agreed to make a second try in June 1770, possibly on advice from English opponents of the Lord North ministry or else to prevent the strongest supporters of the idea in Virginia from accusing the leadership of scuttling it. For a brief time efforts at enforcement were renewed—during the first summer several county committees ordered cargoes returned to England. But compliance was never really more than sporadic, for Chesapeake imports rose again in 1770 to more than £700,000 before the second agreement received an unceremonious burial in the summer of 1771.

The response of Virginians to the issues of the Townshend Act era were in some ways more muted than in many of the colonies, largely because of the absence in the colony of British troops and of aggressive British civil officials. The colony reacted strongly and with virtual unanimity when the occasion seemed to demand it, but it was afforded little opportunity to move beyond political protest until its very belated adoption of nonimportation. Still, developments in Virginia paralleled those in the other major colonies. Its statements of protests, like those elsewhere, emphasized more and more the fundamental question of legislative autonomy in all matters of "internal polity" rather than taxation alone, but then the imperial battles of the 1740s and 1750s had already highlighted that larger issue in Virginia, and

Richard Bland's somewhat neglected pamphlets of 1764 and 1766 had demonstrated the Virginians' early grasp of the question. The Virginia leaders moved some distance, too, with those of the other colonies, in perfecting new techniques of organizing opposition in the face of growing interference with the legislatures. They were quick in responding to the appeal of Massachusetts in the Circular Letter and in moving the whole body of colonial leaders toward greater cooperation across provincial lines, and they moved easily into the pattern of assembling members of the burgesses informally when confronted with dissolution by the governor. Creation of local county committees of inspection as part of the nonimportation agreement, although extremely incomplete, also extended the use of extralegal agencies for local action begun during resistance to the Stamp Act. The prompt collapse of the nonimportation, on the other hand, had the potential for widening the personal and factional disagreements of 1765 and 1766, but in the end was more influential in arousing additional hostility toward the British merchant community in the colony. Virginians had achieved a degree of unity, however fragile, that held in the second phase of the crisis.

*   *   *

When the British ministry, now firmly under the control of Lord North, determined to lessen its difficulties in enforcing the unproductive Townshend duties and to deal instead with an upsurge of radical protest at home and a threat of a new European war, it made no concession on constitutional principle. Lord North's solution, accomplished in April 1770, was to repeal all of the duties except that on tea, leaving it as an affirmation of Parliament's power to tax the colonies. Despite the collapse everywhere of nonimportation and even a growing compliance with payment of the duty on tea, the partial repeal of Townshend's measures no more ended hostility to imperial policy or distrust of the home government than had the repeal of the Stamp Act.

In Virginia, when Governor Botetourt presented the Townshend duty repeal act to the Assembly, he reported that the members unanimously "spurned at the pretended favor" and chose instead to send another petition to the king "as their protestation never to submit silently to the power of the Parliament to tax the colonies." Moreover, the new machinery for customs enforcement remained in place. In 1770 the inspector general for the American Board of Customs Commissioners arrived in Virginia to conduct a detailed investigation. While generally laudatory of the officials' management of their offices, he insisted that lack of personnel permitted too much illegal export of tobacco. Virginians also followed newspaper accounts of incidents involving customs officials elsewhere. The most widely reported incident took place in Rhode Island in 1773, when citizens attacked and burned the revenue cutter *Gaspee* after it ran aground in pursuit of a colonial merchant vessel. British efforts to identify and punish those responsible spurred the establishment of committees of correspondence by the various provincial assemblies to keep one another better informed of further difficulties. Through an exchange of letters between a Virginia legislator, "Squire" Richard Lee, and Massachusetts leaders, Virginia took the lead in the effort. True to the recent spirit of compromise, the committee was widely representative, though a smaller subcommittee charged with carrying on most of the business between sessions was, probably as a matter of convenience, dominated by members from the immediate Williamsburg area.

Other circumstances affecting their relationship with the empire contributed as well to the troubled mood of Virginians. The new governor, the earl of Dunmore, who arrived in 1771 to take up the office vacated by Botetourt's death, from the beginning showed none of his predecessor's ability to get along with the local population. It was a matter of public knowledge that he had been reluctant to leave New York for the Virginia post, and reports that he was a difficult man had preceded him. A more immediate and far more fundamental problem was the outbreak of a sharp credit crisis in the British economy in 1772, putting new pressures on planters to settle their debts and causing the collapse of a number of mercantile houses. The full-scale resumption of trade and the boom in both imports and tobacco exports was all too speculative. There was an essential unhealthiness in the market, with no hint of a really stable prosperity.* The collapse began

---

*The tobacco economy was also seriously affected by devastating floods in the so-called Great Fresh on the James and Rappahannock rivers in the late spring of 1771. Although the Assembly provided some £30,000 to compensate those who had tobacco in the public warehouses that suffered flood damage, many planters experienced such

in some of the Scottish banks, for reasons which were not related to the tobacco trade but which quickly affected it. In the end it damaged the London consignment firms more heavily, because they tended to have larger, longer-term debts outstanding from Virginia planters. With one exception the significant failures among tobacco firms occurred there rather than in Glasgow, but those merchants who survived were hard pressed and moved to tighten the credit they had extended in Virginia. Even a particularly strong, well-connected firm like that of John Norton saw its outstanding credit balances climb from £11,000 in 1769, to £18,000 in 1700, and to £40,000 by 1773.

The Virginia planters had been expanding the amount of their debts since the 1740s, often by extravagant purchases of luxury goods, although the rapid rise in the amount of credit extended by Scots to the smaller planters of the Piedmont was also a critical factor. The wave of speculative trade after 1770 exacerbated an already serious problem, and by the time of independence the total outstanding debt of Virginians had grown to £1,400,000, just a little under half of all the debts owed by North American colonist to British creditors. With the collapse of their own sources of credit, British merchants were by 1773 pressing their Virginia clients for payment, bringing suit against them in the courts of the colony if necessary, and denying most of them additional credit. Without further extensions of credit, sale of land or other assets by planters who were willing to sell or forced to do so by the courts was all but impossible. In the end, the public credit of the provincial government was also endangered, in part from the state of the private economy but also as the consequence of the counterfeiting of Virginia paper notes that were still in circulation. Although a new group of Virginia cargo merchants, who imported goods on consignment and exported tobacco, and some of the greater planters with larger debts and closer relations to the London firms suffered the most, the collapse affected planters at all economic levels. With high numbers of debt suits in the courts and with merchants or their representatives present in the colony, the economic depression offered a very visible ground for discontent.

Except for an occasional step such as creation of the intercolonial

---

heavy losses that Thomas Jefferson believed they had not recovered by the time of the Revolution.

committees of correspondence, which in the end were unable to do much, that strong undercurrent of resentment against imperial policy in the three years after 1770 offered little opportunity for concerted political action against Britain. One effect was to lessen pressure for a unified response from the leadership and instead to make it far easier for divisive or troubling conditions within the colony to surface, as they had in 1766, and to claim a larger share of public attention.

An apparent wave of unrest, for example, broke out among blacks in and around Williamsburg during the 1770s. To judge from advertisements in the *Virginia Gazette*, the number of runaway slaves increased markedly, and accounts of troubles with slaves in the counties of York, James City, and Hanover circulated as far away as Maryland and New York. Authorities in Williamsburg instituted a regular night watch of four persons in 1772, and there was also a patrol in Yorktown, empowered to pick up blacks found on the street at night and hold them until the next day.

The diffuse character of the imperial controversy also permitted a resurgence of a series of political and social issues fought both on the floor of the House and in a series of often vindictive exchanges in the columns of the *Virginia Gazette*, closely resembling those that had taken place in 1766. Once again they threatened to divide the gentry into hostile factions and on this occasion perhaps to penetrate more deeply into the social fabric and to expose those cultural divisions that had become somewhat more apparent in the population at large through the rise of religious dissent.

Amid open criticism of the county courts for their ineffectiveness, the poor performances of its justices, and the low social status of jurors, the Assembly began to consider a sweeping reform of the judicial system, one that would have restricted the General Court to civil cases, instituted new courts of assize for criminal cases, and reduced the authority of the county courts—all changes that would have strengthened the position of professional lawyers at the expense of gentlemen justices. By the end of 1773 the legislation had not passed, however, and the issue stood unresolved.

In the same years the Separate Baptist movement achieved some of its greatest successes. The number of congregations rose dramatically, and in May 1771 an enormous gathering in Orange County formed the Virginia Separate Baptist Association. It was also a time of peak harassment of the Baptists, ranging from newspaper attacks on the denomination as a threat to social order to physical assaults on their ministers as they stood before their congregations. For the first time Baptists showed a desire to win a recognized place within the social and religious order of the colony, most notably by petitioning the Assembly in 1772 to afford them protection from persecution. What they particularly asked was a more explicit and complete application in the colony of the seventeenth-century English Toleration Act. Its enforcement in Virginia rested on an extremely vague provision of a 1705 Virginia statute, and subsequent interpretations of its principles had narrowed rather than liberalized its provisions for allowing public worship by religious dissenters under regulated conditions. The burgesses were no more able to come to a decision on this question than on that of reforming the county courts. Consideration of the toleration issue produced open debate in the House as well as on the outside. Some burgesses now spoke against enforced conformity and for the necessary relationship between free government and free exercise of religion. Yet the bill that passed in 1772 was still restrictive in some of its provisions—dissenters could not, for instance, meet at night or include slaves in their worship services unless masters consented. The lower house voted, moreover, to print the bill for public consideration rather than send it directly to the upper house, so it never passed. The question of settling the religious order of the colony obviously left the leadership divided and unable to reach a clear decision on toleration.

A second religious controversy, arising out of the effort of a minority of the Anglican clergy of the colony to secure the appointment and consecration of a bishop to reside in Virginia, occasioned no such uncertainty among either leaders or people. The episcopacy controversy spilled over into perhaps the most extensive newspaper debate of all the issues of the early 1770s. The lengthy, sometimes harsh exchange owed more, however, to the ardor of a few outspoken clerics on both sides than to either wide public involvement or any likelihood of success in appointing a Virginia bishop. In the summer of 1771 the burgesses found no difficulty in unanimously resolving to extend formal thanks to four clerics who had opposed the episcopate in a clerical convocation, and a few months later the editors of one of the *Gazettes* responded with evident relief to readers' complaints "of their being tired of the Dispute" by declining to publish further writings on it. Although carried on in part within a political framework by reason of the accusation that sending bishops to the colonies would create still another group of British officials bent on curtailing American liberty, the episcopacy controversy ranged well beyond that issue alone, addressing the nature of authority in society in other, equally fundamental ways. Those who argued that bishops were an essential element in a traditional, well-ordered society, one based on rank and hierarchy, were primarily a handful of clerics and perhaps an equally small number of laymen whose statements appeared anonymously in the *Gazette*. Their principal points—first, the completion of the colonial constitution on a true English model required episcopal government in the church, and, second that bishops would provide a means for better discipline of the clergy themselves—ran strongly against the gentry's conception of the established church in Virginia. However much the old elite assumed the Anglican church to be a source of good order and authority, they were not prepared to see bishops as necessary for it to perform that role, any more than they were willing to accept the reasoning of those who argued that a free society demanded complete religious liberty. Richard Bland spoke for the predominant view when he declared: "I profess myself a sincere son of the established church, but I can embrace her Doctrines without approving of her Hierarchy, which I know to be a Relick of the Papal Incroachments upon the Common Law."

Clearly even those members of the gentry most strongly attached to the established Anglican church had long since abandoned any notion that its authority depended on an ecclesiastical hierarchy. They also exhibited almost as much hostility to the Anglican parish clergy in the colony as to the idea of an episcopate, and they had created an established church under de facto lay control. Such authority as the church possessed rested on the elite's own dominance of the parish vestries, and in a sense the leaders did not so much derive a portion of their authority from the church as impart their own social and political authority to it. They had thereby already implicitly rejected one element of the traditional English social order and had weakened the established church as a force in the life of Virginia.

The episcopacy controversy did not in reality prove to be a source of conflict between the political leadership and insurgent forces in the colony. If anything, it revealed such deep-seated hostility to any aspect of British authority that it signaled the movement of the whole colony a step closer to revolution. Issues such as reform of the court system or extension of full religious toleration were another matter, for they remained potentially divisive, though not yet clearly defined in provincial politics.

* * *

Before such domestic issues could be brought into sharper focus, however, the British government brought about a third and final renewal of the imperial crisis that preempted the political arena. That the Tea Act of 1773, the act responsible for reviving colonial opposition, could have provoked the degree of American resistance it did, or that the British would respond as harshly as they did, only demonstrated how irresolvable the conflict had become. The Tea Act was itself not primarily a colonial regulatory measure but rather an effort in good mercantilist fashion to help relieve the financial distress of the East India Company, the giant government-chartered commercial company that enjoyed a monopoly of Britain's trade to the East. The new legislation enabled it to dispose advantageously of a huge unsold inventory of imported tea. The company was now permitted to recover English duties paid on the tea already in English warehouses if it were reexported to the American colonies and there bore the smaller duty still imposed by the remaining Townshend measure. The act also provided that the company might bypass the customary sale of the tea at public auction to all interested merchants and sell it instead directly through its own agents, thereby underselling, in fact excluding from the trade, competing firms.* With these advantages, framers of the legislation anticipated that the company would be able to capture the enormous American market in tea and to end the competition of smuggled tea, on which the government received no duties. Nor did some supporters of the Tea Act fail to note that if the colonists

---

*The rebate of English duties had been offered in previous laws, but direct sale through designated agents was a new provision. The Tea Act was one of the two East India measures passed in 1773, the second being a Regulating Act that extended a large government loan in exchange for a greater degree of government control over the company.

succumbed to the lure of cheaper tea, as they no doubt would, they would be giving the lie to their principled stand against Parliamentary taxation.

Although the East India Company had little difficulty in finding American merchants willing to accept consignments of tea, Patriots in a number of colonies determined to prevent its importation and sale, usually by forcing merchant ships carrying tea in their cargoes to return to England without unloading. In Boston, however, local Patriot activists, thinly disguised as Indians, boarded one of the ships and threw the tea in the harbor in the now-immortalized Boston Tea Party. Initial reactions elsewhere in America were far from uniformly favorable to the Bostonians, since many deplored the destruction of private property as an unnecessarily extreme response. However, when the British countered with a series of restrictive measures against Massachusetts, colonists everywhere fell more strongly in line behind the beleaguered inhabitants of the Bay Colony. The most restrictive features of the Coercive Acts—or, as the colonists often termed them, the Intolerable Acts—fundamentally altered the form of government of Massachusetts under its charter by abolishing the only elected upper house of a colonial assembly and by weakening the independence of its court system. The more immediately damaging measure was, however, the Boston Port Act, which closed the city's busy harbor to all shipping on June 1, 1774, unless compensation was paid by that date to the East India Company. This measure became the great symbolic issue around which Patriots rallied throughout the colonies. Thus, as it turned out, the American response in the summer of 1774 moved the Revolutionary crisis into its last and decisive stage.

The arrival of the news in Williamsburg found the Virginia Assembly already in session and occupied with a crowded agenda, related in a key instance, in fact, to continuing resentment at British suits against Virginia debtors that still flooded the courts of the colony. The status of those courts had been somewhat clouded in any event by the failure of the 1772 reform legislation, but a more pressing problem was the expiration of the annual fee bill in mid-April, shortly before the Assembly met. The lack of a list of prescribed court fees, such as the law regularly included, raised a question in the minds of some as to whether the courts could proceed to sit in civil cases such as debt actions, in which such fees had to be assessed. Both the General Court and the county courts, however, met as usual during April, on the assumption that the upcoming legislature would renew the fee bill retroactively.

When, however, the Committee for Courts and Justice of the House, which Richard Henry Lee chaired, reported on May 10, it omitted a recommendation for renewal of the fee bill, an action often interpreted as an effort on the part of Lee and more outspoken Patriots to close down the civil jurisdiction of the courts and to block further recovery of debts by British creditors. But within a day the full House had overruled Lee's committee, had brought in a new fee bill, and had referred it to another committee, that on Propositions and Grievances. The majority of the House, including the old leadership, seemed determined to keep the courts open, and for almost the first time since 1765 a potentially divisive issue had been introduced into the Revolutionary controversy itself.

Before the Burgesses could complete action on the new bill, news of the crisis in Boston intervened. It had, in fact, reached Williamsburg early enough to be reported in the *Virginia Gazette* of May 12, although the burgesses did not get around to a response for almost two weeks. The leadership was apparently anxious to complete the "Country business" before taking a strong stand and risking dissolution. By late May, however, a small group of burgesses, spearheaded by Thomas Jefferson but including Richard Henry Lee, his brother Francis Lightfoot, and Patrick Henry, met secretly to plan a resolution for a day of fasting and prayer on June 1 to mark the day the Boston Port Act would take effect. There seemed to be a supposition that Dunmore would find such an action more difficult to oppose than a more direct protest, and when Robert Carter Nicholas introduced the resolution, it carried unanimously on May 24. The leaders obviously expected to continue with their remaining business, for the following day, when Richard Henry Lee sought to bring in a set of resolves he had prepared, he reported that he "was prevented from offering them by many Worthy Members who wished to have the public business first finished and who were induced to believe . . . that there was no danger of dissolution before that had happened." But on the second day after the adoption of Nicholas' resolution Dunmore moved to dissolve the Assembly, objecting to the violation of his prerogative for calling fast days and possibly also seeking to prevent any passage of Lee's resolutions. The sequence of events, confused though it was, was important because of the possibility that the old leadership might stall on responding to the Coercive Acts in order to make certain it got a renewal of the fee bill or, conversely, that the insurgents might press for an early stand on the Port Act both to support their fellow colonists and to divert attention from the fee bill or might induce a dissolution before it was passed. But the reconstruction of the events of late May from letters of Richard Henry Lee, an arch-opponent of the fee bill renewal, would seem to suggest that the desire to finish all the regular business of the session was genuine, that he willingly consented to hold back his resolutions, and that the "Worthy Members" had miscalculated on Dunmore's response to the fast day proposal. The outcome, however, left the fee bill issue hanging.

On the other hand, there never seemed to be any doubt, as Lee himself noted, that the reopening of the imperial conflict would once again unify all wings of the leadership in Virginia on some common strategy of resistance. The day after dissolution all but a handful of the former burgesses met, with Peyton Randolph presiding, to adopt an agreement not to use tea or other East India Company products and to join in a call for a meeting of delegates from all the colonies—the key proposals for action contained in Lee's draft resolutions. They held off from a more general trade embargo, but within a few days, after further news from Boston arrived, a smaller gathering of twenty-five or so delegates who still remained in Williamsburg issued a call for another meeting on August 1 to deal with that question.

On June 1 the day of fasting and prayer was observed in Williamsburg and elsewhere in the colony. Those burgesses who remained in Williamsburg went in a body to Bruton Parish Church, followed by townsmen and parishioners, for prayers and a sermon. Then the fast took place, although the unsympathetic John Randolph later commented sarcastically that it had actually only involved putting off the traditional large midday meal until later in the day.

Through the summer of 1774 a series of local county meetings took place, at which those in attendance elected delegates to the August convention, adopted resolutions and instructions to their delegates, and otherwise built up local, popular support against the British. The elections produced no real surprises, as the new convention delegates were generally the same men who had been serving in the House of

Burgesses. On the matter of holding the intercolonial congress and adopting some form of economic embargo, especially a general agreement not to import British goods, disagreement was slight. The issue of the fee bill that had been left unresolved in the May Assembly, however, resurfaced, for a number of mass meetings also demanded the closing of the courts for civil jurisdiction, adding to it a call for nonexportation of Virginia products to England. The intention was to deliver a double blow to British merchant-creditors. In other counties, where leaders like Edmund Pendleton were influential, the resolutions did not address those demands.

No single forum existed in which the issue of closing the courts could be debated, and in the absence of a scheduled session of the Assembly—Dunmore had postponed it to November—no agency was capable of making a decision. Over the summer the question became a matter of wide discussion, however, and not simply in the county mass meetings. At some point Edmund Pendleton prepared a legal opinion arguing that the courts were not under any legal necessity to close for lack of a valid schedule of fees. Thomas Jefferson followed with an analysis of Pendleton's brief which reached the opposite conclusion, arguing that the courts should close for all forms of jurisdiction. Others, Richard Henry Lee in particular, took a middle position, that the courts need only close to civil litigation, meaning especially debt cases. But the fee bill issue was as much political as legal, and the Revolutionary convention assembled as scheduled on August 1 with the question unresolved. In particular, it complicated the adoption of a nonexportation agreement, because to adopt such an agreement without also closing the courts would prevent planters from shipping the tobacco with which they might settle debts, while leaving them vulnerable to debt suits. Yet the convention did not link them: It voted to begin complete nonimportation after November 1, 1774, and, if the imperial dispute were not settled, to adopt nonexportation to England on August 10, 1775. The delegates still refused to recommend blocking debt collections in the courts. Privately, however, the leaders seemed to be reaching some agreement—or bowing to the inevitable. Over the course of the fall, county courts began refusing debt suits, and when the General Court convened for the October session, it recessed its civil proceedings. So by late 1775 the courts were, for all practical purposes, closed to debt suits.

The development was a critical one for Virginia, for it applied one of the most effective weapons of resistance Virginians had in their arsenal. Removal of a principal guarantee possessed by merchants for the security of their trade and their loans probably assured the effectiveness of the economic embargo in a way that signed pledges could never do. The action also marked the first suspension of any duly constituted agency of government, for another nine months would pass before Governor Dunmore would no longer be able to exercise the authority of his office or before the burgesses would be unable to meet. Finally, the act of accommodation by those who had first opposed the partial closing of the courts reaffirmed the unity of the leadership on all measures for opposing imperial policy.

Before adjournment the convention elected delegates to the first Continental Congress, as the proposed intercolonial meeting was coming to be called. The slate included Speaker Randolph, Edmund Pendleton, and Benjamin Harrison from the older Tidewater leadership; two men of considerable seniority and reputation who nevertheless tended to stand somewhat apart from that group, Richard Bland and George Washington; and two more aggressive spokesmen on imperial issues, Richard Henry Lee and Patrick Henry. The attempt at "balance" in the delegation was patent.

Thomas Jefferson, who had been unable to attend the August convention, sent a draft of a statement that he hoped to have adopted as a set of instructions to the Virginia delegation. Although he failed in the objective because of the extreme, uncompromising nature of his remarks, a gathering at the house of Speaker Randolph heard a reading of the essay, which was subsequently published without Jefferson's knowledge as *A Summary View of the Rights of British America*. In it Jefferson brought to the fore the claim for full legislative autonomy of the colonies, introduced sweeping demands for full freedom of trade, and denounced the "connected chain of parliamentary usurpation" in American affairs. Foreshadowing Jefferson's draft of the Declaration of Independence and like it grounded more in moral terms than on an entirely accurate reading of the historical evidence to which it appealed, the *Summary View* was a "radical statement" with which Virginia opinion had to catch up over the succeeding two years, although its presentation in the parlor of Virginia's leader of the old establishment was nonetheless telling.

The restored Raleigh Tavern in Williamsburg was the scene of several extralegal meetings convened by Virginia leaders to carry the Revolutionary movement forward when the governor had dissolved the Assembly or it was not in session. Colonial Williamsburg photograph.

The Virginia delegation, even without the instructions Jefferson would liked to have given them, was active in the first meeting of the Continental Congress. Peyton Randolph served as its presiding officer, and Lee took a prominent part in the forming of a continent-wide agreement, the Continental Association, that combined the economic weapon of nonimportation and nonexportation with prohibitions on gambling, restrictions on the consumption of luxury goods, and other efforts to impose a stern morality on the colonists during the crisis. The Association also called for the organization of local committees in towns and counties to enforce adherence to the agreement. Although Henry argued with his usual force, and not without a little exaggeration, that government in America was already dissolved and that the colonies were free to make new political arrangements, the Congress took no such stand. It still proclaimed its desire for a settlement, but the adoption of a single instrument of economic resistance for all of the colonies was a bold step, one which brought into being a broad revolutionary movement intended to possess genuine coercive powers over the American population.

*   *   *

By the fall of 1774 Virginians had traveled a long road over the decade just passed, perhaps none more so than the group of established leaders of the colony who had held power when it began and who remained for the most part in positions of prominence. Had the demands of pursuing opposition to the most recent round of British measures permitted, or had they been more introspective men than they were, they might have been startled to compare the beginning and ending of the decade. In 1764 they had sat down to frame a series of addresses to the king, the House of Lords, and the House of Commons couched in all the old forms of humble supplication and intended to accommodate their opposition to the proposed Stamp Act within traditional modes of imperial politics. When that effort failed, they had initially betrayed a sense of uncertainty and hesitation. Now in recent months they had formulated trade embargoes (and thereby advanced efforts at the economic independence they had once spurned), had advocated and joined in the formation of an extralegal intercontinental congress, and had deliberately shut down their own courts of law in an area of critical jurisdiction. Perhaps they would have confessed their amazement, but they might also have responded that they contended for much the same broad objective in 1774 as they had in 1764, or for that matter in the early 1750s: to block imperial efforts to restrict their own control of what they would have termed their "internal polity," for that and nothing more.

Yet, more objectively, the decade had wrought an enormous change in imperial relations despite the durability of the ties of sentiment and common culture that remained. For by the summer of 1774 the leadership had raised its level of resistance and the means of effecting it to new levels. An alternative political apparatus, extending from the county level to the Continental Congress, was in place. By its persistence and by the escalation of specific issues and forms of resistance, the imperial crisis that was only dimly perceived at the beginning of the Revolutionary era had become an overwhelming fact in the lives of many Virginia colonists by 1774.

What of that other crisis that had appeared at the beginning of the Revolution, deriving from the first signs of deep changes within the social order of the colony? The old leaders might have looked back a little painfully, with a touch of lingering bitterness, at their ordeal in 1765 and 1766, not to mention more recent controversies in the early 1770s. Unlike the crisis in the imperial world, they would not have been able to see that it had deepened. Among the leadership itself there would still be personal animosities, differences of style and temperament, even among some who had served together since 1764 and earlier, but more so in the case of some of those who had since been added to the ranks. Yet, in both renewals of the imperial crisis, in 1768 and 1774, the adjustments and accommodations necessary to sustain a concerted opposition to the British had been made, most recently in choosing the Virginia delegates to the First Continental Congress and in settling the terms of the nonimportation and nonexportation agreement at the August 1774 convention.

Those among the ranks of more ordinary freemen had been drawn, too, into the imperial crisis, more effectively perhaps by a Patrick Henry than by a more remote, more established leader, but still enlisted in a common endeavor and given perhaps a greater sense of participation in it by the increasing number of county meetings they attended and by the number of instructions and resolutions they were called on to adopt. The evangelical religious revival that set many in this group apart culturally and socially, imparting to them different values and ways of behavior, had not lessened. Indeed, evangelicalism was in a period of maximum growth as the final stages of the Revolution began to unfold, but it did not turn most of the new evangelicals aside from the Revolutionary movement. Nor did the leadership entirely refuse to face the issue of greatest meaning to the evangelicals, greater religious toleration under the laws of the colony. Admittedly it did so reluctantly, uncertainly, but not altogether unwillingly. After 1774 the issue was for the moment swept aside.

One seemed to hear less, too, of that sense of personal crisis among the gentry. Some of its causes had certainly not disappeared. Their economic plight was, if anything, growing worse. Before the end of 1775 Dunmore would by his offer to free slaves who joined him demonstrate that their apprehensions about slavery had some justification. Yet the moral crisis they had lamented had become one of the whole people, of "My Country," as Virginians were fond of referring to their colony, and now found its solution for many in resistance to Britain, more particularly in adherence to the terms of the Association. By pledging themselves to avoid indulgence in luxuries and extravagance and to give up dissipation and idle amusements, such as plays, horseracing, and cockfighting, those who signed the Association could oppose British policy and at the same time reform their lives.

The imperial crisis did not resolve all the other crises, but to a surprising degree it overwhelmed them, even at times subsumed them. What was striking, in looking back over the decade, was the interplay between the two crises, one imperial, one internal, in which every diminution of the imperial crisis released forces for change within while every revival quieted them. Now, at the third reappearance of the imperial dispute, British actions galvanized a degree of unity and energy among the leadership and between the leadership and more ordinary ranks of the population that had not seemed possible a few years earlier.

14

THE REVOLUTIONARY SETTLEMENT

Virginia moved decisively during the summer of 1774 to offer renewed political and economic resistance to the British, yet the apparatus necessary for achieving these ends, extending from local county committees to the Continental Congress at Philadelphia, had only begun to be formed. The work of organizing the county committees to enforce the Continental Association went forward in the closing months of 1774, concentrating in the beginning in the older Tidewater counties and thereby suggesting that the mobilization of opposition to the British still owed as much to a cadre of leaders used to holding tight rein on their localities as it did to a spontaneous outburst of popular enthusiasm. In any event, as least thirty-three counties and three towns, including Williamsburg, established their committees before the end of the year.

In early 1774 some of the more western counties were experiencing another wave of Indian attacks on the borders of settlements, which took attention away from the more remote imperial crisis. Governor Dunmore, in one of the few acts that won him any popularity in the colony, led a successful campaign in the late summer into the western country to subdue the Indians and advance the colony's western land claims. On October 10 General Andrew Lewis, commanding militia forces from southwestern Virginia, won a key victory at Point Pleasant, at the junction of the Kanawha and Ohio rivers, and soon thereafter Dunmore concluded a treaty with the Indians. He returned just before the end of the year, amid expressions of gratitude and approval from the colonists.

However, Dunmore's War was more a temporary diversion than an event that could deflect the course of the Revolutionary movement. During 1775 some of the most familiar and decisive episodes of the Revolution took place. Above all, the clash between British regulars and Massachusetts minutemen at Lexington and Concord in April and the subsequent organization of a Continental Army under the command of George Washington marked the advance of the struggle to one of armed conflict. A parallel series of events, Dunmore's seizure of powder from the Public Magazine in Williamsburg, his flight from the capital and occupation of Norfolk, and a military clash at Great Bridge in December—the "second" battle of the Revolution—took place in Virginia. Yet all the colonies, Virginia included, seemed to hang in a delicate balance between warfare and hope of reconciliation, and only a few Americans would even broach in private the subject of independence. Nevertheless, the logic of circumstance and the continued unwillingness of either side to make substantial concessions began to carry the colonies inescapably toward more organized armed resistance, toward deliberate undermining of British political authority, and, ultimately, toward independence.

*   *   *

However decisive in stirring popular feeling and intensifying opposition those familiar events such as Lexington and Concord, or even more local ones like the Powder Magazine incident at Williamsburg, proved, the crucial year of 1775 was in reality more significant for less dramatic reasons. Over the course of that year the step-by-step development of economic resistance, of extralegal institutions of political control, and of revolutionary military organization converted the American effort from one of sporadic protests against specific acts to a sustained movement by a people capable of fighting a long, difficult war, forming effective governments, administering extensive territories, and in some part reordering American society. That process went forward in Virginia during the year, as it did in one way or another in each of the thirteen colonies.

The surviving records of some of the local committees provide accounts of actions taken not only against suspected violators of the trade embargo but also against those who had pro-British pamphlets in their possession, who spoke or wrote in favor of the British or even criticized members of the Committee of Safety, and who were living extravagantly or engaging in "idle" pleasures like gambling. The Reverend John Wingate, an Anglican clergyman in Orange County, was one of those cited for possession of hostile writings. Another Anglican clergyman received similar treatment for preaching against the Continental Association. David Wardrobe, a young Scottish schoolteacher, had written home an apparently accurate but unflattering account of the burning in effigy of Lord North, the British prime minister, in which he reported on the extent to which the gentry who were managing the event tried in vain to whip up enthusiasm among the onlookers. Until he recanted, Wardrobe faced the loss of Cople Parish Church as his schoolhouse. Williamsburg Patriots erected a scaffold from which they hung a cask of tar and a barrel of feathers and then compelled a number of merchants to appear in front of the display to sign the nonimportation Association.* The Yorktown committee forced a vessel sent out by the prestigious London merchant firm of John Norton to return to England without unloading because its cargo included a small shipment of tea.

Sometimes the actions and statements of offenders were a matter of public record, but on other occasions the committees read private mail or inspected merchants' accounts. It would be too much to find in these activities some uncontrolled reign of terror or to suggest that they always intimidated an otherwise reluctant populace. With county justices prominent among the membership, the committees did not so much supplant the county courts as perform those acts for which the courts themselves had no legal warrant. Nevertheless, the committees could be formidable. At times their members acted with the frenzied fervor of dedicated revolutionaries, but perhaps their main role was that of extending an alternate system of regularly functioning government to the local level, to preserve as much as to undermine order.

Beginning with the August 1774 Convention, the Virginia leaders also moved by stages toward the creation of an extralegal system of government at the provincial level. If anything the problem was more

---

*The Williamsburg incident was the subject of Philip Dawe's anti-American mezzotint *The Alternative of Williamsburg*, issued in London in 1775 and reproduced on p. 340.

THE ALTERNATIVE OF WILLIAMS-BURG.

The Alternative of Williamsburg, a 1775 English mezzotint by Philip Dawe, satirizes the use of the threat of tarring and feathering by Virginia Patriots to force merchants to sign the Association and agree not to import British goods. Colonial Williamsburg photograph.

acute there than in the counties, inasmuch as the burgesses were contending with a hostile governor who could dissolve or refuse to schedule sessions of the Assembly and who also commanded the official militia organization, thereby making it impossible for anyone else legally to call out the military forces of the colony. The Convention of August 1774 had held only a brief session, largely for the specific purpose of organizing an economic embargo and electing a first slate of delegates to the Continental Congress. During 1775, however, additional conventions met in March, June, and December in longer sessions devoted to much more diverse kinds of public business. In the process members converted the Convention into a de facto legislative body for the colony, soon organizing military resistance and passing "ordinances" that were for all practical purposes binding legislation.

With the colony acting in open defiance of Governor Dunmore it became necessary to have some form of executive authority. In July the convention therefore proceeded with the election of a provincial Committee of Safety to administer the affairs of the colony between sessions of the Convention. The committee was an eleven-man body, whose membership reflected something of the same balance between more advanced and more cautious leaders as did the congressional delegation, although the conservative Edmund Pendleton was its president. From the time of its creation in mid-August 1775 until the new state government was organized and installed in power a year later, Pendleton and the committee sat regularly and acted with vigor in directing the Revolutionary effort.

One of the major activities of both the Convention and the Committee of Safety was to raise, equip, and provide for the training of military forces for the defense of the colony. That effort began almost spontaneously at a more local level in the fall of 1774, when a number of counties formed independent military companies, often initially for the purpose of working with the county committees in enforcing the Association. Fairfax County moved first, and others followed until, by mid-1775, there were at least 24 county and 3 town companies, many of the members colorfully outfitted in traditional fringed hunting shirts, often emblazoned across the chest with the motto "Liberty or Death," with bucktails and cockades in their hats, and tomahawks or knives affixed to their belts. Washington became something of a patron of the Fairfax Company, while Edmund

Pendleton presented his Caroline Company with a "very genteel present" of colors, a drum, and two fifes.

The March 1775 Convention turned, not without controversy, to the idea of raising provincial regiments. Many of the old leaders, even though the independent companies were already in many cases in existence, resisted the idea of provincial forces as long as some hope of reconciliation remained. Patrick Henry once again spoke for the opposing proposition, that the "colony be immediately put into a posture of defence." It was in the course of the ensuing debate that he delivered his third celebrated speech containing its concluding line, "Give me liberty, or give me death!" Again Henry carried the day, as he had ten years earlier, and again there was perhaps more difference in style than there was disagreement over objectives in the contest. When the question was settled, the committee to carry out the resolution and organize a military force included both some who had supported Henry's initial resolution and some who had opposed it.

Before the committee could begin to organize provincial regiments the first armed clash occurred at Lexington and Concord, and at almost the same time a similar incident was narrowly averted in Virginia. On the night of April 20, 1775, Governor Dunmore, using men from the British naval vessel *Magdalen*, ordered the removal under cover of night of the supply of guns and powder stored in the Public Magazine in Williamsburg so that it would not fall into the hands of the rebel forces now being raised. The discovery of the small force prevented their removal of more than a portion of the supplies, mainly twenty kegs of powder, but it touched off a period of alarm and tension in the little capital town. As the news spread, two groups of independent companies, a large gathering of forces from a number of counties that were assembled at Fredericksburg, and a single, smaller detachment of the Hanover Company under the command of Patrick Henry, prepared to make separate marches on Williamsburg. Local Patriot leaders in the capital, anxious to forestall real violence and no doubt equally anxious not to contribute further to Henry's reputation as a forceful leader, managed to calm the town populace and head off the march of either group. Henry's men had, however, come within a few miles of Williamsburg before they could be turned back. The situation seemed sufficiently alarming that Dunmore, who contributed to the unrest by his own excitability, soon gave up on a session of the Assembly he had called, fled the governor's residence, and at Yorktown took refuge aboard the *Fowey*, a British man-of-war.

The formation of a provincial military force was more urgent now than ever before, for Dunmore had made it clear that he intended to subdue the colony and reestablish his control. Ultimately the Convention decided to establish two regiments and, after a close vote, to give Patrick Henry command of the 1st Virginia Regiment and overall command of the whole force, while William Woodford, an associate of Edmund Pendleton and commander of the Caroline independent company, received command of the 2nd Virginia Regiment. By early fall of 1775 Henry had taken up his assignment in Williamsburg. Despite shortages in supplies of all kinds, especially gunpowder, volunteers came in over the succeeding weeks, as did a number of units from the existing independent companies.

Reinforced by a small contingent of regular British troops and additional naval vessels, Dunmore had in the meantime moved his base to the strongly Loyalist Norfolk area. With the advantage of naval superiority, his basic strategy became that of raiding plantations along the extensive shoreline of the colony, seizing supplies and carrying off slaves. In early November he made good on an earlier threat and issued a proclamation offering freedom to all slaves who would desert their masters and join his forces. The offer stung the colonists far more deeply than almost any of the governor's other unpopular acts. Even the outwardly satirical, jocular comments that filled the *Virginia Gazette* betrayed a sense of rage and apprehension, and every report of blacks arrested on their way to join the governor received notice. The proclamation clearly had an effect, and the governor soon formed his Ethiopian Regiment, a company of some three hundred black soldiers commanded by white officers.

The threatening situation at Norfolk forced the Committee of Safety even before the end of October to move troops to the area to attempt to hold Dunmore in check. Continuing their ongoing battle over Henry's military command, committee members voted to send William Woodford and the 2nd Regiment, augmented by several of the independent companies, and to make Woodford independent of Henry's command. By early December, Woodford's troops were reinforced by three companies from Henry's regiment, and a North Carolina regiment was expected momentarily.

As the net tightened, Dunmore determined to move before the rebels outnumbered him by more than the two-to-one ratio they already enjoyed. The governor counted on a nucleus of some two hundred British regulars, drawn from the 14th Regiment and sailors and marines from the ships, to give him some advantage, even if the untested Loyalists and the black regiment that made up the rest of his force performed less well. On December 8, the British moved out from Norfolk, marching about twelve miles south to Great Bridge, where they already had a small fortification overlooking the bridge across a branch of the Elizabeth River and the long causeway beyond that led south across swampland. Woodford had occupied all the solid, high ground to the south of the causeway, so a battle could only take place if the British made a risky attack across the narrow causeway in full face of the Americans. Woodford lacked the artillery or naval support that the British could command and was able to do no more than delay while awaiting a British move. The British regular officers with Dunmore did not like the prospect of attacking under such conditions, but the governor evolved a strategy of using the black troops for a diversion against the American rear so that the regulars could make a frontal attack on the presumably distracted forces. For some reason the black troops were sent instead to guard an exposed point, but the regulars were nonetheless ordered out to confront the Americans. Even with the American works only lightly manned at the beginning of the fight and despite the bravery of the British, Woodford's men turned the British back in half an hour and then came out of their breastworks to bring in and treat the British wounded, drawing a salute from the senior regular British officer.

After nightfall on December 9 the defeated British moved back to a now exposed and vulnerable Norfolk, which Dunmore soon had to abandon. The American occupation that followed occasioned widespread plundering by the American forces and all but complete destruction of the town by burning. The men who had fought with discipline and honor at Great Bridge could not be kept under control in the aftermath of their victory or in the taunting presence of the British and Loyalists safely aboard their ships in sight of the Norfolk waterfront.

Dunmore still possessed the necessary naval force to continue his raids on plantations along Virginia's extensive waterways. For a number of months he kept up the effort, always hoping for and indeed demanding from British authorities the forces he needed to mount a full-scale campaign to retake the empire's largest colony. As time went by, crowded conditions aboard the ships produced terrible suffering and disease, especially among the blacks, while the naval officers, completely estranged from the difficult and unrealistic Dunmore, argued for abandoning Virginia and sailing to a safe port such as New York. By the time the weakened and demoralized force had come ashore to set up a final camp at Gwynn's Island, the governor had ceased to be more than a nuisance, albeit a destructive one. His political authority had long since crumbled in the wake of the Powder Magazine incident, and his defeat at Great Bridge destroyed his ability to pose a serious military threat. Facing an American invasion of Gwynn's Island, Dunmore and his men finally departed in July 1776 for New York, ironically almost at the same time the Continental Congress was adopting and signing the Declaration of Independence.

William Woodford's victory did not end the need to continue to build up the military defenses of the colony as well as to support the Continental forces. There was always the chance that Dunmore would get his reinforcements—a sizable expedition had, for instance, stopped in Hampton Roads in early February 1776 but, to the governor's dismay, had almost immediately sailed for North Carolina. The objective of a stronger Virginia military force was, however, not easily attainable. Discipline among sometimes enthusiastic but raw and rebellious troops was a problem, as the fiery aftermath of the occupation of Norfolk had shown. Adequate supplies of arms, clothing, and food continued to be difficult to find, especially after the Committee of Safety decided in January 1776 to raise an additional seven regiments.

Too, the committee's efforts to circumvent Patrick Henry's nominal command of the forces still rankled adherents of the popular orator. On the eve of the battle at Great Bridge, Henry had moved to assert his authority over Woodford by demanding to receive information directly from him. Woodford declined to provide it except through the Committee of Safety. For all practical purposes the committee rebuffed Henry, for while it directed Woodford to keep Henry informed of the condition of his forces, it also ruled that he would be subject to Henry's orders only if neither the Convention nor the Committee of Safety were in session—a circumstance everyone understood to be highly unlikely. The Henry supporters retaliated as best they could, by dropping Edmund Pendleton from first to fourth among those elected to the new Committee of Safety. Pendleton retained the chairmanship, however. The issue came to a showdown in the creation of the new regiments the following month, for the committee directed that three general officers for the Virginia regiments, one major general and two brigadiers, should be named by the Continental Congress, with the committee commissioning all the lesser officers. The action reduced Henry to colonel of the original 1st Regiment without any overall command, and Henry resigned rather than accept the new commission. His own regiment was profuse in its expression of loyalty to him, giving him a farewell dinner at the Raleigh Tavern and threatening to demand their own discharges until Henry calmed them.

Whatever personal bitterness the controversy left, it did not measurably affect the continuing military preparation, but controversy of another sort broke out in March, when the imperious, disputatious English-born officer, General Charles Lee, arrived in Williamsburg as commander of all the Continental forces in the South. Relations were strained at first between the Committee of Safety and Lee, who was predictably critical of everything he found and apt to do what he pleased. Over the course of the next few months he began to get along better, took a hand in improving the defenses of the colony, and then, when he moved to South Carolina, took some of the Virginia troops with him.

The colony's military effort thus progressed some distance toward the establishment of a more disciplined, trained military force, one that successfully engaged the British on Virginia soil and was joined to the larger Continental effort by deployment beyond the borders of the colony. In a political sense, too, the Revolutionary movement achieved an equivalent level of active, sustained resistance by erecting the machinery for carrying out most of the regular functions of local and provincial government in defiance of Crown authority.

*   *   *

The ultimate success of resistance depended on the extent to which it might attract and hold a broad base of support in the population at large and avoid encouraging the formation of sizable groups who opposed the Revolution. In an era of more limited communication, less literacy, and greater isolation of an essentially rural population, it is never easy to measure the impact of great public events on the larger body of people. Perhaps nowhere in the colonies was it more difficult to gauge popular response to the Revolutionary movement than in Virginia, with its vast distances, unusually small urban population, and lack of representative institutions of local government. Yet, just as evangelicals had begun to stimulate a heightened popular consciousness in religious and cultural matters, so did the imperial crisis, especially in this final phase, begin to stir a stronger popular political consciousness. A means of some importance for expressing such sentiments already existed in the traditional county court, militia muster, and election days, although the role of the people at large on those occasions was sometimes more nearly passive. Now the formation of independent military companies and the initial provincial regiments rested on volunteers, and young men came forward in those first heady days in a mood of high excitement. People, perhaps in many cases in larger numbers than simply those landholders who were eligible to vote for burgesses, gathered in county conventions and mass meetings. Even if they often elected to the provincial conventions the same leaders who had served in the regular Assembly, they also simultaneously adopted resolutions and instruction that involved them more directly with the issues of the day and charged their leaders much more explicitly with carrying out the popular will. The selection of county committees had a similar effect. Even though frequently composed primarily of members of the old county elite, including those who had served as justices, the committees were popularly elected. Although voters at county conventions might on occasion turn old leaders out of office, the main effect of the mobilization of popular opinion in support of the Revolutionary cause was not so much a direct threat to the leadership as the infusion of a new, somewhat more popular spirit in politics.[*]

[*]Rhys Isaac (in *The Transformation of Virginia*) has dealt suggestively with the way in which "patterned forms of communal action"—for example, the observance of the Day of Fasting and Prayer on June 1, 1774, or the adoption of resolutions at county conventions—served to mobilize the people by forms of public dramatization. He has suggested, too, that such ceremonial events could serve either to stir those in the elite culture (as when the Williamsburg Troop of Horse rode out with "order, good

Even with a wide base of popular support for the Revolution, two sources of disunity remained. First, given the determined response of Governor Dunmore, a sizable Loyalist movement in the colony could well have raised the specter of the Revolution's becoming a full-fledged civil war. The bulk of Loyalist sentiment in Virginia lay in a concentrated area, among the merchants of Norfolk, Portsmouth, and the Eastern Shore, many of whom were English or Scots without permanent ties to the colony. The fighting around Norfolk and the somewhat vindictive destruction of the town by the Virginia forces suggested what might conceivably have happened more widely in different circumstances. Many of the Tidewater Loyalists, however, fled with Dunmore or on their own, although the area, occupied by later British expeditions on several occasions during the war, remained a trouble spot. Loyalists who were more closely identified with Virginia remained relatively few, although they included a number of individuals or families of great prominence, including members of the Wormeley, Grymes, and Byrd families, Attorney General John Randolph, and the deputy receiver general of Crown revenues, Richard Corbin. The native Loyalists tended to be persons of extremely conservative temperament or those who had held offices by royal appointment. Although a number served on the Governor's Council, they did not form an organized force attempting to restore Crown authority as much as a collection of individuals who dropped out of active politics and sometimes paid a heavy price for their refusal to embrace the Patriot cause. Later in the Revolutionary War, strong pockets of Loyalism on the southwestern frontier brought bitter local conflict in that region at a time when the Revolution faced some of its darkest days, but state leaders continued to have a powerful group of local allies in the west with whom they could work. While violence in the region was serious, the problem was not as disruptive to the state as a whole as were the repeated British invasions of the Tidewater.

The second potential source of civil conflict within Virginia was, of course, the slave population, for Dunmore's proclamation revealed the

---

discipline, and regularity" to meet Speaker Randolph on his return from the Continental Congress in May 1775) or to appeal more directly to popular elements (as in the rallying to the independent military companies of volunteers clad in their hunting shirts).

extent to which blacks glimpsed the prospect of the freedom denied them by the Virginia leadership. Nor did the example of the hardship, disease, and death that so many Virginia black fugitives suffered during Dunmore's last days in Virginia deter thousands of other slaves from fleeing to the British side whenever British forces were operating in Virginia, even in the face of the threat of imprisonment, other harsh punishment, or execution at the hands of the Patriots. Yet the British made it increasingly obvious that their main purpose in seizing blacks or encouraging them to run away was to plunder American property and secure a ready source of labor, not to play the role of liberators. By removing many of their slaves from areas threatened by the British and sometimes by enlisting skilled blacks in the Revolutionary service, often as seamen, Virginians were increasingly able to deal with the serious problem of runaway blacks and to forestall any threat of revolt. In the end, two potent sources of serious internal division—Loyalism and slave resistance—were largely nullified. Nowhere in America was the degree of unity with which the leadership of the colony and the larger part of its population approached independence any more complete.

* * *

No less striking was the reluctance of the Virginia leadership to face the ultimate step of separation from the empire even while it systematically demolished British political authority within the colony. Whether revealed in the efforts of Edmund Pendleton to prevent the closing of the courts, in the fulminations of an aging and politically inactive Landon Carter against Thomas Paine's ringing call for independence in *Common Sense,* or in the reluctance of Patrick Henry to take the step without assurance of foreign support, the mood seemed to run against the final, irrevocable act. Once again the leaders of the colony seemed as hesitant as they had been more than ten years earlier to make a bold, decisive move. Once again, however, their deepest beliefs and the logic of the steps they had already taken left them little choice unless the British offered some compromise. Not only did officials in the home government decline to make significant concessions in the peace negotiations that had already occurred, but they began to take active measures to suppress what they believed to be an illegal revolt. As early as August 1775 a proclamation declaring the colonies in a state of rebellion opened the way for punishment of American leaders under British treason statutes, and later in the year the American Prohibitory Act stopped all commerce by the colonies and declared colonial ships subject to seizure until Americans submitted. Too, so far as the Patriot leaders were concerned, the speech of George III at the opening of the fall 1775 session of Parliament demonstrated beyond all doubt the king's own sympathy with the acts of his ministers and destroyed a last symbolic and psychological tie with the imperial world—a hope that the king might intervene personally on behalf of faithful colonial subjects to reverse the policies of a corrupt Parliament and to restore the order and harmony of a free empire. Every British response undermined the possibility that Americans might ever again be effective in a world of imperial politics.

During the early months of 1776 the idea of separation therefore gained ground more rapidly. At least one Virginia delegate to the Continental Congress, Richard Henry Lee, had been in regular contact with more outspoken proponents of independence from other colonies, but Congress still lacked a majority willing to declare for it openly. The sentiment in Virginia for complete separation from the empire seemed to grow almost spontaneously, more than from the deliberate efforts of any of its leaders. As the time of the next Virginia Convention, scheduled for May 6, drew closer, county meetings one by one began to elect delegates and at the same time to instruct them to work for independence. Although some of the old leaders faced strong opposition, only the extremely conservative Carter Braxton seems to have failed to win a seat. Richard Henry Lee, George Mason, and possibly Edmund Pendleton himself, had close calls, but Pendleton survived to become the president of the Convention, defeating a rival, Thomas Ludwell Lee, whom the Henry partisans supported.

After a few days devoted to discussion of pressing military business, debate on independence began on May 14. With Patrick Henry now having given his firm support, only the Treasurer Robert Carter Nicholas remained a known opponent, though he, too, would yield in the end. Delegates had before them alternate proposals for pursuing the objective of independence, however. One passed by the immediate question of independence to recommend the preparation of a declaration of rights and a new plan of government, while the other asserted the necessity for independence but made no provision for forming a new government. To these Henry added an additional idea: that the Virginia delegation in Congress "be enjoined in the strongest and most positive manner to exert their ability in procuring an immediate, clear and full Declaration of Independency." In the end Pendleton combined all into a single, wordy, and scarcely stirring resolution that provided both for instructing the Virginia delegates in Philadelphia to propose that Congress declare the colonies independent and for appointing a committee of the convention to draft a constitution and declaration of rights for Virginia. The resolution passed unanimously on May 15. Richard Henry Lee soon introduced the motion for independence in Congress, and it carried on July 2. Thomas Jefferson, of course, took a leading part in composing the formal Declaration of Independence. However reluctant its leaders had been only months earlier, the role of Virginia in the adoption of independence became preeminent.

Nor did the delegates at Williamsburg wait for Congress to pass Lee's resolution or adopt Jefferson's declaration. The day after the May 15 resolution passed they watched a parade of Virginia soldiers, read their resolution aloud, drank the inevitable patriotic toasts (held on this occasion to a restrained total of three), raised the "Union Flag of the American states" over the capitol, and treated the soldiers. Pendleton immediately appointed a committee to prepare the constitution and declaration of rights and then on May 17 reinforced it by adding a late arrival, George Mason, who proved to be the principal participant in the work. The full convention received the draft of the Declaration of Rights on May 27 and adopted it on June 12. The plan of government took longer, but it was reported out on June 24 and approved on June 29. A day later the Convention picked the first occupant of the weak governor's office provided for by the new constitution, choosing Patrick Henry by fifteen votes over Thomas Nelson, who had been serving as president of the old Governor's Council. Some have wondered whether Henry's opponents, by placing him in an office which he himself had denounced as a "mere phantom," did not thereby gain the sweetest revenge of all. Finally, at a last session on July 5 the Convention struck from the services in the Book of Common Prayer, the prescribed order of worship in the Anglican church, all references to the king, the royal family, and royal authority, a small though significant alteration which presaged the religious transformation that the Revolution would bring to Virginia.

Independence had been declared and a new government put in place with a speed that belied the usual hesitancy of the Virginia leaders. The colonial era had ended.

The events that occurred in Williamsburg in the spring and summer of 1776 were significant for the future of the new state, but it was no less true that, in the interplay of events between Williamsburg and Philadelphia, Virginia leadership was decisive in the ultimate success of the Revolutionary movement throughout the colonies. Peyton Randolph, the Virginia Speaker and legislative leader, was the clear choice of the First Continental Congress to serve as its president. In the next year, 1775, delegates to the Second Continental Congress elected Washington as commander of the Continental Army, a position he retained throughout the War for Independence. In 1776 Richard Henry Lee as sponsor of the resolution for independence of July 2 and Thomas Jefferson as author of the Declaration of Independence continued the tradition. George Mason's Virginia Declaration of Rights pointed the way to the subsequent United States Bill of Rights, which was initially proposed by James Madison as a series of amendments to the federal Constitution, of which he had been a principal author. The record was one of Virginia's shining accomplishments.

*   *   *

Although the members of the Virginia Convention no doubt departed Williamsburg in the summer of 1776 feeling both relief at having escaped the always oppressive summer heat of the capital and a sense of satisfaction at having carried through the first and fundamental step in the political revolution they sought, they could not have failed to recognize that they, like all Americans, had only begun the War for Independence on which the ultimate success of their efforts depended. As that struggle dragged on through the remainder of the decade and into the 1780s, the problems of raising, supplying, and keeping an army in the field while sustaining the morale of a war-weary population became ever more overwhelming. British occupation of parts of the state after 1779 and the threat of persistent pockets of Loyalism made those problems more immediate.

From Dunmore's flight in mid-1776 until the middle of 1779, when Admiral Sir George Collier and General Edward Matthews invaded the

George Mason (1725–1792) was the author of the Virginia Declaration of Rights and an active participant in drafting the Virginia Constitution of 1776 and the Federal Constitution of 1787, although in the end he opposed ratification of the latter. The portrait at the Virginia Historical Society is a copy made in 1857 by Louis M. D. Guillaume of an earlier copy by Dominic Boudet of an original 1750 portrait by John Hesselius that was destroyed in a fire. Reproduced by permission of the Society.

Chesapeake, Virginia remained free from British attack apart from sporadic naval and privateering raids along the coast. Then, from the fall of 1780, British incursions into the state became all but continuous until the American victory at Yorktown. General Alexander Leslie first led an invasion up the James River. No sooner had he departed than Benedict Arnold, who had by this time deserted to the British, arrived with another body of troops, to be reinforced in early 1781 by General William Phillips. While the Americans sought to oppose these attacks with forces led at one time or another by General Henry Lee, Baron von Steuben, the marquis de Lafayette, and Anthony Wayne, they were seldom successful in containing enemy raids, and Virginians living in the areas affected suffered heavy losses of tobacco, slaves, horses, and cattle. When Lord Cornwallis moved a much larger force into the state in May 1781 and when the Franco-American armies under Washington and the comte de Rochambeau and the French fleet under Admiral de Grasse determined to oppose him at Yorktown, the state became for the first time the scene of a major battle and a critical victory, concluded on October 19, 1781. The serious effects of the earlier invasions on both the economy and morale of the state should not, however, be underestimated—on one occasion Thomas Jefferson, while serving as governor, narrowly escaped capture by fleeing Monticello.

The weakness of the state government, above all of the governor's office, and economic dislocation from collapse of the tobacco market, inflation, and British depredations, compounded military problems. Yet somehow the new state, along with the nation, survived and in the final Treaty of Paris of 1783 made good on its claim to independence. Whatever the difficulties at home, Virginia's contribution to that success was notable, symbolized by nothing so much as the military command of the Continental Army that George Washington held throughout the war and by his climactic victory at Yorktown, only a dozen miles from the old colonial capital where the Convention had set in motion the final steps toward American independence.

By 1781 the state capital was at Richmond, a small, struggling village as Williamsburg had once been, located fifty miles farther west at the falls of the James River. The legislature had voted to make the move in the preceding year, an act that had its own symbolic meaning. It indicated, first of all, how much, with growth of population and spread of settlement, the political center of gravity had shifted in the state. Moreover, the decision to relocate the capital suggested how much the Revolution—in a political and social rather than military sense—continued to unfold throughout the war years and into the decade or two that followed peace. The exact dimensions of that ongoing revolutionary process are, however, not easily fixed, and efforts to measure the consequences of the Revolution will no doubt always produce different conclusions.

*   *   *

The example of Virginia has sometimes seemed to suggest that the changes were hardly so sweeping as altogether to justify the very term "revolution." True, the decision for independence and the replacement of monarchical government with republican forms were notable in a world dominated by empires and kings. The two steps resolved at once the most visible, sharply defined aspect of the crisis Virginians faced. Yet both occurred so rapidly and with so little disagreement among those committed to the Patriot cause that they appeared almost instinctive reactions, an all but inevitable consequence of colonial growth in material wealth and political autonomy under a social order in which class lines among whites were never completely rigid and in which the traditional highest ranks of royalty and nobility were lacking altogether. Republicanism also constituted a more logical expression of the ideal of virtuous, responsible government to which Americans had for so long been ideologically committed.

The adoption of the Virginia Declaration of Rights displayed similar characteristics. By spelling out in a series of sixteen articles both the fundamental principles on which free government ought to rest and the rights that such governments owed to the individual citizen, the convention took another step that was revolutionary in its day. The delegates took those fundamental precepts out of the realm of theory and enshrined them, albeit in the most general of terms, in written constitutional law. The Virginia Declaration of Rights thereby set a precedent and became a direct influence on the Bill of Rights added to the federal Constitution of 1791 as well as on those added to many later state and foreign constitutions. Yet, with the possible exception of the uncompromisingly worded sixteenth article on freedom of religion, it was clear in the debate on the Declaration of Rights that its framers intended to set down principles to which they had long adhered, however incompletely, rather than to extend or impart new meaning to them.

Too, given the capacity of the old leadership of the colony to overcome its own doubts and to place itself at the head of the movement, the Revolution in Virginia—with allowance for the removal of those few who held office by Crown appointment and for the normal turnover that would inevitably occur over a quarter of a century—produced far less displacement of political leadership than has generally characterized revolutions. Nor did the structure of the new government, as outlined in the constitution of 1776, drastically alter the forms and institutions that had prevailed in the late colonial era, apart, of course, from the elimination of every vestige of royal authority. The governorship became a markedly weaker office, as Patrick Henry noted to his discomfort—henceforth the chief executive was elected annually by the legislature, restricted to three consecutive years of service, and denied the veto. A stricter application of the doctrine of separation of powers substituted for the old Governor's Council three distinct bodies, the Senate as the upper house of the Assembly, a new high court of appeals, and a separate privy council to advise the governor. The new lower house of the legislature, the House of Delegates, bore, however, a strong resemblance in composition and mode of election to the old House of Burgesses, for the Convention retained a property qualification for voting and officeholding. The structure of county government, based on appointed justices, remained intact.

Yet, however limited their intentions and their actions in the summer of 1776, Virginians, in common with other Americans, had for at least three reasons taken a step with greater implications than they could have foreseen. First, the very act of repudiation of imperial authority by a people who had possessed such deep psychological and cultural attachments to England promised to have important longer-range effects. In particular, the Virginia gentry's perception of themselves and of their place in society, their long-standing involvement in Anglo-American as much as provincial and local politics, and their economic position—indeed much about their status in the old order—had been dependent on that connection. More ordinary colonists may have had a less direct sense of the relationship, but all lived to some extent in an imperial world that was now cast aside. Too, the republican principles that the colonists espoused had about them, as perhaps all revolutionary ideologies do, a certain transforming quality. That is to say, one used them to justify specific and immediate objectives, in this instance separation and establishment of independent civil government, but those who resort to such fundamental principles often find overlooked vestiges of the old order, discover the logical necessity of making further reforms, or otherwise make unanticipated changes in carrying out the revolution. In such a manner they may be carried beyond their original purposes. Finally, wide hostility to British policies drew disparate groups into the Revolutionary movement. For more than a decade the imperial controversy swept aside a variety of tensions and pressures that had been gaining ground within the society of late colonial Virginia. Yet the two periods of domestic controversy that erupted during lulls in the imperial contest had already suggested how difficult it might be to suppress those questions much longer.

Perhaps the clearest example of the way in which the logic of revolutionary ideas can take revolutionaries beyond their original intentions lay in the vast effort to revise the entire law code of the state. Independence necessitated at least enough alteration in statutory law to eliminate references to Crown authority and other remnants of the old imperial system, but in the hands of its chief proponent, Thomas Jefferson, the revision became a welcome opportunity to reform the code more thoroughly and to bring it more fully into accord with the new republican order. It was not to be the work of a day, or even a session or two of the legislature. Jefferson and some of his associates began the task in 1779, and it occupied the lawmakers, as they found time to take up various individual measures, throughout much of the decade of the 1780s. Although Jefferson, who was no longer in the legislature but abroad in France for much of the time, saw it as a comprehensive reform—perhaps *the* reform that the Revolution would accomplish in Virginia—others regarded the process as a piecemeal enactment of legislation as needed. Some laws passed in the form Jefferson wanted, others with major amendments, and still others not at all. Since at one time or another virtually every reform measure undertaken required legislation—the status of blacks, religion, education, the court system, criminal justice—Jefferson was right in thinking of law revision along with the constitution itself, as central to the Revolutionary achievement in Virginia. Yet it is important, too, to understand the piecemeal way in which legislators approached the undertaking in order to appreciate the mixed results.

Of the aspects of the revision that passed most easily, Jefferson took particular pride in the abolition of two feudal remnants in the law of land tenure: primogeniture, which in the absence of other provisions in a will gave all the land owned by a deceased father to the eldest son; and entail, which in order to keep a family estate intact over many generations prevented heirs from disposing of the landed property they inherited. Jefferson saw both as outmoded props of the old landed gentry; but in truth Virginians had rarely employed the device of primogeniture in a society where land was so freely available, and colonial assemblies had almost routinely permitted the breaking of entails. It was the kind of reform that brought legal theory in line with social reality, rather than one that brought revolutionary doctrine to bear on an actual grievance. There was, on the other hand, somewhat more substance in the revision of the criminal code of the state, which was perceived as introducing a greater degree of humaneness to the sometimes harsh punishment of crime.

The question of an overburdened court system and the alleged inadequacy of the county justices surfaced in the 1780s, especially after the justices were all but overwhelmed with a backlog of cases at the end of the war in 1783. In Jefferson's absence from the state, James Madison began the fight for additional courts, carrying one bill by the tie-breaking vote of the Speaker of the House of Delegates only to have it challenged and defeated in the next session of the legislature. Finally, at the end of 1787 he succeeded in winning approval for the establishment of a new layer of district courts, but the county courts also remained very much alive, championed particularly by newer justices in some of the inland, noncommercial counties.

Legislators received Jefferson's elaborate plans for limited public support for education in Virginia with scant enthusiasm, and the legislation he devised to accomplish that end was never effective. Similarly, the two largest disadvantaged groups in colonial society— women of all social ranks and blacks—derived few legal benefits from the Revolutionary settlement. The debate at the Convention over the first article of the Declaration of Rights, which declared all men "by

This portrait of Thomas Jefferson was painted by Charles Willson Peale in 1791 at a time when Jefferson was in his late 40s and serving as Secretary of State. Of all the Jefferson likenesses this one is most succesful in capturing the mood and the spirit of the Jefferson who carried out the Revolutionary settlement in his native state. Courtesy of Independence National Historical Park.

nature equally free and independent," specifically raised the question of the applicability of the principle to slaves, but the point was quickly swept aside in the response that it applied only to those who were constituent members of society, as slaves were not. Although Jefferson himself was unable to envision the absorption of large numbers of emancipated blacks into Virginia society, he found appealing the idea of liberating those born in the state in the future, provided that they could be recolonized in Africa. Few were as willing to give up black labor. On the other hand, the legislature readily agreed to prohibit the importation of additional slaves from Africa or other states, less for humanitarian reasons than from an apprehension that the increase would endanger control of an already perilously large black population. A few blacks who had served the Revolutionary cause with particular distinction were able to gain freedom by special acts of the legislature, one example being James Lafayette, a black who had served as a spy for the marquis de Lafayette and who assumed the general's name upon winning freedom. A much larger number, more than 10,000, were emancipated by individual planters who had been influenced by the antislavery beliefs of the early evangelical movement. In 1782 the statutory law of the state regularized such voluntary manumissions, but the law was rescinded in 1805. Thereafter owners could free slaves only if they also transported them outside the state.

Both the number of blacks who had voluntarily fled to the British and the circumstances surrounding an unsuccessful slave uprising, led by a black craftsman, Gabriel Prosser, which almost erupted in Richmond in 1800, offered some evidence, however, that black Virginians had been deeply touched by the political message of the Revolution. Depositions taken in the trials after Gabriel's Rebellion abounded with statements like that of John Mayo's slave George, who spoke of "a society to fight the white people for freedom." After 1775 runaway slaves also began to flee more often to the North, with the intention of reaching states where slavery was being gradually abolished. The pronouncement of universal human freedom made by the Revolutionary generation would continue to work its influence; yet, as the nineteenth century opened, the institution of black slavery was fixed more rigidly than ever in the social order of Virginia.

The impact of the Revolution on the position of Virginia women remains less completely explored than its effect on blacks, but general studies of the experience of women throughout the American states suggest that they gained few additional legal and political rights. Certainly, like so many other groups in the population, women seemed to have been stirred by the Revolutionary controversy to a new awareness of public issues. At the lower ranks of white society one consequence was the frequency with which both married and single women followed their men who went into military service. "Camp follower" in its modern usage has become an excessively unfavorable term for these women of the army, for many suffered the same hardships of disease, hunger, and inadequate clothing as the men did, while performing much of the necessary domestic and menial work of the encampment, such as cooking, nursing the sick, and washing clothes. In the middle and upper ranks of society the most characteristic response of women was to form distinct organizations and associations—sometimes called Daughters of Liberty—first to promote enforcement of nonimportation and nonconsumption of British goods and then to collect funds or supplies for the American troops. As early as July 1769 the *Virginia Gazette* noted with the "greatest pleasure" that the "Association of Ladies meets with the greatest encouragement in every county that we have yet heard from." Five years later the paper included an appeal to Virginia women from their "sisters and country-women" of South Carolina for abstention from luxury goods, especially tea. Martha Washington served as a coordinator of the association organized in May 1780 to support the Continental troops; while much of its work centered in Pennsylvania, some Virginians were active members. Upon reflection one must conclude, however, that those women who labored in the military camps had, in effect, transferred their performance of traditional domestic work—at wages often lower than those paid for the hire of slaves—to a new and more difficult setting, while the organizations of more genteel women in some respects fulfilled the traditional feminine role of moral exhortation more than they signaled a larger involvement in political issues.

As the imperial crisis moved to independence and a new political settlement, the question of the extent to which women gained new legal rights or found themselves occupying new social and cultural roles became more significant. Thus in 1777 Hannah Lee Corbin wrote her brother Richard Henry Lee to ask his support for suffrage for widows. Lee consented, although he expressed the belief that they already possessed the right. Lee was perhaps correct that the Virginia suffrage provisions, like those of most states, defined property requirements without specifying that only male property owners could vote, but except for a brief time in postrevolutionary New Jersey, voting by women remained a rare exception. An even more substantial question was that of defining the right of women to act independently in legal actions concerning their ownership of property. For the minority of single women or widows who owned businesses or other real property—the *feme sole* of legal terminology—there was no issue. In the more frequent case of married women—the *feme covert* in law—the prevailing principle was that husband and wife were one and that the husband controlled all the property of the two, even that which the wife had brought to the marriage from her own family. Exceptions, based especially on the acceptance of equity principles in Virginia, were made from time to time, by agreements between husband and wife that the courts accepted. The revisions of statutory common law that accompanied the Revolution in Virginia, on the other hand, made no change in principle. If anything, the increasing influence there as elsewhere of Sir William Blackstone's *Commentaries on the Law of England*, which placed an extremely restricted interpretation on the rights of women in English law, also weakened the legal position of American women after the Revolution.

There was a sense, as Linda Kerber has pointed out, in which the Revolution encouraged a new ideal of the "Republican Mother" who was to "play a political role through the raising of a patriotic child." But as Kerber also concluded, "The Republican Mother was to encourage in her sons civic interest and participation. She was to educate her children and guide them in the paths of morality and virtue. But she was not to tell her male relatives for whom to vote. She was a citizen but not really a constituent."

Historians are beginning to find evidence, too, that sometime after the Revolution some women gradually began to achieve a greater degree of autonomy in their personal lives. Fewer widows, for example, may have remarried and may thereby have retained control of their property. Mary Marshall Bolling, whom Suzanne Lebsock has described in a study of free women in Petersburg between the Revolution and the Civil War, provides an unusual example. Widowed about 1777, when she was perhaps 40 years of age, she did

THE REVOLUTIONARY SETTLEMENT

not remarry but continued to manage a very large estate, actively made new investments, and was responsible for numerous public benefactions before her death in 1814. Lebsock notes, however, that such independence was exceptional before the 1830s, and the number of widows who did not remarry remained small until then, although the number increased thereafter. The Revolution may have produced few immediate changes in the status of women, but a case can be made that it began to arouse a stronger consciousness of identity among many women, a consciousness which gained momentum in the nineteenth century.

The outcome of the Revolution hardly seemed to affect either the structure of social classes or the patterns of landownership in Virginia. Individuals lost or gained from the fortunes of war, but no distinct class was either displaced or brought to new prominence. A predominantly rural, agrarian society continued to prevail, even with the revival or rise of a few commercial centers such as Alexandria, Norfolk, and Richmond, aided more by a continued increase in the trade in grain and other foodstuffs than by any full-scale recovery of tobacco. The war indeed dealt the economy of Tidewater Virginia an all but mortal blow, and the continuing commerce in tobacco centered much more on the newer Piedmont and Southside regions. Those same areas became more influential in the politics of the state as well, although at the same time their leaders—so uncertain in their authority before the Revolution— came more and more to resemble the old Tidewater elite. The coincidence was never complete, but in their increasing affluence, their adoption of larger-scale slave holding, and their achievement of a more secure and accepted status, if not necessarily in learning and other ornaments of high culture, they changed markedly. In some areas, notably in the more northern reaches of the Valley and to some extent along the upper James, older Tidewater families also often maintained their position.

In one respect, however—the place of religion in the lives of the citizens and its relationship to the state—the society and culture of Virginia changed dramatically. The striking increase in the number of evangelicals—Separate Baptists, New Light Presbyterians, and Methodists—in the last years before the Revolution had already challenged the established Anglican Church. The extent to which evangelicals, apart from many Methodists, also supported the Patriot cause, indeed imparted much of the same evangelical fervor to it as to religion, made it scarcely conceivable that they would not press for greater freedom of worship and greater equality among the various churches. Independence, moreover, required redefinition of the status of an established church closely tied to England. Virginia Anglicans had in reality long since taken de facto control of the church in Virginia away from British political or ecclesiastical authorities. Yet a majority of them still supported it, often less out of deep faith than out of the conviction that it was a part of a moral civic order, dispensing charity and helping to sustain a well-regulated, virtuous society.

With the adoption of independence the old leadership revealed its dilemma: suggesting in its modest revisions in the language of the Book of Common Prayer that it hoped to continue the established church and yet, carried along by the logic of the new republican order and the arguments of the young James Madison, proclaiming "the free exercise of religion" in Article 16 of the Declaration of Rights. Baptists, among others, lost no time in seizing the opening, petitioning the House of Delegates at its first meeting in the fall of 1776 that "the burden of ecclesiastical establishment, . . . as well as every other yoke, may be broken and that the oppressed may go free." The legislators, however, maintained the ambivalence of the Convention by enacting a permanent exemption of dissenters from taxes to the established church while reasserting the principle of establishment and the right of the legislature to regulate meetings for public worship.

A complete resolution of the issue required another decade, but the law of 1776, in ending compulsory taxation, all but rendered disestablishment inevitable. Jefferson, who returned from Congress to sit in the new legislature, spoke for the small but influential group of Enlightenment rationalists among the leadership who, no less than the radical evangelicals, desired total disestablishment. So the two groups—one small in number but intellectually compelling, desirous of freeing the republic from all religious interference; the other, numerous and also powerful in their indispensability to the revolutionary cause but determined to protect "true religion" from the interference of the state—joined forces. Already they had implanted in the preamble of the first 1776 law on religious taxation on uncompromising statement denying that public morality and public support of religion were inseparably linked. The legislative majority of 1776 did not crumble immediately, however, for it enjoyed support that extended beyond the old Anglican elite. Its argument that a virtuous republic did depend, in fact, on public encouragement of religion, more broadly conceived than any single denomination, indeed underlay the religious settlement that prevailed in the Revolution in virtually every state but Virginia, if we may judge from the continuation of the Congregational establishment in parts of New England and the religious tests for officeholding and constitutional definitions of the state as Christian and Protestant that prevailed elsewhere. In Virginia more conservative dissenters, especially among the Presbyterians, joined forces with the remaining adherents of Anglicanism on the broad principle of taxation for the support of all recognized denominations. For once Patrick Henry and Edmund Pendleton found themselves on the same side.

The debate between the two groups crested at two distinct times. In 1779, as part of the general revision of the laws, a first version of Jefferson's bill to establish complete, unqualified religious freedom was introduced in the House of Delegates. When it failed, opponents introduced a countermeasure that would have taxed all for the support of the denomination of their choice and affirmed that "the Christian Religion shall in all times coming be deemed the established Religion of this Commonwealth"; it, too, died. All that the legislators could agree on was a further whittling away of the old Anglican establishment while leaving it in possession of its properties and retaining the vestry's responsibility for public charity. With the war ended, the contest was renewed in 1784, but over the next two years support for the general religious taxation eroded in the face of an unprecedented flood of hostile petitions. In 1786 the Statute for Religious Freedom, guided now in the legislature by James Madison but still embodying Jefferson's language, passed with overwhelming support. For the practice of religion the meaning of Jefferson's statute was unmistakable—henceforth there would be no public support for or regulation of any religious body in Virginia. Disestablishment stood, with the formation of republican government itself, as one of the most marked changes that the Revolution had brought within Virginia.

The Revolution, in effect, brought Virginia a degree of religious freedom that exceeded that of any other state in the nation. Much as in the case of political independence and republican government, this achievement marked a sudden, sweeping change and yet at the same time appeared to be the logical culmination of a slow, long-term evolution of the social and cultural order. The leaders of that order once again responded with a degree of accommodation not unlike that which had so often characterized their political behavior. The acceptance of such a reconstruction of the religious life of the Virginia populance, as Herbert Sloan and Peter Onuf have observed, perhaps contained an element of expediency, constituting "a timely step to eliminate from politics the one issue—religious sectarianism—that could have brought about a successful electoral challenge to the leading families in the counties of Virginia." For that matter, it is by no means certain that the old elite saw religious establishment as fundamental to its position. Pressed, its members might instinctively defend it as part of the proper and traditional order of things. Yet in many of their actions they also demonstrated how much of its force had already been undermined. They had adjusted much earlier to the dominance of county leadership by Old Light Presbyterians in some counties in the Valley. They appeared more uncertain than unyielding in the abortive toleration debate of 1772. From 1776 they had ceased to fight for an Anglican monopoly, as exemplified by their acceptance of general assessment to support all religious bodies. Indeed, their own commitment to Anglicanism had already remarkably weakened in the face of their deepening hostility toward their own clergy, their emphatic rejection of episcopacy, the inroads of Enlightenment principles among the younger men in their ranks, and the indifference of many to its forms of public worship and theology. The legal position of the established church was not unlike that of primogeniture and entail—something that no longer seemed vital. Both the logical thrust of revolutionary ideology and dissenter pressures carried disestablishment along at a faster pace, but its achievement was scarcely a struggle to the death. Anglicanism survived only in the weakened Protestant Episcopal church, which suffered a final and particularly devastating blow in the confiscation of its remaining properties and endowments in 1802, but it did not take the old leadership down with it. In breaking the imperial bonds that had shaped much of the structure of life in colonial Virginia, the Revolution appeared likely to make profound changes, religious freedom along with republican government being among the most far-reaching in their implications for the new order. Yet in the end the Revolutionary settlement was no less striking for the continuities with the old order that it preserved.

15

EPILOGUE:
THE IRONY OF VICTORY

Thomas Jefferson, more profoundly revolutionary than many of his Virginia contemporaries, found the absence of sweeping reform that seemed to characterize the Revolution in Virginia troubling. While serving the new Confederation government as minister to France in the mid-1780s, he prepared answers to a series of queries from a French official, François Marbois, about his native state, about its natural features and geography, but no less about its society and government. In 1785 he completed a first version of what he entitled *Notes on the State of Virginia* and circulated it privately. Then in 1786 an edition in French appeared, followed the next year by a more authoritative English edition. Despite his pride in the Revolution, appreciation of the natural features of the state, and excitement about the beacon of republicanism he thought Virginia might become, he nevertheless regretfully spelled out in some detail a program of reform that he believed remained unfulfilled. Not even the satisfaction of being able to include the full text of the statute for religious freedom in an appendix, and in later editions to note its successful enactment, overcame his disappointment. At that Jefferson's was a modest program, calling mostly for further revision of constitutional and political forms by a new convention that would amend and properly ratify the 1776 constitution, restore a better balance between legislature and governor, open the right to vote to more citizens, and equalize representation in the Assembly in proportion to population instead of giving each county an equal number of delegates. Still holding out for gradual emancipation and colonization as the answer to slavery, Jefferson did not otherwise address the character of the larger society. Almost certainly, though, he must have thought that reforming the franchise and representation in the legislature would bring about further social improvement, as would the provisions that he still hoped to make for public education and libraries. How different was his mood from that of 1776, when he sat in Philadelphia composing the Declaration of Independence and all the while chafing at his absence from the Virginia Convention in Williamsburg, where he believed the serious business of forming the new order was taking place.

Jefferson's sense that the Revolution remained incomplete and unfulfilled in Virginia was understandable and not without insight. He was writing, however, less than a decade after the adoption of the new state constitution and scarcely two years after the conclusion of the treaty that confirmed American independence. The Revolution had not necessarily run its course. Jefferson fixed his attention, moreover, on constitutional forms and statutory law. While they can reveal much about the underlying structure and values of a society, the language of such public formulations also has a tendency to remain traditional and unchanging even while accommodating altered patterns of thought and behavior.

In a word, it is not a simple matter, once we move beyond laws and political institutions, to determine the extent to which the Revolution had actually transformed Virginia. Lacking as yet full-scale studies of social change in the state during the Revolution, we must again begin with the question of leadership. The circle of established political and social leaders of prerevolutionary Virginia—though often hesitant and challenged by vocal opponents, and all but overwhelmed by the difficulties of the war years—appeared, if anything, to have reinforced its position by its ultimate success. Certainly individual members of the group were displaced for reasons other than the normal attrition of age and death. Sometimes whole families, the Nelsons of York County and others from the older Tidewater region, suffered loss of economic and political position. Yet, Jackson Main's examination of the hundred wealthiest families of the 1780s found that something over half still resided in the Tidewater, concentrated along those portions of the Potomac, Rappahannock, and James rivers just below the fall line. However, almost as many were living in the Piedmont, though concentrated along the upper valleys of the same three river systems, and the continuing wealth of many of the Tidewater families depended heavily on their lands in a number of newer Piedmont counties.

Moreover, the political climate of the 1780s did not altogether restore the harmony of the late colonial era. Despite a failure to extend the suffrage, the enlargement of popular political participation that had accompanied the imperial struggle was not undone. More openly contested and tumultuous elections became common. Legislative sessions during the decade became the scene of closely contested battles, which the leadership generally lost. Jefferson's frustration in the *Notes on Virginia* recorded, after all, his failure and that of his associates to achieve some of the most cherished objectives of the revision of the laws of the state.

Whatever authority the leadership lost within the state, it more than recovered in the decisive influence on the new national government of the group of younger Virginia leaders who had come to prominence in the Revolution. James Madison, fresh from his sponsorship of the Jeffersonian program in the Virginia legislature, became the principal author of the new federal Constitution, his working plan for that document known to contemporaries as the Virginia Plan. As a congressman he also shaped the federal Bill of Rights. George Washington, the revered military leader of the War for Independence, presided over the convention that framed the Constitution and then served by virtual acclamation as the first president of the government it created. Jefferson, emerging rapidly as a principal figure in that government and the leader of one of the two loosely formed coalitions that appeared in national politics, was the third president; Madison and James Monroe, the fourth and fifth, respectively, before the Virginia dynasty ended. John Marshall, the most confirmed nationalist of the group, became the first chief justice to bring the Supreme Court to its central role in the federal government by establishing its power to decide the constitutionality of legislation and executive acts. If their youth, their spirit of innovation, and their ease in working in a national rather than a local setting set them apart from many in the preceding generation of Virginia leaders, they were nevertheless unmistakable products of the same cultural milieu, though none came directly from the inner circle of older leaders. Their rise to such prominence in the course of the Revolution scarcely suggested an elite that had been overthrown or entered a state of decline, although it had been in some respects transformed by a generational change and the experience of waging the struggle for independence.

In the 1790s, fortified by that national prestige, those associated with Madison and Jefferson also triumphed over popular and localist leaders who had opposed them on the state level and over a smaller group of Virginia Federalists. The reestablishment of their dominance in state politics suggested, as Herbert Sloan and Peter Onuf have remarked, "how an old ruling class refashioned itself to changing times." If Daniel Jordan's study of Virginians who served in the early federal congresses is an indication, the new generation of leaders resembled in wealth, social rank, and outlook their predecessors who dominated prerevolutionary provincial politics.

Yet the preference of Jefferson and many of the younger group of Revolutionary leaders for the national scene, coupled—despite a deep attachment to Virginia—with an undercurrent of despair at the failure to complete the Revolution, was prophetic. Like most Americans in the half century after independence, most Virginians cloaked the great events of recent memory with a patriotic aura and enshrined them in history. The ongoing transformation for which Jefferson had hoped did not, however, occur. The Revolution remained in some respects frozen in time, while in others social and cultural changes went in altogether another direction.

Those who led the Revolution in Virginia and sought to carry it to completion had few successors among the next generation of Virginians. The men who come most readily to mind, like John Taylor of Caroline or John Randolph of Roanoke, made their reputations as permanent dissenters, brilliant but idiosyncratic defenders of the particular interests of Virginia and resolute opponents of broad national policies. The members of the earlier dynasty reflected two opposing political tendencies, Washington and Marshall becoming Federalists, favoring the close association of Virginia with nationalizing policies, the others becoming Republicans, broadly committed to ensuring the position of an independent yeomanry as the base of a republic with weaker central authority. Nevertheless, both brought Virginia into one or the other of the major currents of early nineteenth-century American political development as her later leaders did not.

With the establishment of religious freedom the evangelical triumph seemed complete, the more so with the rapid rise of Methodism, which began to emerge on the eve of independence and grew rapidly after the war, taking its place alongside the Baptist and earlier evangelical movements. Certainly evangelicals established complete dominance of the religious life of the state and placed their lasting imprint on its popular culture. Yet characteristic values and attitudes of evangelical-ism—stern moralism, egalitarianism, and emphasis on individual, voluntary action rather than on the consensual action of an ordered community—in the end failed to reorder society to the extent that they had promised to do. Striking as the effects of those values may have been when one looks, for example, at a county court day, with itinerant preachers competing for attention with the old amusements and drinking or with turbulence and rowdiness the order of the day at elections, it seems problematical whether the evangelicals worked any great change on several stubborn, vital features of Virginia society. The frequency with which prominent evangelicals began to assume posi-tions of leadership themselves, in the process of taking on such marks of the old elite as greater affluence, finer houses, and increased ownership of slaves is telling, slave holding especially so. By the early nineteenth century Baptists and Methodists abandoned their early hostility to the institution, and they, too, left unshaken the predom-inantly rural, agrarian, and slave-holding character of Virginia society as well as the pattern of leadership that flowed from it.

It is also true that the breaking of the imperial bond, however easy and logical it had seemed, and the hardships of a long, difficult war exacted a high price from Virginians, introducing negative effects beyond the control of the most determined members of the leadership. The most obvious was the economic stagnation that followed the wartime collapse of the tobacco trade. Although both Britons and Virginians rushed to reopen the trade after the peace, neither its partial revival, centering in the Piedmont region more than Tidewater, nor further growth in the raising of grain and foodstuffs successfully revived the old prosperity. Shrinking opportunity produced extensive migration out of the state by whites and blacks alike—slaves either carried by masters who were moving or sold because their labor was no longer needed. The flow of migration spread westward to Kentucky and across southern Indiana and Illinois and southward to the new lands of the lower South. In some respects the truly dynamic element of Virginia's nineteenth-century leadership was provided by that numerous group of native-born Virginians who achieved prominence in those states to which they had migrated. In an even more subtle manner—also tied in part to economic decline but linked as well to the destruction of the old cultural bonds to the metropolitan center of the empire and to a lack of primary concern in evangelical culture for secular learning—Virginia became increasingly provincial in outlook, increasingly isolated from newer intellectual currents of the day.

Thus the Virginia colony that perhaps stood at a high point of its development at the middle of the eighteenth century was transformed by the experience of the Revolution, but in an ambivalent manner. However troubled by the signs of crisis, its leaders demonstrated as strong an attachment to republican principles as those of any state, broke off imperial ties that were perhaps more vital than those of any other mainland colony, proclaimed doctrines of political and religious liberty as strongly as anyone, and furnished far more than their share of the first generation of national leadership. Yet the state remained only lightly touched by the social and economic changes of the Revolutionary and early national eras. Its agrarian, slave-holding regime was left substantially intact, even reinforced in some respects by economic decline and a growing provincialism. In the late colonial and Revolutionary era Virginia and the leaders it produced left a legacy to the whole nation—a legacy that within its own borders endured in tradition but faded in reality.

BIBLIOGRAPHY

This essay has as its primary objective the presentation of a guide to the extensive literature of Virginia history that is selective rather than exhaustive and reasonably accessible to students and general readers. It also emphasizes more recent work published in the last two or three decades. The bibliographies in some of the studies cited below will offer guidance to the reader who wishes to examine the older literature more thoroughly. At the same time the essay departs to some extent from these guidelines by including some older works that remain of first importance, by including references to more specialized and less easily obtainable studies that nonetheless offer the best treatment of certain specific topics, and by providing references to unpublished dissertations that the authors have found especially helpful in the preparation of this volume.

In the interest of brevity, two areas of historical study that are important for understanding the context in which the Virginia colony developed are largely unrepresented in the bibliography. First, the history of England from the late sixteenth century to the late eighteenth century is, of course, a vital background to all that transpired in that nation's oldest and largest New World colony, but an adequate treatment of English bibliography would more than double the length of the present essay. Recent historians are aware, too, of how much the tidewater regions of Maryland and Virginia developed as a single Chesapeake society. Much of the newer Chesapeake social and economic history often treats the two colonies together, whatever the differences in their political and religious systems. Where these new works give substantial attention to Virginia, they are cited below, but there remains a large body of other excellent work devoted to Maryland alone that is useful in understanding the development of Virginia. The bibliography in Aubrey C. Land, *Colonial Maryland: A History* (Millwood, New York, 1981), a companion volume in the same series as this one, provides a helpful introduction.

BIBLIOGRAPHICAL REFERENCES AND GUIDES

There is no single authoritative bibliography of colonial Virginia of recent date. Much like colonial Virginia historical writing itself, bibliographical discussions of the subject tend to be separated into seventeenth- and eighteenth-century components. For seventeenth-century bibliography an excellent starting point is the "Critical Essay on Authorities" in Wesley Frank Craven, *The Southern Colonies in the Seventeenth Century, 1607–1689* (Baton Rouge, 1949). Obviously a great deal of new work has appeared since its publication. The newer work is surveyed in Thad W. Tate, "The Seventeenth-Century Chesapeake and Its Modern Historians," in Tate and David L. Ammerman, eds., *The Chesapeake in the Seventeenth Century* (Chapel Hill, 1979). For eighteenth-century bibliography before 1763 a useful beginning is the listing in volume II of Richard L. Morton, *Colonial Virginia* (Chapel Hill, 1960), although it, too, requires updating by the use of the bibliographies in some of the more recent studies in that period of Virginia history. The footnote references in Thad W. Tate, "The Coming of the Revolution in Virginia . . . ," *William and Mary Quarterly*, 3rd ser., XIX (1962), 323–343, provide a bibliography of the 1763–1776 era to its date of publication. That listing can be updated in the appropriate sections of this bibliographical essay.

Two especially valuable indexes to Virginia materials are Earl Gregg Swem, comp., *Virginia Historical Index*, 2 vols. (Roanoke, 1934–1936) and Lester J. Cappon and Stella F. Duff [Neiman], eds., *Virginia Gazette Index, 1736–1780*, 2 vols. (Williamsburg, 1950). Emily J. Salmon, ed., *A Hornbook of Virginia History* (Richmond, 1983; 3rd ed.), contains both a brief historical survey and a number of useful lists of persons, places, population figures, etc. William G. and Mary Newton Stanard, eds., *The Colonial Virginia Register* (Albany, 1902; repr. Baltimore, 1965), contains fuller lists of various colonial officeholders, which is helpful but neither entirely complete nor accurate. Lyon Gardiner Tyler, *Encyclopedia of Virginia Biography*, 5 vols. (New York, 1915), also has some inaccuracies and a confusing organization, but it remains a good source of useful brief biographical sketches of some colonial Virginians who have not received full-scale biographies. A new and authoritative Virginia biographical dictionary is in preparation at the Virginia State Library. Nell Marion Nugent, *Cavaliers and Pioneers: Abstracts of Virginia Land Patents and Grants, 1623–1732*, 3 vols. and suppl. (Richmond, 1934–1980), is also useful.

Two valuable guides to Virginia portraits are Alexander Wilbourne Weddell, ed., *A Memorial Volume of Virginia Historical Portraiture, 1585–1830* (Richmond, 1930) and Virginius Cornick Hall, Jr., *Portraits in the Collection of the Virginia Historical Society* (Charlottesville, 1981). Jane D. Carson, ed.,

Travelers in Tidewater Virginia, 1700–1800: A Bibliography (Charlottesville, 1965), provides an informative listing. The famous John White drawings of the Indians whom the Roanoke Island colonists encountered in North Carolina in the 1580s are also thought to depict reliably the dress and style of life of eastern Virginia Indians at the time of English colonization. There is an excellent and inexpensive modern edition: Paul Hulton, *America 1585: The Complete Drawings of John White* (Chapel Hill, 1984). Although the time period is somewhat late, the many drawings and sketches in Edward C. Carter II et al., eds., *The Virginia Journals of Benjamin Henry Latrobe, 1795–1798*, 2 vols. (New Haven and London, 1977), tell us a great deal about the landscape and character of life in Virginia in the late colonial period. Lester J. Cappon, Barbara Bartz Petchenik, and John Hamilton Long, eds., *Atlas of Early American History: The Revolutionary Era, 1760–1790* (Princeton, 1976), contains a number of valuable Virginia maps. On the important theme of tobacco cultivation and marketing, see Jerome E. Brooks, ed., *Tobacco, Its History Illustrated by the Books, Manuscripts and Engravings in the Library of George Arents, Jr. . . . .*, 5 vols. (New York, 1937–1952).

PRIMARY SOURCES

Research into the history of early Virginia ultimately rests on several categories of surviving manuscript records and printed materials from the colonial period: (1) the private correspondence of leading individuals or mercantile firms, (2) Williamsburg's newspaper, the *Virginia Gazette*, published by a succession of editors between 1736 and 1780, plus a number of almanacs, pamphlets, and other titles printed on the *Gazette's* press, (3) the great body of British public records pertaining to Virginia and imperial affairs generally, (4) the records of the colony's own provincial government, chiefly those of the two houses of the Assembly and the land patents, (5) a scattered group of vestry books and parish registers for some of the parishes of the Anglican church, which provide the only systematic records of births, marriages, and deaths, and (6) a rich body of county records, which survive for a sufficient number of colonial counties to provide a reliable sample of the wills, inventories of estates, court records, and the like that enable us to understand the character of society and the temper of everyday life better than any other source.

A thorough examination of those sources and a few others would require research in a number of major depositories. Within the United States these include especially the Virginia Historical Society and the Virginia State Library in Richmond, the Alderman Library of the University of Virginia, the

Library of Congress, the Henry E. Huntington Library in San Marino, California, and the libraries of the Colonial Williamsburg Foundation and the College of William and Mary in Williamsburg. British records are found in the Public Record Office, the British Library, and in numerous county record offices and private collections.

For the serious researcher the task of examining these records is eased by the existence of published guides to a number of the depositories listed above, by the union catalog of manuscripts issued by the Library of Congress, and by the issuance of microform copies of some collections. The microfilm edition of the extant issues of the *Virginia Gazette* is especially useful (see above for the companion index). The Virginia Colonial Records Project, founded in 1957 at the time of the Virginia 350th anniversary celebration of the Jamestown settlement, has produced microfilm copies of a large portion of the extensive public and private records pertaining to Virginia that are in British depositories. Copies may be consulted at the University of Virginia, the Virginia State Library, and the Colonial Williamsburg Foundation.

The study of Virginia history is facilitated, too, by a number of modern printed editions of important sources. Their existence makes the task of the professional scholar easier and makes it possible for the student or general reader at least to sample the original sources, thereby gaining an understanding of the history of early Virginia that can be acquired in no other way.

The preparation of a number of important sets of public records of the colony began early in the twentieth century under the editorship of Henry R. McIlwaine, in some cases continuing under various successors. These editions include: *Executive Journals of the Council of Colonial Virginia*, 6 vols. (Richmond, 1925–1966); *Journals of the House of Burgesses of Virginia, 1619–1776*, 13 vols. (Richmond, 1905–1915); *Legislative Journals of the Council of Virginia*, 3 vols. (Richmond, 1918); and *Minutes of the Council and General Court of Colonial Virginia*, 2nd ed. (Richmond, 1979). The larger part of the laws enacted in the colony were compiled by William Waller Hening in *The Statutes at Large . . .* , 13 vols. (Richmond, 1809–1823), but Waverly Winfree has provided an important addendum in *The Laws of Virginia, Being a Supplement to Hening's The Statutes at Large, 1700–1750* (Richmond, 1971). Warren M. Billings and Jon Kukla have compiled further omitted seventeenth-century statutes in separate articles entitled "Some Acts Not in Hening's *Statutes . . .* ," *Virginia Magazine of History & Biography*, 83 (1975), 22–76, 77–97.

There are only a few editions of court records. R. T. Barton, ed., *Virginia Colonial Decisions: The Reports by Sir John Randolph and Edward Barradall of the Decisions of the General Court of Virginia, 1728–1741*, 2 vols. (Boston, 1909), provides some information for the high court of the colony, for which the records are largely lost. Susie M. Ames edited two volumes of seventeenth-century Accomac-Northampton records in *County Court Records of Accomack-Northampton, Virginia, 1632–1640* (Washington, D.C., 1954) and *County Court Records of Accomack-Northampton, Virginia, 1640–1645* (Charlottesville, 1973). Peter C. Hoffer has more recently edited a group of criminal records for Richmond County from March 10, 1701/11 to 1754 in *Criminal Proceedings in Colonial Virginia* . . . (Athens, Georgia, 1984).

There is a collection of records of one royal governor in a modern edition: George Reese, ed., *The Official Papers of Francis Fauquier, Lieutenant Governor of Virginia, 1758–1768*, 3 vols. (Charlottesville, 1980–1983). The papers of the late seventeenth-century governor, Lord Howard of Effingham, have been edited by Warren M. Billings and will be published in the near future. John C. Van Horne has also edited *The Correspondence of William Nelson as Acting Governor of Virginia, 1770–1771* (Charlottesville, 1975).

A significant group of records of slave importations into Virginia appear in Elizabeth Donnan, ed., *Documents Illustrative of the Slave Trade to America*, vol. 4 (Washington, D.C., 1935), which should now be supplemented with Walter E. Minchinton, Celia King, and Peter Waite, eds., *Virginia Slave-Trade Statistics* (Richmond, 1984). G. Melvin Herndon, *William Tatham and the Culture of Tobacco* (Coral Gables, Florida, 1969), contains a facsimile reprint of Tatham's *Historical and Practical Essay on the Culture and Commerce of Tobacco* (1800), the standard treatise on Virginia's most important colonial crop.

When one turns to documentary editions that cover specific time periods in Virginia history, the first years of settlement at Jamestown are especially well served. The classic writings of Captain John Smith have recently appeared in a new edition, Philip L. Barbour, ed., *The Complete Works of Captain John Smith*, 3 vols. (Chapel Hill, 1986). Barbour was also editor of *The Jamestown Voyages Under the First Charter, 1606–1609* (London, 1969). William Strachey, *The Historie of Travell into Virginia Britania* (1612), ed. Louis B. Wright and Virginia Freund (London, 1953), is also valuable. David B. Quinn, ed., *The Roanoke Voyages, 1584–1590*, 2 vols. (Cambridge, 1955), has material of Virginia interest, as does the edition of Richard Hakluyt's 1589 *Principall Navigations, Voyages and Discoveries of the English Nation*, prepared by Quinn and R. A. Skelton (Cambridge, 1965). Susan Myra Kingsbury, ed., *The Records of the Virginia Company of London*, 4 vols. (Washington, D.C., 1906–1935) is an indispensable record of the commercial company that first colonized Virginia.

There are fewer edited sources for the remainder of the seventeenth century. Warren M. Billings, ed., *The Old Dominion in the Seventeenth Century: A Documentary History of Virginia, 1606–1689* (Chapel Hill, 1975), provides a useful sampling with explanatory commentaries. Clarence Walworth Alvord and Lee Bidgood, eds., *The First Explorations of the Trans-Allegheny Region by the*

Virginians, 1650–1674 (Cleveland, 1912), chronicles the important internal explorations of Virginia in the mid-seventeenth century, although William P. Cumming, ed., *The Discoveries of John Lederer* . . . (Charlottesville, 1958) is better on that important figure, perhaps the first European to ascend to Blue Ridge in Virginia. For Bacon's Rebellion, Charles M. Andrews, ed., *Narratives of the Insurrections, 1675–1690* (New York, 1915), remains the best collection of sources. Richard Beale Davis, ed., *William Fitzhugh and His Chesapeake World, 1676–1701: The Fitzhugh Letters and Other Documents* (Chapel Hill, 1963), is the best record of an individual Virginian of the seventeenth century. Gilbert Chinard, ed., *A Huguenot Exile in Virginia* . . . (New York, 1934), contains interesting observations on the colony by a traveler of the late seventeenth century.

There are modern editions of three informative accounts of Virginia dating from the late seventeenth and early eighteenth centuries, all bearing very similar titles: Henry Hartwell, James Blair, and Edward Chilton, *The Present State of Virginia and the College*, ed. Hunter D. Farish (Princeton, 1940); Robert Beverley, *The History and Present State of Virginia*, ed. Louis B. Wright (Chapel Hill, 1947); and Hugh Jones, *The Present State of Virginia*, ed. Richard L. Morton (Chapel Hill, 1956).

The eighteenth-century planter who has left the most remarkable literary record is William Byrd II. Two of his three published diaries pertain to years he spent in Virginia: *The Secret Diary of William Byrd of Westover, 1739–1741*, ed. Louis B. Wright and Marion Tinling (Richmond, 1941), and *Another Secret Diary of William Byrd of Westover, 1739–1741*, ed. Maude H. Woodfin (Richmond, 1942). There are several editions of his prose writings, which pertain mostly to natural history and his travels into the interior regions of the colony; the most recent is *The Prose Works of William Byrd of Westover*, ed. Louis B. Wright (Cambridge, Massachusetts, 1966). There is also a collection of his correspondence and that of his father William I and son William III, spanning almost a century, in *The Correspondence of the Three William Byrds of Westover, Virginia, 1684–1776*, ed. Marion Tinling, 2 vols. (Charlottesville, 1977). In addition to their historical interest the William Byrd II materials also constitute the largest single body of literary materials for colonial Virginia, although none were published in Byrd's lifetime. Among the few other modern editions of colonial Virginia literary sources are Richard Beale Davis, ed., *The Colonial Virginia Satirist: Mid-Eighteenth-Century Commentaries on Politics, Religion, and Society*, in *Transactions of the American Philosophical Society*, new ser., vol. 57, pt. 1 (1967), 1–74, and James A. Servies and Carl R. Dolmetsch, eds., *Poems of Charles Hansford* (Chapel Hill, 1961).

The other planter diary that rivals Byrd's and perhaps presents an even richer picture of the cultural milieu of the Virginia planter is *The Diary of*

Colonel Landon Carter of Sabine Hall, 1752–1778, ed. Jack P. Greene, 2 vols. (Charlottesville, 1965). Two briefer but interesting journals, kept in each instance by plantation tutors who came to Virginia from elsewhere and lived briefly in the colony, are Hunter D. Farish, ed., *Journals and Letters of Philip Vickers Fithian, 1773–1774: A Plantation Tutor of the Old Dominion* (Williamsburg, 1957), and Edward M. Riley, ed., *The Journal of John Harrower, An Indentured Servant in the Colony of Virginia, 1773–1776* (Williamsburg, 1963).

Useful for natural science in colonial Virginia are Joseph A. and Nesta Ewan, eds., *John Banister and His Natural History of Virginia, 1678–1692* (Urbana, Illinois, 1970); Edmund and Dorothy S. Berkeley, eds., *The Reverend John Clayton: A Parson with a Scientific Mind: His Scientific Writings and Other Related Papers* (Charlottesville, 1965); and Earl Gregg Swem, ed., *Brothers of the Spade: Correspondence of Peter Collinson of London, and of John Custis, of Williamsburg, Va., 1734–1746* (Barre, Massachusetts, 1957).

Virtually all of the rich body of records pertaining to the economic history of the colony remains in manuscript, but Frances Norton Mason, ed., *John Norton & Sons, Merchants of London and Virginia* (Richmond, 1937), provides a good selection of the papers of one of the leading consignment firms in the Virginia tobacco trade. Most of Norton's papers fall, however, in the Revolutionary era.

Just as edited source material is particularly rich for the first years in which the colony was founded, it is also especially plentiful for the years of the Revolutionary crisis. A recent and very full compilation of documentary evidence for the political history of the movement toward independence is William J. Van Schreeven, Robert L. Scribner, and Brent Tarter, eds., *Revolutionary Virginia: The Road to Independence*, 7 vols. (Charlottesville, 1973–83).

Another particularly rich vein of material on Revolutionary Virginia is contained in the edited letters and papers of many of the leading participants. For some of the major figures who had long national careers, recent and authoritative new multivolume editions are in progress. Most are complete for the years before 1783, and the references that follow cite only the volumes for that period. For George Washington, W. W. Abbot, ed., *The Papers of George Washington: Colonial Series*, 4 vols. to date (Charlottesville, 1983–1984), covers the period to October 1757, and the *Revolutionary War Series*, 1 vol. to date (Charlottesville, 1985), provides material for June–September 1775. Donald Jackson and Dorothy Twohig, eds., *The Diaries of George Washington*, 6 vols. (Charlottesville, 1976–1979), includes the Virginia and Revolutionary years in the first three volumes. For Thomas Jefferson, the current edition is Julian P. Boyd, ed., *The Papers of Thomas Jefferson*, vols. 1–6 (Princeton, 1950–1952); for James Madison, William T. Hutchinson and William M. E.

Rachal, eds., *The Papers of James Madison*, vols. 1–7 (Chicago, 1962–1971); and for John Marshall, Herbert A. Johnson, ed., *The Papers of John Marshall*, vol. 1 (Chapel Hill, 1974).

There are also collections of the papers of three important figures whose principal activities occurred at the provincial and state level: James C. Ballagh, ed., *The Letters of Richard Henry Lee*, 2 vols. (New York, 1911–1914); David J. Mays, ed., *The Letters and Papers of Edmund Pendleton*, 2 vols. (Charlottesville, 1967); and Robert A. Rutland, ed., *The Papers of George Mason*, 3 vols. (Chapel Hill, 1970).

Two very informative volumes for the Revolutionary period, both of which have been extensively used in the final chapters of this volume, are Arthur H. Shaffer, ed., *Edmund Randolph, History of Virginia* (Charlottesville, 1970) and Thomas Jefferson, *Notes on the State of Virginia*, ed. William Peden (Chapel Hill, 1955).

SECONDARY STUDIES: GENERAL

For a general narrative of colonial Virginia to 1763 that possesses scholarly depth Richard L. Morton, *Colonial Virginia*, 2 vols. (Chapel Hill, 1960) remains the standard work. There is also a useful political narrative in Alf J. Mapp, Jr., *The Virginia Experiment: The Old Dominion's Role in the Making of America 1607–1781* (La Salle, Illinois, 1974; 2nd ed.).

A few histories that are intended for a more popular audience, and comprehend the whole sweep of Virginia history, are also of interest. The opening chapters of Louis D. Rubin, Jr., *Virginia: A Bicentennial History* (New York, 1971), include a good condensed account of the colonial era. Virginius Dabney, *Virginia: The New Dominion* (New York, 1971), and the older Matthew Page Andrews, *Virginia: The Old Dominion* (Garden City, New York, 1937), provide interesting perspectives on Virginia history. Marshall Fishwick, *Virginia: A New Look at the Old Dominion* (New York, 1959), takes a somewhat more iconoclastic view of the writing of Virginia history. The interpretation of colonial Virginia outlined by Daniel J. Boorstin, *The Americans: The Colonial Experience* (New York, 1958), 97–143, is of continuing interest, in part because it effectively captures the perspective of much historical scholarship of the 1950s.

So much new work on the society and culture of early Virginia has appeared since the early 1970s, however, that none of these earlier works can bring the reader fully abreast of present-day perspectives on the history of colonial Virginia. The work that comes closest to accomplishing that end is Edmund S. Morgan, *American Slavery, American Freedom: The Ordeal of Colonial Virginia*

(New York, 1975). Only the last two or three chapters concern the eighteenth century, but the author's provocative analysis of the interrelationship of a labor system that largely depended on unfree workers and a strong commitment to political freedom among Virginia colonial landowners illuminates much about the wider history of the colony. Darrett B. and Anita H. Rutman, *A Place in Time: Middlesex County, Virginia; 1650–1750* (New York, 1984), which concentrates on the late seventeenth century, is particularly effective in helping the reader to understand how Virginia society developed and functioned at a more local level. In a second volume, subtitled *Explicatus*, the Rutmans provide a more detailed and technical supplementary discussion for specialists.

A great deal of the newer work must, however, still be read in shorter essays and journal articles or in books that cover a more restricted period of time. Such work will be cited below in the appropriate sections of this essay. In addition to the more scholarly articles that have appeared in such journals as *The Virginia Magazine of History and Biography* (hereafter cited as *VMHB*), *The William and Mary Quarterly* (hereafter cited as *WMQ*), *The Journal of Southern History*, and others, readers should also know that *Virginia Cavalcade*, an illustrated and popular magazine of Virginia history published by the Virginia State Library, consistently includes well-illustrated and authoritative articles on all phases of the history of Virginia.

There are also a number of more topical studies that span most, if not all, of the seventeenth and eighteenth centuries. One of the most interesting is Arthur P. Middleton, *Tobacco Coast: A Maritime History of Chesapeake Bay in the Colonial Era* (Baltimore and London, 1984; repr. ed.). For agriculture, see Lewis C. Gray, *History of Agriculture in the Southern United States to 1860*, 2 vols. (Washington, D.C., 1933). The classic work of Avery O. Craven, *Soil Exhaustion as a Factor in the Agricultural History of Virginia and Maryland, 1606–1860* (Urbana, Illinois, 1926), while still important, probably exaggerates the extent of soil exhaustion before 1800. Thomas P. Abernethy, *Three Virginia Frontiers* (Baton Rouge, 1940), remains a brief but informative introduction to the major phases of the expansion of Virginia from 1607 forward. A somewhat overlooked and valuable book is Sarah S. Hughes, *Surveyors and Statesmen: Land Measuring in Colonial Virginia* (Richmond, 1979).

The pertinent sections of John J. McCusker and Russell R. Menard, *The Economy of British America, 1607–1789* (Chapel Hill, 1985) are now the best introduction to the economy of early Virginia and also include in their footnotes an excellent guide to the bibliography. For indentured servant labor, see Abbot E. Smith, *Colonists in Bondage* (Chapel Hill, 1947), and the more recent work of David Galenson, *White Servitude in Colonial America* (Cambridge, 1981). General works on blacks in early America that are especially useful for Virginia include Winthrop D. Jordan, *White Over Black: American Attitudes Toward the Negro, 1550–1812* (Chapel Hill, 1968); A. Leon Higginbotham, Jr., *In the Matter of Color: Race and the American Legal Processes: The Colonial Period* (New York, 1978); Edgar A. Toppin, *A Biographical History of Blacks in America Since 1528* (New York, 1971); Herbert A. Gutman, *The Black Family in Slavery and Freedom, 1750–1925* (New York, 1976); and Ira Berlin, "Time, Space, and the Evolution of Afro-American Society in British Mainland North America," *American Historical Review*, XXXV (1980), 44–78. James C. Ballagh, *A History of Slavery in Virginia* (Baltimore, 1902), remains of some use for sketching in the legal framework of slavery. For questions of economy and labor, the more recent literature appears in the topical sections of this essay.

The scholar who has written most extensively on the literary and intellectual life of the Virginia colony and all of the colonial South is Richard Beale Davis. See especially his *Literature and Society in Early Virginia, 1608–1840* (Baton Rouge, 1973), *A Southern Colonial Bookshelf: Reading in the Eighteenth Century* (Athens, Georgia, 1979), and his comprehensive magnum opus, *Intellectual Life of the Colonial South, 1585–1763*, 3 vols. (Knoxville, 1978). A brief provocative discussion that runs somewhat counter to Davis's high estimate of the cultural life of colonial Virginia is Carl Bridenbaugh, *Myths and Realities: Societies of the Colonial South* (Baton Rouge, 1952), 1–53. For religious life George MacLaren Brydon, *Virginia's Mother Church and The Conditions Under Which It Grew*, 2 vols. (Richmond, 1947–1952), provides a detailed and sympathetic account of the Anglican Church in the colony.

Several other important topics—among them law, politics, and society—are notably missing from this list of general studies of major topics, because the best work on them deals with particular themes or more limited periods of time and is cited below.

SECONDARY STUDIES: 1607–1689

In addition to the studies by Edmund S. Morgan and Darrett and Anita Rutman, which have been previously cited, the history of seventeenth-century Virginia is unusually well served by a number of older works that remain of first importance. The Virginia chapters of Wesley Frank Craven, *The Southern Colonies in the Seventeenth Century, 1607–1689* (Baton Rouge, 1949), constitute an excellent introduction. The two studies by Philip Alexander Bruce, *Economic History of Virginia in the Seventeenth Century*, 2 vols. (New York, 1896), and *Institutional History of Virginia in the Seventeenth Century*, 2 vols. (New York, 1910), rest on extensive research in the original records. Even those historians who would not agree with every interpretation of Thomas J.

Wertenbaker recognize that his three major works are a remarkable achieve-
ment, especially for their pioneering investigation of the seventeenth-century
Virginia social order: *Patrician and Plebeian in Virginia, or, The Origin and
Development of the Social Classes of the Old Dominion* (Charlottesville, 1910);
Virginia Under the Stuarts, 1607–1688 (Princeton, 1914); and *The Planters of
Colonial Virginia* (Princeton, 1922). All have been reprinted in a single volume
entitled *The Shaping of Colonial Virginia* (New York, 1958).

Susie M. Ames, *Studies of the Virginia Eastern Shore in the Seventeenth Century*
(Richmond, 1940), is a useful local history, thoroughly grounded in the
county records. William L. Shea, *The Virginia Militia in the Seventeenth Century*
(Baton Rouge, 1983), examines military organization from settlement
through Bacon's Rebellion. Earl G. Swem, ed., *The Jamestown 350th
Anniversary Booklets* (Williamsburg, 1957), is a convenient collection of
twenty-three brief treatments of a variety of subjects on the seventeenth
century.

There are two collections of original essays that contain important
contributions on Virginia: James M. Smith, ed., *Seventeenth-Century America*
(Chapel Hill, 1959) and the previously cited Tate and Ammerman, eds.,
Chesapeake in the Seventeenth Century.

Similarly, one of the best introductions to the English background of the
colonization of Virginia is another essay volume: K. R. Andrews, N. P.
Canny, and P.E.H. Hair, eds., *The Westward Enterprise: English Activities in
Ireland, the Atlantic and America* (Liverpool, 1978). See especially the essays by
Carole Shammas, "English Commercial Development and American Colonization, 1520–1620"; Nicholas Canny, "The Permissive Frontier: The Problem of Social Control in English Settlements in Ireland and Virginia,
1550–1660"; and Warren M. Billings, "The Transfer of English Law to
Virginia, 1606–1650." All of David B. Quinn's extensive work on English
exploration and discovery bears in one way or another on the first permanent
English settlement at Jamestown, but especially important are chaps. 13 and
18 of *North America from Earliest Discovery to First Settlement* (New York, 1978),
Part V of *England and the Discovery of America, 1481–1620* (New York, 1974),
and his recent *Set Fair for Roanoke: Voyages and Colonies, 1584–1606* (Chapel
Hill and London, 1985). The bibliography for English history in the period
of overseas expansion is extensive, but two useful introductions are Geoffrey
Elton, *England Under the Tudors* (London, 1961), and A. L. Rowse, *The
England of Elizabeth* (New York, 1951). The Spanish presence in Virginia
before the English settlement is poorly documented, but see Clifford M. Lewis
and Albert J. Loomie, *The Spanish Jesuit Mission in Virginia, 1570–1572*
(Chapel Hill, 1953), and Carl Bridenbaugh, *Jamestown, 1544–1699* (New
York, 1980).

As interest in the native peoples of North America has grown, scholarship on the subject has shifted away from discussions of colonial Indian policy, which dominated the older literature, toward more searching examination of Indian culture and of intercultural contacts between Indians and European settlers. Nancy O. Lurie opened up that subject for Virginia in an essay of enduring significance, "Indian Cultural Adjustment to European Civilization," in Smith, ed., *Seventeenth-Century America*. Two more general discussions with significance for Virginia are Gary B. Nash, *Red, White, and Black: The Peoples of Early America* (Englewood Cliffs, New Jersey, 1974), and Francis P. Jennings, *The Invasion of America: Indians, Colonialism, and the Cant of Conquest* (Chapel Hill, 1975). The chapters by Christian Feest in William C. Sturtevant, gen. ed., *Handbook of North American Indians: Northeast*, vol. XV (Washington, D.C., 1978), 240–289, provide a brief authoritative account of the Indians of the mid-South region. Philip L. Barbour, *Pocahontas and Her World* (Boston, 1970), treats the famous Indian princess. Two studies of Indian-white relations from different perspectives are Bernard W. Sheehan, *Savagism and Civility: Indians and Englishmen in Colonial Virginia* (Cambridge and New York, 1980), and Karen O. Kupperman, *Settling With the Indians: The Meeting of English and Indian Cultures in America, 1580–1640* (Totowa, New Jersey, 1980). From the periodical literature, see especially Gary B. Nash, "The Image of the Indian in the Southern Colonial Mind," *WMQ*, 3rd ser., XXIX (1972), 197–230; J. Frederick Fausz, "The 'Barbarous Massacre' Reconsidered: The Powhatan Uprising and the Historians," *Explorations in Ethnic Studies*, I (1978), 16–36; and Alden T. Vaughan, " 'Expulsion of the Salvages': English Policy and the Virginia Massacre of 1622," *WMQ*, 3rd ser., XXXV (1978), 57–84.

The founding of Virginia and the brief period of Virginia Company rule from 1607 to 1624 has also received extensive attention. Much of it has focused on Captain John Smith, especially in Philip L. Barbour, *The Three Worlds of Captain John Smith* (Boston, 1964); Alden T. Vaughan, *American Genesis: Captain John Smith and the Founding of Virginia* (Boston, 1975); and Everett H. Emerson, *Captain John Smith* (New York, 1971). Morgan, *American Slavery, American Freedom*, is also of central importance. Wesley F. Craven, *Dissolution of the Virginia Company: The Failure of a Colonial Experiment* (New York, 1932), remains the standard treatment of the Virginia Company and its vicissitudes.

There are three important articles on the problems of survival in the early years of the colony: Carville Earle, "Environment, Disease, and Mortality in Early Virginia," in Tate and Ammerman, eds., *Seventeenth-Century Chesapeake*, chap. 3; Karen O. Kupperman, "Apathy and Death in Early Jamestown," *Journal of American History*, vol. 66 (1979), 24–40; and Darrett B. Rutman and Anita H. Rutman, "Of Agues and Fevers: Malaria in the Early Chesapeake," *WMQ*, 3rd ser., XXIII (1976), 31–60. Two other articles are helpful in understanding the building of order and social structure in the first years of the colony: Darrett B. Rutman, "The Virginia Company and Its Military Regime," in Rutman, ed., *The Old Dominion: Essays for Thomas Perkins Abernethy* (Charlottesville, 1964), 1–20, and Sigmund Diamond, "From Organization to Society: Virginia in the Seventeenth Century," *American Journal of Sociology*, LXIII (1958), 457–475.

Three other figures from the Jamestown years besides John Smith are represented by full-length biographies: S. G. Culliford, *William Strachey, 1572–1621* (Charlottesville, 1965); Richard Beale Davis, *George Sandys: Poet Adventurer* (New York, 1955); and William S. Powell, *John Pory, 1572–1636: The Life and Letters of a Man of Many Parts* (Chapel Hill, 1977).

The middle and later years of the seventeenth century have received recent attention in a number of articles and essays that deal especially with society and labor. Apart from a continuing interest in the era of Bacon's Rebellion, there have been few books published for the period other than those by Morgan and the Rutmans already cited. One exception is Wesley F. Craven, *White, Red, and Black: The Seventeenth-Century Virginian* (Charlottesville, 1971), a brief study that anticipated some of the themes of the work in social history that began to appear soon after its publication.

The thrust of much of this new attention to the early Virginia social order emphasizes its instability and sometimes ruthless exploitation of unfree labor, at first white servants and then black slaves. Irene D. Hecht, "The Virginia Muster of 1624/25 as a Source of Demographic History," *WMQ*, 3rd ser., XXX (1973), 65–92, analyzes the implications of the demographic character of the small population that survived Virginia company rule. One aspect of the turbulence of life in the colony is discussed in Clara Ann Bowler, "Carted Whores and White Shrouded Apologies: Slander in the County Courts of Seventeenth-Century Virginia," *VMHB*, LXXXV (1977), 411–426. T. H. Breen offers an interpretation of the effect of social conditions on the prevailing value system of the population in "Looking Out for Number One: Conflicting Values in Early Seventeenth-Century Virginia," *South Atlantic Quarterly*, LXXVIII (1979), 342–360.

A full understanding of the implications of the new work in the social history of the Chesapeake requires the examination of a number of articles by Darrett and Anita Rutman, Kevin Kelly, Lois Carr, Russell Menard, Lorena Walsh, Gloria Main, and others. Much of this work—the Rutmans and Kelly are exceptions—deals principally with Maryland but has equivalent significance for Virginia. Representative essays by several of these scholars (Lorena Walsh on marriage and family, the Rutmans on parental death, Kelly on settlement patterns, and Carr and Menard on immigration and opportunity) appear in Tate and Ammerman, eds., *Seventeenth-Century Chesapeake.*

Another essay from the same volume by James Horn, "Servant Immigration to the Chesapeake in the Seventeenth Century," is one of several important essays on the social origins of those who came to Virginia. The others include Mildred Campbell, "Social Origins of Some Early Americans," in Smith, ed., *Seventeenth-Century Virginia*, and David W. Galenson, " 'Middling People' or 'Common Sort'?: The Social Origins of Some Early Americans Reexamined," *WMQ*, 3rd ser., XXXV (1978), 499–524. Campbell replies, *ibid.*, 525–540, and there is an additional informative exchange, *ibid.*, XXXVI (1979), 264–286. One of the best statements on the nature and extent of the opportunity that the Chesapeake afforded immigrants, especially those who came as servants, is Russell R. Menard, "From Servant to Freeholder: Status Mobility and Property Accumulation in Seventeenth-Century Maryland," *WMQ*, 3rd ser., XXX (1973), 37–64.

At one time historians of the black experience in seventeenth-century Virginia were especially concerned with how and when slavery developed in the first mainland English colony to which blacks came. There is a convenient summary and review of the earlier literature for that question in Paul C. Palmer, "Servant into Slave: The Evolution of the Legal Status of the Negro Laborer in Colonial Virginia," *South Atlantic Quarterly*, LXV (1966), 355–370. The recent book by T. H. Breen and Stephen Innes, *"Myne Owne Ground": Race and Freedom on Virginia's Eastern Shore, 1640–1676* (New York, 1980), is an important reminder of the presence of a significant free black population in early Virginia. Increasingly, however, attention has turned to the last decade or two of the seventeenth century when slavery was already established but when the black population began to increase dramatically from new importations and slaves began to replace white servants as the predominant labor force in the colony. The completion of that important transition did not occur until the eighteenth century. In addition to Morgan, *American Slavery, American Freedom*, there is an important periodical literature that traces the origins and early stages of that transition. Especially important are Russell R. Menard, "From Servants to Slaves: The Transformation of the Chesapeake Labor System, 1680–1710," *Southern Studies*, XVI (1977), 355–390; Menard, "The Tobacco Industry in the Chesapeake Colonies, 1617–1730: An Interpretation," *Research in Economic History*, V (1980), 109–177; Richard R. Beeman, "Labor Forces and Race Relations: A Comparative View of the Colonization of Brazil and Virginia," *Political Science Quarterly*, LXXXVI (1971), 609–636; and T. H. Breen, "A Changing Labor Force and Race Relations in Virginia, 1660–1710," *Journal of Social History*, VII (1973), 3–25.

Even those historians who have stressed demographic failure and social

instability in seventeenth-century Virginia have always given some recognition to the strategies by which settlers sought in custom and in law to combat
the problem. Still other historians seem to deny that political and social
institutions were ever as weak as the new social historians have sometimes
suggested. Thus Virginia Bernhard, "Poverty and the Social Order in
Seventeenth-Century Virginia," *VMHB*, LXXXV (1977), 141–155, finds a
high degree of social concern for the poor. Warren M. Billings traces "The
Growth of Political Institutions in Virginia, 1634 to 1676," in *WMQ*, 3rd
ser., XXXI (1974), 225–242, and Wesley F. Craven reviews the political
development of the colony positively in " ' . . . And So the Form of
Government Became Perfect,' " *VMHB*, LXXVII (1969), 131–145. The
strongest criticism of the social historians for their overemphasis of instability
occurs in Jon Kukla, "Order and Chaos in Early America: Political and Social
Stability," *American Historical Review*, vol. 90 (1985), 275–298.

It seems clear, however, that Virginia had to undergo a painful adjustment
of its political order in Bacon's Rebellion in 1676, although there is little
agreement about the precise nature of the process in the large body of
literature on the causes and significance of the rebellion. Craven, *Southern
Colonies in the Seventeenth Century*, is very helpful in understanding the
background of the rebellion, as is Warren M. Billings, "The Causes of Bacon's
Rebellion: Some Suggestions," *VMHB*, LXXVIII (1970), 409–435, which
draws on his more extensive " 'Virginias Deploured Condition,' 1660–1676:
The Coming of Bacon's Rebellion" (Ph.D. diss., Northern Illinois University,
1968). Bernard Bailyn, "Politics and Social Structure in Virginia," in Smith,
ed., *Seventeenth-Century America*, is a seminal essay which discusses the
development of political leadership through several stages during the century
and places the rebellion in that context.

Thomas J. Wertenbaker, *Torchbearer of the Revolution: The Story of Bacon's
Rebellion and Its Leader* (Princeton, 1940), strongly advances the view that
Nathaniel Bacon led a popular protest against an autocratic governor, while
Wilcomb E. Washburn defends Governor Berkeley no less vigorously in *The
Governor and the Rebel: A History of Bacon's Rebellion in Virginia* (Chapel Hill,
1954). Stephen S. Webb provides an uncompromising restatement of
Wertenbaker's view in Book One of *1676: The End of American Independence*
(New York, 1984). Also useful is Jane D. Carson, *Bacon's Rebellion,
1676–1696* (Jamestown, Virginia, 1976). The aftermath of the rebellion in
the years between its collapse and the Glorious Revolution have been
somewhat neglected by historians, although Morgan, *American Slavery,
American Freedom*, is important for that period, as is Wilcomb E. Washburn,
"The Effect of Bacon's Rebellion on Government in England and Virginia,"
United States National Museum Bulletin, CCXXV (1963), 137–152.

Finally, there is some important work on intellectual and cultural topics for the seventeenth century. In addition to the work of Richard Beale Davis, cited before, Howard Mumford Jones and Sue Bonner Walcutt, *The Literature of Virginia in the Seventeenth Century* (Charlottesville, 1968; 2nd ed.), and Louis B. Wright, *The First Gentlemen of Virginia: Intellectual Qualities of the Early Colonial Ruling Class* (San Marino, California, 1940), remain important. On the place of religion in the colony, see Perry Miller, "The Religious Impulse in the Founding of Virginia: Religion and Society in the Early Literature," *WMQ*, 3rd ser., V (1948), 492–522, and VI (1949), 24–41, and Darrett B. and Anita H. Rutman, "The Evolution of Religious Life in Early Virginia," *Lex et Scientia: The International Journal of Law and Science*, XIV (1978), 190–240. William H. Seiler, "The Anglican Parish in Virginia," is in Smith, ed., *Seventeenth-Century America*.

SECONDARY STUDIES: 1689–1750

To date, historians have produced relatively few narratives of Virginia history from the end of Bacon's Rebellion to the middle of the eighteenth century. Biographical literature is similarly thin compared with the periods before and after. In addition to the few published works, this study, as a result, is dependent on a number of unpublished theses and dissertations that are not easily available to the general reader, but whose contributions we must acknowledge. Among published works, John C. Rainbolt, *From Prescription to Persuasion: Manipulation of Seventeenth-Century Virginia Economy* (Port Washington, New York, 1974), analyzes the maturing of Virginia politics at the end of the century with special attention to the controversy over the formation of towns. It may be supplemented by two unpublished dissertations: Martin H. Quitt, "Virginia House of Burgesses, 1660–1706: The Social, Educational, and Economic Bases of Political Power" (Ph.D. diss., Washington University, 1970) and D. Alan Williams, "Political Alignments in Colonial Virginia Politics, 1698–1750" (Ph.D. diss., Northwestern University, 1959). Janis M. Horne reveals Governor Gooch's political skills in "The Opposition to the Virginia Tobacco Inspection Act of 1730" (Honors thesis, College of William and Mary, 1977). Jack P. Greene, *The Quest for Power: The Lower Houses of Assembly in the Southern Royal Colonies, 1689–1776* (Chapel Hill, 1963), traces the rise of the House of Burgesses; Robert E. and B. Katherine Brown, *Virginia, 1705–1786: Democracy or Aristocracy?* (East Lansing, 1964), and Lucille B. Griffith, *The Virginia Houses of Burgesses, 1750–1774* (University, Alabama, 1970) track down the extent of the suffrage; and Charles S. Sydnor, *Gentlemen Freeholders: Political Practices in Washington's Virginia* (Chapel Hill, 1952), describes election procedures in a delightful style.

In addition to the seminal work of Philip Bruce on the economic history of seventeenth-century Virginia cited above, Jacob M. Price massively documents the growth of the North Atlantic tobacco industry in *France and the Chesapeake: A History of the French Tobacco Monopoly, 1674–1791, and of Its Relationship to the British and American Tobacco Trade*, 2 vols. (Ann Arbor, 1973), and succinctly analyzes its role in capital formation, and the resulting problem of debt in the Chesapeake, in *Capital and Credit in British Overseas Trade: The View from the Chesapeake, 1700–1776* (Cambridge, Massachusetts, 1980). See also Price's "The Rise of Glasgow in the Chesapeake Tobacco Trade, 1707–1775," *WMQ*, 3rd ser., XI (1954), 179–199; James H. Soltow, "Scottish Traders in Virginia, 1750–1775," *Economic History Review*, XII (1959), 83–98; and Aubrey Land, "Economic Behavior in a Planting Society: The Eighteenth-Century Chesapeake," *Journal of Southern History*, XXXIII (1967), 469–485. Russell Menard accounts for secular trends in the Chesapeake industry in a number of articles conveniently listed in McCusker and Menard, *Economy of British America*, p. 429, already cited. John M. Hemphill III reviews the effects of British business cycles on the Chesapeake trade and describes the colony's involvement with Robert Walpole's Excise Bill in *Virginia and the English Commercial System, 1689–1733: Studies in the Development and Fluctuations of a Colonial Economy under Imperial Control* (New York, 1985). For the shift from the cultivation of tobacco to grain, which occurred first in Maryland and later in Virginia, see Paul G. E. Clemens, *The Atlantic Economy and Colonial Maryland's Eastern Shore: From Tobacco to Grain* (Ithaca, 1980), and David C. Klingaman, *Colonial Virginia's Coastwise and Grain Trade* (New York, 1975).

Philip Bruce also pioneered in the social history of the early colony with his *Institutional History of Seventeenth-Century Virginia*. Three recent community studies are the Rutmans' *A Place in Time: Middlesex County, Virginia*; Kevin Kelly's essay on Surry county, appearing in Tate and Ammerman, eds., *Chesapeake in the Seventeenth Century*, pp. 183–205; and for a later period, Richard R. Beeman's *The Evolution of the Southern Backcountry: A Case Study of Lunenburg County, Virginia, 1746–1832* (Philadelphia, 1984). A comprehensive study of social development in the early Chesapeake, with particular reference to Afro-American society, is Allan Kulikoff, *Tobacco and Slaves: The Development of Southern Cultures in the Chesapeake Colonies, 1680–1800* (Chapel Hill, 1986). Wesley Frank Craven offers insights into the pattern of white and black immigration in *White, Red, and Black*. The best study of white servitude is Galenson, *White Servitude in Colonial America*. Kulikoff's work cited above is the best on the social effects of the introduction of slavery. For the ideological aspects of the latter, see Jordan, *White Over Black*. Wertenbaker, *Planters of Colonial Virginia*, analyzes the quit rent roll of 1704 and notes the straits of the small farmer. See also D. Alan Williams, "The Small Farmer in Eighteenth-Century Virginia Politics," *Agricultural History*, XLIII (1969), 91–101.

The best study of the Northern Neck proprietorship is Douglas Southall Freeman, *George Washington*. Vol. I: *The Young Washington* (New York, 1949), appendix I-1, 2. Other biographical works are Leonidas Dodson, *Alexander Spotswood, Governor of Virginia, 1710–1722* (Philadelphia, 1932); Pierre Marambaud, *William Byrd of Westover, 1674–1744* (Charlottesville, 1971); Louis Morton, *Robert Carter of Nomini Hall: A Tobacco Planter of the Eighteenth Century* (Charlottesville, 1945); and Parke Rouse, *James Blair of Virginia* (Chapel Hill, 1971). Madelaine C. Kadubowski, "The Administration of Lieutenant-Governor Hugh Drysdale, 1722–1726" (M.A. thesis, College of William and Mary, 1967) fills a gap in the literature. Brief lives of Virginia governors before their appointments are in Stephen S. Webb, *The Governors-General: The English Army and the Definition of the Empire, 1569–1681* (Chapel Hill, 1979).

In addition to Richard B. Davis's three volumes on *Intellectual Life in the Colonial South*, his "The Intellectual Golden Age in the Colonial Chesapeake Bay Country," *VMHB*, LXXVIII (1970), 131–143, is a good overview. Louis B. Wright, *First Gentlemen of Virginia*, examines the contents of the libraries collected by Chesapeake planters. For the contemporary interest in science, see Brooke Hindle, *The Pursuit of Science in Revolutionary America, 1735–1789* (Chapel Hill, 1956).

The standard works on architecture are: Hugh S. Morrison, *Early American Architecture, From the First Colonial Settlements to the National Period* (New York, 1952); John W. Reps, *Tidewater Towns: City Planning in Colonial Virginia and Maryland* (Charlottesville, 1972); Marcus Whiffen, *The Eighteenth-Century Houses of Williamsburg: A Study of the Architecture and Buildings in the Colonial Capital of Virginia* (Williamsburg, 1960), and *The Public Buildings of Williamsburg, Colonial Capital of Virginia: An Architectural History* (Williamsburg, 1958); Thomas T. Waterman and John A. Barrows, *Domestic Colonial Architecture of Tidewater Virginia* (New York, 1969); and Waterman, *The Mansions of Virginia, 1706–1776* (New York, 1945). See also the important recent study, Cary Carson et al., "Impermanent Architecture in the Southern American Colonies," *Winterthur Portfolio*, 16 (1981), 135–196; and Henry B. Glassie, *Folk Housing in Middle Virginia: A Structural Analysis of Historic Artifacts* (Knoxville, 1978).

SECONDARY STUDIES: 1750–1783

The remarkable expansion of the Virginia colony into the Piedmont and Shenandoah Valley regions of the colony after 1720 was a central influence on all phases of the subsequent development of eighteenth-century Virginia that has somehow failed to receive full due from historians. Morton, *Colonial Virginia*, provides a convenient and relatively detailed narrative of the process, and there are additional details for the Shenandoah Valley in Thomas P. Abernethy, "The First Transmontane Advance," in James S. Wilson and others, eds., *Humanistic Studies in Honor of John Calvin Metcalf* (Charlottesville, 1941). Kulikoff, *Tobacco and Slaves*, is important for the subject, and Beeman, *Evolution of the Southern Backcountry*, provides a case study of a new Southside county, Lunenburg. Robert D. Mitchell, *Commercialism and Frontier: Perspectives on the Early Shenandoah Valley* (Charlottesville, 1977), is a work of first importance by a historical geographer. The last phase of this expansionism before the outbreak of the Revolution, the extensive speculation in lands beyond the Allegheny mountains, has to be examined for the most part in older works such as Kenneth P. Bailey, *The Ohio Company of Virginia and the Westward Movement, 1748–1792* (Glendale, California, 1939), and Alfred P. James, *The Ohio Company: Its Inner History* (Pittsburgh, 1959). In a recent article Marc Egnal treats the division between expansionists and non-expansionists as a central theme in "The Origins of the Revolution in Virginia: A Reinterpretation," *WMQ*, XXXVII (1980), 401–428.

The greater concern of most recent historians with internal changes in the society and economy of Virginia has tended to downplay the effects of colonial policy and imperial political relations on the development of the Revolutionary controversy, a subject that once loomed very large in the writings of early American historians. Whatever the underlying causes of the Revolution, changing imperial relationships provided at the least the immediate setting in which the crisis erupted. In any reexamination of the imperial origins of the Revolution, the best starting point is Jack P. Greene, "An Uneasy Connection: An Analysis of the Preconditions of the American Revolution," in Stephen G. Kurtz and James H. Hutson, eds., *Essays on the American Revolution* (Chapel Hill, 1973), 32–80. Three other studies that, like Greene's, examine the question for all the colonies but have important implications for Virginia, are Bernhard Knollenberg, *Origin of the American Revolution, 1759–1766* (New York, 1960); James A. Henretta, *"Salutary Neglect": Colonial Administration under the Duke of Newcastle* (Princeton, 1972); and Alan Rogers, *Empire and Liberty: American Resistance to British Authority, 1755–1763* (Berkeley, 1974).

The specific manifestations of increasing tensions in imperial relations that developed in Virginia—British reactions to the 1748 revision of the Virginia law code, the Pistole Fee controversy, the Parsons' Cause, and reaction to the end of the Seven Years' War—are best studied through a series of articles and essays pertaining to one or another of these issues. They include: Gwenda Morgan, " 'The Privilege of Making Laws'; The Board of Trade, The Virginia

Assembly and Legislative Review, 1748–54," *Journal of American Studies*, X (1976), 1–15; Jack P. Greene, ed., "The Case of the Pistole Fee . . . ," *VMHB*, LXVI (1958), 399–422; Glenn Curtiss Smith, "The Affair of the Pistole Fee, Virginia, 1752–1775," *ibid.*, XLVIII (1940), 209–221; Gwenda Morgan, "Virginia and the French and Indian War: A Case Study of the War's Effect on Imperial Relations," *ibid.*, LXXXI (1973), 23–48; and Jack P. Greene, "The Seven Years' War and the American Revolution: The Causal Pattern Reconsidered," in Peter Marshall and Glyn Williams, eds., *The British Atlantic Empire Before the American Revolution* (London, 1980), 85–105. Two biographies of the Virginia governor who served during the Pistole Fee controversy and the first years of the Seven Years' War are also useful: Louis K. Koontz, *Robert Dinwiddie* (Glendale, California, 1941) and John R. Alden, *Robert Dinwiddie: Servant of the Crown* (Charlottesville, 1973).

The recent bibliography for various sources of internal tension that developed within Virginia is more extensive. A background for the feelings of uncertainty, sense of failure, and suspicion of British politics that seemed to affect the Virginia gentry is laid in a number of works on the ideological origins of Revolution that examine the strong attachment of virtually all colonial Americans to conceptions of civic virtue and morality. Bernard Bailyn, *Ideological Origins of the American Revolution* (Cambridge, Massachusetts, 1967), is an important example. Gordon S. Wood, "Rhetoric and Reality in the American Revolution," *WMQ*, 3rd ser., XXIII (1966), 3–32, brings this interpretation directly to bear on the Virginia elite. Jack P. Greene, "Society, Ideology, and Politics: An Analysis of the Political Culture of Mid-Eighteenth-Century Virginia," in Richard M. Jellison, ed., *Society, Freedom, and Conscience* . . . (New York, 1976), 14–76, finds a broader range of concerns among the gentry, of which this ideological aspect is but one. Greene's "Character, Persona, and Authority: A Study of Alternative Styles of Leadership in Revolutionary Virginia," in W. Robert Higgins, ed., *The Revolutionary War in the South: Power, Conflict, and Leadership* . . . (Durham, 1979), 3–42, is also useful.

Richard R. Beeman, "Robert Munford and the Political Culture of Frontier Virginia," *Journal of American Studies*, XII (1978), 169–183, is especially valuable for understanding the more turbulent politics of some of the newer interior counties, as is his study of Lunenburg county, *Evolution of the Southern Backcountry*. The text of *The Candidates* is available as edited by Jay B. Hubbell and Douglass Adair in *WMQ*, 3rd ser., V (1948), 217–257. The unsettling effect of the decline of tobacco on the gentry is the principal theme of T. H. Breen, *Tobacco Culture: The Mentality of the Great Tidewater Planters on the Eve of the Revolution* (Princeton, 1985). Growing dissatisfaction with the functioning of the county court system on the eve of the Revolution is but one important theme in A. G. Roeber, *Faithful Magistrates and Republican Lawyers: Creators of Virginia Legal Culture, 1680–1810* (Chapel Hill, 1981).

Daniel Blake Smith, *Inside the Great House: Planter Family Life in Eighteenth-Century Chesapeake Society* (Ithaca and London, 1980), discusses among other things a shift away from the patriarchal authority of fathers in gentry families. Jan Lewis, *The Pursuit of Happiness: Family and Values in Jefferson's Virginia* (Cambridge, 1983), focuses on the post-Revolutionary period but begins at the middle of the eighteenth century and disagrees with Smith's periodization of changing family values. See also Edmund S. Morgan, *Virginians at Home: Family Life in the Eighteenth Century* (Williamsburg, 1952).

For the rise of religious dissent in Virginia, Wesley M. Gewehr, *The Great Awakening in Virginia, 1740–1790* (Durham, 1930), is the standard narrative, but the recent study by Rhys Isaac, *The Transformation of Virginia, 1740–1790* (Chapel Hill, 1982), treats the rise of the Separate Baptists in a much more provocative manner, arguing that they fundamentally reordered the society and culture of Virginia. For Isaac that development is one, if not the most, significant consequence of the Revolution in Virginia, and hence his study is more a reinterpretation of the entire Revolutionary era than a study in religious history alone. J. Stephen Kroll-Smith, "Transmitting a Revival Culture: The Organizational Dynamic of the Baptist Movement in Colonial Virginia, 1760–1777," *Journal of Southern History*, L (1984), 551–568, complements Isaac's discussion. George W. Pilcher, *Samuel Davies: Apostle of Dissent in Colonial Virginia* (Knoxville, 1971), is also helpful for Presbyterianism.

In addition to the work cited earlier on blacks in Virginia, Gerald W. [Michael] Mullin, *Flight and Rebellion: Slave Resistance in Eighteenth Century Virginia* (New York, 1972), is an important contribution to understanding the unsettling effects of slavery in the later eighteenth century. Philip J. Schwarz, "Slaves and Crime in Late Eighteenth-Century Virginia," *VMHB*, XC (1982), 283–309, is also helpful. Robert McColley, *Slavery and Jeffersonian Virginia* (Urbana, Illinois, 1964), deals primarily with the post-Revolutionary period but is pertinent here as well.

When one turns from the background to the Revolution and focuses on the immediate events of the crisis in the years from 1763 to 1776, the literature is not as full, apart from biographies of many of the major and some of the minor Virginia leaders. One of the biographies, David J. Mays, *Edmund Pendleton: A Biography*, 2 vols. (Cambridge, Massachusetts, 1952), provides both a study of that significant figure in state affairs and the best overall account of the political crisis. Hamilton J. Eckenrode, *The Revolution in Virginia* (Boston and New York, 1916), is an older and briefer account that stresses a high degree of conflict among more conservative and more radical supporters of the Revolution in the colony. Carl Bridenbaugh, *Seat of Empire: The Political Role of Eighteenth-Century Williamsburg* (New York, 1958), shares Eckenrode's perspective and emphasizes the Revolutionary crisis as it unfolded in the capital of the colony. Isaac, *Transformation of Virginia*, should, as noted above, be read as a very sweeping reinterpretation of the Revolution in Virginia.

Like Mays, *Edmund Pendleton*, the multivolume biographies of Thomas Jefferson, James Madison, and George Washington provide full accounts of those events of the Revolution in Virginia in which their subjects participated. Dumas Malone, *Jefferson and His Time*, 6 vols. (Boston, 1948–1981), covers Jefferson's Virginia career, including the war governorship and effort to reform the law code of Virginia, in Volume I, *Jefferson the Virginian*. Volumes I–III of Irving Brant, *James Madison*, 6 vols. (Indianapolis and New York, 1941–1961), examine Madison's career to 1800. Freeman, *George Washington*, cited above, devotes three volumes to Washington's Virginia years up to 1775 and two to his military leadership of the Revolution. For those who prefer a more compressed treatment of the three men, the following are excellent one-volume biographies: John R. Alden, *George Washington: A Biography* (Baton Rouge and London, 1984); Ralph Ketcham, *James Madison: A Biography* (New York, 1971); and Merrill D. Peterson, *Thomas Jefferson and the New Nation: A Biography* (New York, 1970). Richard R. Beeman, *Patrick Henry: A Biography* (New York, 1974), although briefer than some other Henry biographies, is the most up-to-date and the best for placing his career in its full context. Robert A. Rutland, *George Mason: Reluctant Statesman* (New York, 1961), and Helen H. D. Miller, *George Mason: Gentleman Revolutionary* (Chapel Hill, 1975), are the most recent studies of the author of the Virginia Declaration of Rights. Louis W. Potts, *Arthur Lee: A Virtuous Revolutionary* (Baton Rouge, 1981), treats a Virginia leader who lived in London for much of the Revolutionary crisis but played an influential role on the American side. Alonzo T. Dill, *Carter Braxton, Virginia Signer: A Conservative in Revolt* (Lanham, Maryland, 1983), makes the most of the limited sources available for one of Virginia's most conservative Patriots. Emory G. Evans, *Thomas Nelson of Yorktown: Revolutionary Virginian* (Charlottesville, 1975), is a good account of another of the leaders at the state level. Bernard Mayo, *Myths and Men: Patrick Henry, George Washington, Thomas Jefferson* (Athens, Georgia, 1959), contains incisive essays on the three men and their reputations that deserve to be better known than they are. Finally, during the Bicentennial of the Revolution the Virginia Independence Bicentennial Commission sponsored a group of brief biographies of principal participants in the Revolution, including several who have not received successful full-length biographies.

Some of the specific events of the Revolutionary crisis are treated in articles and essays. Eugene M. Del Papa, "The Royal Proclamation of 1763: Its Effect upon Virginia Land Companies," *VMHB*, LXXXIII (1975), 406–411, briefly reexamines the effect of the Proclamation of 1763 in restricting westward expansion. Joseph A. Ernst has discussed the Currency Act in two articles and the John Robinson scandal in a third: "Genesis of the Currency Act of 1764: Virginia Paper Money and the Protection of British Investments," *WMQ*, 3rd ser., XXII (1965), 33–74; "The Currency Act Repeal Movement: A Study of Imperial Politics and Revolutionary Crisis, 1764–1767," *ibid.*, 3rd ser., XXV (1968), 177–211; and "The Robinson Scandal Redivivus: Money, Debts, and Politics in Revolutionary Virginia," *VMHB*, LXXVII (1969), 146–173. Jack P. Greene and Richard M. Jellison also discuss the Currency Act in "The Currency Act of 1764 in Imperial-Colonial Relations, 1764–1776," *WMQ*, 3rd ser., XVIII (1961), 485–518.

For the Patrick Henry resolves against the Stamp Act, Edmund S. and Helen M. Morgan, *The Stamp Act Crisis: Prologue to Revolution* (Chapel Hill, 1953), 88–98, is an important account. J. A. Leo Lemay adds significant information in "John Mercer and the Stamp Act in Virginia, 1764–1765," *VMHB*, XCI (1983), 3–38. The series of domestic controversies that followed repeal of the Stamp Act are illuminated in Jack P. Greene, "'Virtus et Libertas': Political Culture, Social Change, and the Origins of the American Revolution in Virginia, 1763–1776," in Jeffrey J. Crow and Larry E. Tise, eds., *The Southern Experience in the American Revolution* (Chapel Hill, 1973), 55–108; Jack P. Greene, "The Attempt to Separate the Offices of Speaker and Treasurer in Virginia, 1758–1776," *VMHB*, LXXI (1963), 11–18; Carl Bridenbaugh, "Violence and Virtue in Virginia, 1766: or The Importance of the Trivial," *Proceedings of the Massachusetts Historical Society*, LXXVI (1964), 3–29 [an account of the Chiswell murder case]; and J. A. Leo Lemay, "Robert Bolling and the Bailment of Colonel Chiswell," *Early American Literature*, VI (1971), 99–142.

The events of 1767–1770 surrounding the Virginia reaction to the Townshend duties and other measures of that period have not been the subject of any recent publications, although an unpublished paper by Joseph Ernst on the politics of interest in Revolutionary Virginia is an important statement on the nonimportation agreements of the period. Joseph R. Frese, ed., "The Royal Customs Service in the Chesapeake, 1770: The Reports of John Williams, Inspector General," *VMHB*, LXXXI (1973), 280–318, covers an overlooked inspection of Virginia customs enforcement. Richard O. Curry, "Lord Dunmore and the West: A Re-evaluation," *West Virginia History*, XIX (1958), 231–243, treats Dunmore as a champion of colonial rights in the West.

The domestic issues that arose in 1771–1773 affecting religion and the court system are best covered in Isaac, *Transformation of Virginia*, and Roeber, *Faithful Magistrates*, respectively. Three articles, all from the *Virginia Magazine of History and Biography*, are useful for the last stages of the Revolutionary controversy: Larry Bowman, "The Virginia Committees of Safety, 1770–1776," LXXIX (1971), 322–337; Michael D. Pierce, "The Independence Movement in Virginia, 1775–1776," LXXX (1972), 442–452; and William E. White, "The Independent Companies of Virginia, 1774–1775," LXXXVI (1978), 149–162. The significance of the issue of renewal of the fee bill is discussed in George M. Curtis III, "The Role of the Courts in the Making of the Revolution in Virginia," in James Kirby Martin, ed., *The Human Dimension of Nation-Making* (Madison, Wisconsin, 1976), and is further illuminated in Frank L. Dewey's forthcoming study, *Thomas Jefferson, Lawyer.*

The question of the relevance to the movement for independence of the huge debts owed by Virginia planters to British merchants does not rest on any single event, but the debt question came to something of a climax in the aftermath of the British credit crisis of 1772, which is examined in Richard B. Sheridan, "The British Credit Crisis of 1772 and the American Colonies," *Journal of Economic History*, XX (1960), 161–186. Jacob M. Price, *Capital and Credit in British Overseas Trade*, plays down the seriousness of the crisis for the efforts to collect debts from Virginians. Isaac S. Harrell, *Loyalism in Virginia* (Durham, 1926), is, despite its title, a study of planter debts that attributes to them a significant influence on the Revolutionary movement. Two articles by Emory G. Evans in the *William and Mary Quarterly* are more skeptical of their importance: "Planter Indebtedness and the Coming of the Revolution in Virginia," 3rd ser., XIX (1962), 511–533, and "Private Indebtedness and the Revolution in Virginia, 1776 to 1796," 3rd ser., XXVIII (1971), 349–374.

Robert M. Calhoon, *The Loyalists in Revolutionary America, 1760–1781* (New York, 1973), 458–466, offers an excellent brief account of Virginia Loyalism. Adele Hast, *Loyalism in Revolutionary Virginia: The Norfolk Area and the Eastern Shore* (Ann Arbor, 1982), is a careful study. For the threat of frontier Loyalism, see Emory G. Evans, "Trouble in the Backcountry: Disaffection in Southwest Virginia during the American Revolution," in Ronald Hoffman, Thad W. Tate, and Peter J. Albert, eds., *An Uncivil War: The Southern Backcountry during the American Revolution* (Charlottesville, 1958), 179–212. For an example of a Loyalist family, see George M. Curtis III, "The Goodrich Family and the Revolution in Virginia, 1774–1776," *VMHB*, LXXIV (1976), 49–74.

The Virginia Convention of May 1776 which adopted the resolution for independence, the new state constitution, and the Virginia Declaration of Rights is more celebrated than written about. In most respects the biographies of Madison, Jefferson, and Mason cited above remain the fullest accounts. See also John E. Selby, "Richard Henry Lee, John Adams, and the Virginia Constitution of 1776," *VMHB*, LXXXIV (1976), 387–400. His forthcoming study, *Revolution in Virginia, 1775–1783*, will provide a fuller account of both the events leading to independence and the years of military struggle in Virginia than we now have.

The longer-range consequences of the Revolution in Virginia are equally difficult to trace in the existing literature. There is a suggestive overview in Herbert Sloan and Peter Onuf, "Politics, Culture, and the Revolution in Virginia: A Review of Recent Work," *VMHB*, XCI (1983), 259–284. Thanks to Rhys Isaac, *Transformation of Virginia*, and Thomas E. Buckley, *Church and State in Revolutionary Virginia, 1776–1787* (Charlottesville, 1977), the important question of religious change is more thoroughly studied than any other aspect of the subject.

A. G. Roeber, *Faithful Magistrates*, covers changes in the court system, placing a stronger emphasis on the displacement of the county courts than many other scholars would concede. J. R. Pole, "Representation and Authority in Virginia from the Revolution to Reform," *Journal of Southern History*, XXIV (1958), 16–50, is a valuable discussion. Aspects of the revision of the law code, in Jefferson's mind the fundamental means for reforming the society and government of Virginia, are treated in the following articles: C. Ray Keim, "Primogeniture and Entail in Colonial Virginia," *WMQ*, 3rd ser., XXV (1968), 545–586; Charles T. Cullen, "Completing the Revisal of the Laws in Post-Revolutionary Virginia," *VMHB*, LXXXII (1974), 84–99; and Kathryn Preyer, "Crime, the Criminal Law and Reform in Post-Revolutionary Virginia," *Law and History Review*, I (1983), 53–85. Robert P. Thomson, "The Reform of the College of William and Mary, 1763–1780," *Proceedings of the American Philosophical Society*, CXV (1971), 187–213, is an important case study in the failures and successes of Jefferson's attempts to reform education in the new state.

In addition to Gerald Mullin, *Flight and Rebellion*, Benjamin Quarles, *The Negro in the American Revolution* (Chapel Hill, 1961), gives attention to blacks in Revolutionary Virginia. See also Richard S. Dunn, "Black Society in the Chesapeake, 1776–1810," in Ira Berlin and Ronald Hoffman, eds., *Slavery and Freedom in the Age of the American Revolution* (Charlottesville, 1983). For women in Revolutionary Virginia it is necessary to use more general works, in particular Linda K. Kerber, *Women of the Republic: Intellect and Ideology in Revolutionary America* (Chapel Hill, 1980), and Mary Beth Norton, *Liberty's Daughters: The Revolutionary Experience of American Women, 1750–1800* (Boston, 1980). See also pp. 614ff. of Norton's "The Evolution of White Women's Experience in Early America," *American Historical Review*, LXXXIX (1984), 593–619. Suzanne Lebsock, *The Free Women of Petersburg: Status and Culture in a Southern Town, 1784–1860* (New York and London, 1984), is a work of first importance, although it covers the immediate post-Revolutionary period relatively briefly.

The brief comments in this volume regarding the extent of change in the leadership of Virginia after the Revolution were intended to be suggestive rather than to open up a full discussion of the subject, but the following will provide the reader who wishes to look further with a good beginning: Jackson T. Main, "The Distribution of Property in Post-Revolutionary Virginia," *Mississippi Valley Historical Review*, XLI (1954), 241–258; Richard R. Beeman, *The Old Dominion and the New Nation, 1788–1801* (Lexington, Kentucky, 1972); and Daniel P. Jordan, *Political Leadership in Jefferson's Virginia* (Charlottesville, 1983).

In conclusion, it is not simply for rhetorical effect that the author of the epilogue of this volume turned for an overall assessment of the consequences of the Revolution in Virginia to what is perhaps the first systematic statement on the subject, Thomas Jefferson's *Notes on the State of Virginia*, for it may, after all, still be the best place to begin.

INDEX